# BEGINNING
# TONAL DICTATION

# BEGINNING TONAL DICTATION

*by*

## Thomas L. Durham
*Brigham Young University*

WAVELAND
PRESS, INC.
Prospect Heights, Illinois

For information about this book, write or call:
Waveland Press, Inc.
P.O. Box 400
Prospect Heights, Illinois 60070
(847) 634-0081

Printed in the United States of America

7   6   5   4

# TABLE OF CONTENTS

# PREFACE

*Beginning Tonal Dictation*, written for first year music theory programs, contains a regulated group of pitch, rhythm, melodic and harmonic dictation exercises designed for use in and out of the classroom. **This manual differs from other ear training books because students can check their work immediately--they cover the answer to the left with a piece of scratch paper, and remove it to check their work.**

Although theory and ear training programs vary from school to school, teachers unanimously affirm the importance of dictation (aural) skills in music education. The ability to *hear with the eye and see with the ear* separates the most able musicians from the average. Dictation exercises prevail as the best gauge of aural acuity. These exercises boil down to three basic skills: writing out a rhythmic succession, a melodic succession, and a harmonic progression. This manual focuses on those skills only, leaving other peripheral exercises to alternate authors and texts.

*Beginning Tonal Dictation* contains two units--each unit has ten sections. Individual sections have a FOCUS which concentrates on a particular intervalic, rhythmic, metric, and harmonic concept (see Table of Contents). Students hear the instructor play an example, write out what was played, then compare their answers against the instructor's key. This process eliminates the instructor's time-consuming task of calling out the detailed answers, and provides for immediate feedback to the student.

In each section, pitch, rhythm, and melodic exercises appear before the harmonic materials. **In all exercises, students should take a piece of scratch paper, and cover up the "Instructor's Key" until they are ready to check their answers.** The following instructions will benefit those using this text:

## PITCH

Unit 1: Students write out the second note of four different melodic intervals. Instructors may ask students to analyze the interval below the exercise. These intervals occur on exactly the same pitches in the melody below the rhythm exercise.

Unit 2: Students write out the second and third note of three different pitch exercises. One of the three note-patterns appears in the melody below the rhythm exercise.

# RHYTHM

Unit 1: Students hear the instructor play a short, usually four-bar melody and are given beginning and ending note values in a staff with a neutral (rectangular) clef. Then they write out only the rhythm of the melody. This rhythm features a particular pattern mentioned in the FOCUS. Similar patterns will occur in the melody below the rhythm exercise. Rests are used in exercises 3 and 7, and ties appear in exercises 4 and 8 in the rhythm and melody examples.

Unit 2: Exercises are twice as long as they were in the previous unit. Accordingly, there are only half as many examples. Rests and ties occur in exercises 2 and 4 respectively.

# MELODY

Unit 1: Having completed the pitch and rhythmic portions of the exercise, students now write out a four-bar melody which combines the pitch and rhythmic concepts of the previous exercises. The first and last notes are given to the students as a reference. Melodies numbered 1-4 begin in C-Major and progress to other major keys with more and more accidentals. Melodies numbered 5-8 begin in A-minor and progress through other minor keys similarly. Both treble and bass clefs appear.

Unit 2: As with rhythm, these exercises are now twice as long as they were in the previous unit. The students are given the first and last pitches, and a few more along the way for reference. Exercises 1 and 2 feature major keys while exercises 3 and 4 use minor. Again, rests and ties are found in exercises 2 and 4 respectively. Both treble and bass clefs appear.

# HARMONY

Units 1 and 2: The harmonic dictation exercises follow. Students listen to a group of from three to seven chords, writing them out on a grand staff provided to the right of the answers. The first chord is given in its four-part arrangement. The instructor may have the class write out all four parts, only the outer voices, or merely the Roman numeral analysis. If the class finds the exercise too difficult, the instructor may give them a chord or two along the way, or parts of chords.

A variety of keys and ranges is used, and the examples become increasingly longer and more difficult. Each section contains a subheading "A" for major keys and "B" for minor. All sections focus on a particular chord, group of chords, or inversion. The students are expected to retain past concepts, because any chord previously encountered might appear in later exercises.

## TO THE INSTRUCTOR:

Because dictation can sometimes become monotonous, you may wish to vary your approach to the use of these materials. The following suggestions will diversify your normal routine:

1. **Error Detection**--Prior to class, add some accidentals to the pitch exercise, change the rhythm exercise in a few places, and modify a few pitches and rhythms in the melody. Then ask the students to watch the instructor's page and locate the errors in the exercises as you play the "wrong" version through.

2. **Error dictation from memory**--Prior to class, prepare the pitch, rhythm, and melody exercises as in #1 above. This time, have the students close their books as you play the example with the wrong notes or rhythms you added. The students should then open their books, look at the exercise you played and then *from memory* attempt to iden-tify the errors.

3. **Interval identification**--Have the students examine the intervals on the instructor's page. Play an interval on different pitches whose quantity, quality and contour resemble an interval in the instructor's key. Then ask the students to match the interval you played with the one *similar* to it in the book.

4. **Harmonic error detection**--As in #1 above, alter a few of the notes in a harmonic dictation exercise and ask the students to locate the error.

5. **Harmonic error detection from memory**--Prepare a harmonic dicta-tion exercise as in #3 above. Again, (as in #2 above) have the students close their books as you play the example, wrong notes and all. Then have the students open their books and mark the errors *from memory*.

6.  **Separate voices**--Instead of having the students write out the harmonic dictation in four parts, ask them to write out only the tenor, or any other single part. Or have them complete the outer voices, the inner voices, or any combination of voices.

7.  **Harmonic scramble**--Have the students examine a harmonic exercise in the instructor's key. As you play the example, scramble the order by playing the chords *out of sequence* in a predetermined order. The students should write "1" below the first chord played, "2" below the second and so on. Blanks already exist for this exercise because these spaces are normally used for the analysis of the chord above when taking harmonic dictation.

8.  **Non-harmonic tones**--As the students watch the instructor's key in a harmonic dictation, add two or three non-harmonic tones to the exercise, and ask the students to identify them, write them in, or both. Outer voices tend to be easier than inner voices, so be sure to include examples of both.

TO THE STUDENT:

These materials can be used outside of class very easily, with two students assisting each other. One can play the role of the instructor at a piano, while the other practices dictation. If a student has already filled in the rhythm and melody answers on a particular page, it might be useful to reverse the rhythm and melody examples when practicing outside of class. In other words, have your partner play the melody exercise while you write down its rhythm, then listen to the rhythm exercise and write down its melody. These can both be done on a blank sheet of music manuscript paper. Both rhythm and melody were composed with the principles of the FOCUS in mind. A practice room or any quiet room with a piano gives ample privacy for such a session.

Any student can improve his or her aural skills, but ear training takes patience. Understand that with time and practice, improvement will come. The time it takes will be justified by the satisfaction you feel with improved aural acuity. Although these skills are not music in themselves, they will significantly inform the music you write, analyze, conduct, and perform.

ACKNOWLEDGEMENTS:

This book benefited from the generous assistance of colleagues, student instructors, teaching assistants, and hundreds of students at Brigham Young University.  In addition, the University Press of America granted permission for the author to use his own harmonic progressions from an earlier publication under their copyright.

# UNIT 1

# PRIMARY
# TONAL DICTATION

# SECTION 1

FOCUS: m2, M2, -- ♩ ♩ -- $\frac{2}{4}$

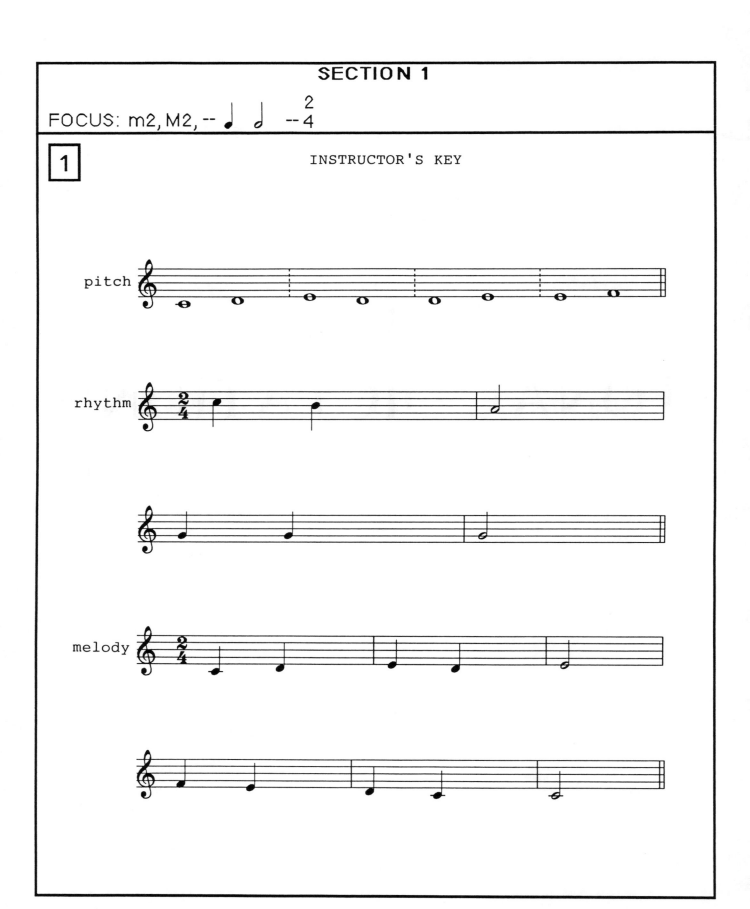

# SECTION 1

FOCUS: m2, M2, -- ♩ ♩ -- $\frac{2}{4}$

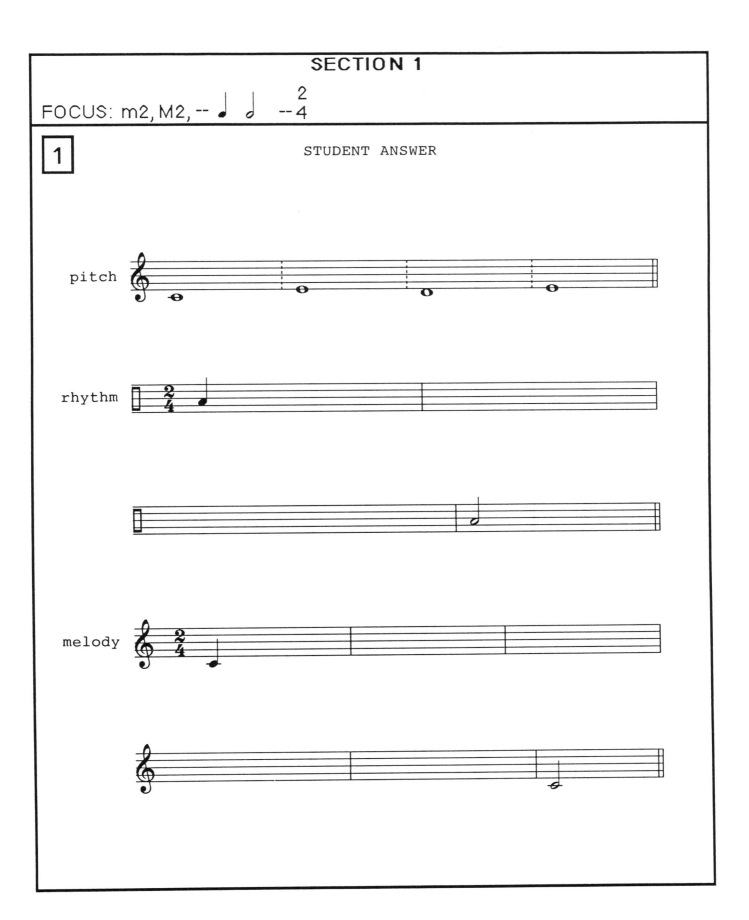

# SECTION 1

FOCUS: m2, M2, -- ♩ ♩ -- 2/4

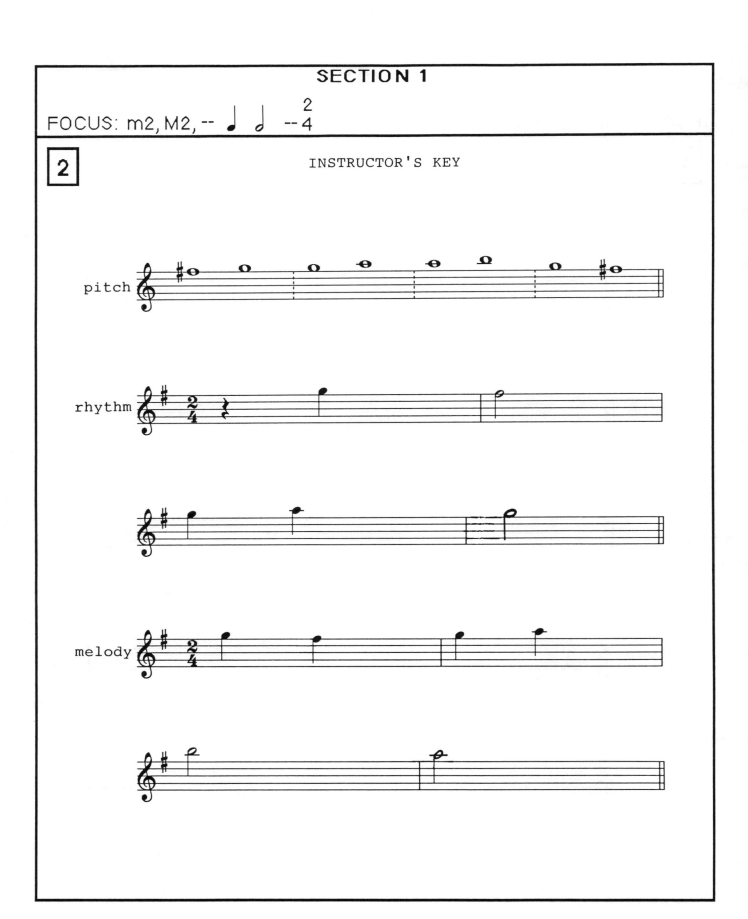

2  INSTRUCTOR'S KEY

pitch

rhythm

melody

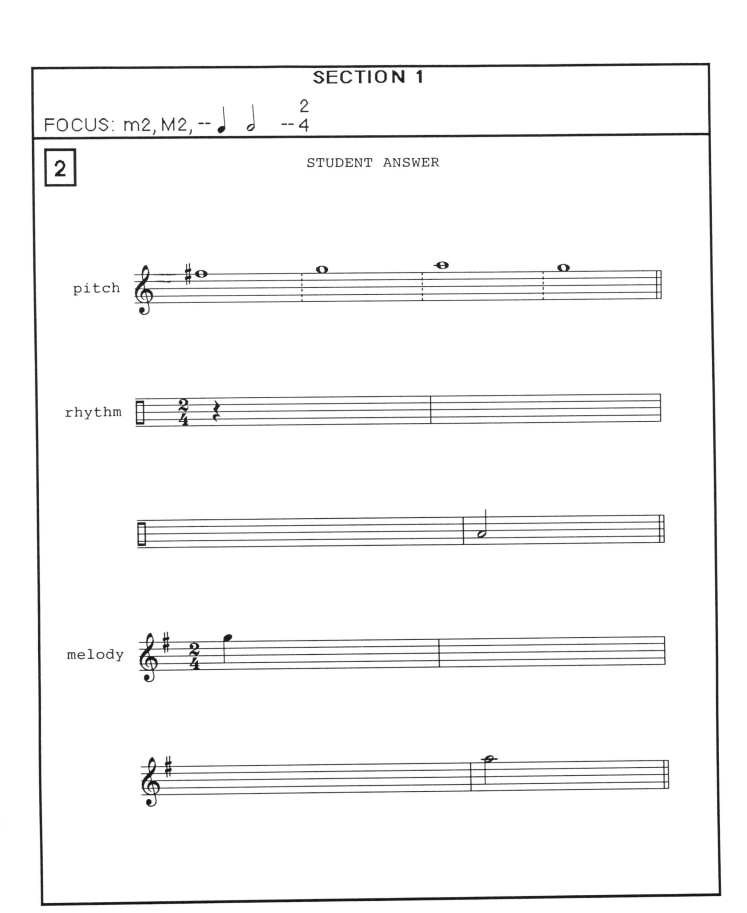

# SECTION 1

FOCUS: m2, M2, -- ♩ ♩ -- $\frac{2}{4}$

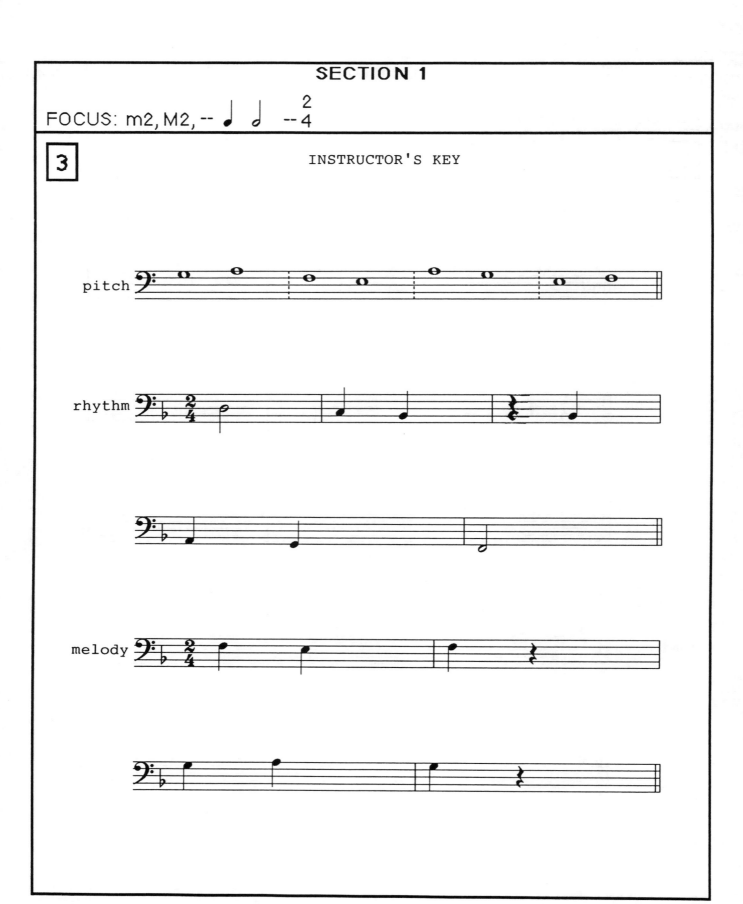

INSTRUCTOR'S KEY

# SECTION 1

FOCUS: m2, M2, -- ♩ ♩ -- $\frac{2}{4}$

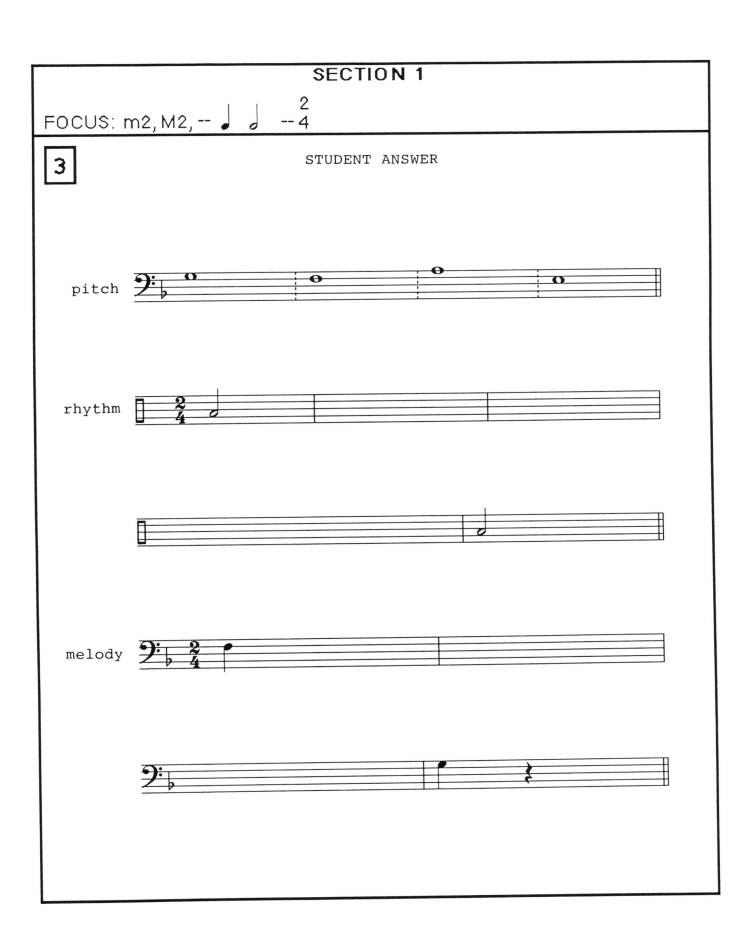

# SECTION 1

FOCUS: m2, M2, -- ♩ ♩ -- $\frac{2}{4}$

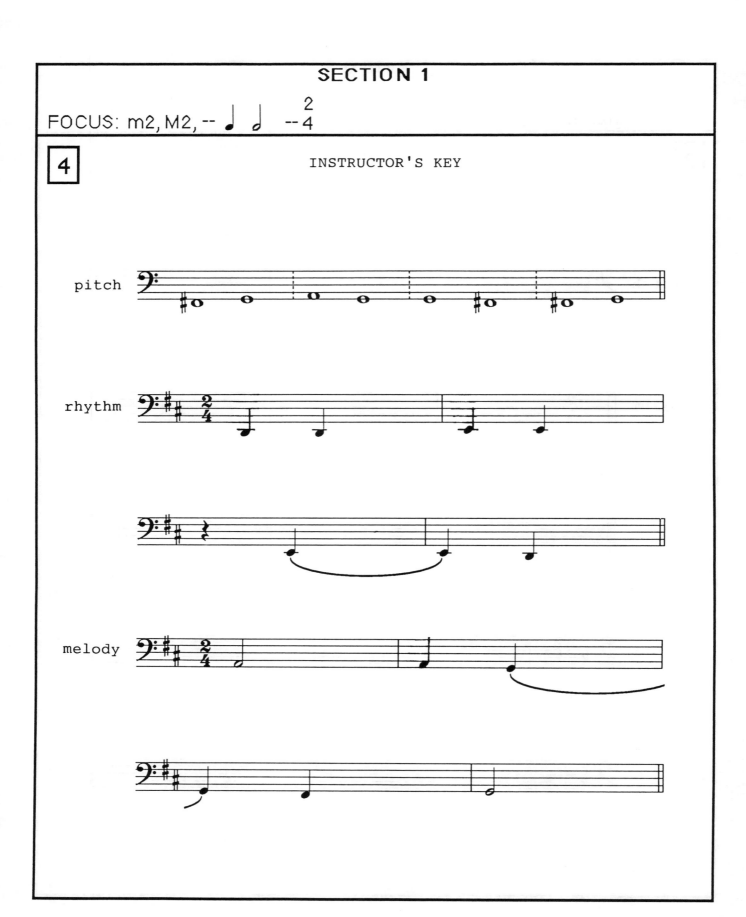

# SECTION 1

FOCUS: m2, M2, -- ♩ 𝅗𝅥 -- $\frac{2}{4}$

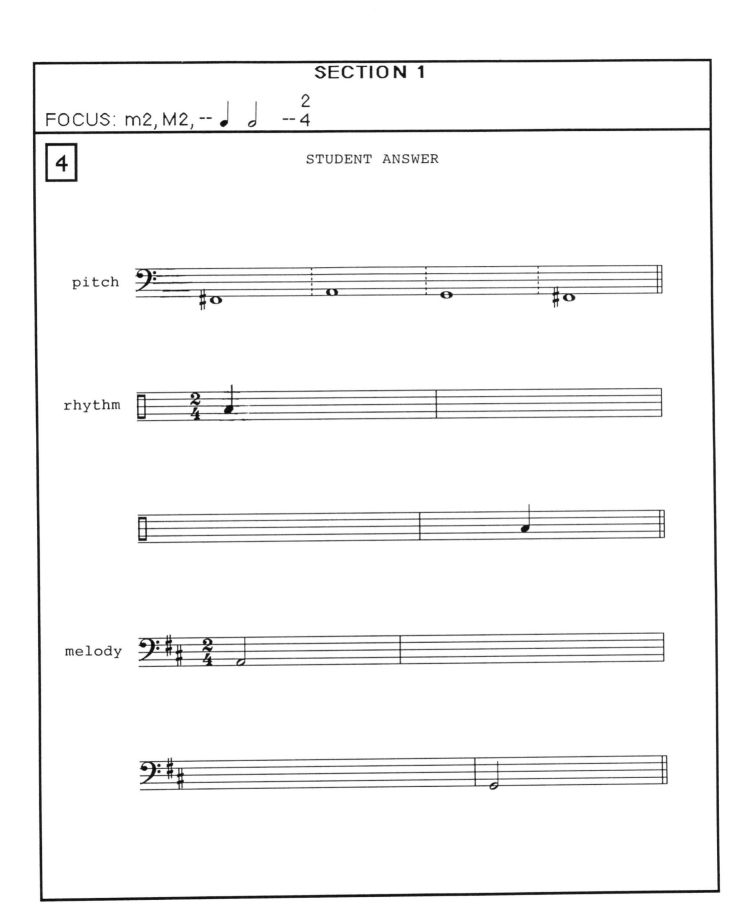

# SECTION 1

FOCUS: m2, M2, -- ♩ ♩ -- $\frac{2}{4}$

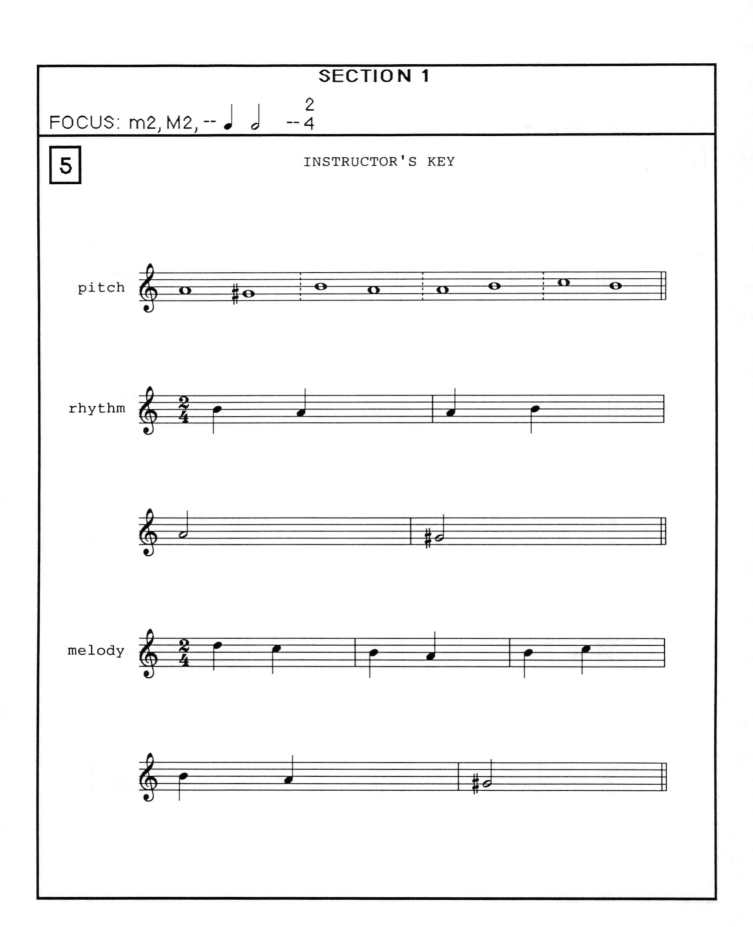

INSTRUCTOR'S KEY

10

# SECTION 1

FOCUS: m2, M2, -- ♩ ♩ -- $\frac{2}{4}$

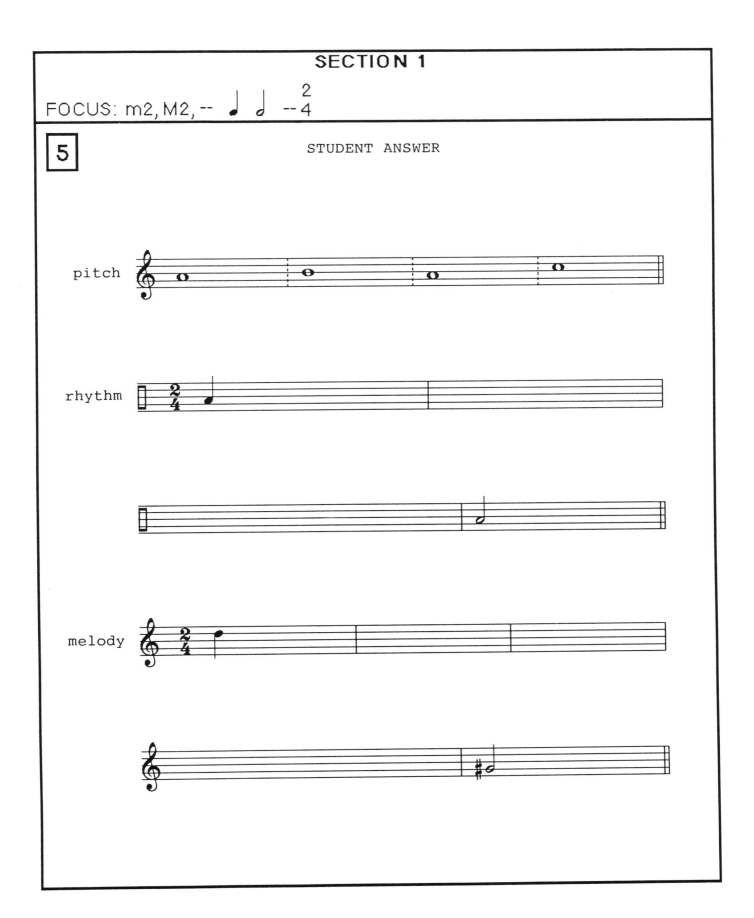

# SECTION 1

FOCUS: m2, M2, -- ♩ ♩ -- $\frac{2}{4}$

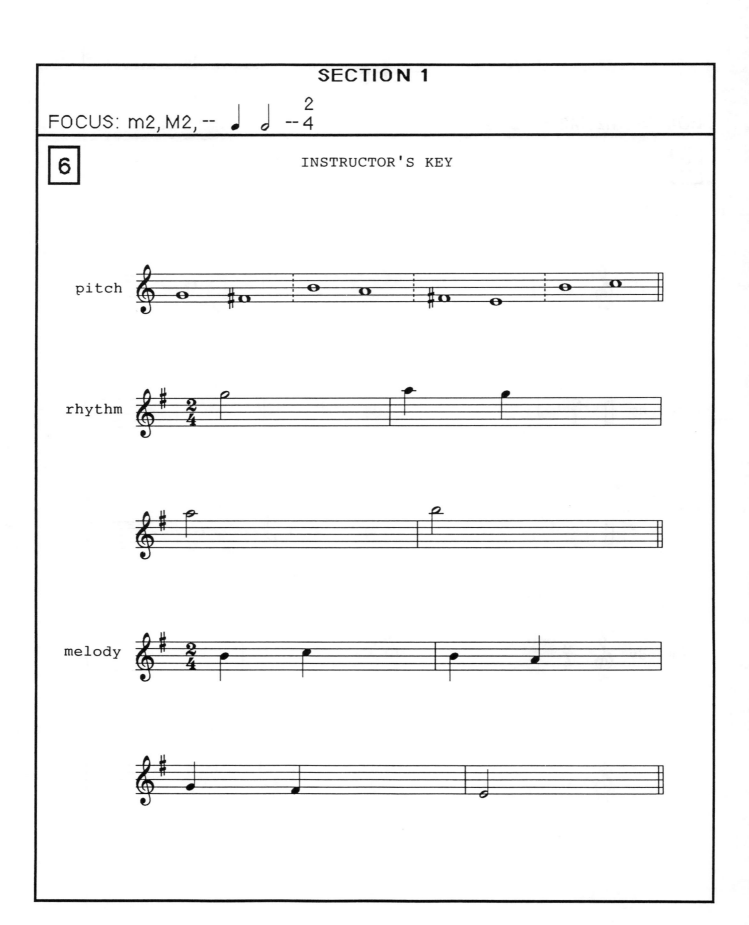

INSTRUCTOR'S KEY

pitch

rhythm

melody

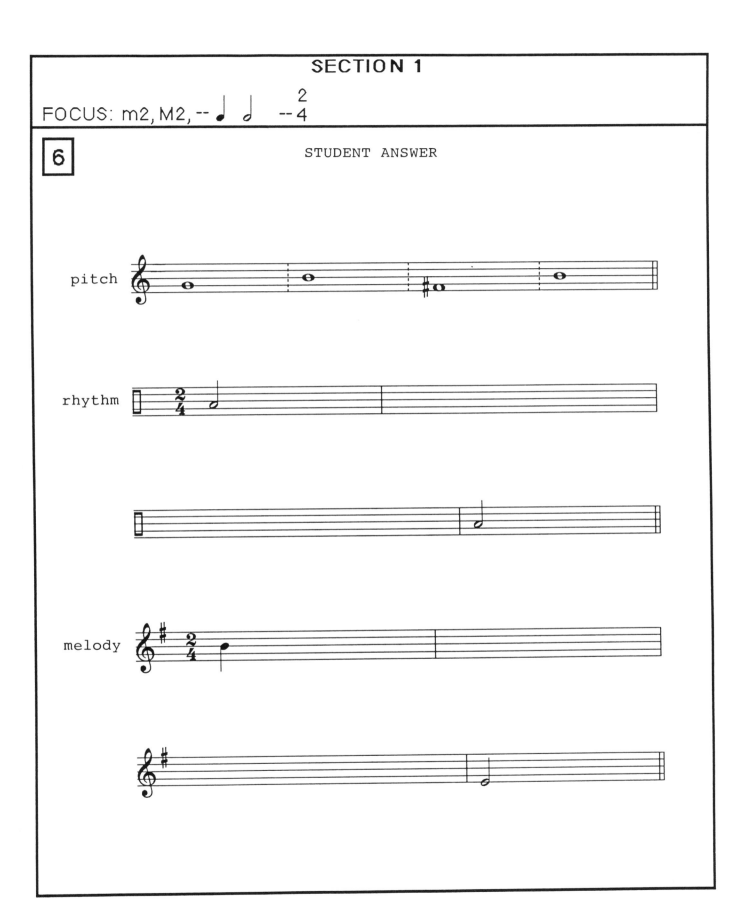

# SECTION 1

FOCUS: m2, M2, -- ♩ ♩ -- $\frac{2}{4}$

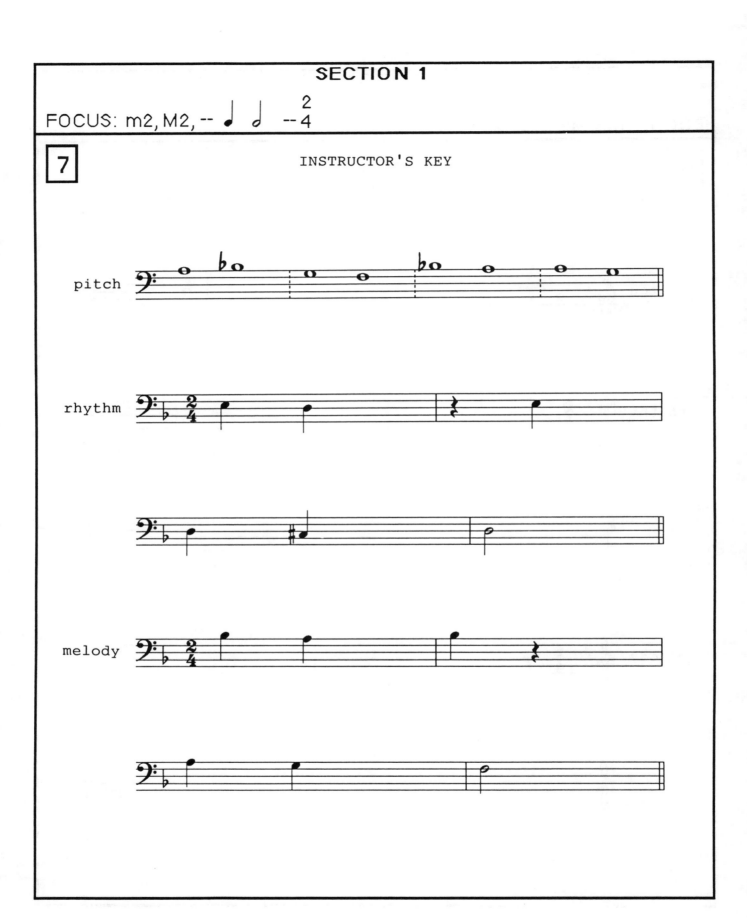

# SECTION 1

FOCUS: m2, M2, -- ♩ ♩ -- 2/4

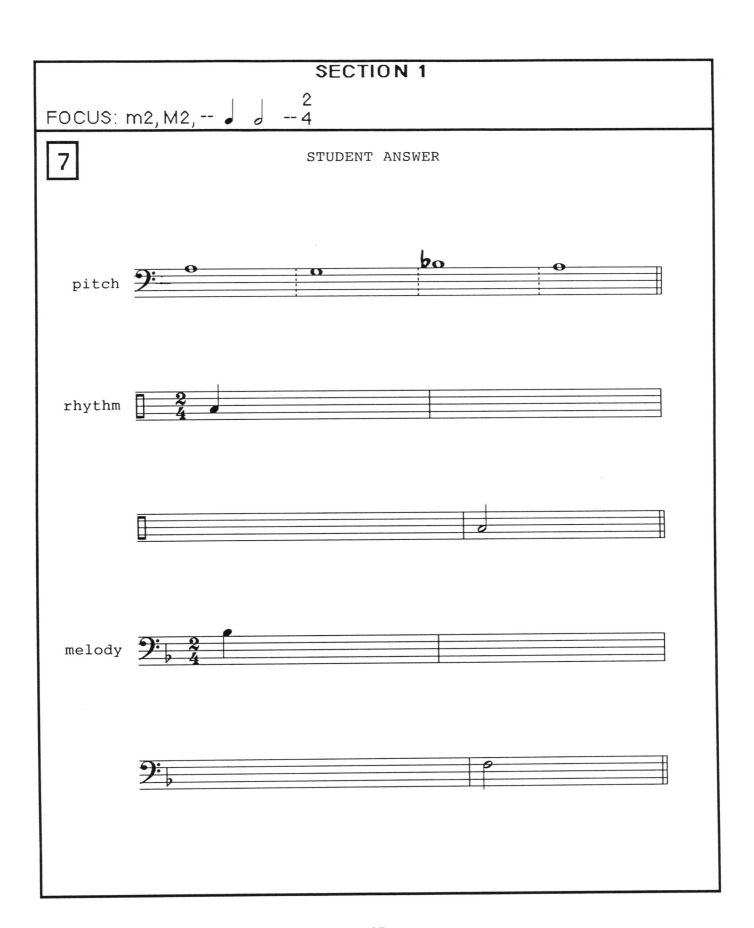

15

# SECTION 1

FOCUS: m2, M2, -- ♩ ♩ -- 2/4

8  INSTRUCTOR'S KEY

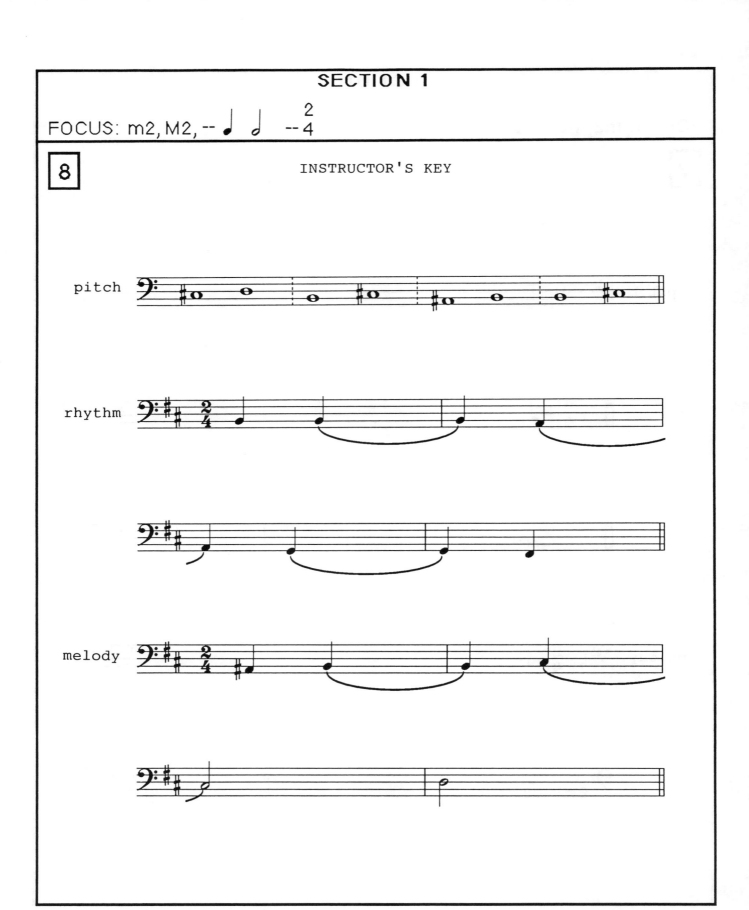

# SECTION 1

FOCUS: m2, M2, -- ♩ ♪ -- $\frac{2}{4}$

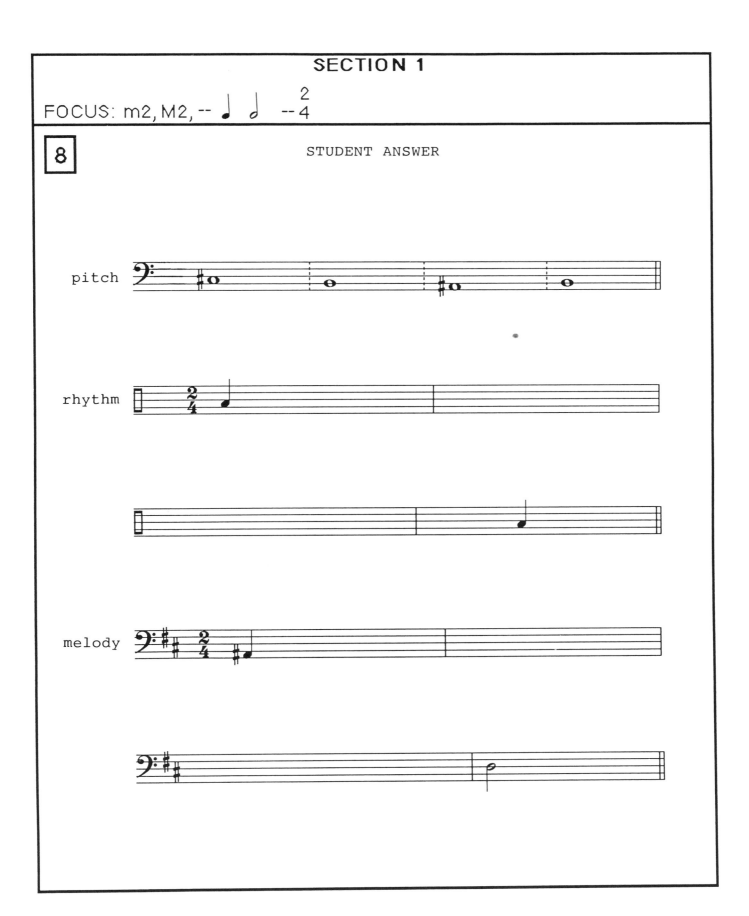

# SECTION 1A

FOCUS: Tonic, Dominant,
root position

INSTRUCTOR'S KEY:

STUDENT ANSWER:

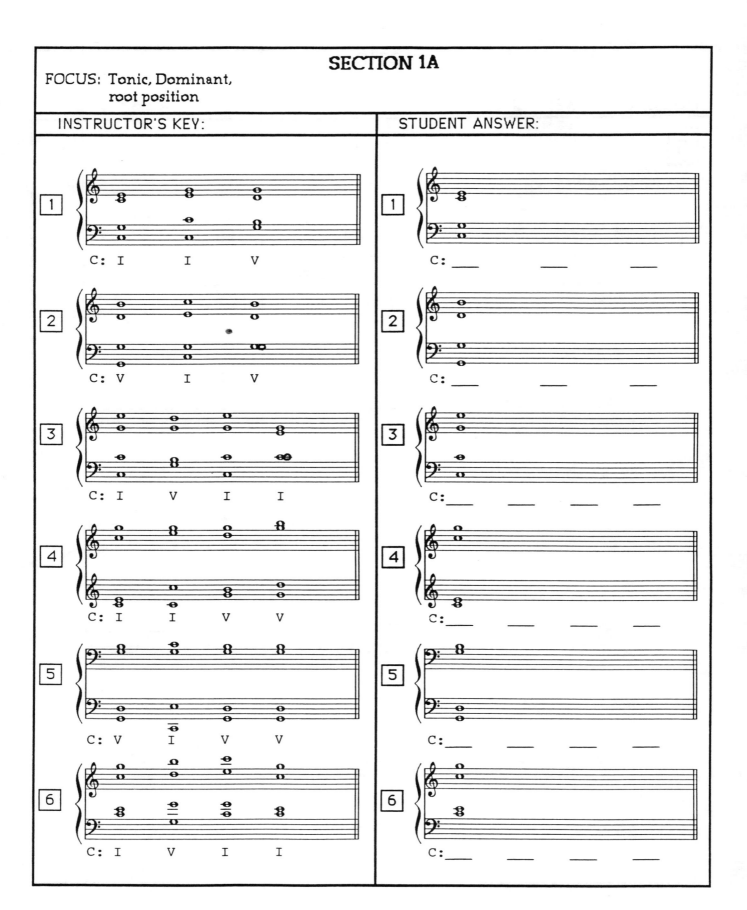

# SECTION 1 A

FOCUS: Tonic, Dominant,
root position

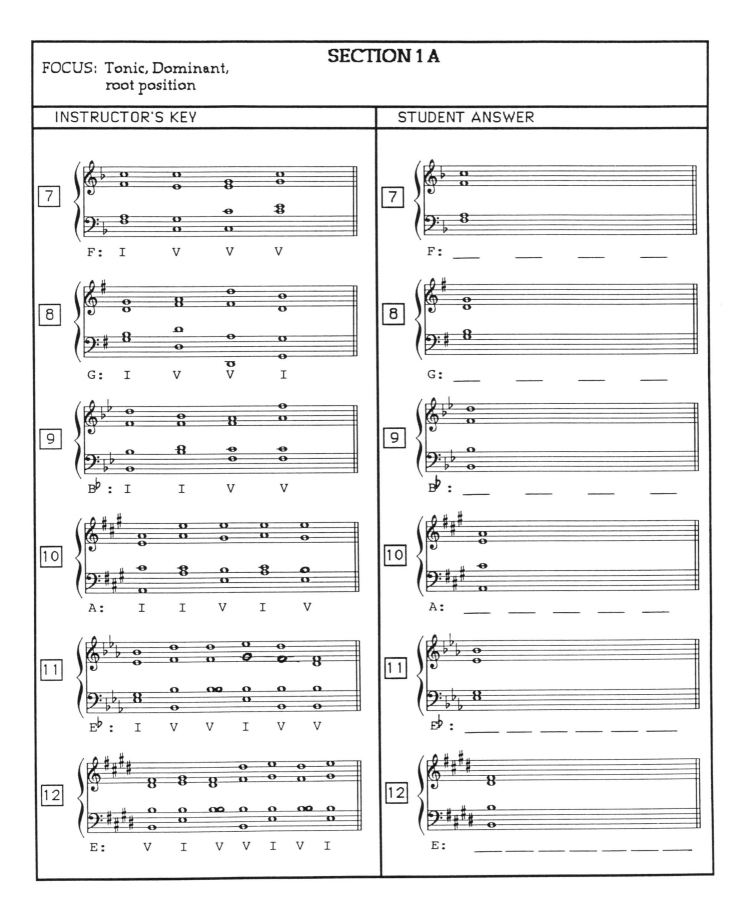

INSTRUCTOR'S KEY

STUDENT ANSWER

7  F: I   V   V   V

8  G: I   V   V   I

9  B♭: I   I   V   V

10  A: I   I   V   I   V

11  E♭: I   V   V   I   V   V

12  E: V   I   V   V   I   V   I

7  F: ___ ___ ___ ___

8  G: ___ ___ ___ ___

9  B♭: ___ ___ ___ ___

10  A: ___ ___ ___ ___ ___

11  E♭: ___ ___ ___ ___ ___ ___

12  E: ___ ___ ___ ___ ___ ___ ___

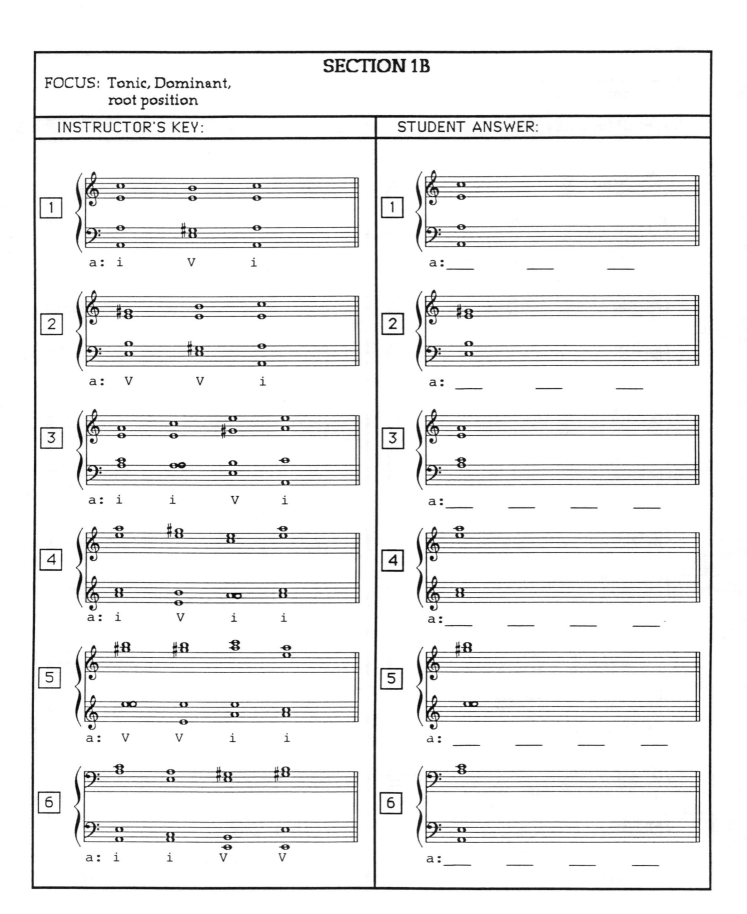

# SECTION 1B

FOCUS: Tonic, Dominant,
root position

INSTRUCTOR'S KEY:

STUDENT ANSWER:

20

# SECTION 1B

FOCUS: Tonic, Dominant,
root position

| INSTRUCTOR'S KEY | STUDENT ANSWER |
|---|---|

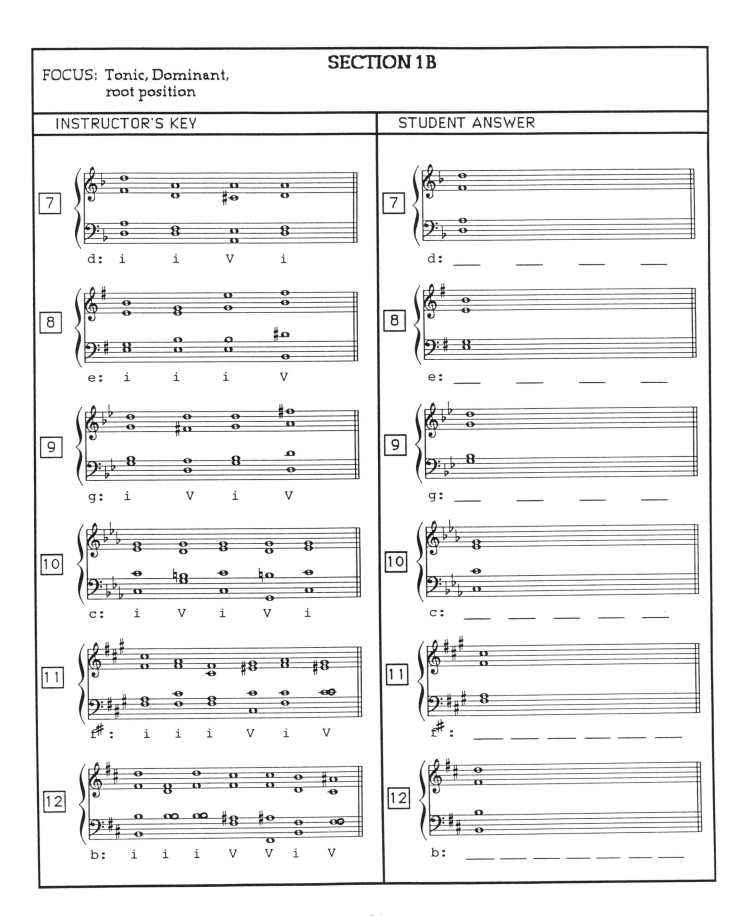

**7** d: i    i    V    i

**7** d: ___  ___  ___  ___

**8** e: i    i    i    V

**8** e: ___  ___  ___  ___

**9** g: i    V    i    V

**9** g: ___  ___  ___  ___

**10** c: i    V    i    V    i

**10** c: ___  ___  ___  ___  ___

**11** f#: i   i   i   V   i   V

**11** f#: ___  ___  ___  ___  ___  ___

**12** b: i   i   i   V   V   i   V

**12** b: ___  ___  ___  ___  ___  ___  ___

# SECTION 2

FOCUS: m3, M3 -- ♩. -- 3/4

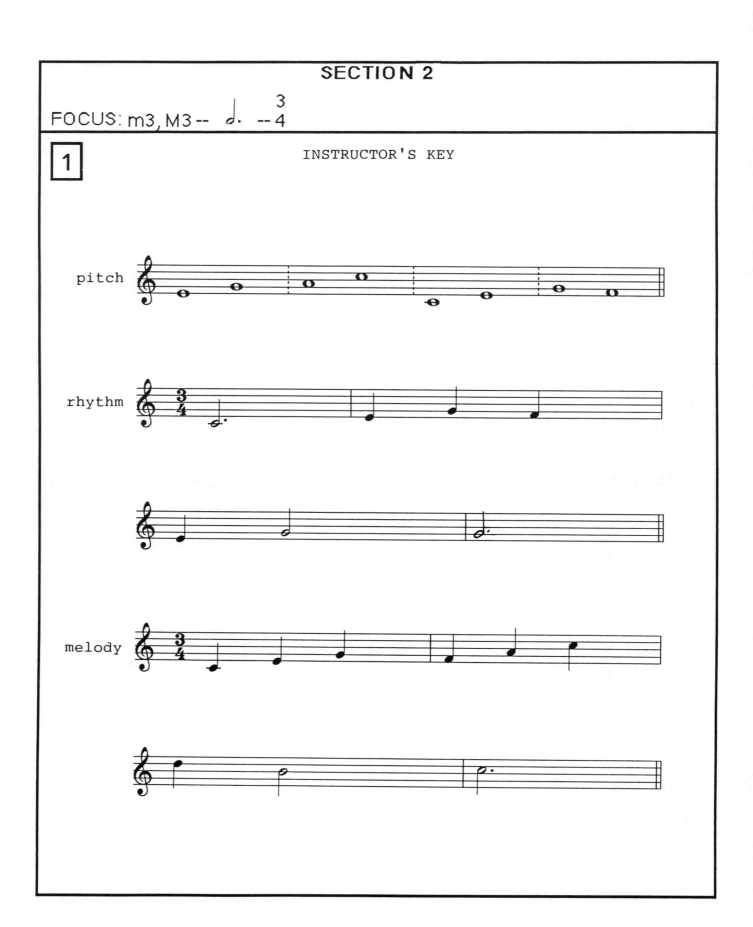

INSTRUCTOR'S KEY

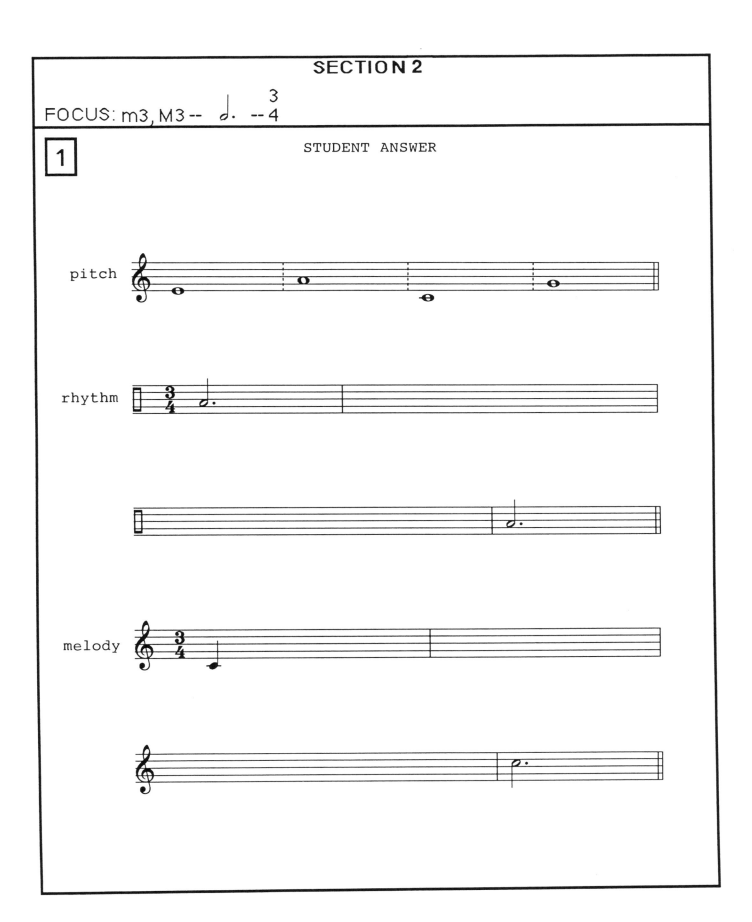

# SECTION 2

FOCUS: m3, M3 -- ♩. -- $\frac{3}{4}$

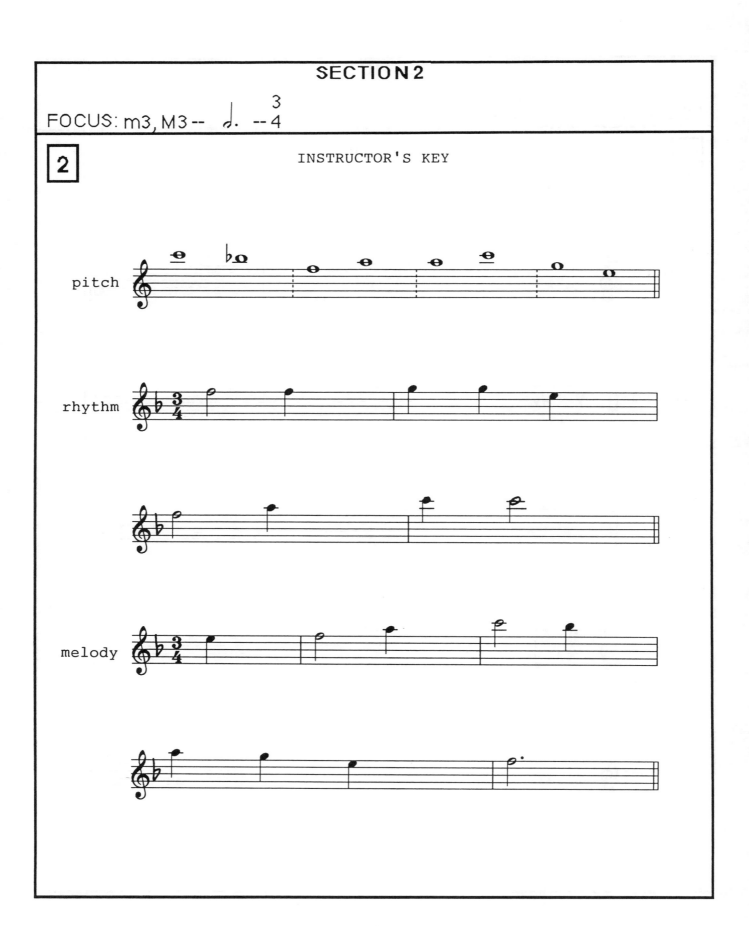

pitch

rhythm

melody

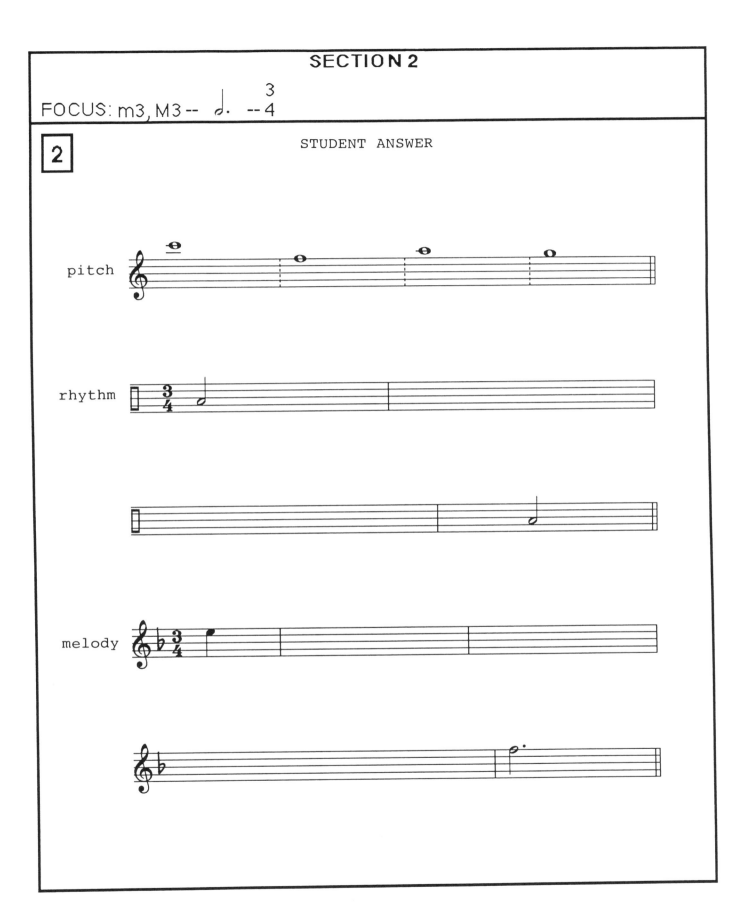

FOCUS: m3, M3 -- ♩. -- 3/4

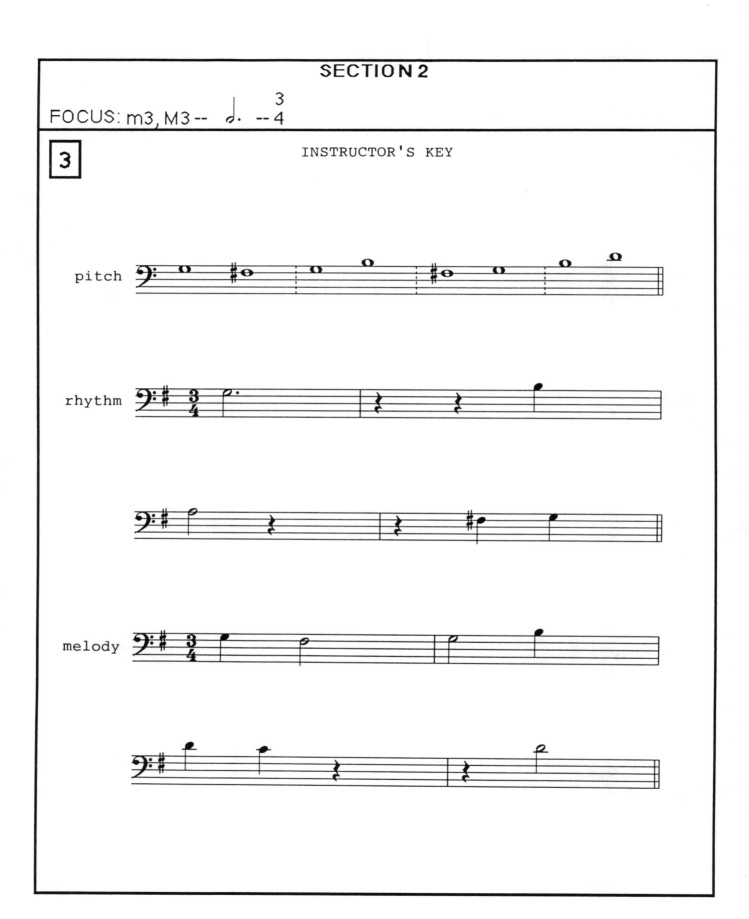

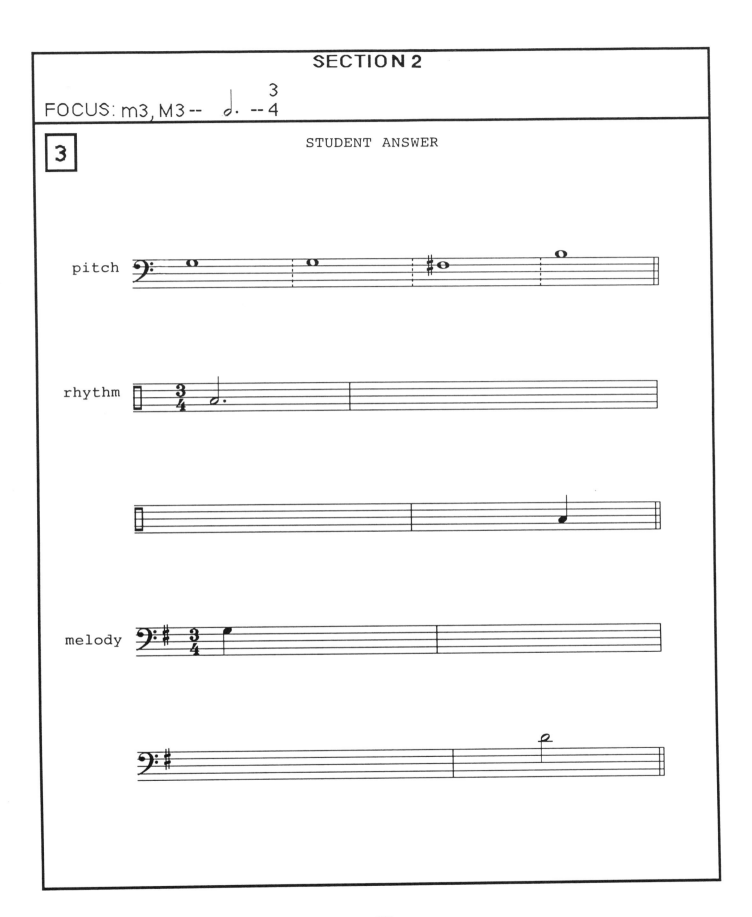

# SECTION 2

FOCUS: m3, M3 -- 𝅗𝅥. -- 3/4

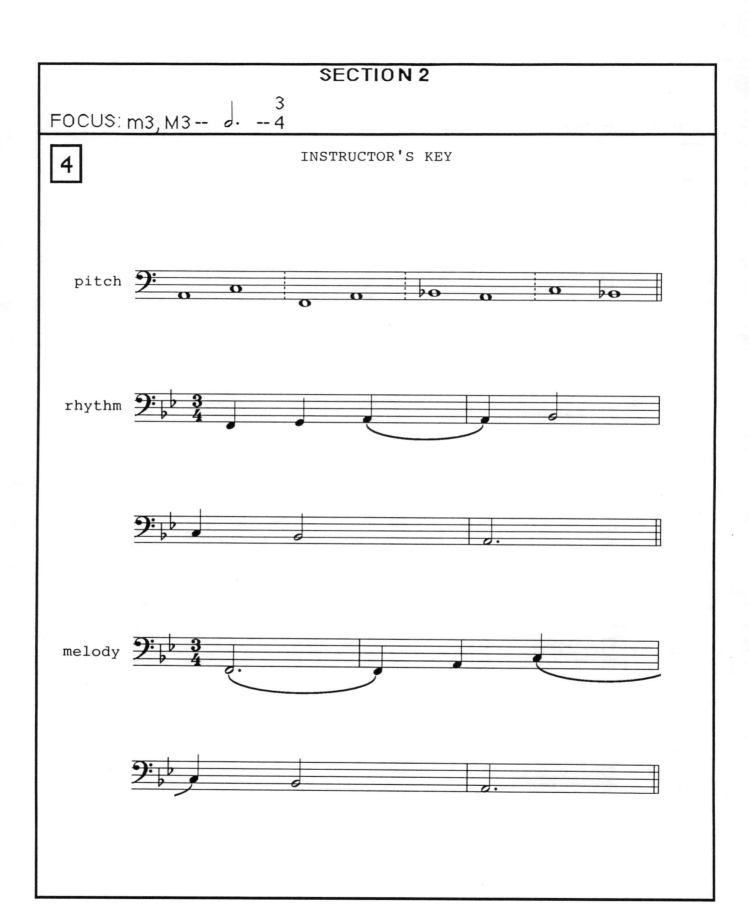

INSTRUCTOR'S KEY

28

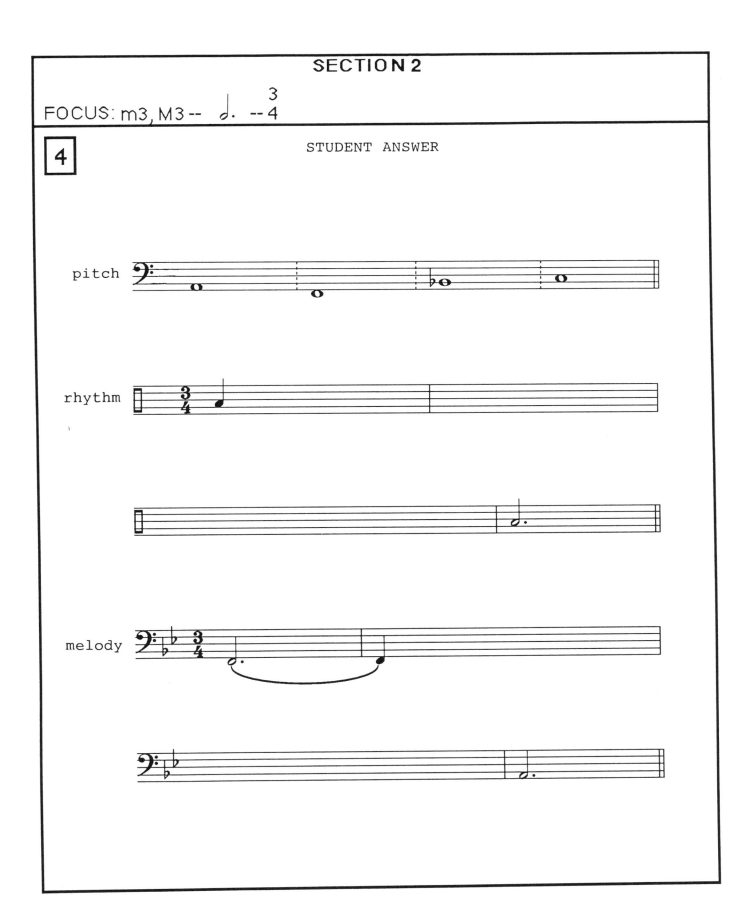

FOCUS: m3, M3 -- ♩. -- 3/4

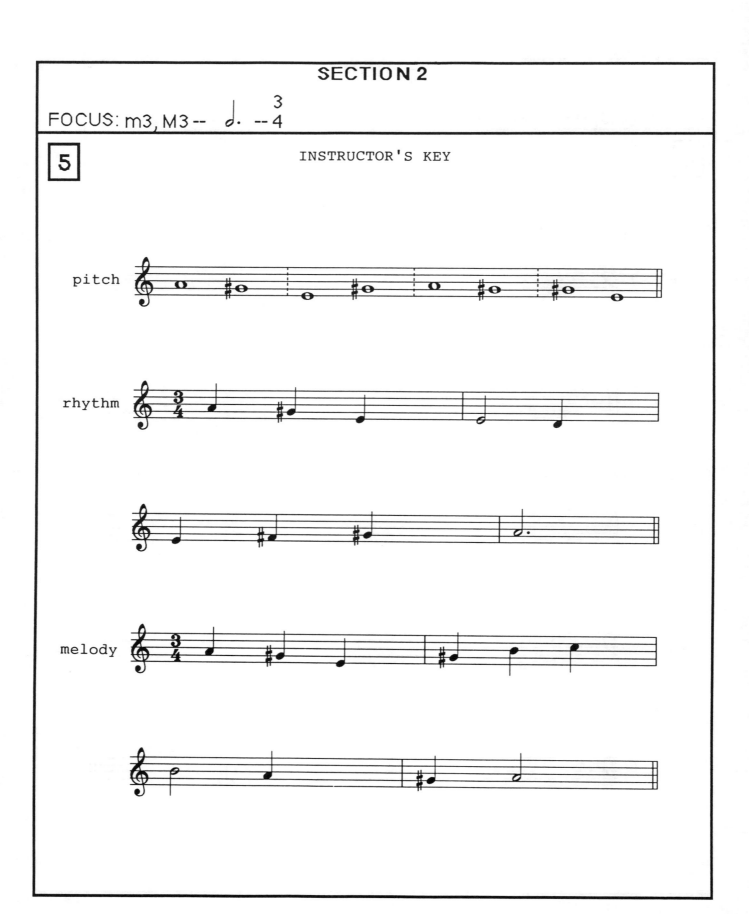

INSTRUCTOR'S KEY

# SECTION 2

FOCUS: m3, M3 -- 𝅗𝅥. -- 3/4

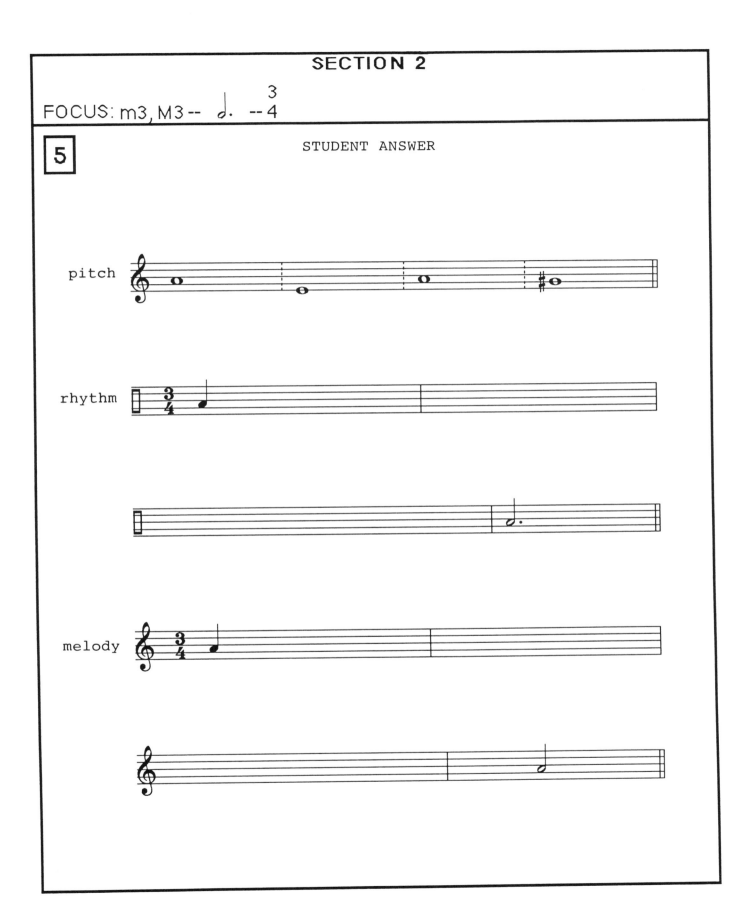

# SECTION 2

FOCUS: m3, M3 -- ♩. -- 3/4

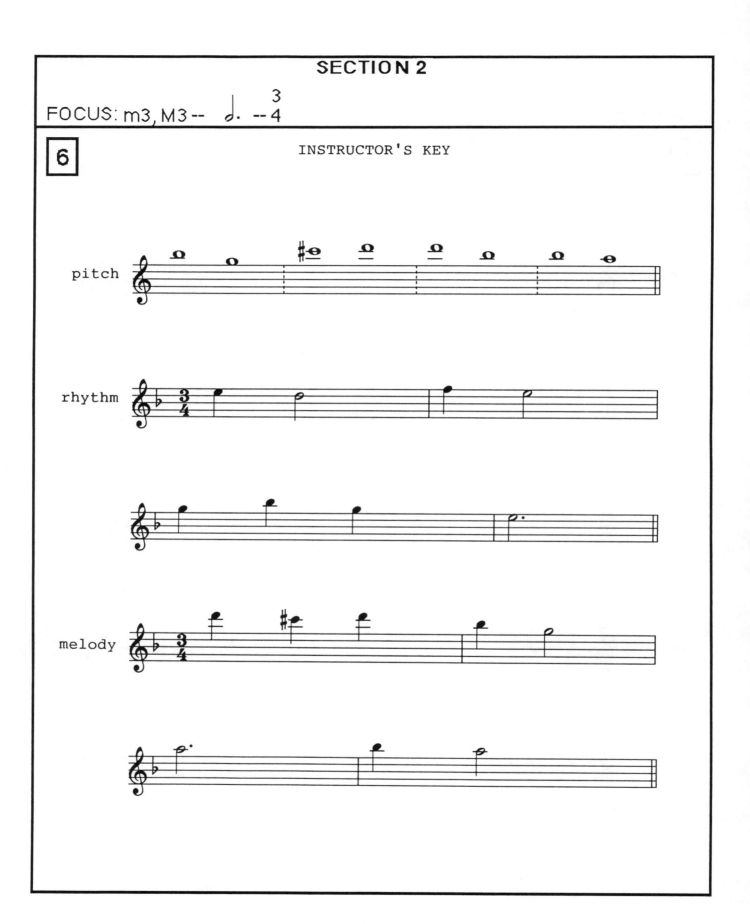

# SECTION 2

FOCUS: m3, M3 -- 𝅗𝅥. -- 3/4

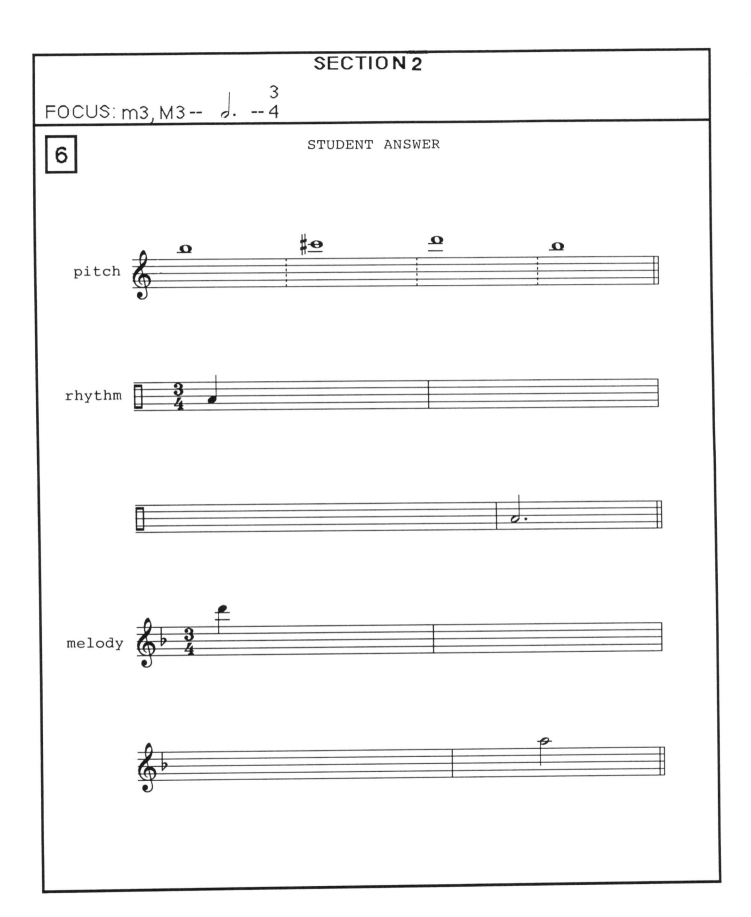

# SECTION 2

FOCUS: m3, M3 -- ♩. -- ³₄

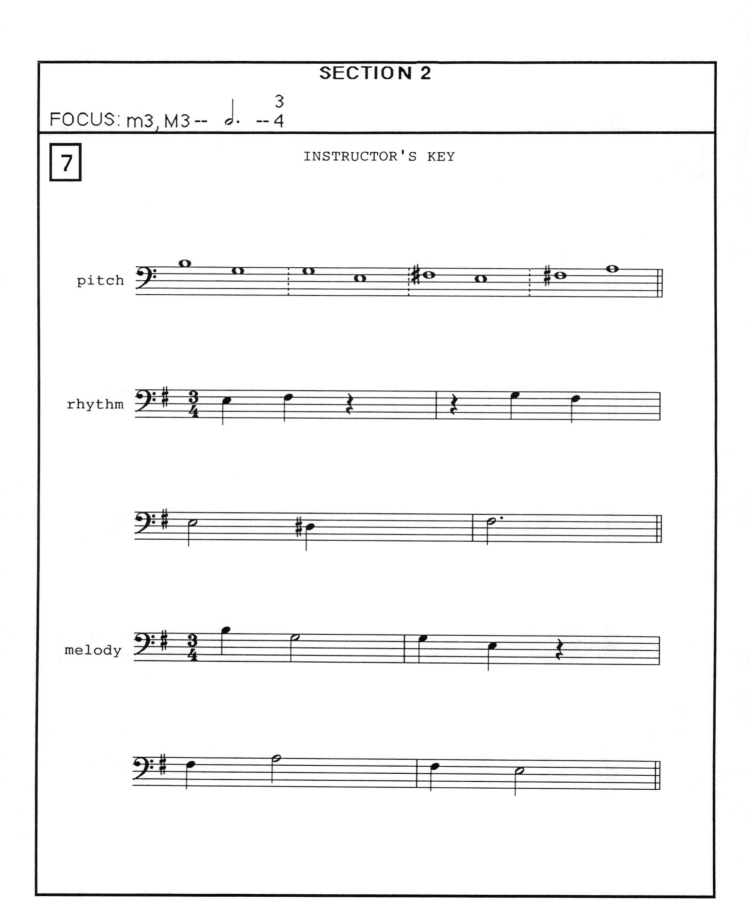

INSTRUCTOR'S KEY

pitch

rhythm

melody

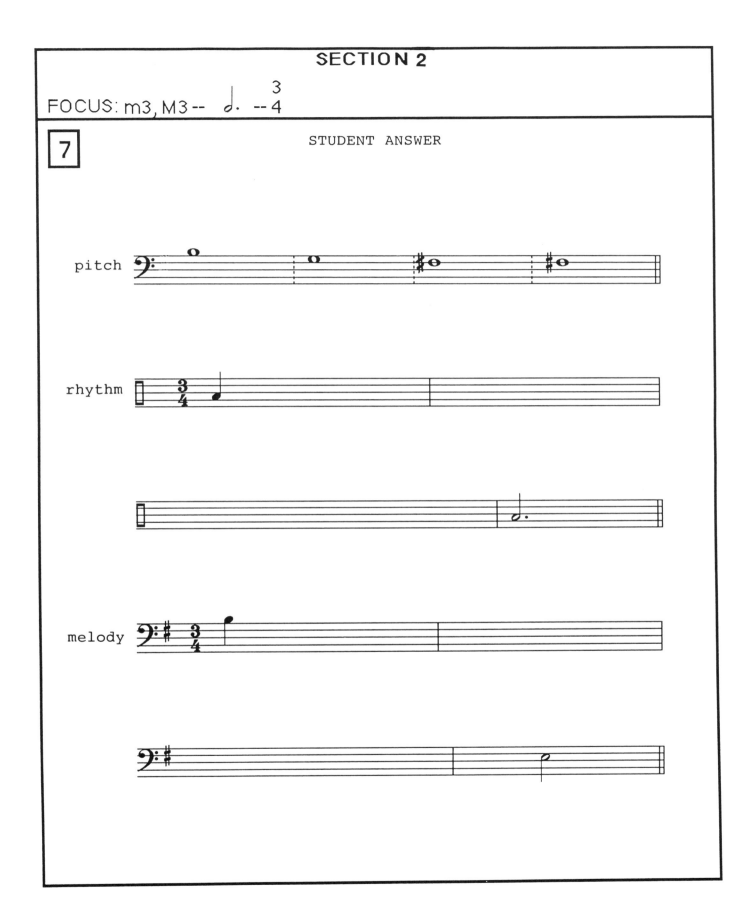

FOCUS: m3, M3 -- 𝅗𝅥. -- 3/4

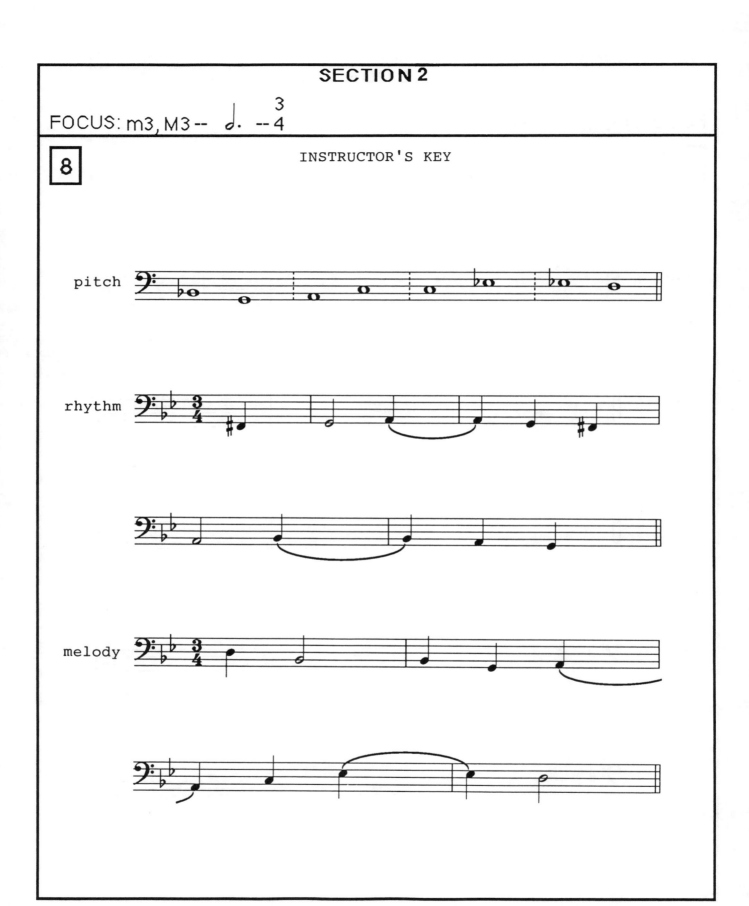

8   INSTRUCTOR'S KEY

# SECTION 2

FOCUS: m3, M3 -- ♩. -- 3/4

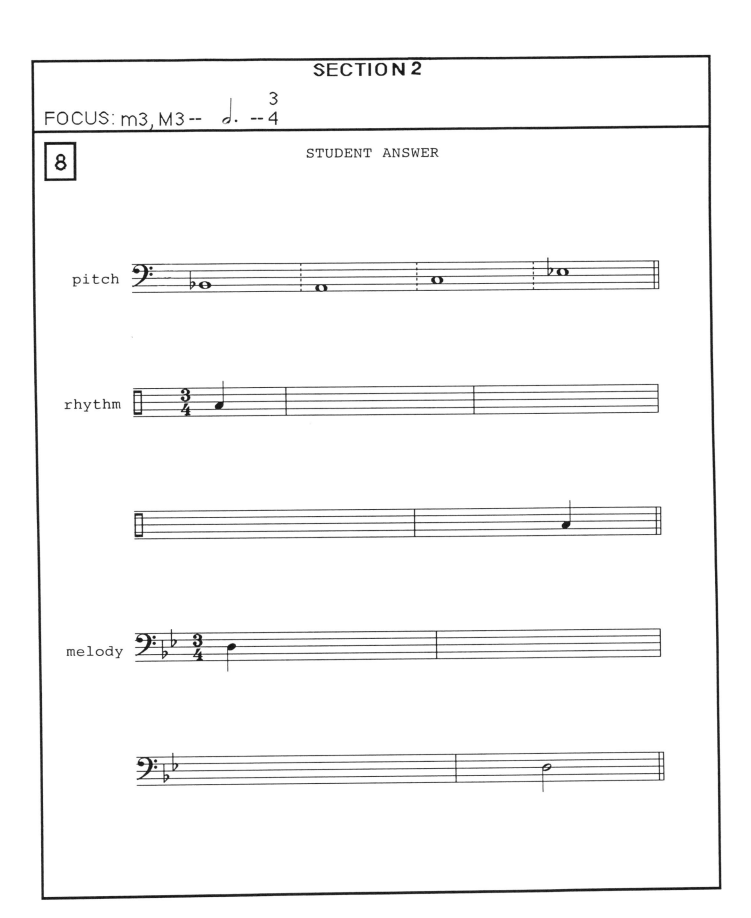

# SECTION 2A

**FOCUS:** Tonic, Subdominant, root position

| INSTRUCTOR'S KEY: | STUDENT ANSWER: |
| --- | --- |

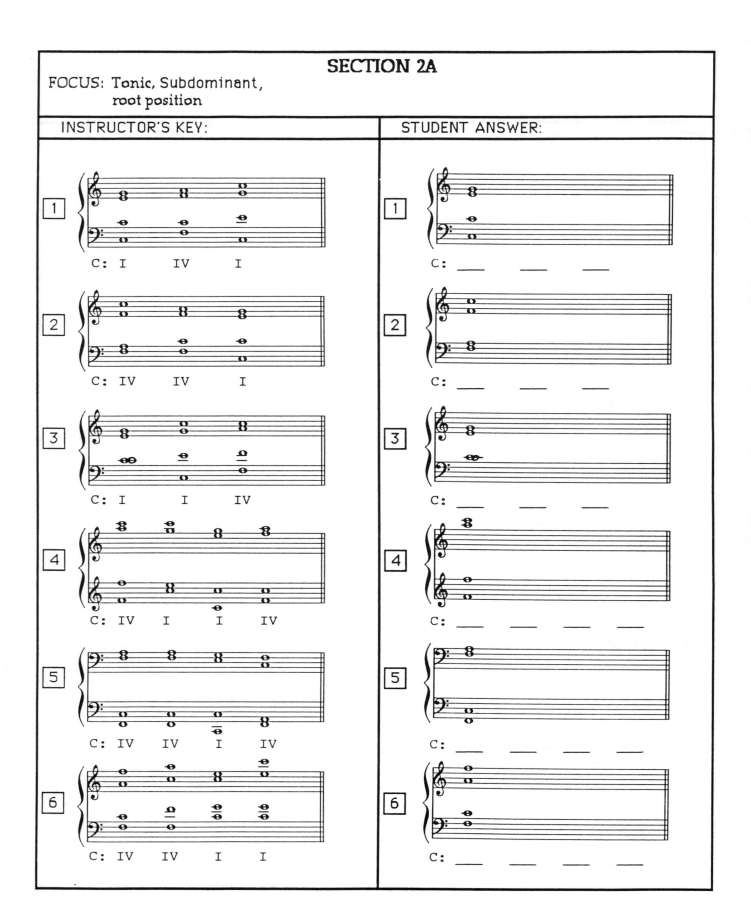

1   C: I   IV   I

2   C: IV   IV   I

3   C: I   I   IV

4   C: IV   I   I   IV

5   C: IV   IV   I   IV

6   C: IV   IV   I   I

# SECTION 2A

FOCUS: Tonic, Subdominant,
root position

| INSTRUCTOR'S KEY | STUDENT ANSWER |
|---|---|

**7**  A:  I   IV   I   IV

**7**  A: ___ ___ ___ ___

**8**  A♭:  I   I   I   IV

**8**  A♭: ___ ___ ___ ___

**9**  D:  IV   IV   I   I

**9**  D: ___ ___ ___ ___

**10**  B♭:  I   I   IV   I   IV

**10**  B♭: ___ ___ ___ ___ ___

**11**  G:  IV   I   IV   I   I   IV

**11**  G: ___ ___ ___ ___ ___ ___

**12**  F:  IV   IV   I   IV   I   I   IV

**12**  F: ___ ___ ___ ___ ___ ___ ___

# SECTION 2B

FOCUS: Tonic, Subdominant,
root position

INSTRUCTOR'S KEY:

STUDENT ANSWER:

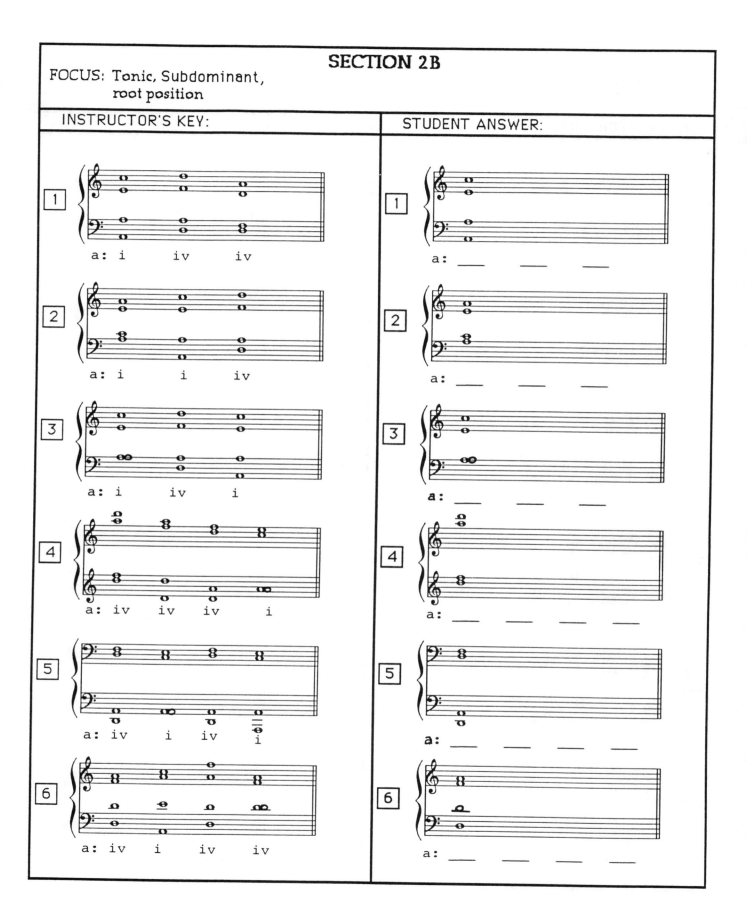

1  a:  i    iv    iv

1  a: ___  ___  ___

2  a:  i    i    iv

2  a: ___  ___  ___

3  a:  i    iv    i

3  a: ___  ___  ___

4  a:  iv   iv   iv    i

4  a: ___  ___  ___  ___

5  a:  iv   i   iv    i

5  a: ___  ___  ___  ___

6  a:  iv   i   iv   iv

6  a: ___  ___  ___  ___

40

# SECTION 2B

FOCUS: Tonic, Subdominant,
      root position

| INSTRUCTOR'S KEY | STUDENT ANSWER |
|---|---|

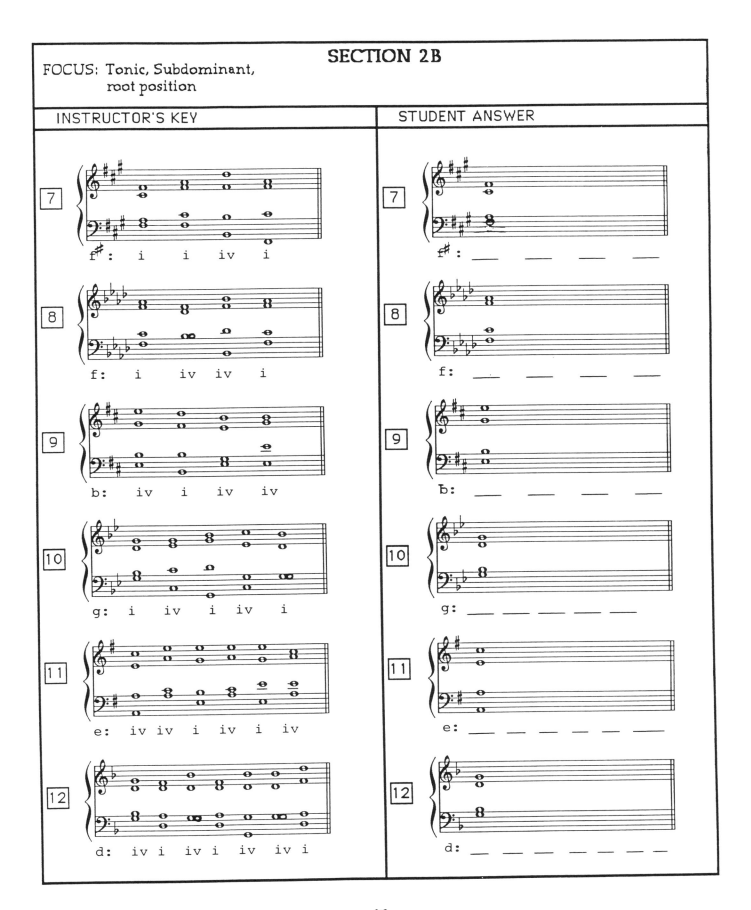

7    f♯ :  i    i    iv    i

8    f :  i    iv    iv    i

9    b :  iv    i    iv    iv

10    g :  i    iv    i    iv    i

11    e :  iv  iv    i    iv    i    iv

12    d :  iv  i   iv  i   iv   iv  i

41

# SECTION 3

FOCUS: P8 -- ♩♪ -- $\frac{2}{4}$, $\frac{3}{4}$

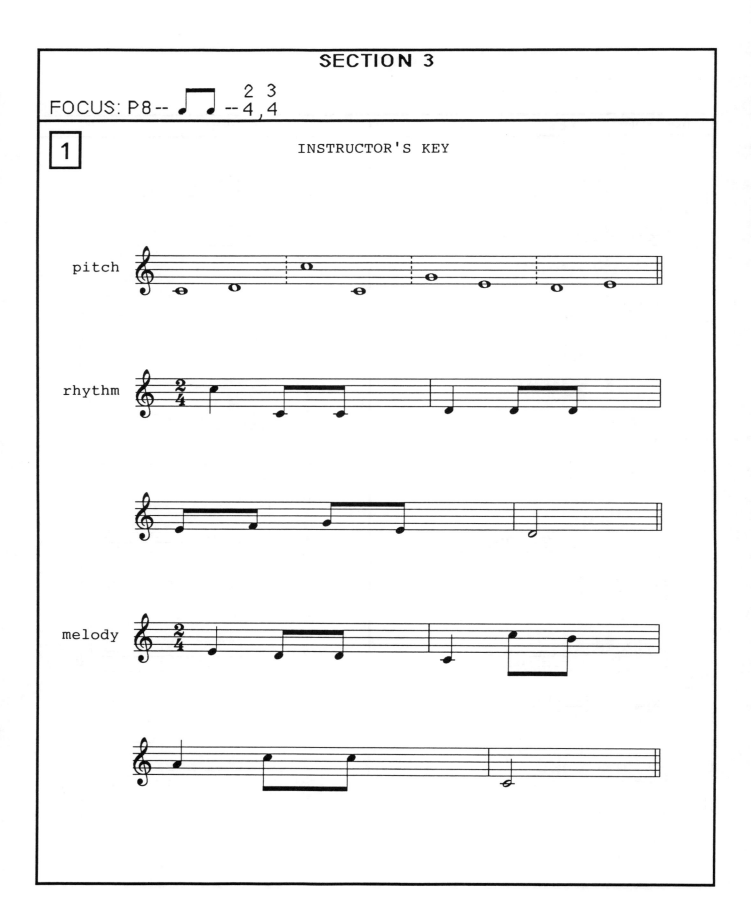

# SECTION 3

FOCUS: P8 -- ♪♪ -- 2/4, 3/4

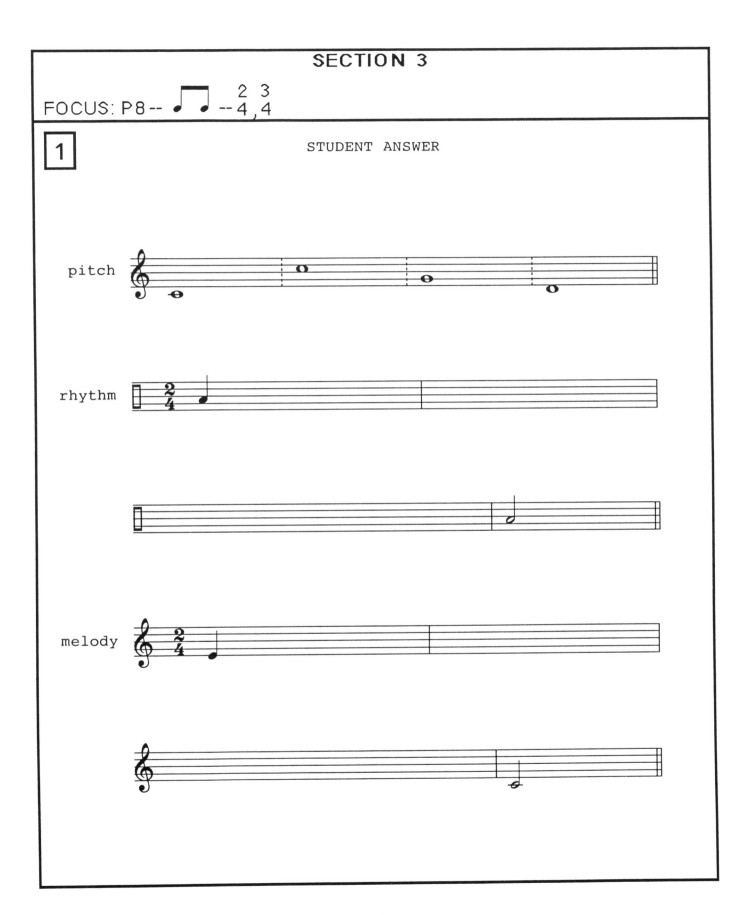

# SECTION 3

FOCUS: P8 -- ♩♩ -- $\frac{2}{4}$, $\frac{3}{4}$

2    INSTRUCTOR'S KEY

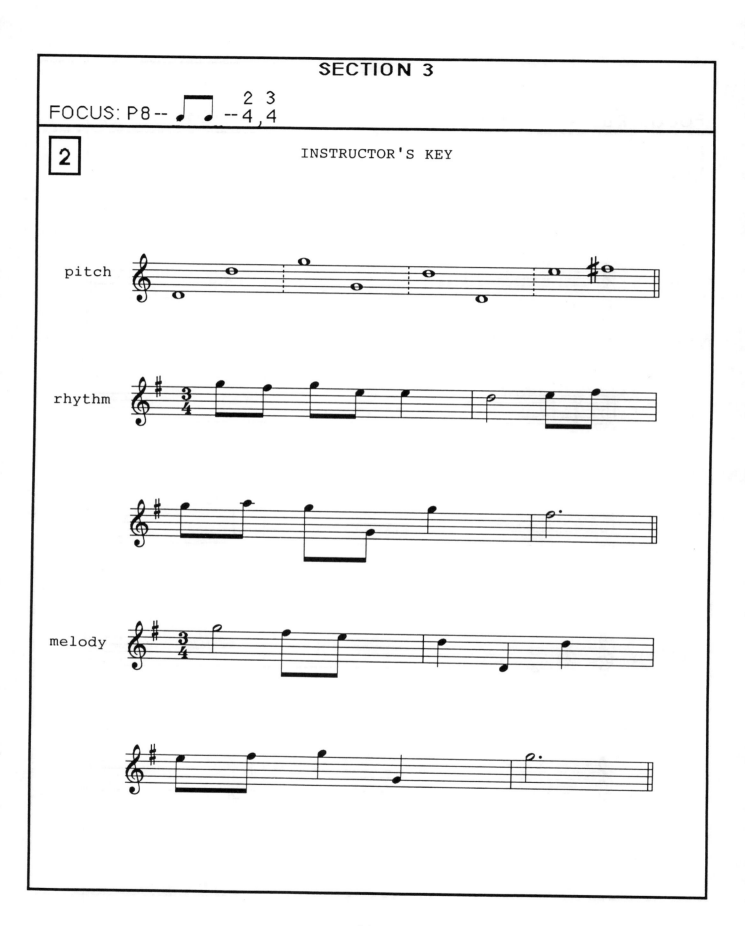

# SECTION 3

FOCUS: P8 -- ♫ -- $\frac{2}{4}$, $\frac{3}{4}$

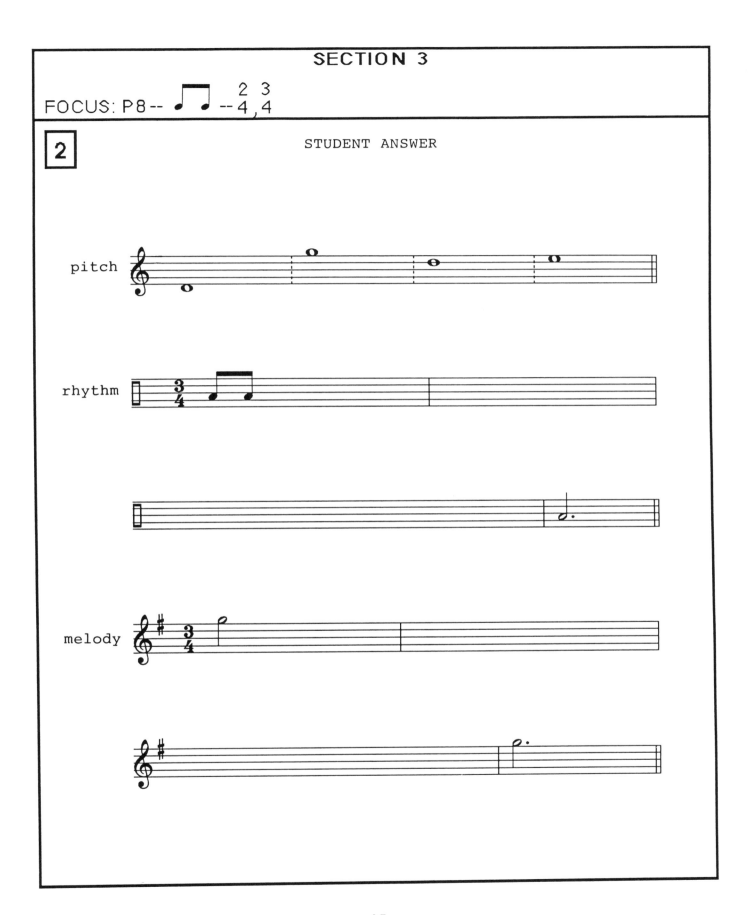

45

# SECTION 3

FOCUS: P8 -- ♪♪ -- $\frac{2}{4}, \frac{3}{4}$

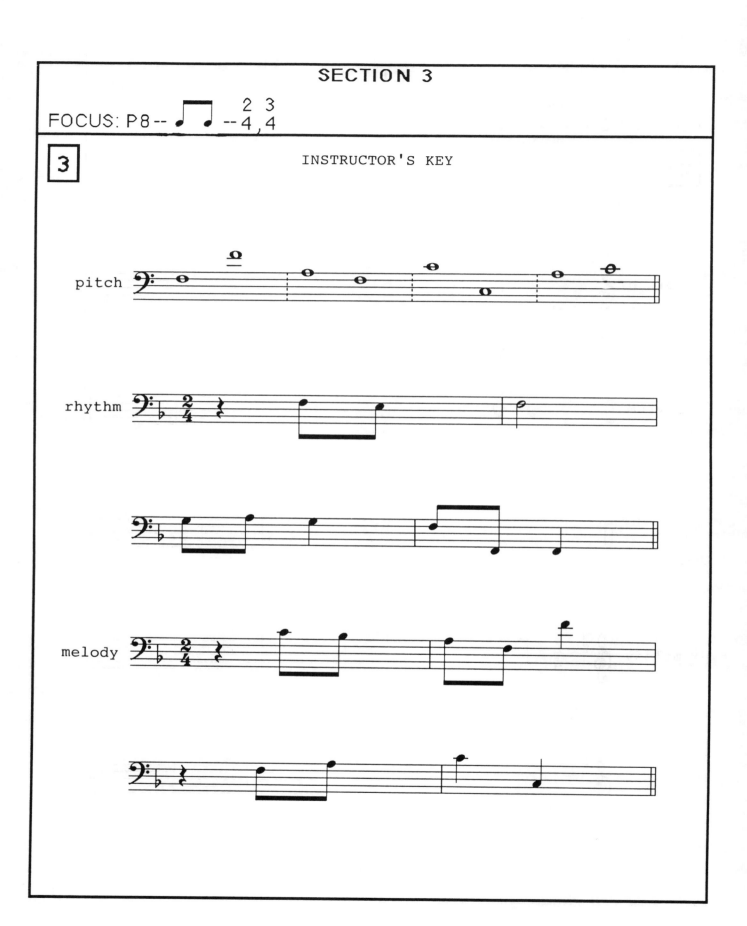

INSTRUCTOR'S KEY

pitch

rhythm

melody

# SECTION 3

FOCUS: P8 -- ♪ ♪ -- 2/4, 3/4

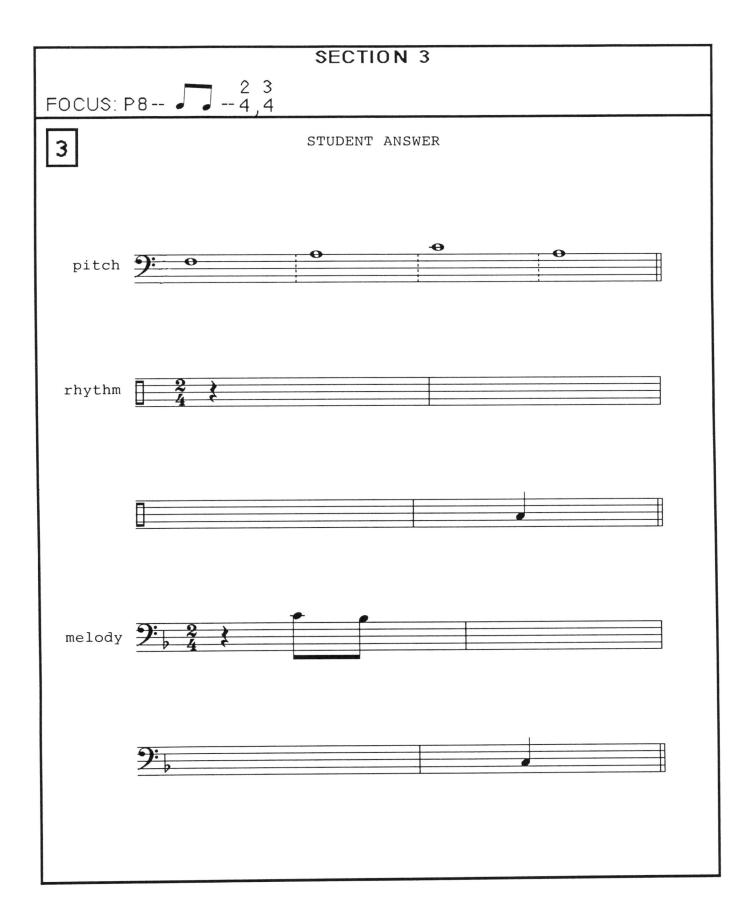

STUDENT ANSWER

pitch

rhythm

melody

# SECTION 3

FOCUS: P8 -- ♪ ♪ -- $\frac{2}{4}, \frac{3}{4}$

**4**           INSTRUCTOR'S KEY

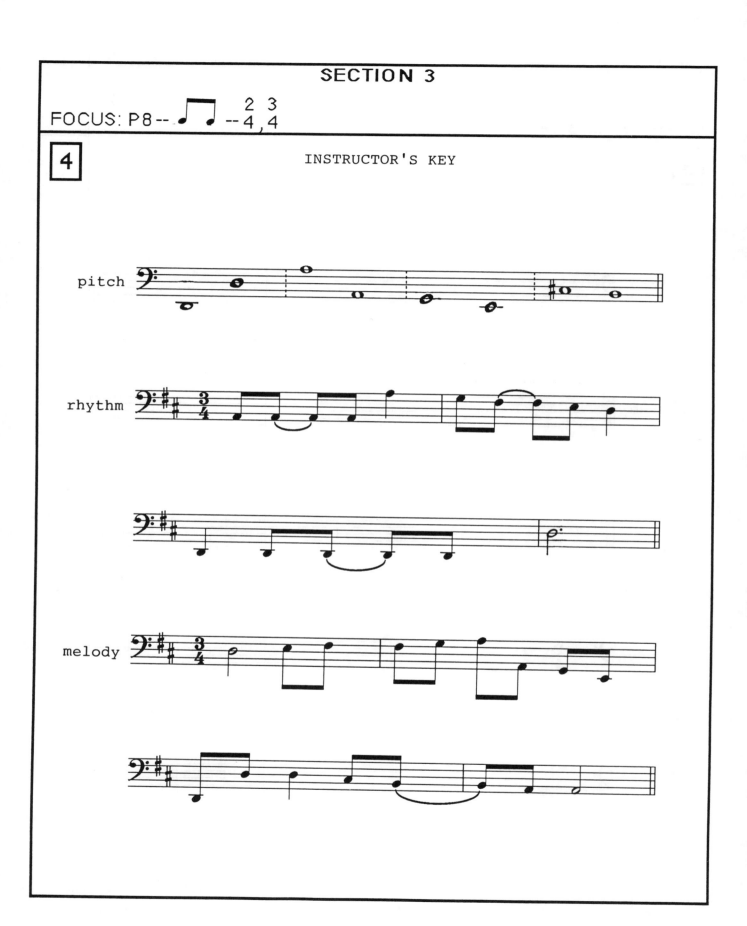

48

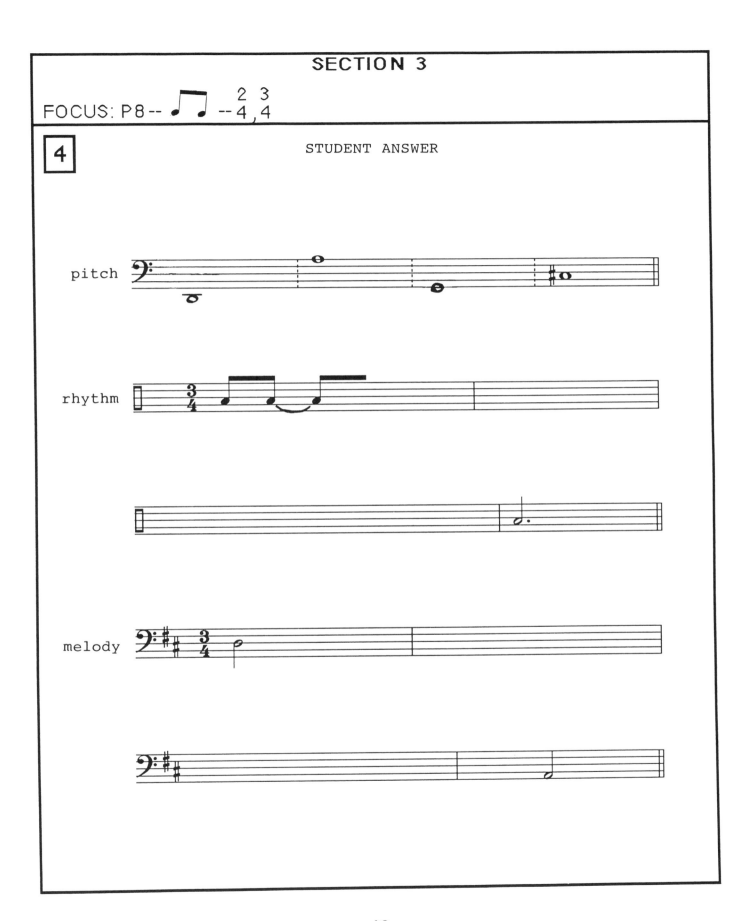

# SECTION 3

FOCUS: P8 -- ♪ ♪ -- $\frac{2}{4}$, $\frac{3}{4}$

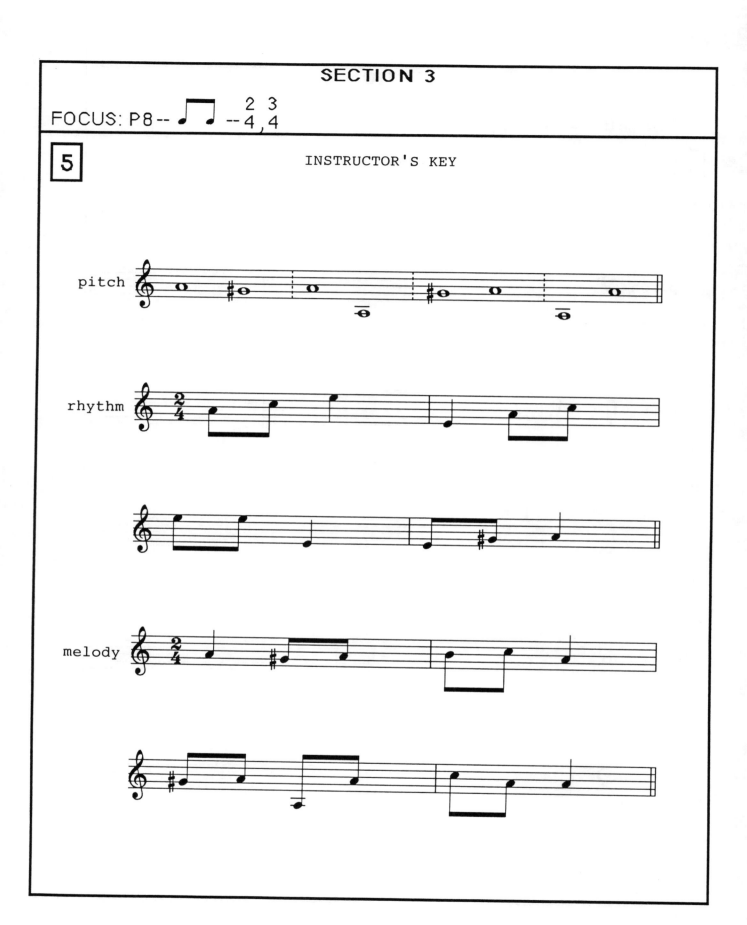

5

INSTRUCTOR'S KEY

pitch

rhythm

melody

50

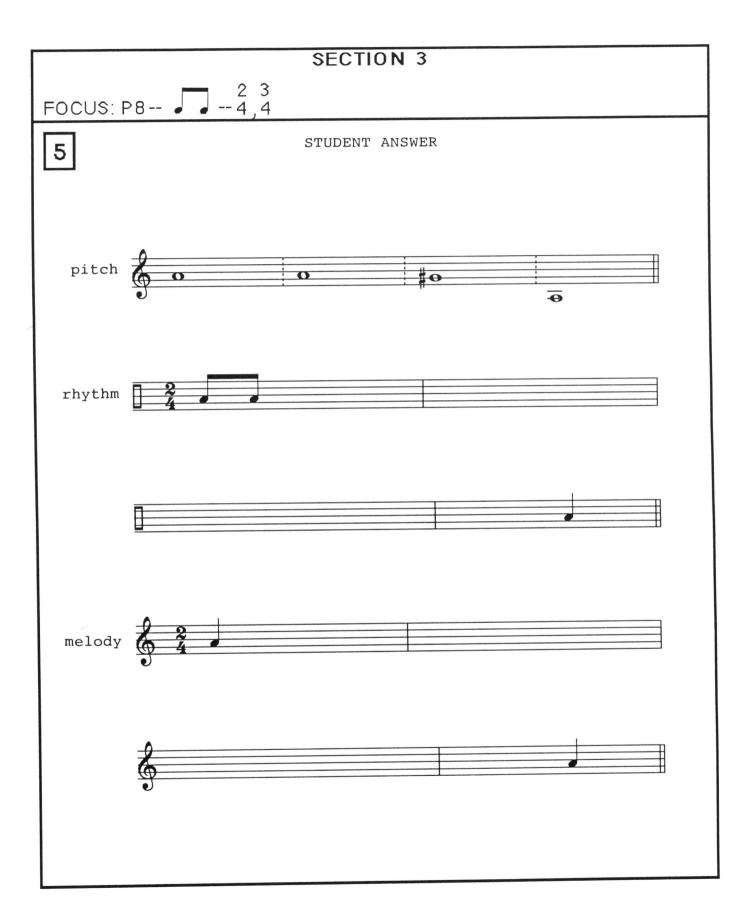

# SECTION 3

FOCUS: P8 -- ♩ ♩ -- 2/4 , 3/4

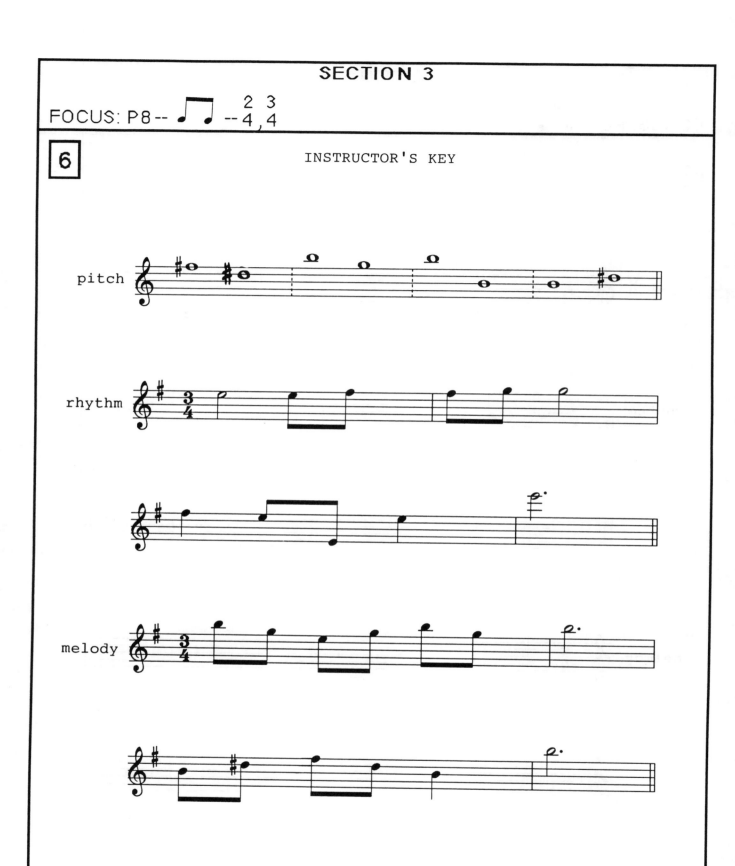

**6**

INSTRUCTOR'S KEY

pitch

rhythm

melody

52

# SECTION 3

FOCUS: P8 -- ♩ ♩ -- $\frac{2}{4}$, $\frac{3}{4}$

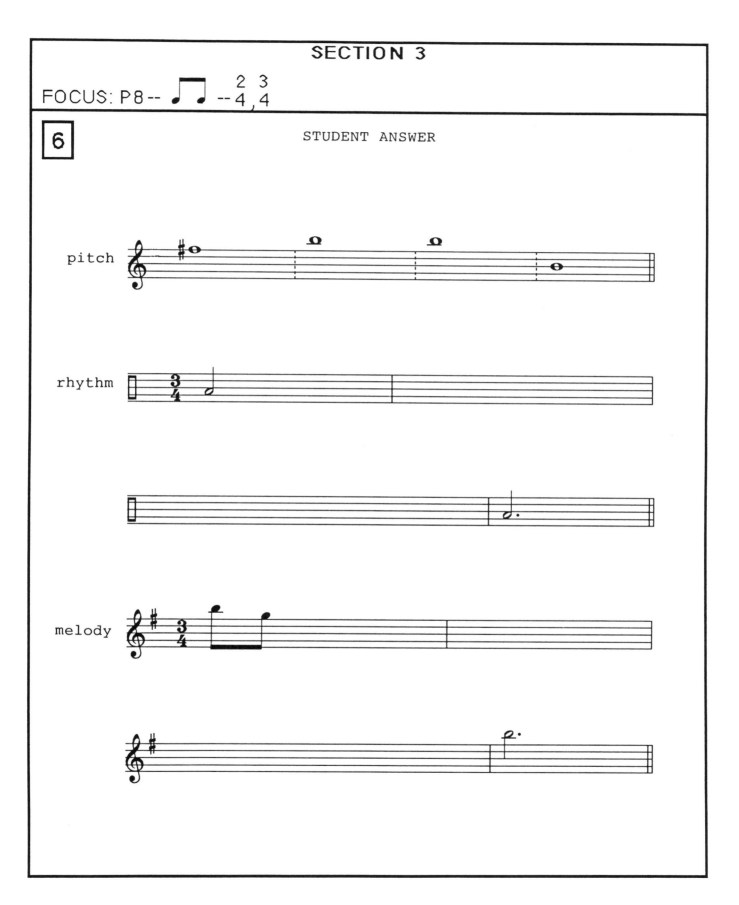

6

STUDENT ANSWER

pitch

rhythm

melody

53

# SECTION 3

FOCUS: P8-- ♪♪ --²⁄₄, ³⁄₄

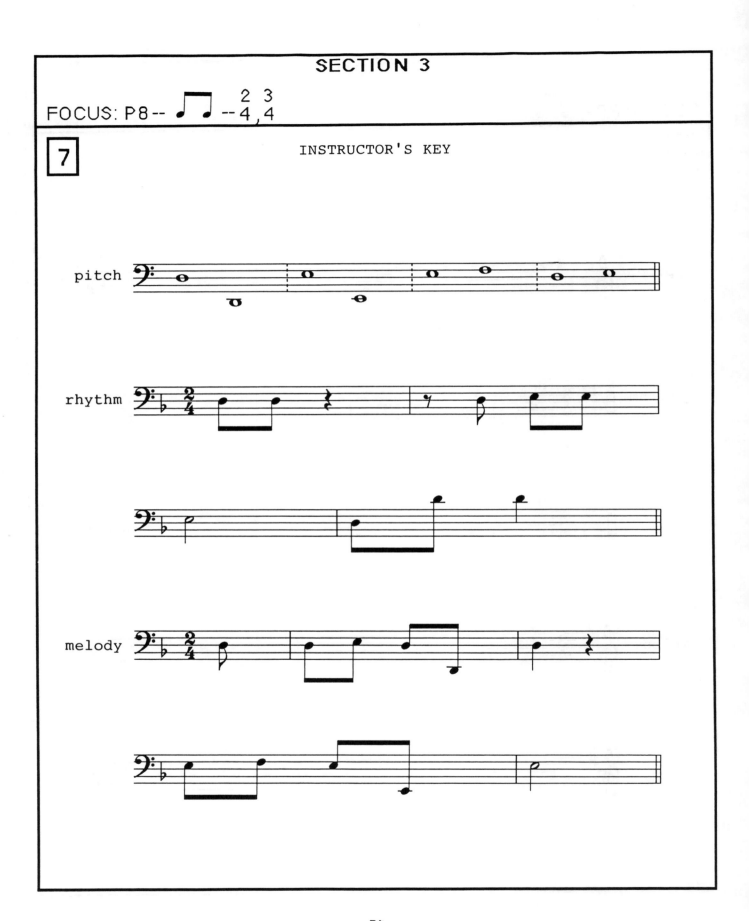

7

INSTRUCTOR'S KEY

pitch

rhythm

melody

54

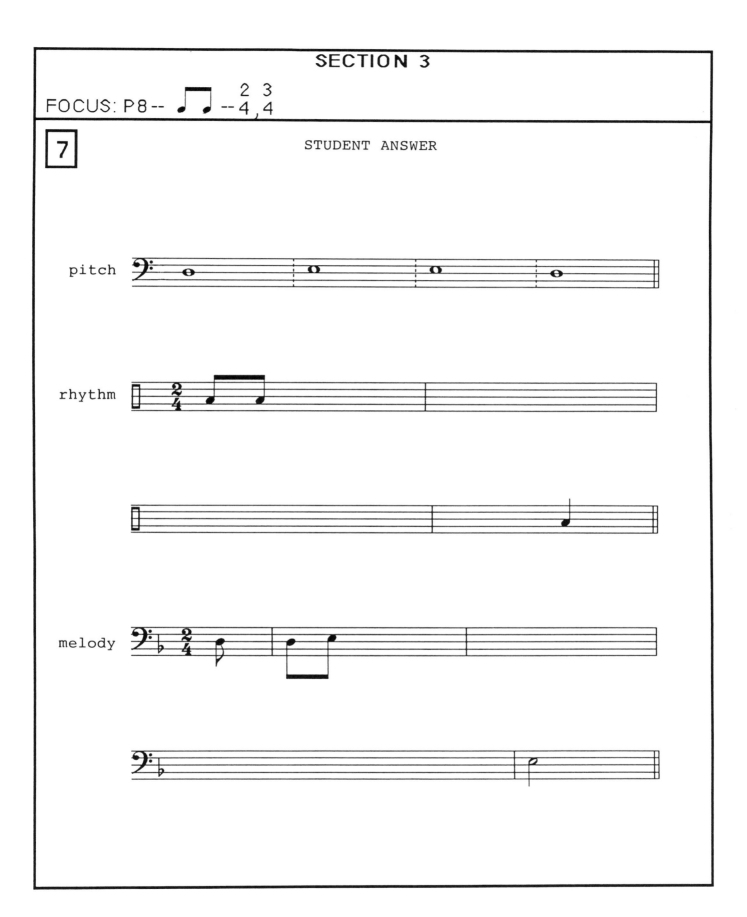

55

# SECTION 3

FOCUS: P8-- ♩♩ --2/4, 3/4

8

INSTRUCTOR'S KEY

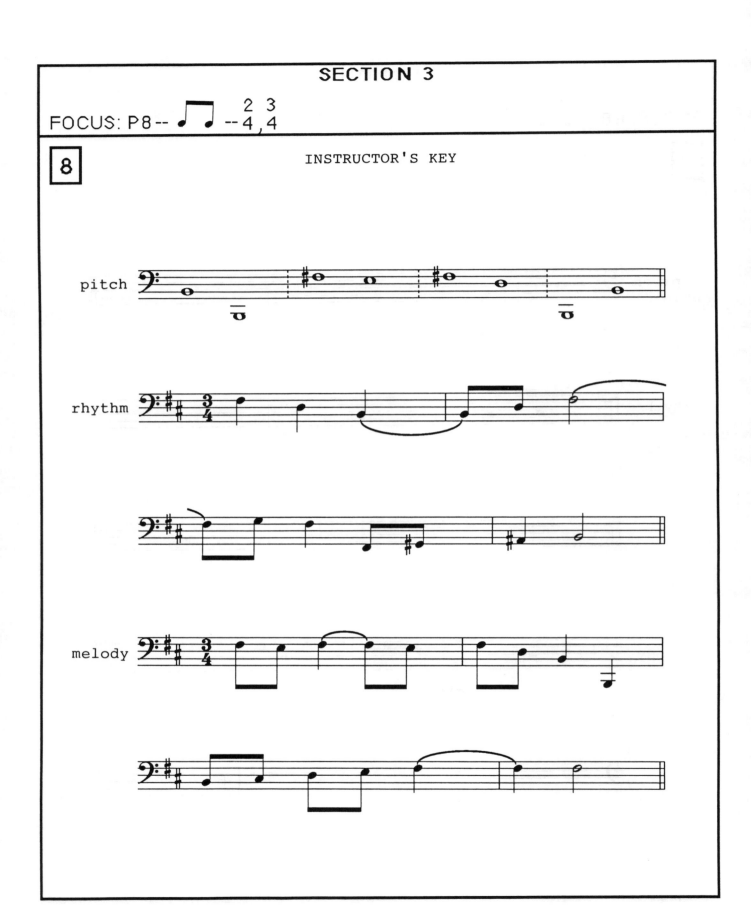

56

# SECTION 3

FOCUS: P8 -- ♪♪ -- 2/4 , 3/4

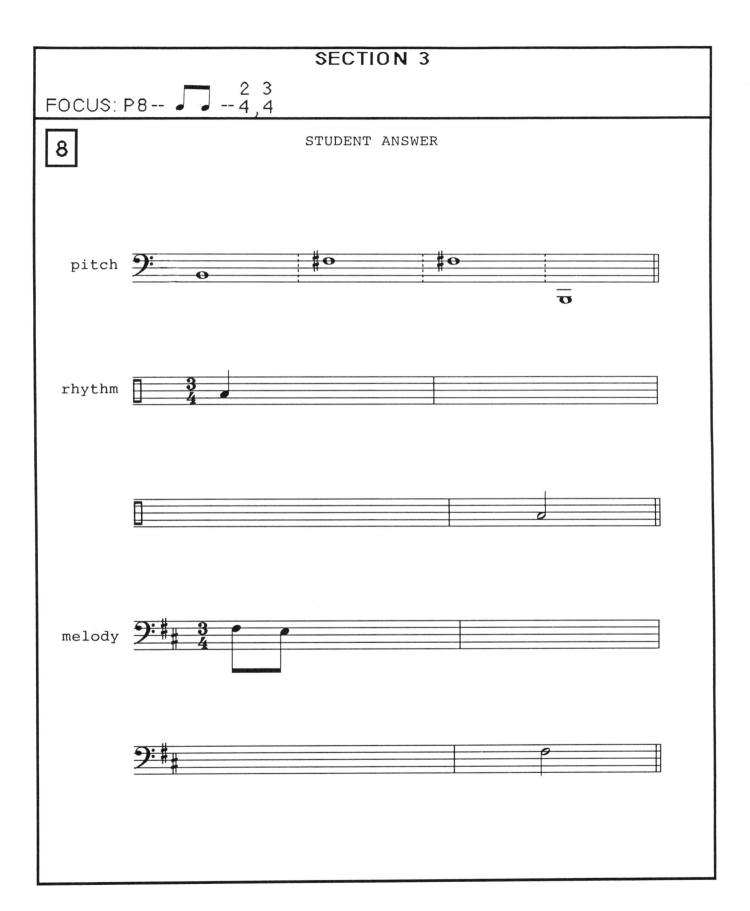

# SECTION 3A

FOCUS: Primary Triads,
       root position

INSTRUCTOR'S KEY:                    STUDENT ANSWER:

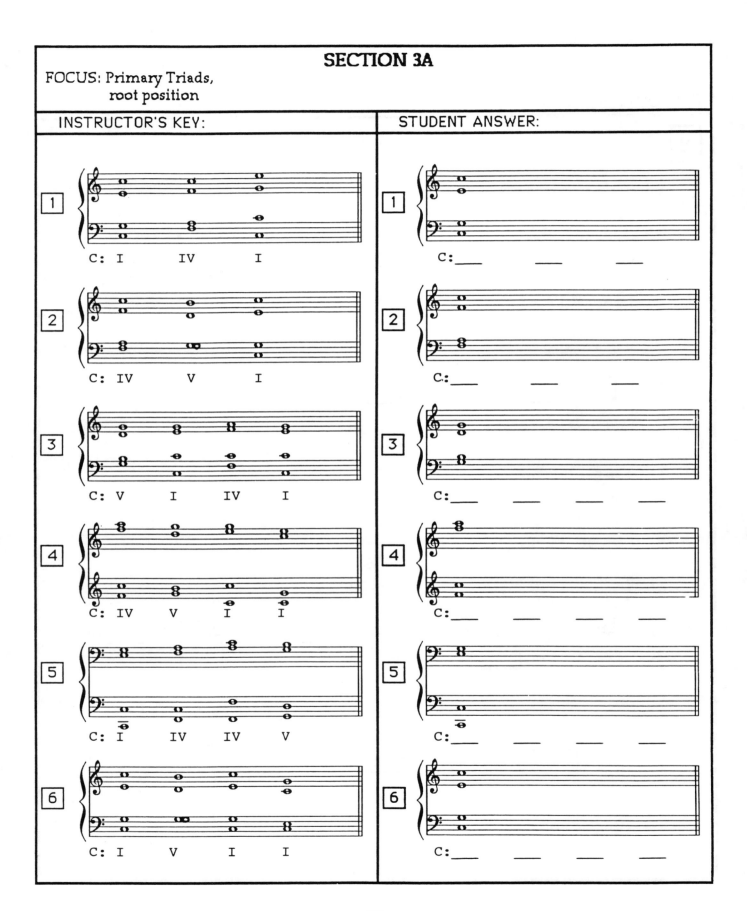

1   C: I       IV      I          1   C: ___      ___     ___

2   C: IV      V       I          2   C: ___      ___     ___

3   C: V    I    IV    I          3   C: ___   ___   ___   ___

4   C: IV    V     I    I         4   C: ___   ___   ___   ___

5   C: I    IV    IV    V         5   C: ___   ___   ___   ___

6   C: I    V     I     I         6   C: ___   ___   ___   ___

58

# SECTION 3A

**FOCUS:** Primary Triads, root position

| INSTRUCTOR'S KEY | STUDENT ANSWER |
|---|---|

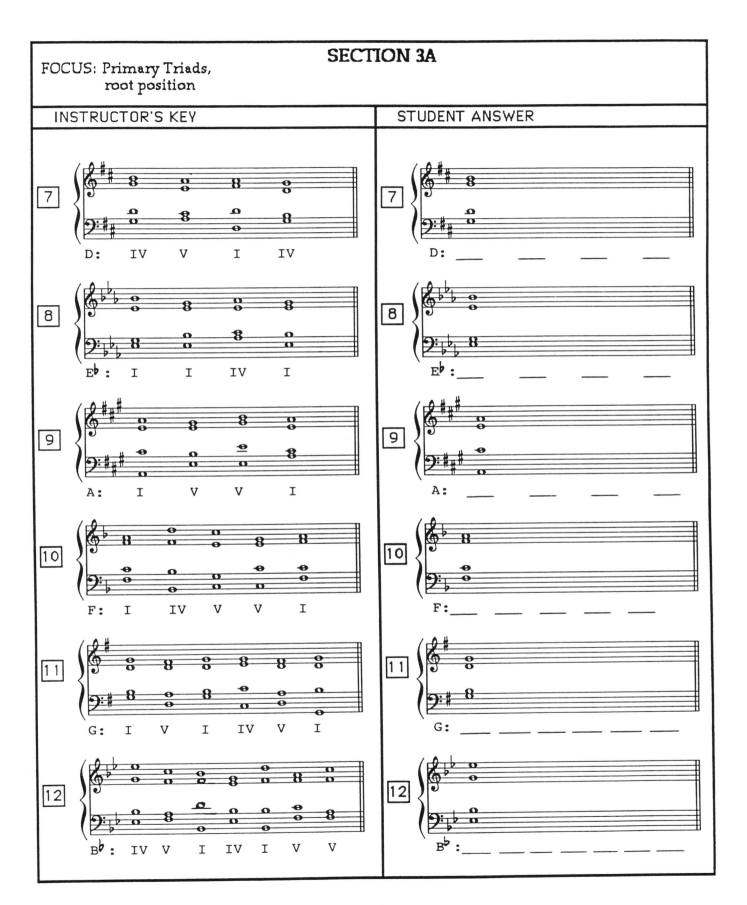

7  D:  IV  V  I  IV        7  D: ___ ___ ___ ___

8  E♭:  I  I  IV  I        8  E♭: ___ ___ ___ ___

9  A:  I  V  V  I          9  A: ___ ___ ___ ___

10  F:  I  IV  V  V  I     10  F: ___ ___ ___ ___ ___

11  G:  I  V  I  IV  V  I  11  G: ___ ___ ___ ___ ___ ___

12  B♭:  IV  V  I  IV  I  V  V   12  B♭: ___ ___ ___ ___ ___ ___ ___

# SECTION 3B

FOCUS: Primary Triads,
root position

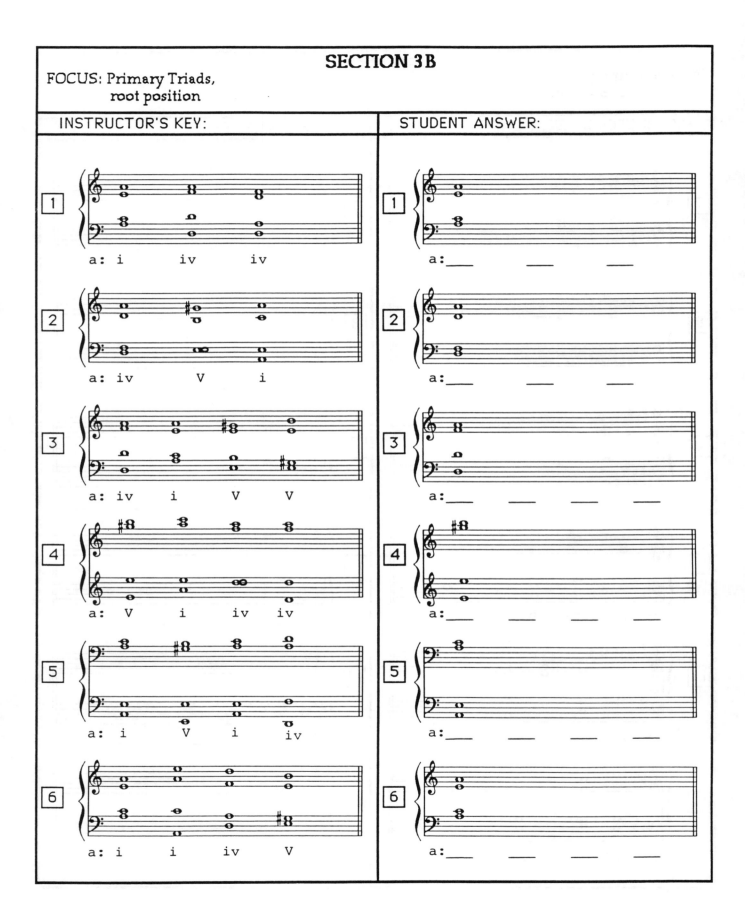

| INSTRUCTOR'S KEY: | STUDENT ANSWER: |
|---|---|

1  a: i  iv  iv

2  a: iv  V  i

3  a: iv  i  V  V

4  a: V  i  iv  iv

5  a: i  V  i  iv

6  a: i  i  iv  V

1  a:___ ___ ___

2  a:___ ___ ___

3  a:___ ___ ___ ___

4  a:___ ___ ___ ___

5  a:___ ___ ___ ___

6  a:___ ___ ___ ___

# SECTION 3B

FOCUS: Primary Triads,
        root position

| INSTRUCTOR'S KEY | STUDENT ANSWER |
|---|---|

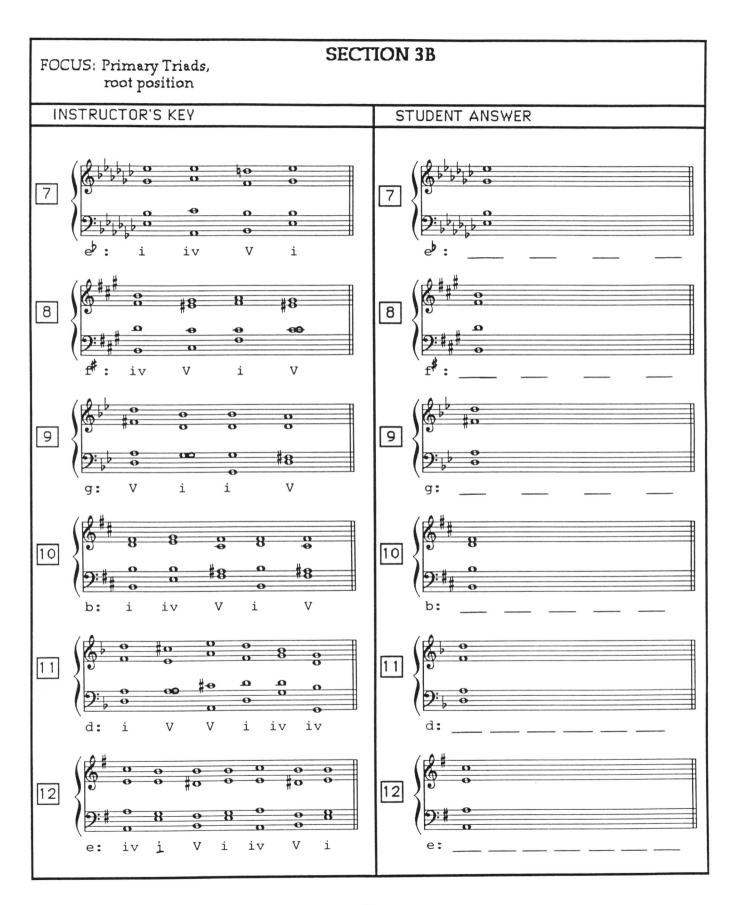

7  eᵇ :  i   iv   V   i        7  eᵇ : ___ ___ ___ ___

8  f♯ :  iv   V   i   V        8  f♯ : ___ ___ ___ ___

9  g:  V   i   i   V           9  g: ___ ___ ___ ___

10  b:  i   iv   V   i   V     10  b: ___ ___ ___ ___ ___

11  d:  i   V   V   i   iv   iv   11  d: ___ ___ ___ ___ ___ ___

12  e:  iv   i   V   i   iv   V   i   12  e: ___ ___ ___ ___ ___ ___ ___

# SECTION 4

FOCUS: P5 -- ♪.♪,♩. -- 4/4

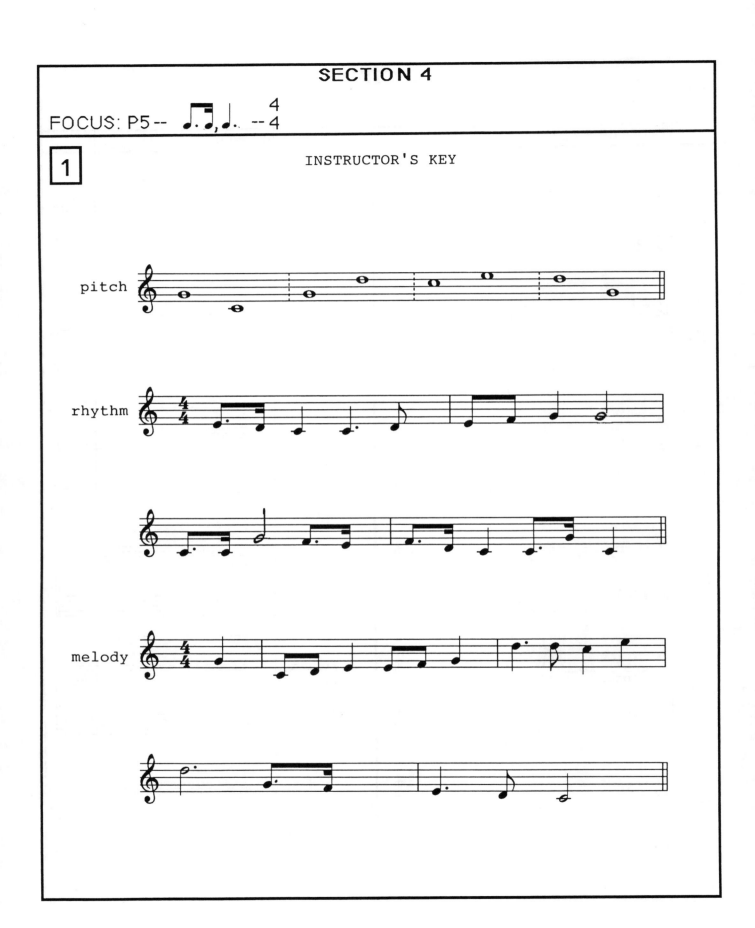

**1** INSTRUCTOR'S KEY

pitch

rhythm

melody

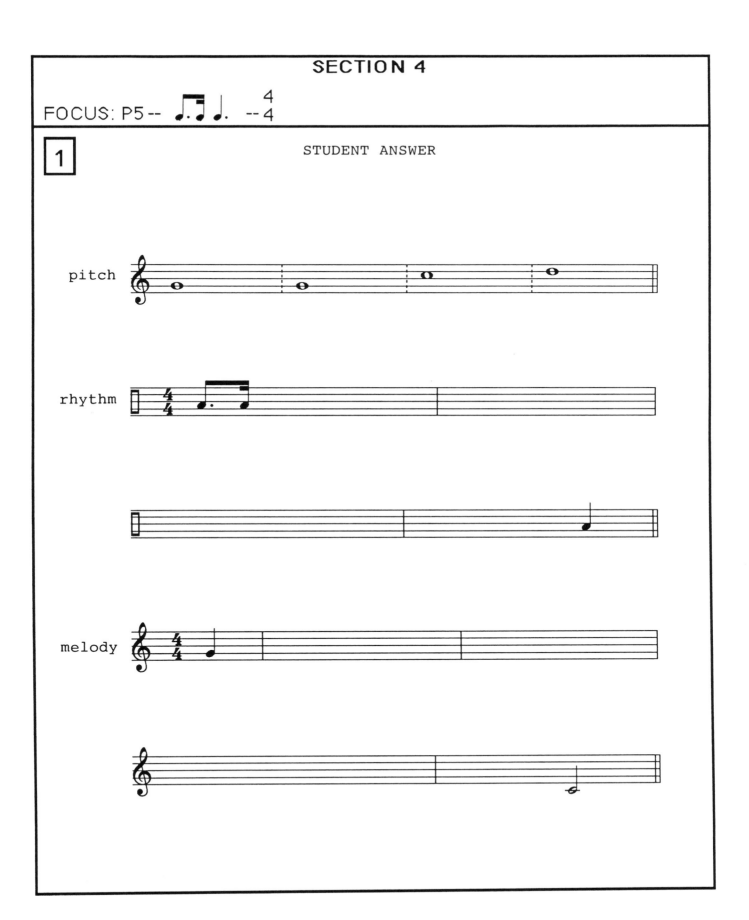

# SECTION 4

FOCUS: P5 -- ♪. ♪ ♩. -- $\frac{4}{4}$

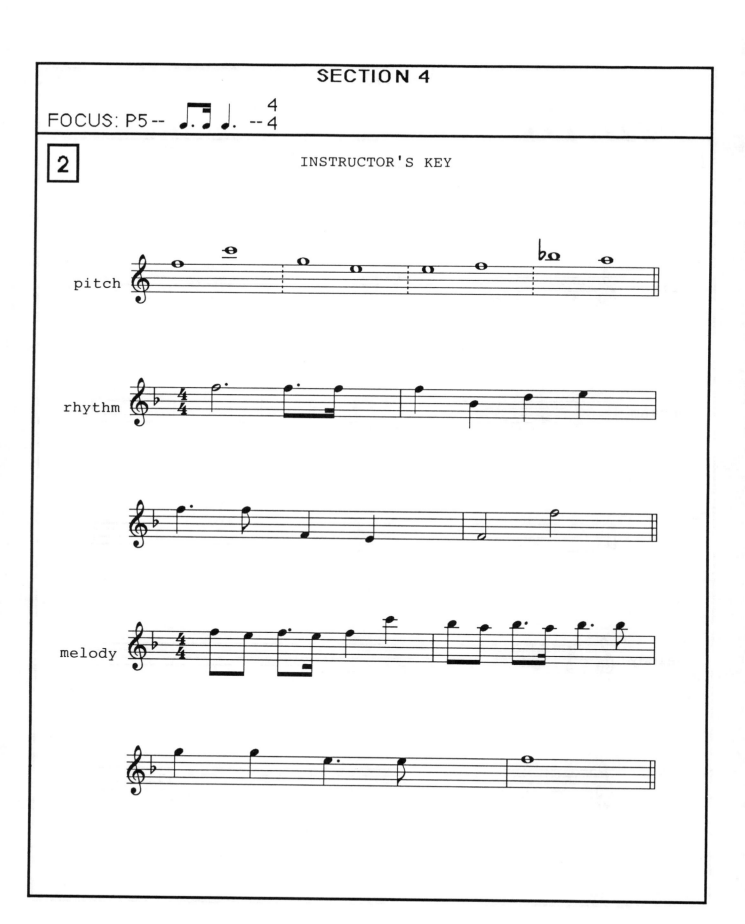

2  INSTRUCTOR'S KEY

pitch

rhythm

melody

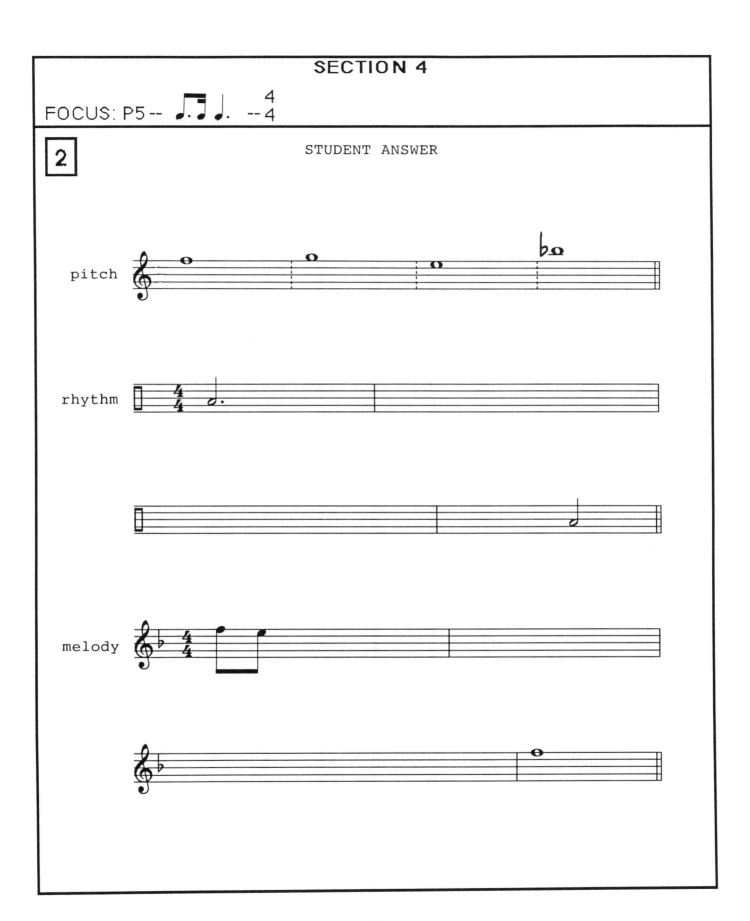

SECTION 4

FOCUS: P5

STUDENT ANSWER

pitch

rhythm

melody

# SECTION 4

FOCUS: P5 -- ♪.♪ ♩. -- 4/4

INSTRUCTOR'S KEY

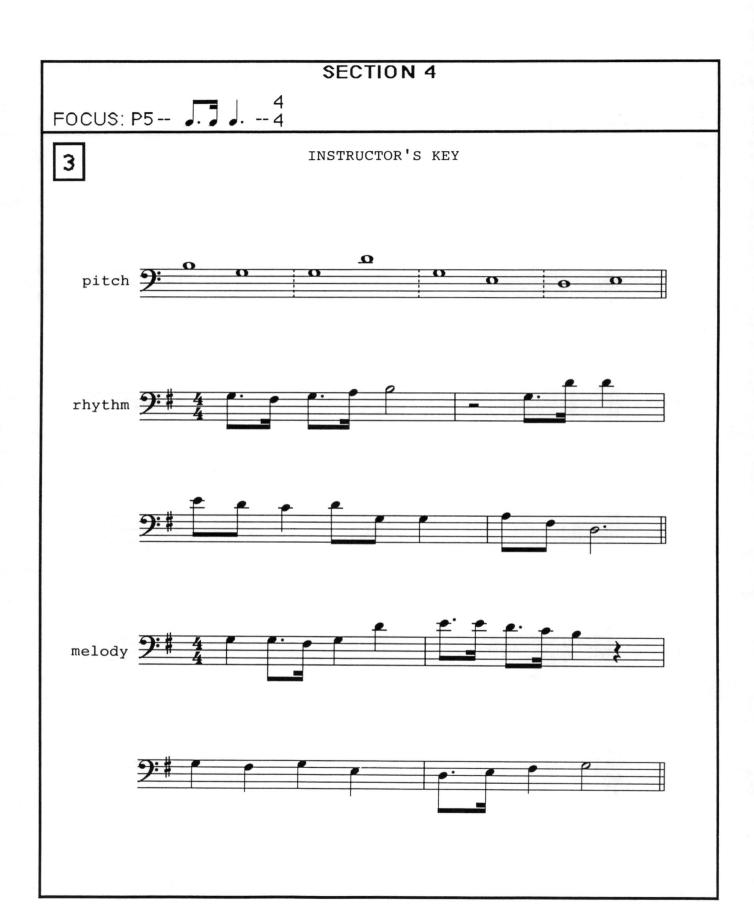

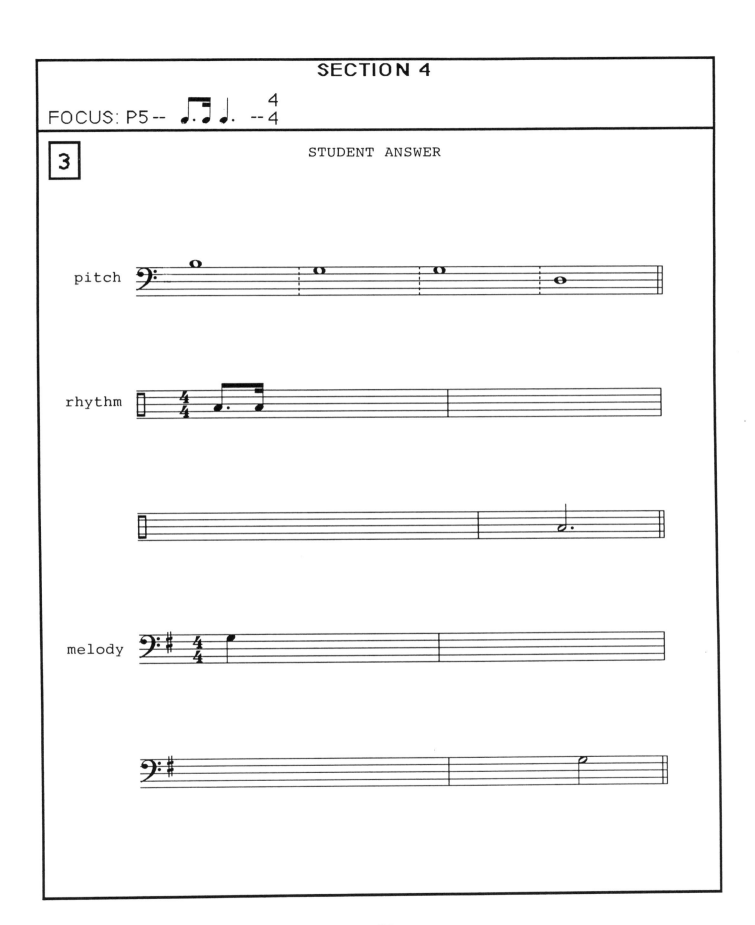

# SECTION 4

FOCUS: P5 -- ♪. ♩ ♩. -- $\frac{4}{4}$

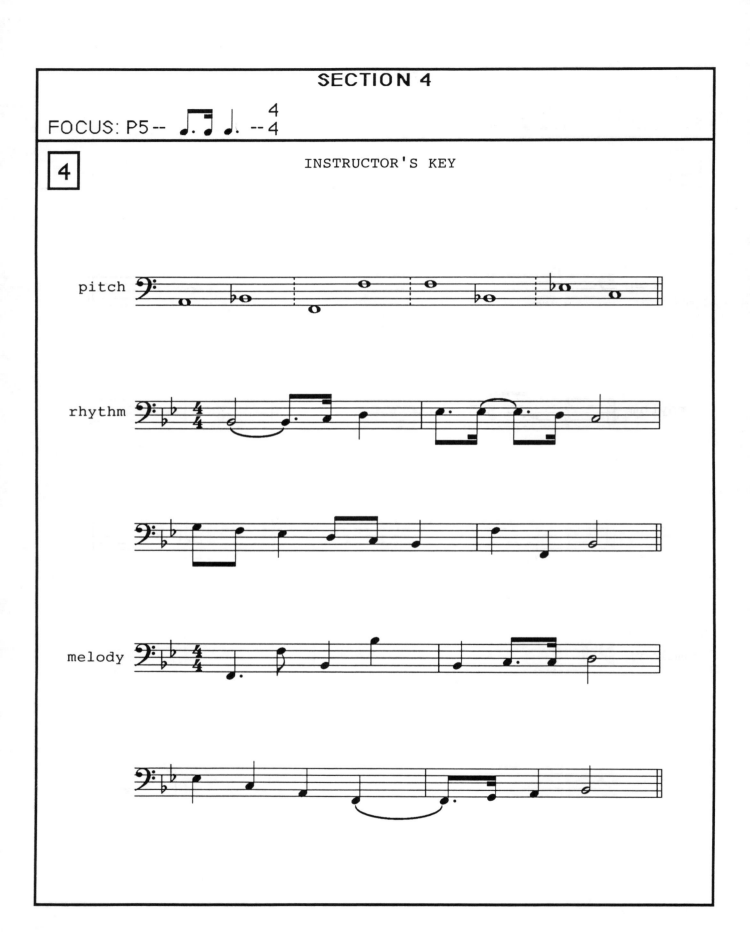

4

INSTRUCTOR'S KEY

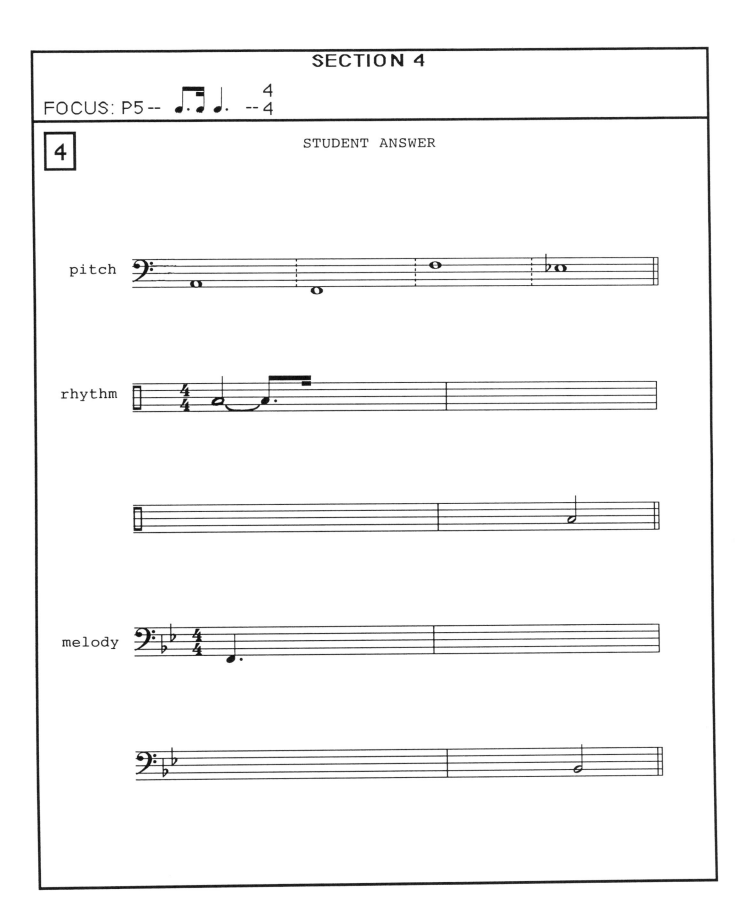

# SECTION 4

FOCUS: P5 --  ♪. ♪  ♪. -- 4/4

**5**                                     INSTRUCTOR'S KEY

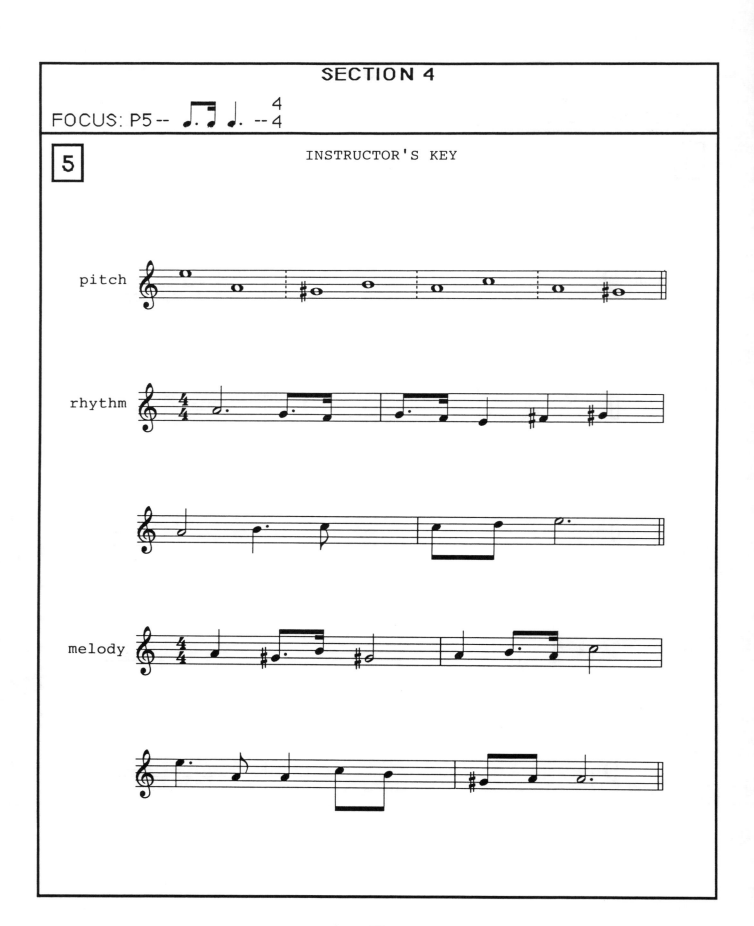

# SECTION 4

FOCUS: P5 -- 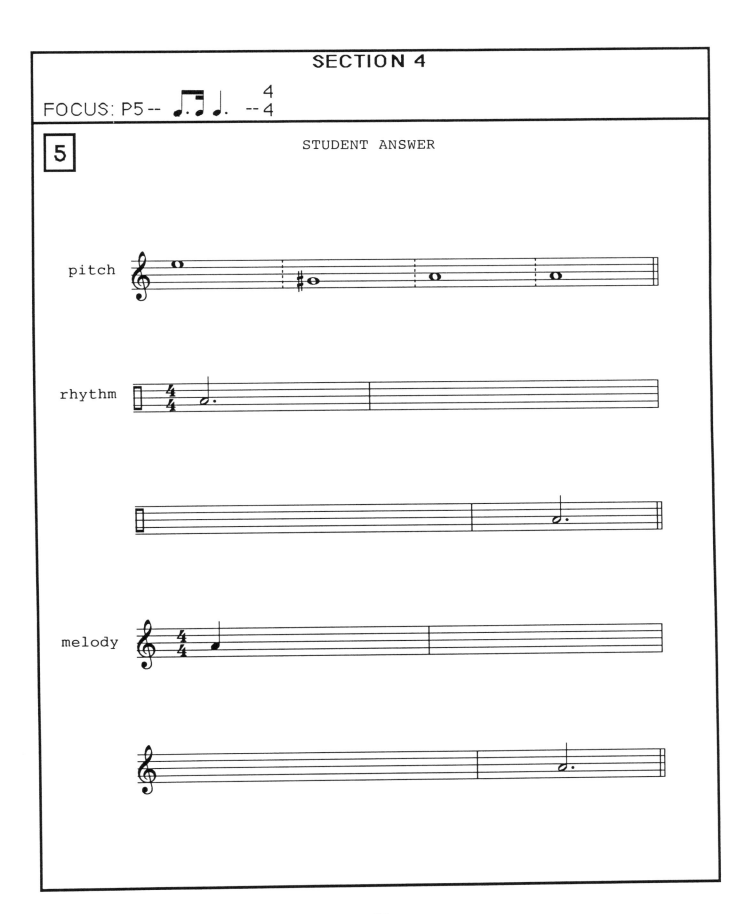 -- 4/4

STUDENT ANSWER

5

pitch

rhythm

melody

# SECTION 4

FOCUS: P5 -- ♪. ♪ ♩. -- 4/4

6    INSTRUCTOR'S KEY

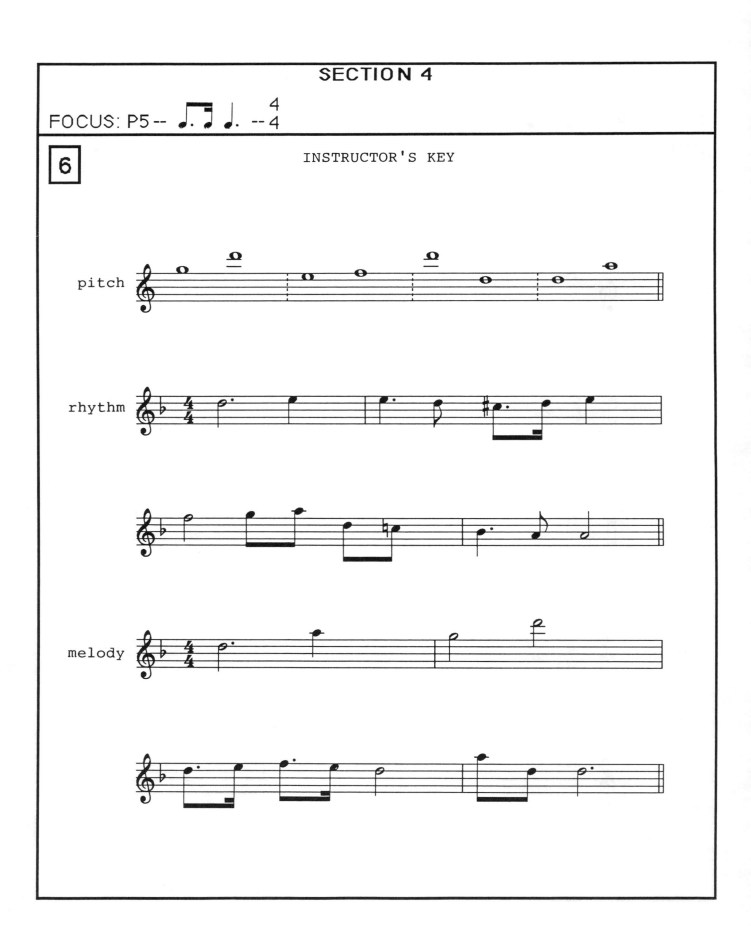

72

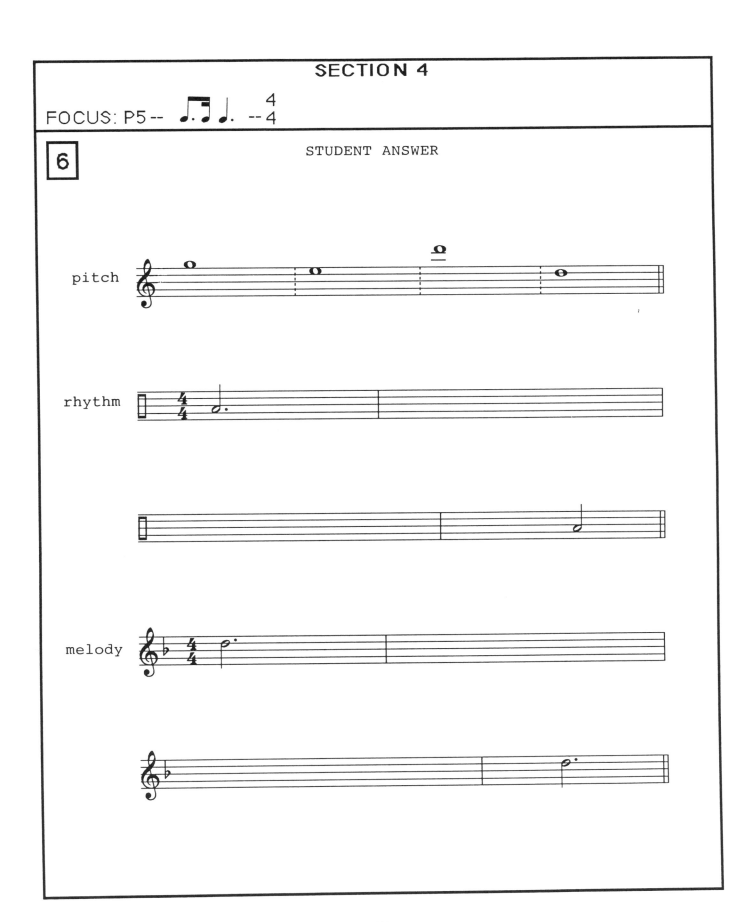

# SECTION 4

FOCUS: P5 -- ♪. ♪ ♩. -- 4/4

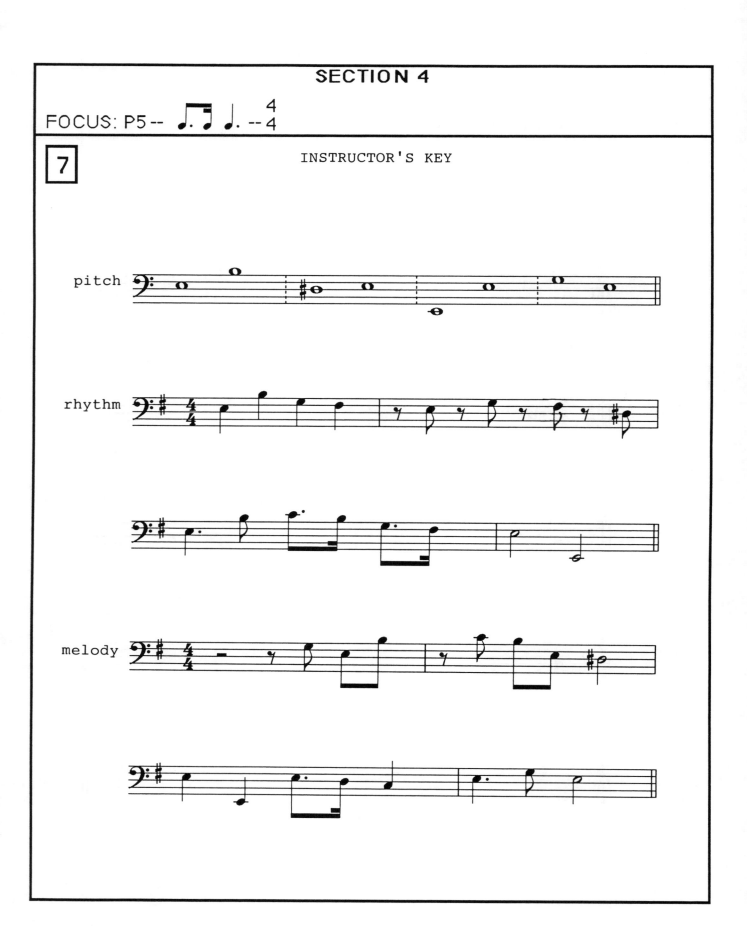

7

INSTRUCTOR'S KEY

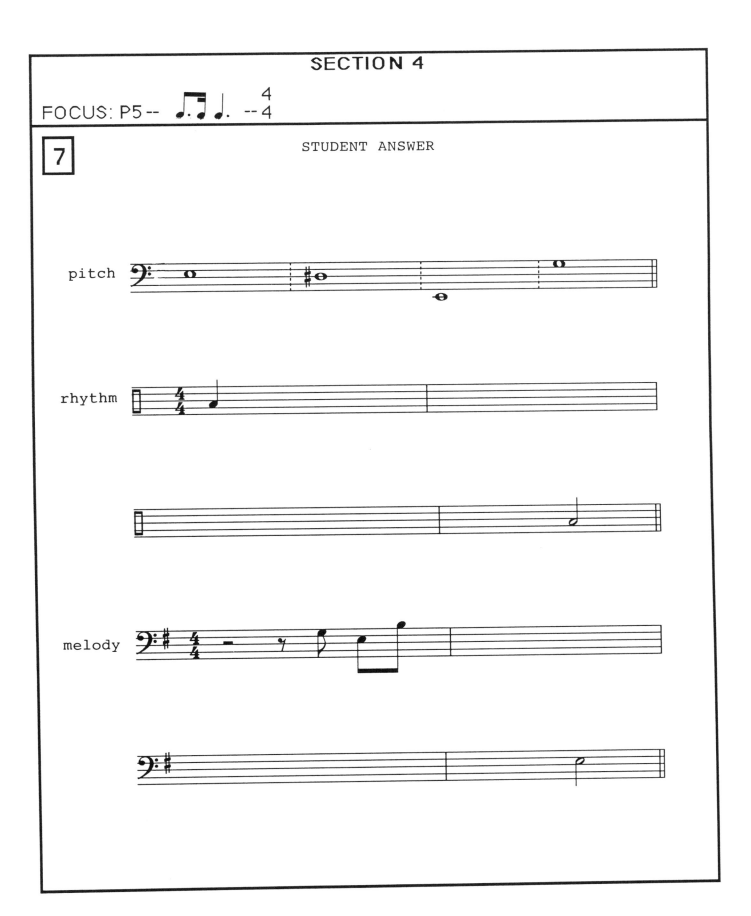

FOCUS: P5 -- ♩. ♪ ♩. -- 4/4

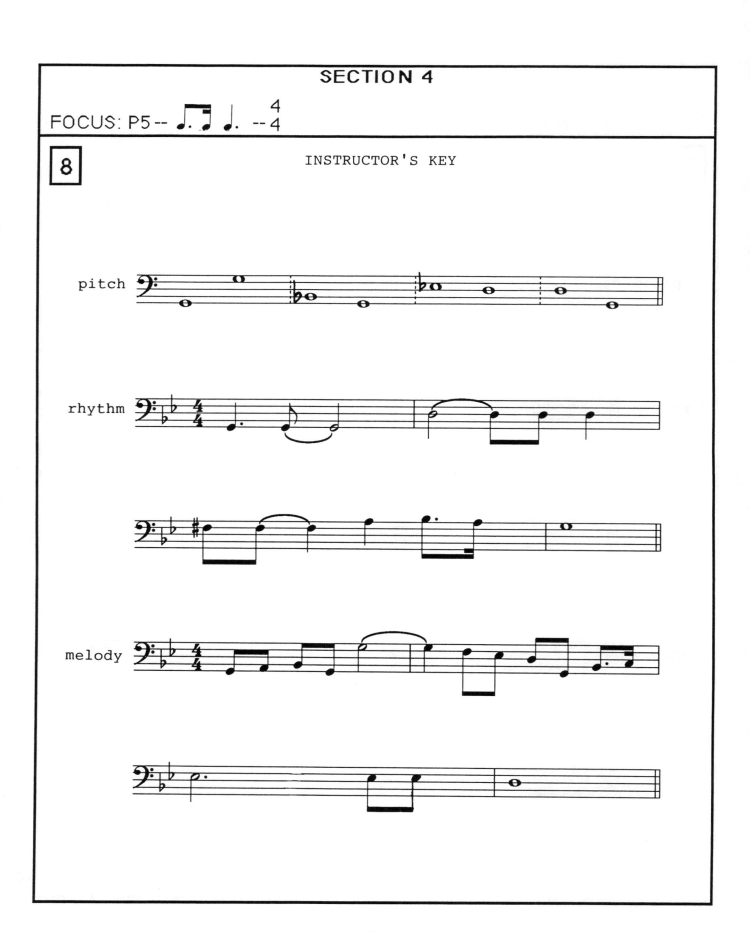

8    INSTRUCTOR'S KEY

pitch

rhythm

melody

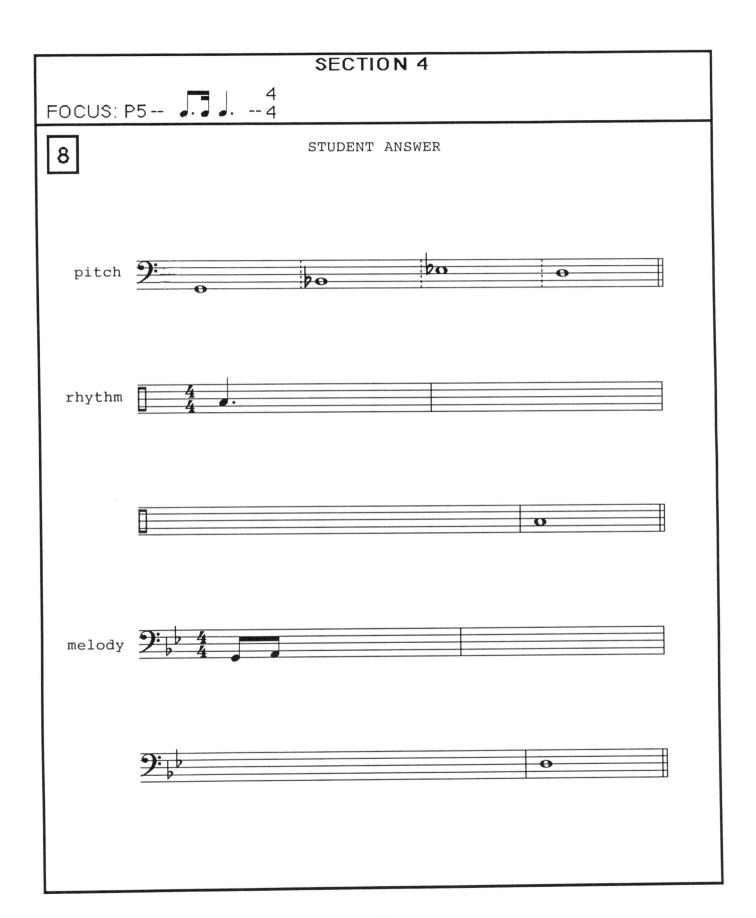

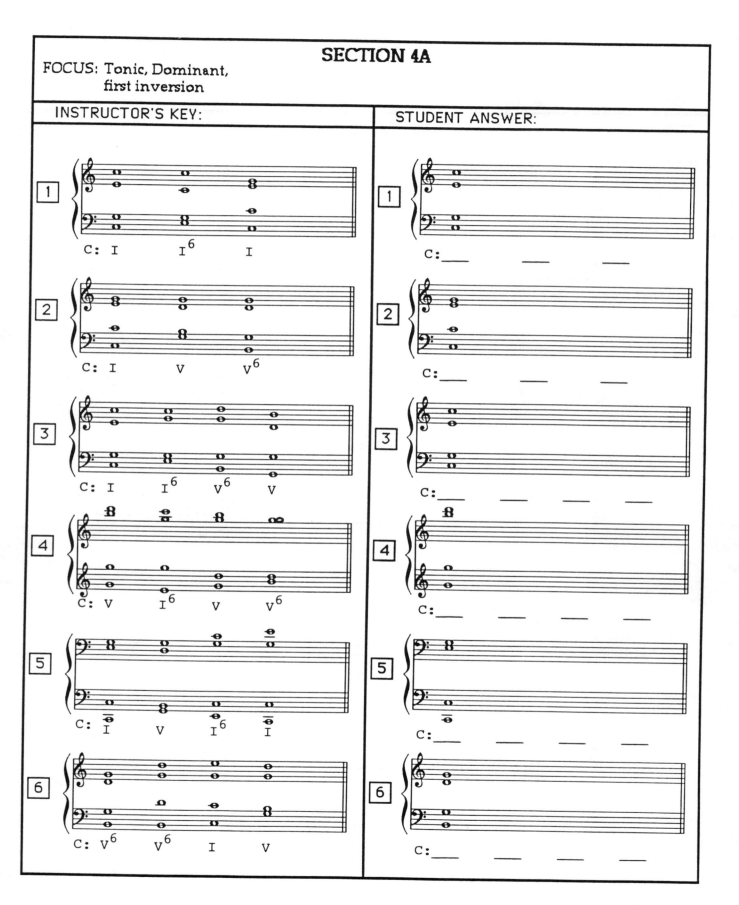

# SECTION 4A

**FOCUS:** Tonic, Dominant, first inversion

**INSTRUCTOR'S KEY:**

1. C: I    I⁶    I
2. C: I    V    V⁶
3. C: I    I⁶    V⁶    V
4. C: V    I⁶    V    V⁶
5. C: I    V    I⁶    I
6. C: V⁶    V⁶    I    V

**STUDENT ANSWER:**

1. C:___ ___ ___
2. C:___ ___ ___
3. C:___ ___ ___ ___
4. C:___ ___ ___ ___
5. C:___ ___ ___ ___
6. C:___ ___ ___ ___

78

# SECTION 4A

FOCUS: Tonic, Dominant,
first inversion

| INSTRUCTOR'S KEY | STUDENT ANSWER |
|---|---|

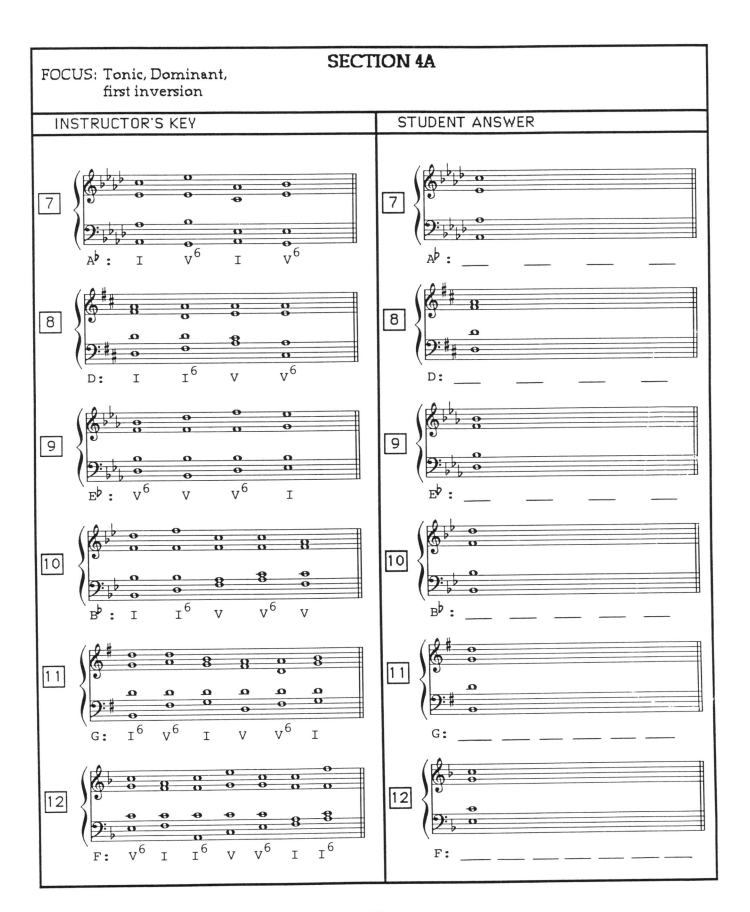

7  A♭:  I   V⁶   I   V⁶

7  A♭: ___ ___ ___ ___

8  D:  I   I⁶   V   V⁶

8  D: ___ ___ ___ ___

9  E♭:  V⁶   V   V⁶   I

9  E♭: ___ ___ ___ ___

10  B♭:  I   I⁶   V   V⁶   V

10  B♭: ___ ___ ___ ___ ___

11  G:  I⁶   V⁶   I   V   V⁶   I

11  G: ___ ___ ___ ___ ___ ___

12  F:  V⁶   I   I⁶   V   V⁶   I   I⁶

12  F: ___ ___ ___ ___ ___ ___ ___

79

# SECTION 4B

**FOCUS:** Tonic, Dominant, first inversion

INSTRUCTOR'S KEY:  STUDENT ANSWER:

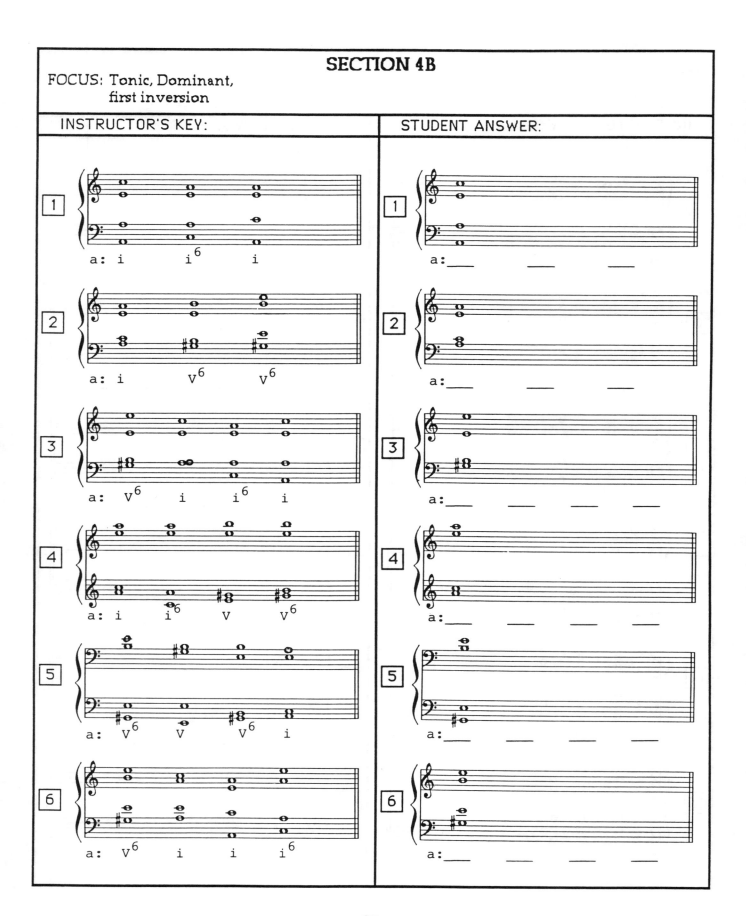

# SECTION 4 B

FOCUS: Tonic, Dominant,
first inversion

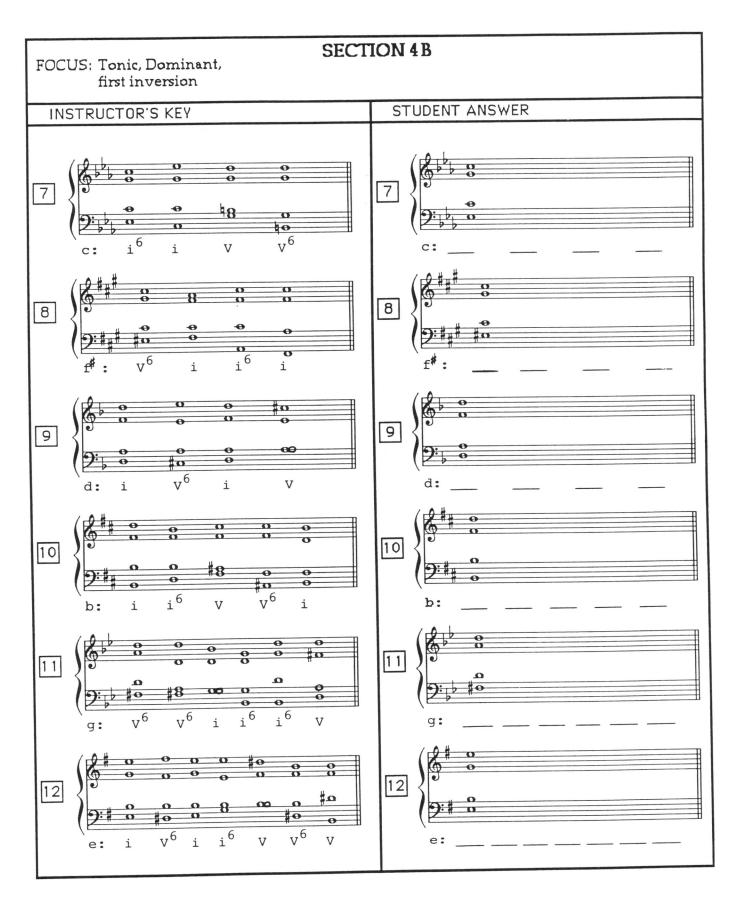

| INSTRUCTOR'S KEY | STUDENT ANSWER |

7  c:  $i^6$  i  V  $V^6$

7  c: ___  ___  ___  ___

8  f#:  $V^6$  i  $i^6$  i

8  f#: ___  ___  ___  ___

9  d:  i  $V^6$  i  V

9  d: ___  ___  ___  ___

10  b:  i  $i^6$  V  $V^6$  i

10  b: ___  ___  ___  ___

11  g:  $V^6$  $V^6$  i  $i^6$  $i^6$  V

11  g: ___  ___  ___  ___  ___  ___

12  e:  i  $V^6$  i  $i^6$  V  $V^6$  V

12  e: ___  ___  ___  ___  ___  ___  ___

81

# SECTION 5

FOCUS: P4 -- ♩♪♪♪ var. -- $\overset{2\ 3\ 4}{4,4,4}$

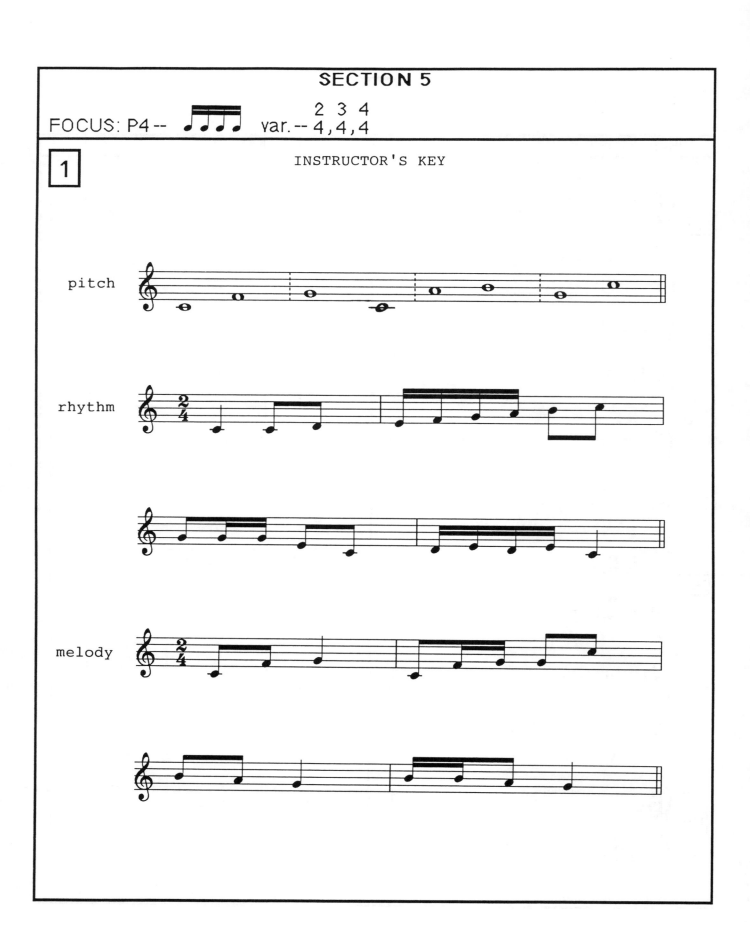

# SECTION 5

FOCUS: P4 -- ♪♪♪♪  var. -- $\overset{2}{4}, \overset{3}{4}, \overset{4}{4}$

STUDENT ANSWER

1

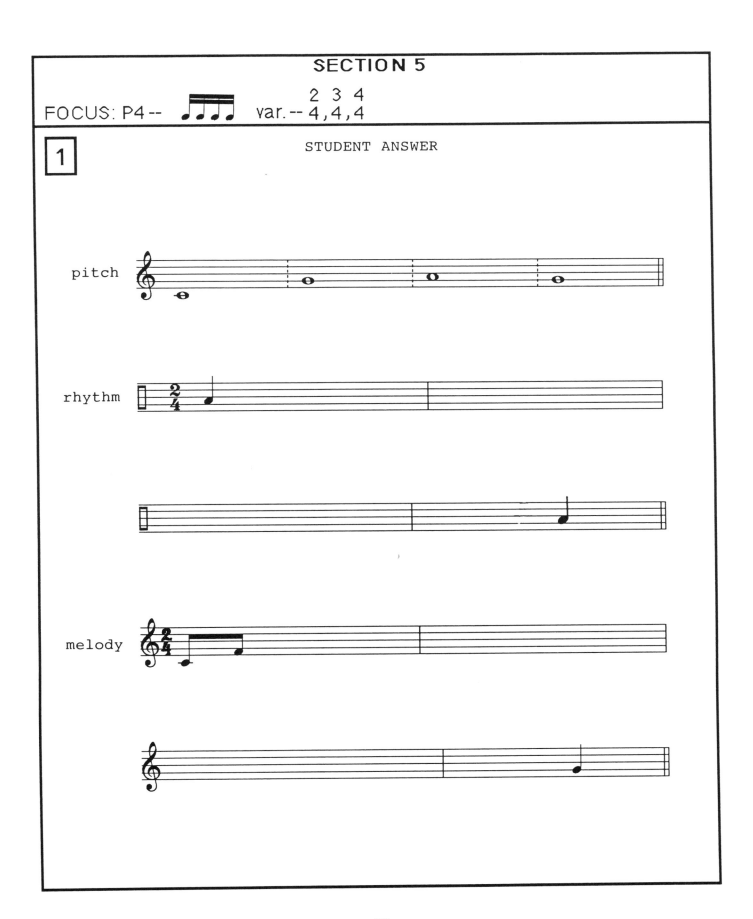

pitch

rhythm

melody

# SECTION 5

FOCUS: P4 -- ♪♪♪♪ var. -- $\overset{2\ 3\ 4}{4,4,4}$

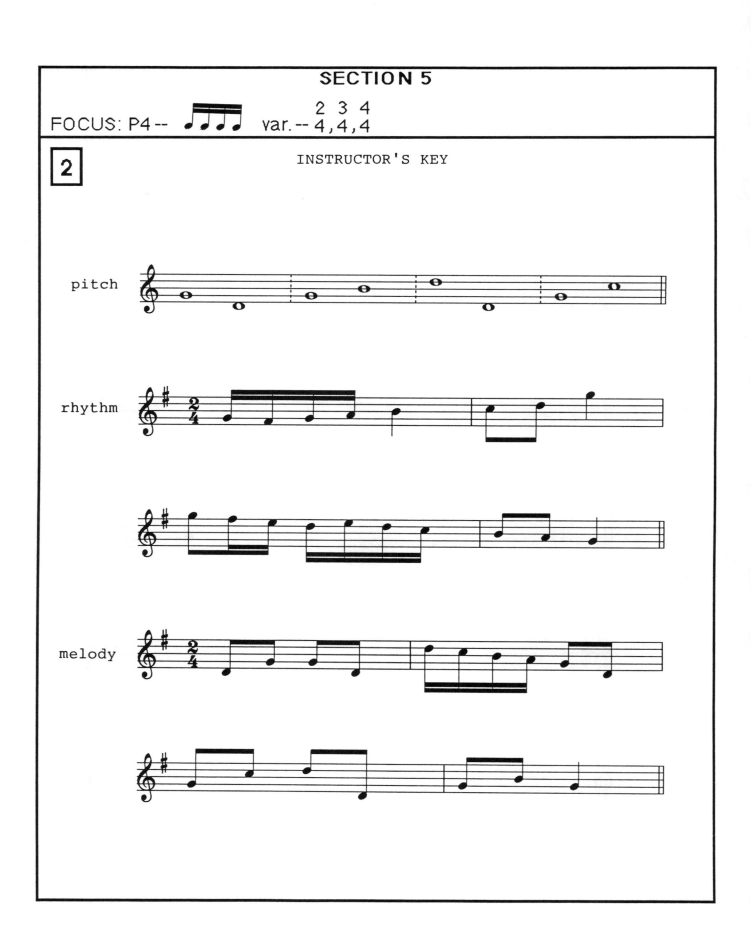

2         INSTRUCTOR'S KEY

pitch

rhythm

melody

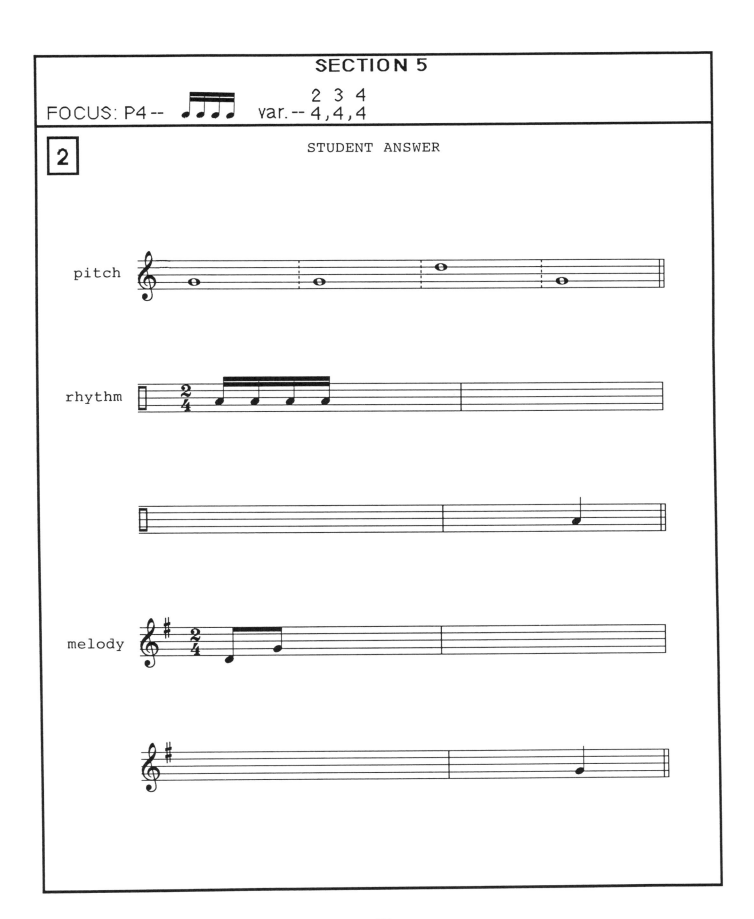

# SECTION 5

FOCUS: P4 -- ♪♪♪♪  var. -- 4,4,4 (over 2 3 4)

INSTRUCTOR'S KEY

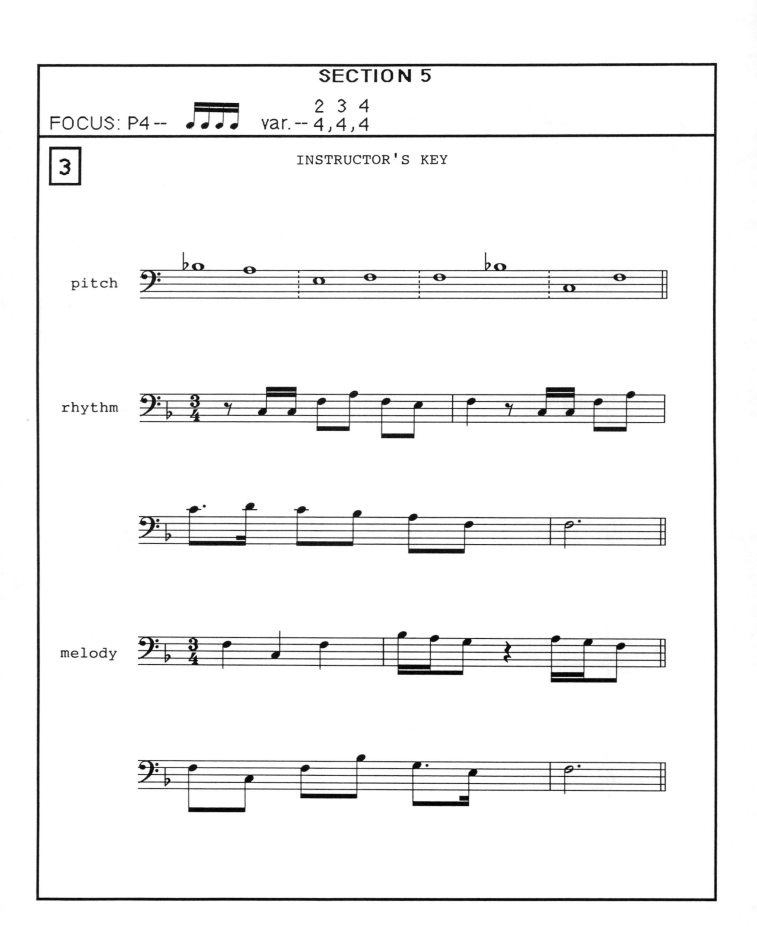

pitch

rhythm

melody

86

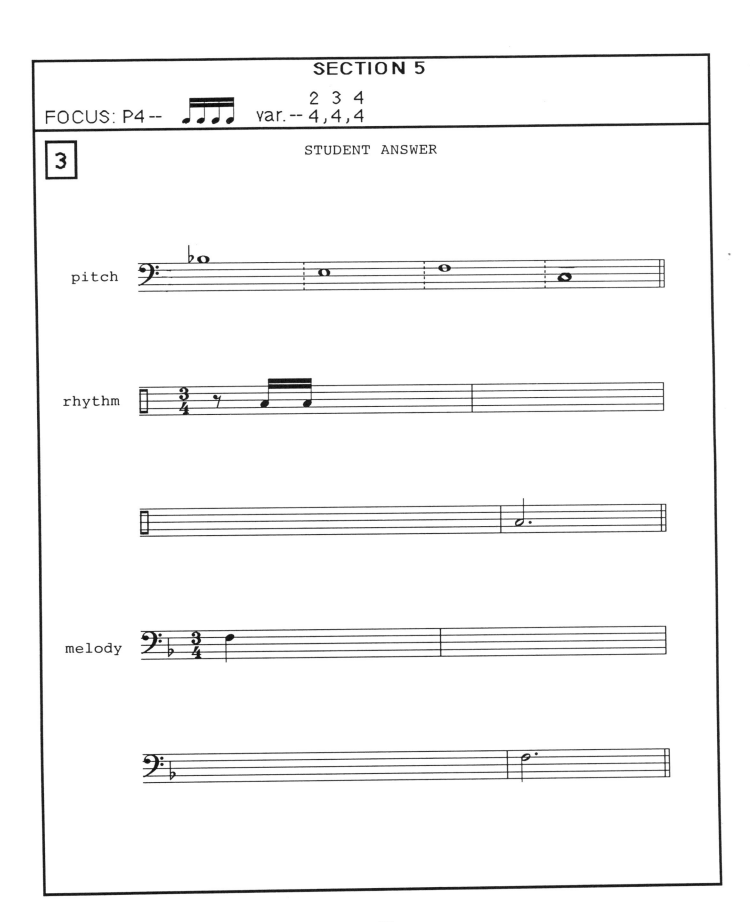

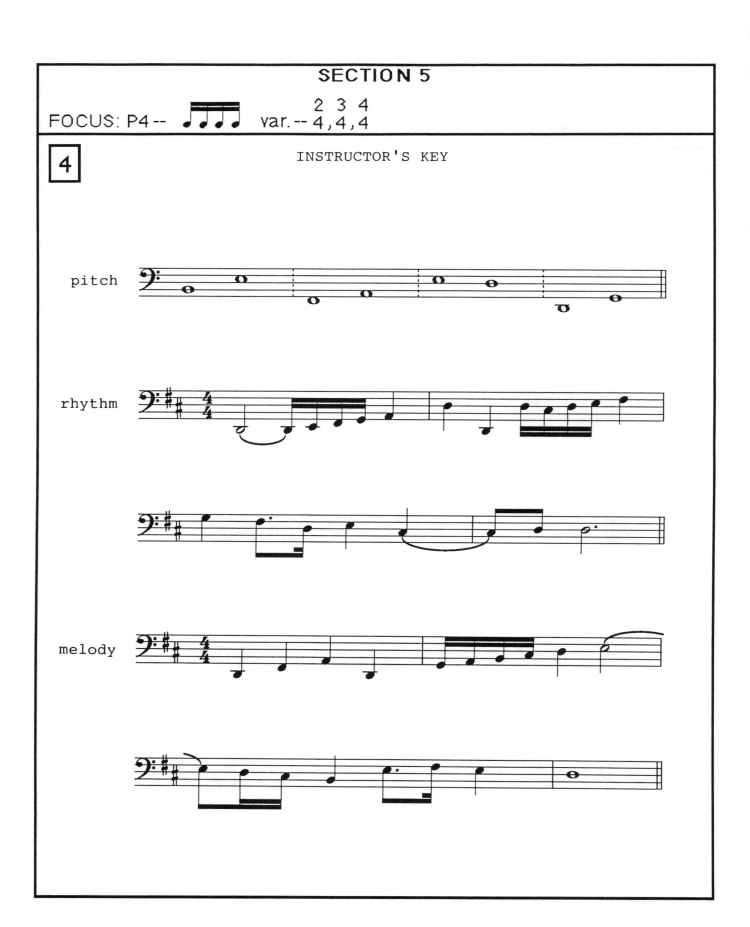

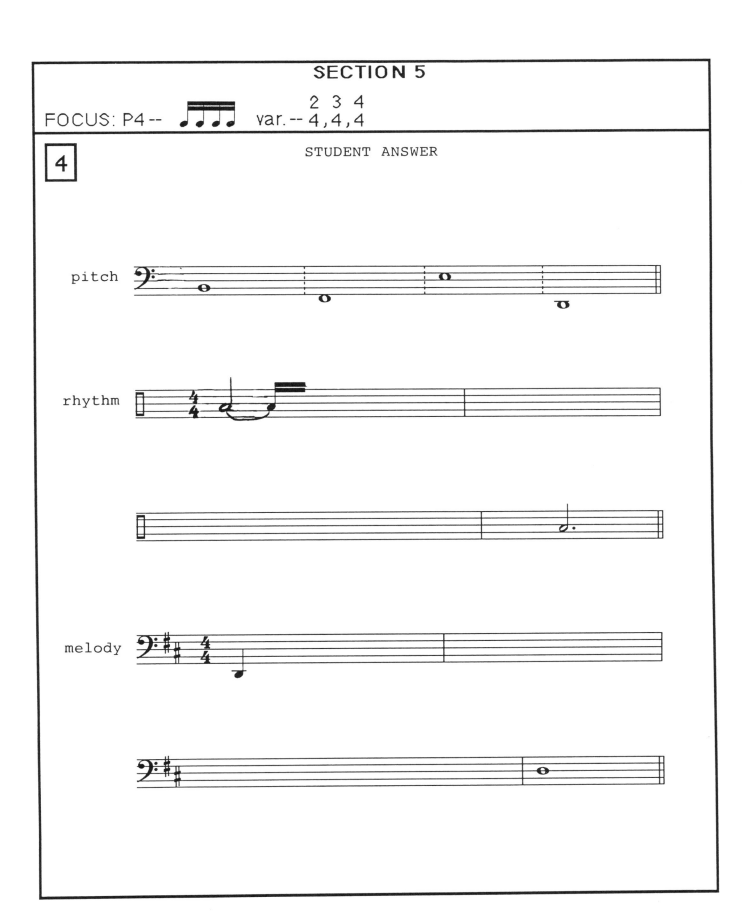

# SECTION 5

FOCUS: P4 -- ♩♩♩♩  var. -- 2 3 4
4,4,4

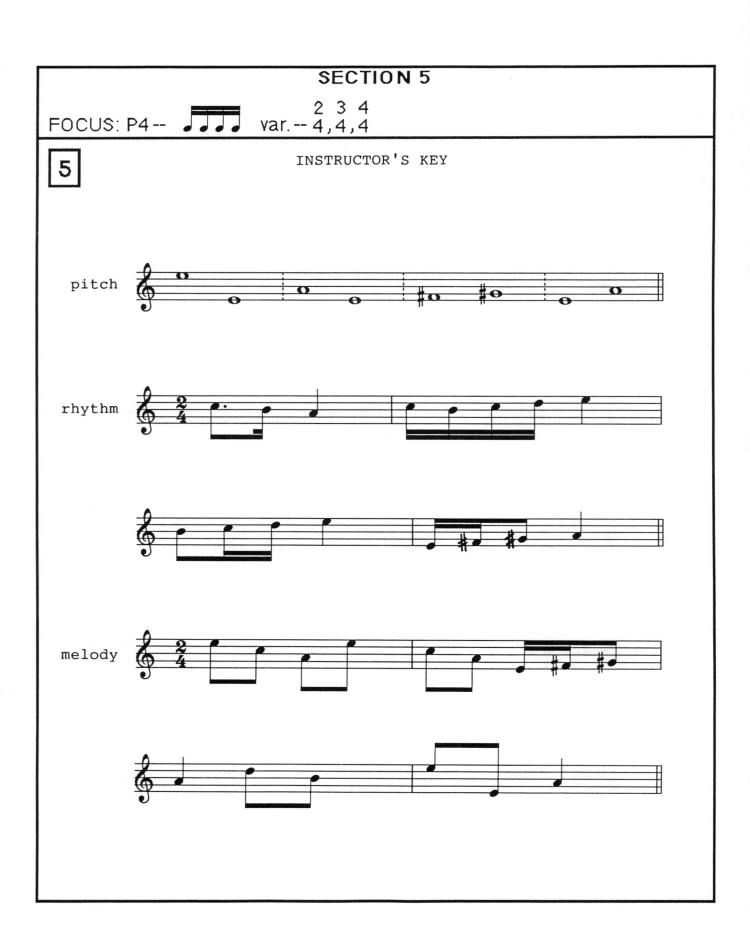

INSTRUCTOR'S KEY

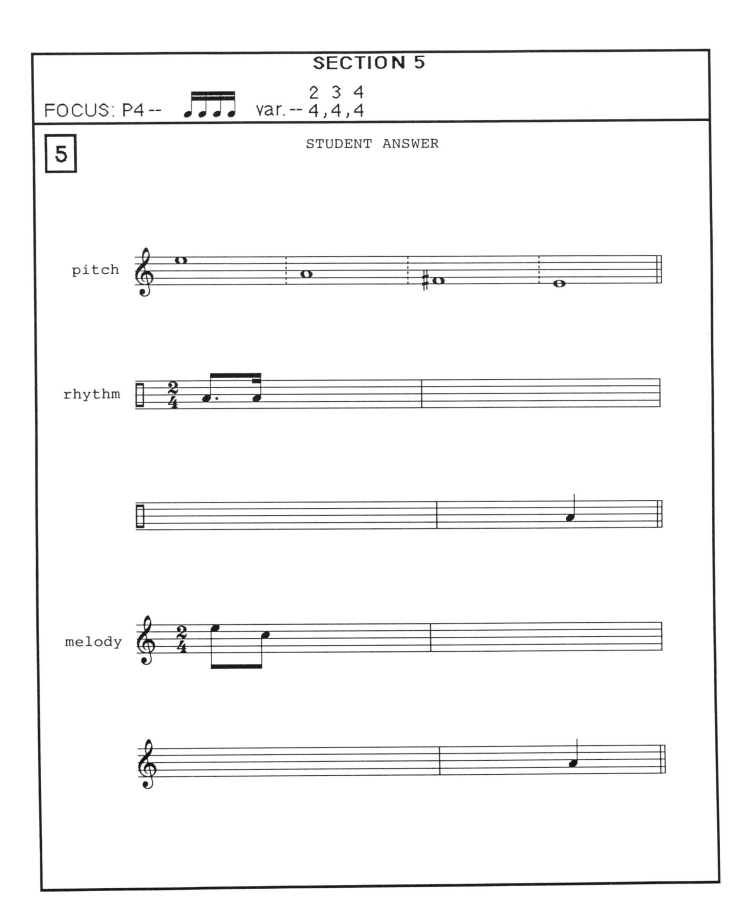

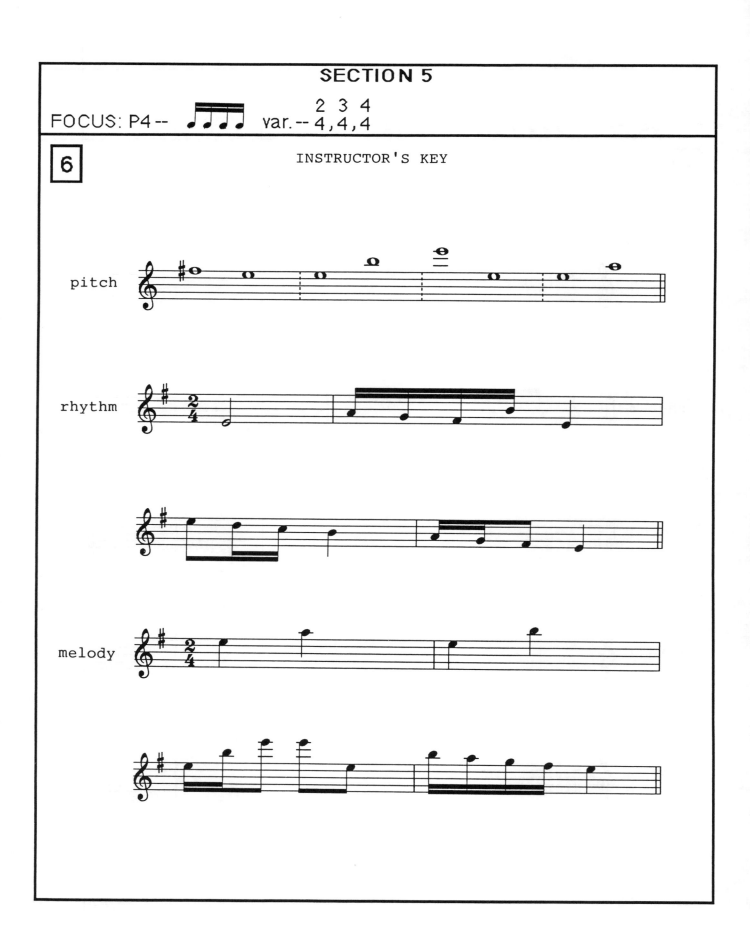

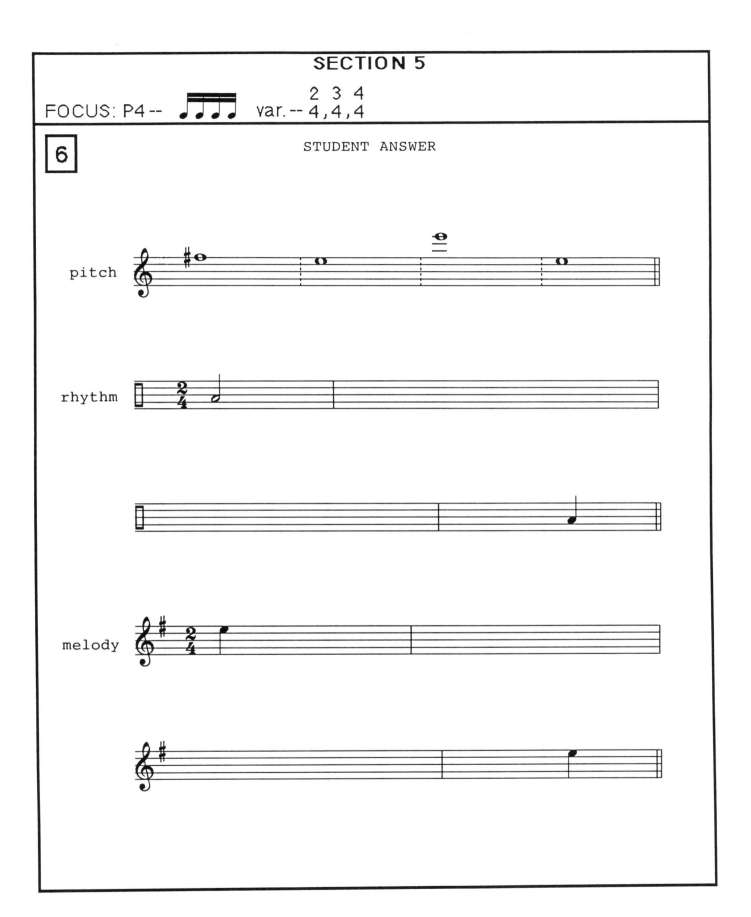

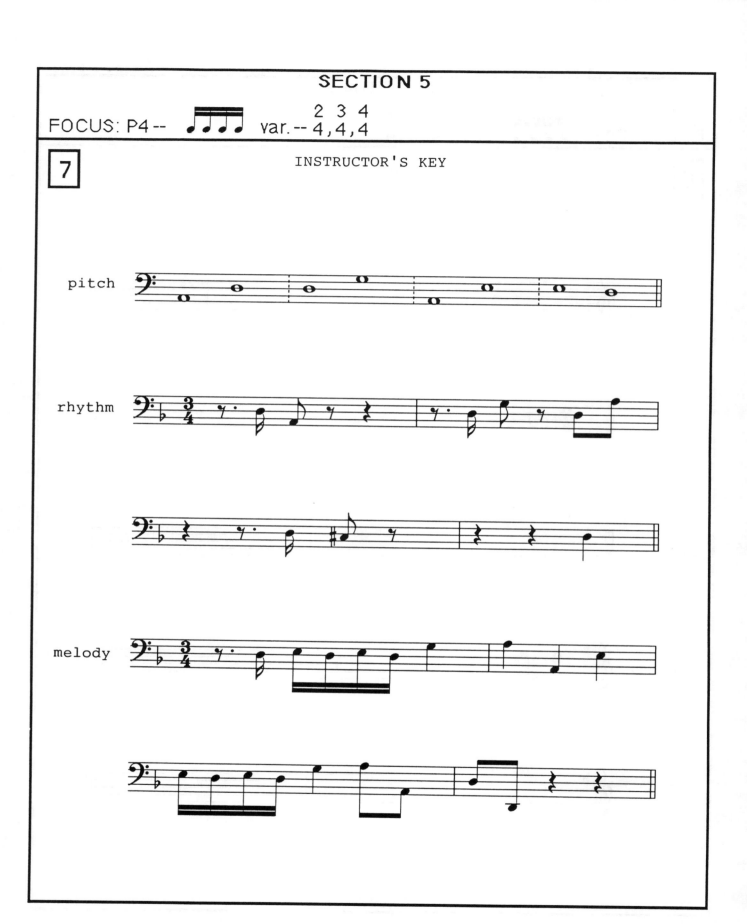

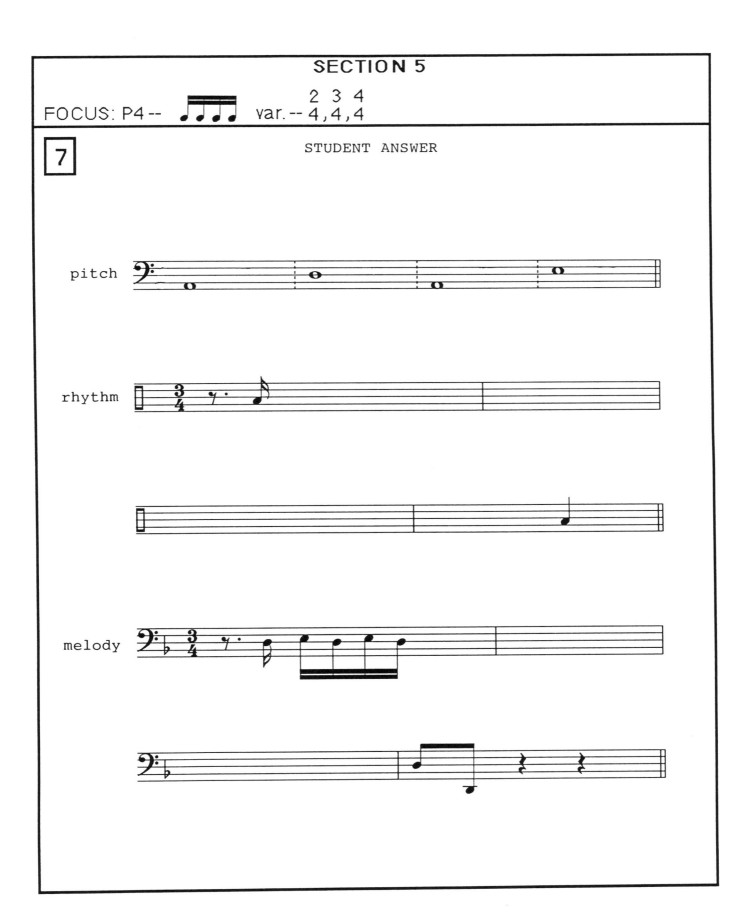

# SECTION 5

FOCUS: P4 -- ♪♪♪♪ var. -- 2 3 4 / 4, 4, 4

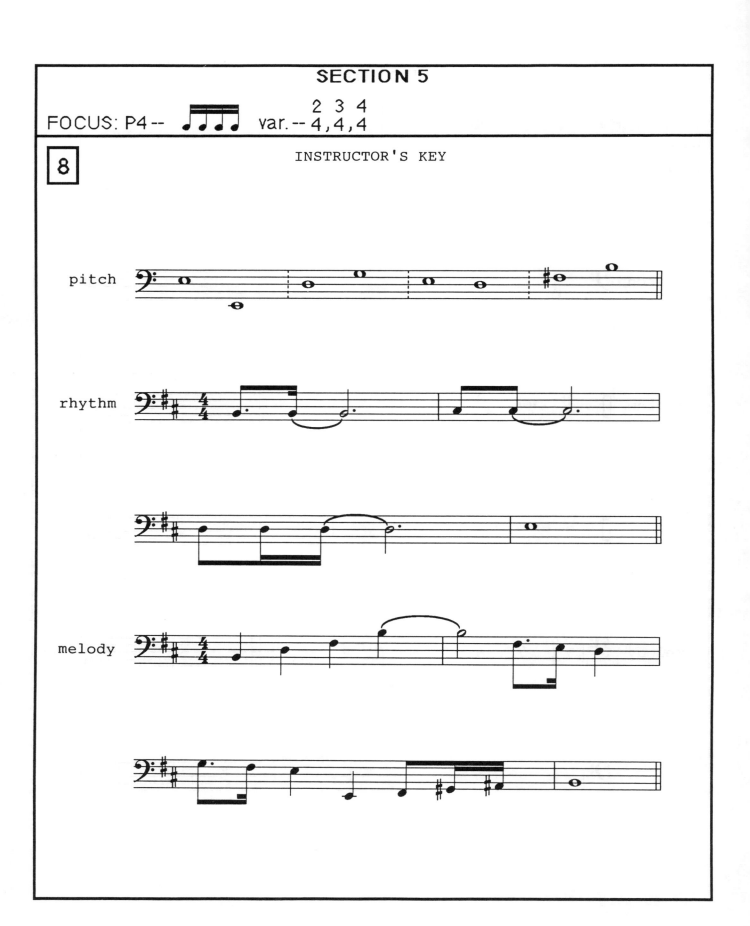

INSTRUCTOR'S KEY

# SECTION 5

FOCUS: P4 -- ♪♪♪♪   var. -- 4,4,4
                       2 3 4

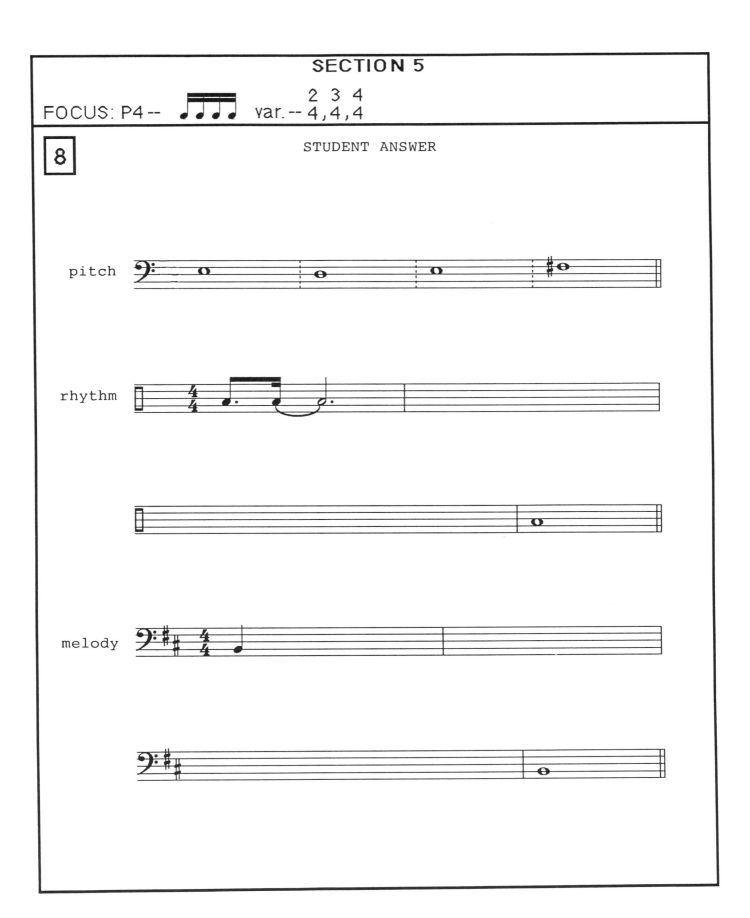

STUDENT ANSWER

8

pitch

rhythm

melody

# SECTION 5A

FOCUS: Tonic, Subdominant,
first inversion

INSTRUCTOR'S KEY:    STUDENT ANSWER:

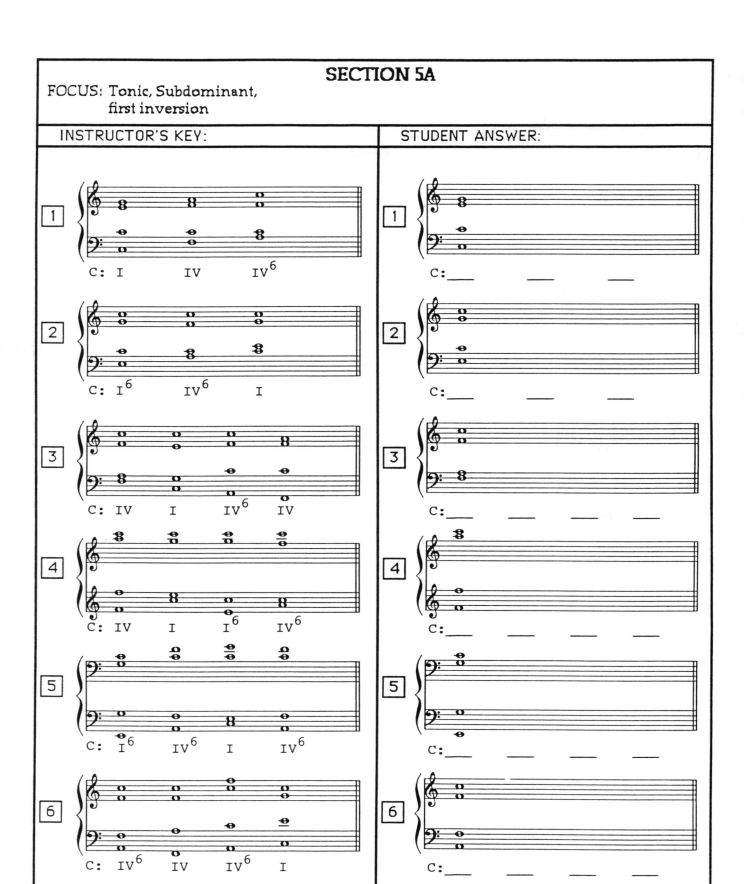

1. C: I    IV    IV⁶      1. C:___  ___  ___

2. C: I⁶    IV⁶    I      2. C:___  ___  ___

3. C: IV    I    IV⁶    IV    3. C:___  ___  ___  ___

4. C: IV    I    I⁶    IV⁶    4. C:___  ___  ___  ___

5. C: I⁶    IV⁶    I    IV⁶    5. C:___  ___  ___  ___

6. C: IV⁶    IV    IV⁶    I    6. C:___  ___  ___  ___

# SECTION 5A

FOCUS: Tonic, Subdominant,
first inversion

| INSTRUCTOR'S KEY | STUDENT ANSWER |
| --- | --- |

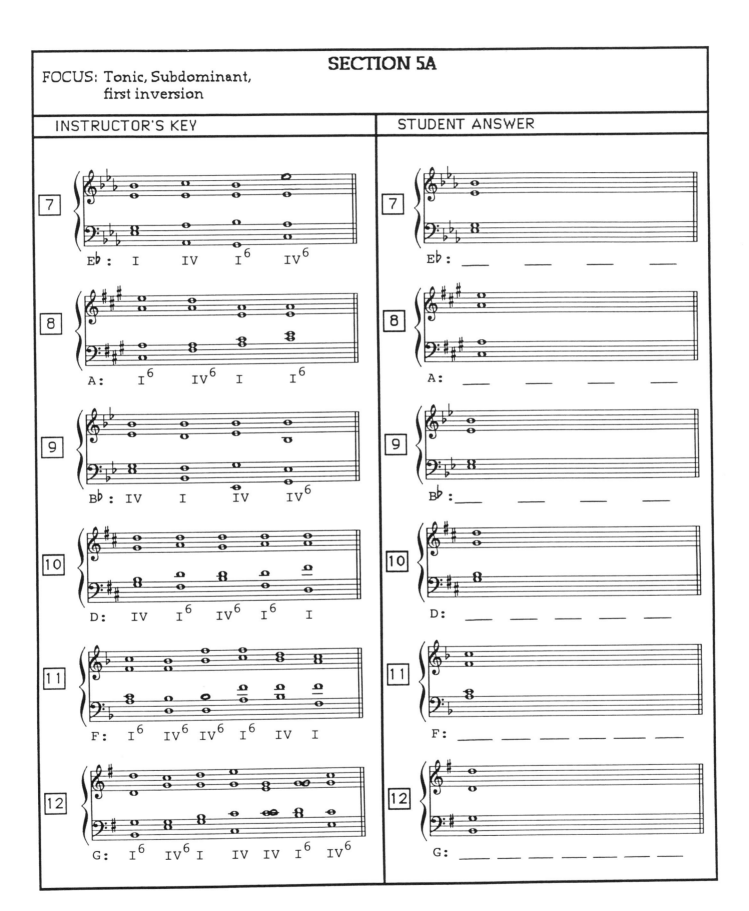

7  Eb: I    IV    I⁶   IV⁶

7  Eb: ___  ___  ___  ___

8  A: I⁶   IV⁶  I    I⁶

8  A: ___  ___  ___  ___

9  Bb: IV   I    IV   IV⁶

9  Bb: ___  ___  ___  ___

10  D: IV   I⁶   IV⁶  I⁶   I

10  D: ___  ___  ___  ___  ___

11  F: I⁶   IV⁶  IV⁶  I⁶   IV   I

11  F: ___  ___  ___  ___  ___  ___

12  G: I⁶   IV⁶  I   IV   IV   I⁶   IV⁶

12  G: ___  ___  ___  ___  ___  ___  ___

# SECTION 5B

FOCUS: Tonic, Subdominant,
first inversion

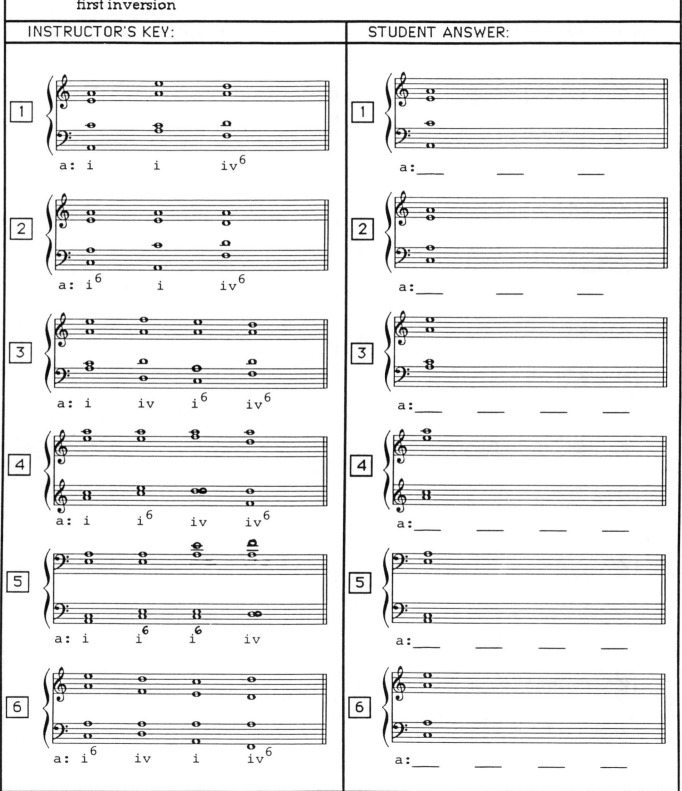

INSTRUCTOR'S KEY:

STUDENT ANSWER:

1.  a: i    i    iv⁶
    a:___ ___ ___

2.  a: i⁶   i    iv⁶
    a:___ ___ ___

3.  a: i    iv   i⁶   iv⁶
    a:___ ___ ___ ___

4.  a: i    i⁶   iv   iv⁶
    a:___ ___ ___ ___

5.  a: i    i⁶   i⁶   iv
    a:___ ___ ___ ___

6.  a: i⁶   iv   i    iv⁶
    a:___ ___ ___ ___

# SECTION 5B

FOCUS: Tonic, Subdominant,
first inversion

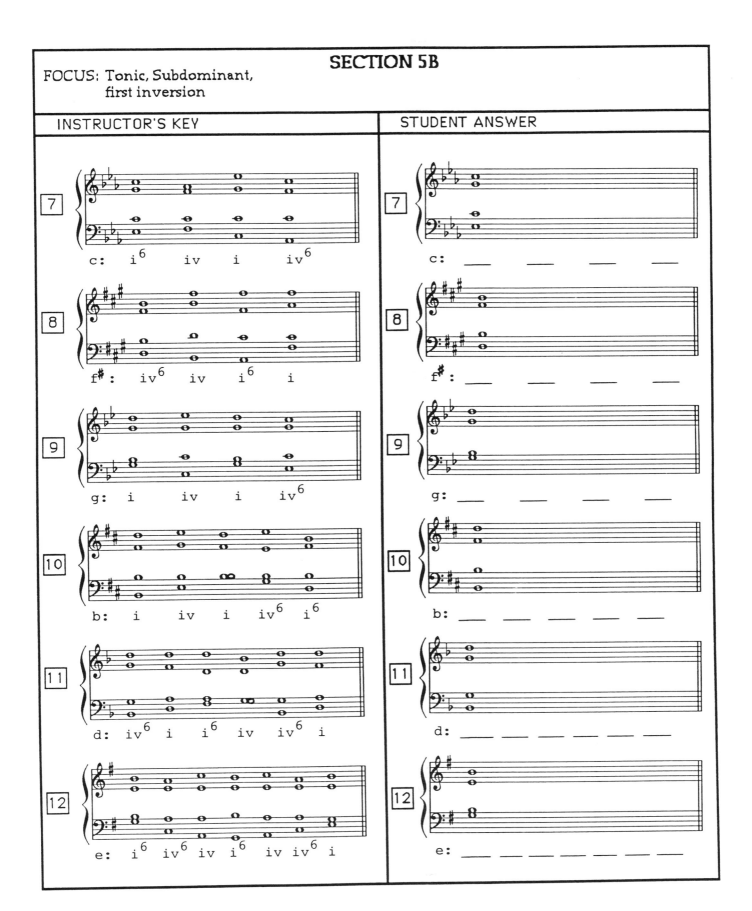

# SECTION 6

FOCUS: m6 -- 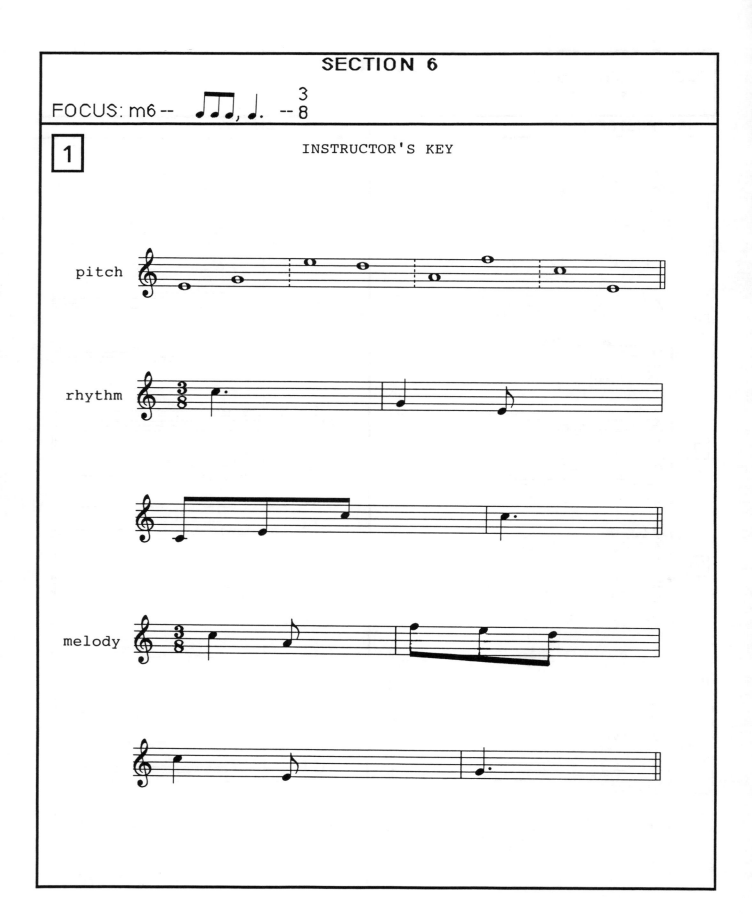 -- 3/8

1    INSTRUCTOR'S KEY

# SECTION 6

FOCUS: m6 --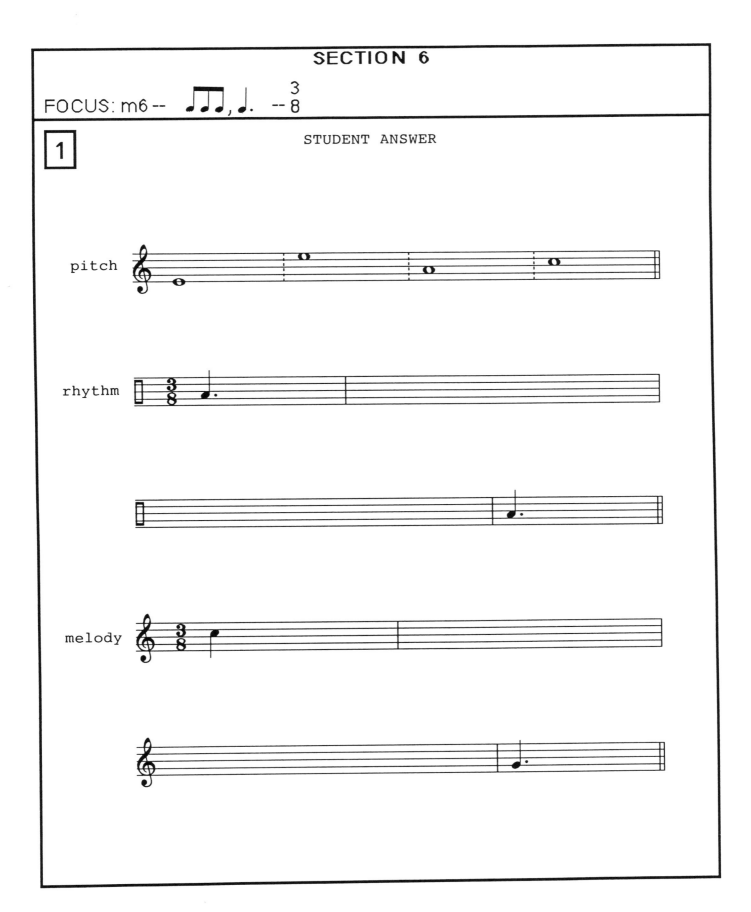

STUDENT ANSWER

**1**

103

FOCUS: m6 -- 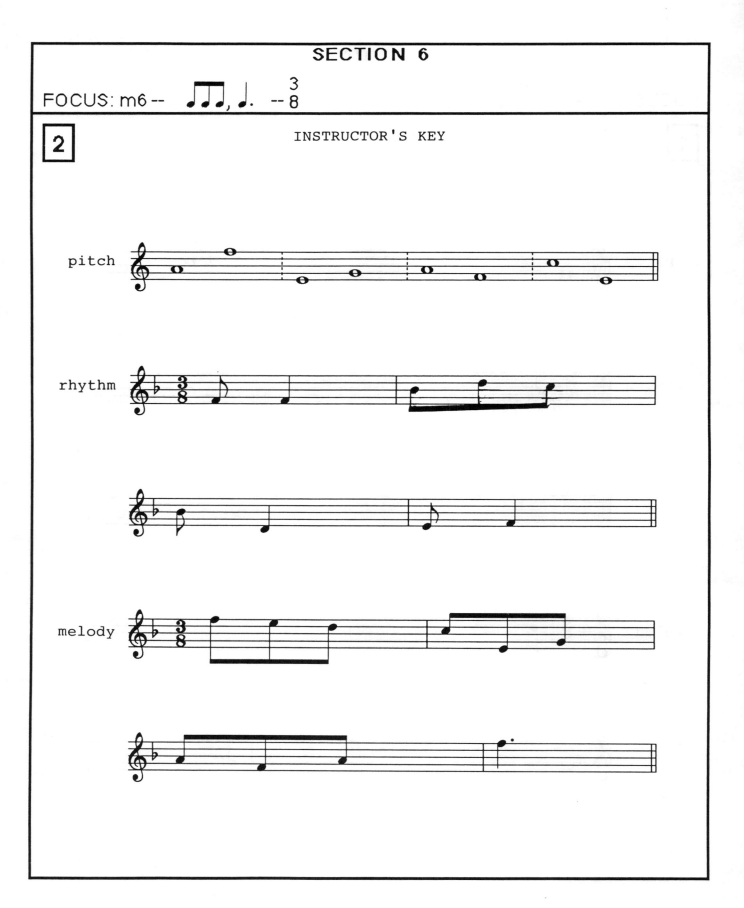 , 𝅘𝅥. -- 3/8

2

pitch

rhythm

melody

# SECTION 6

FOCUS: m6 -- 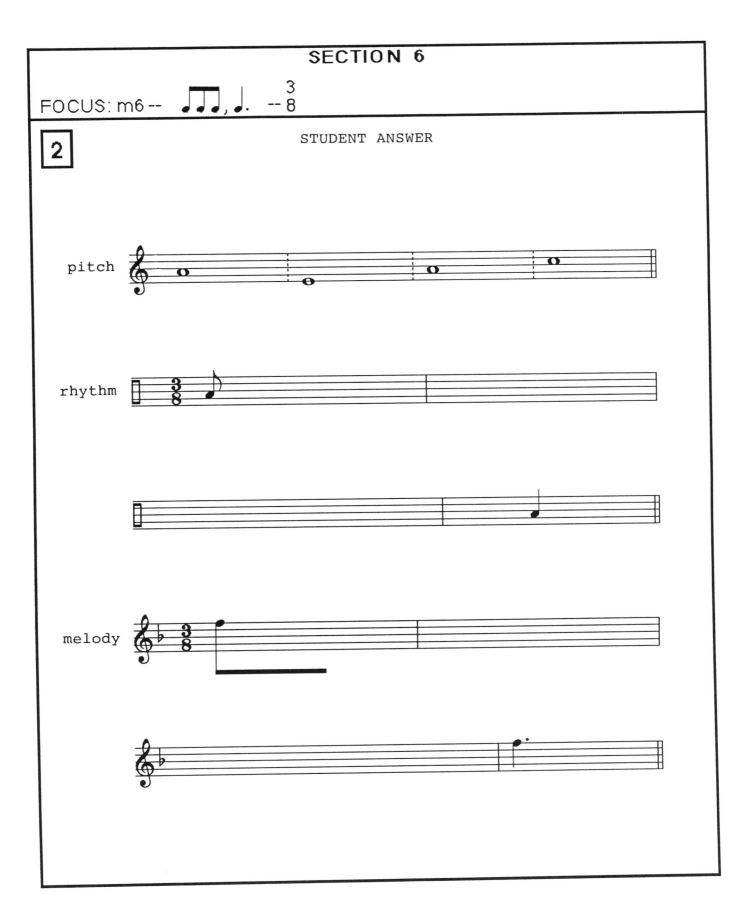 -- 3/8

STUDENT ANSWER

2

pitch

rhythm

melody

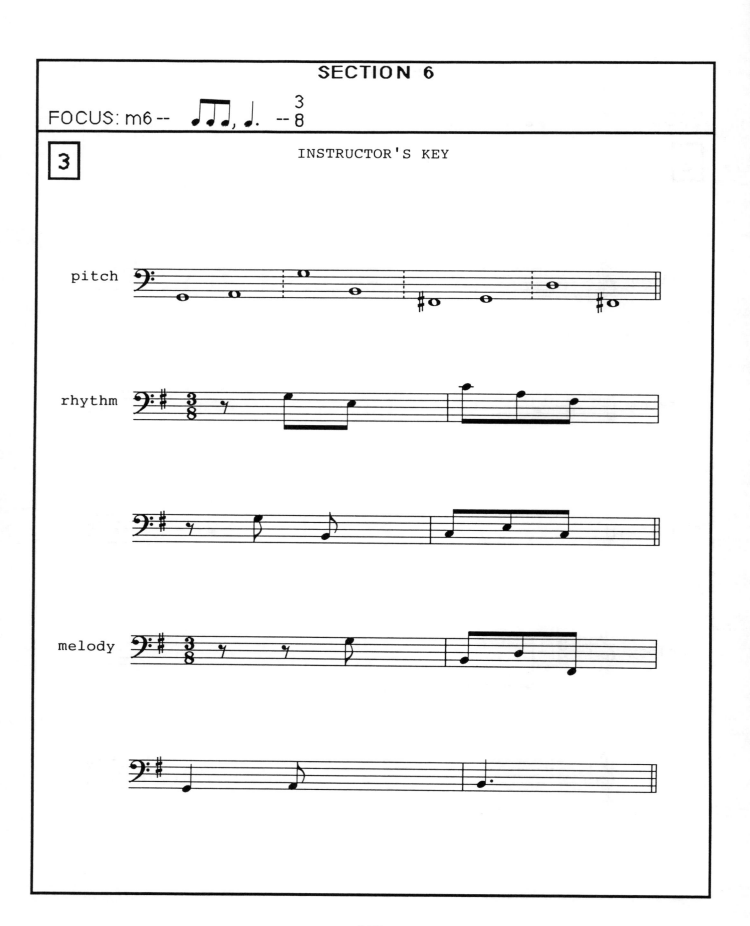

# SECTION 6

FOCUS: m6 -- 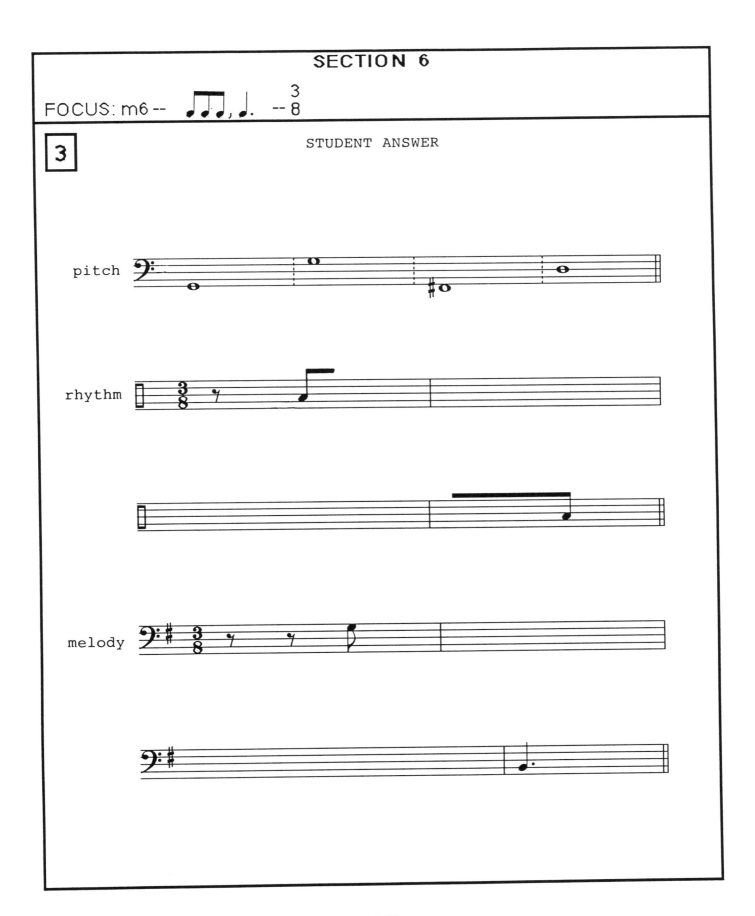 , ♩. -- 3/8

## 3

STUDENT ANSWER

# SECTION 6

FOCUS: m6 -- ♩♩♩, ♩. -- 3/8

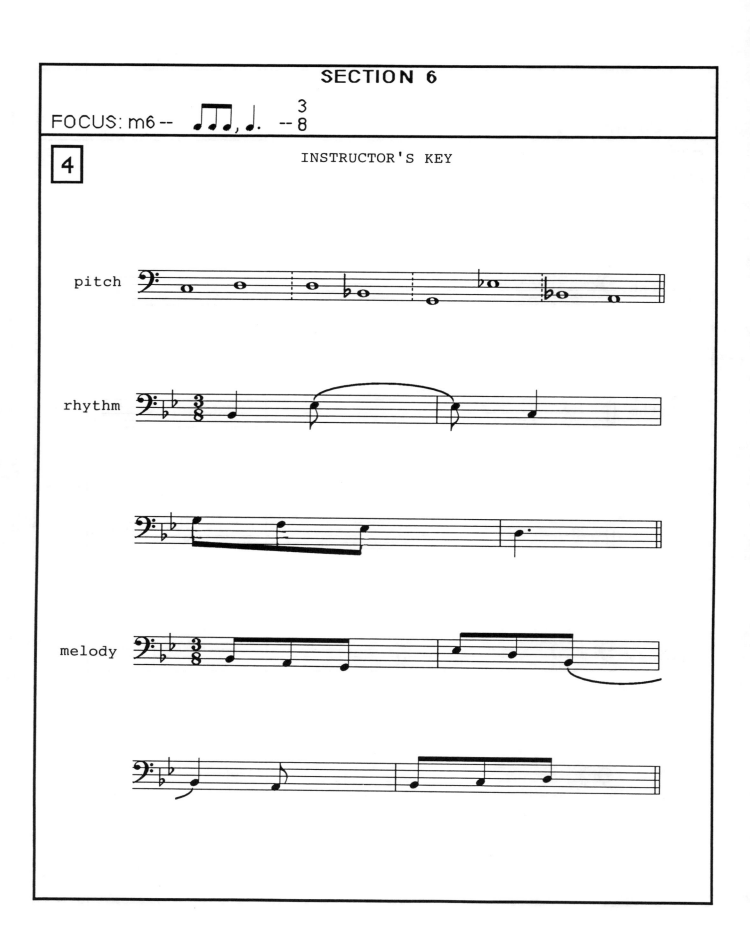

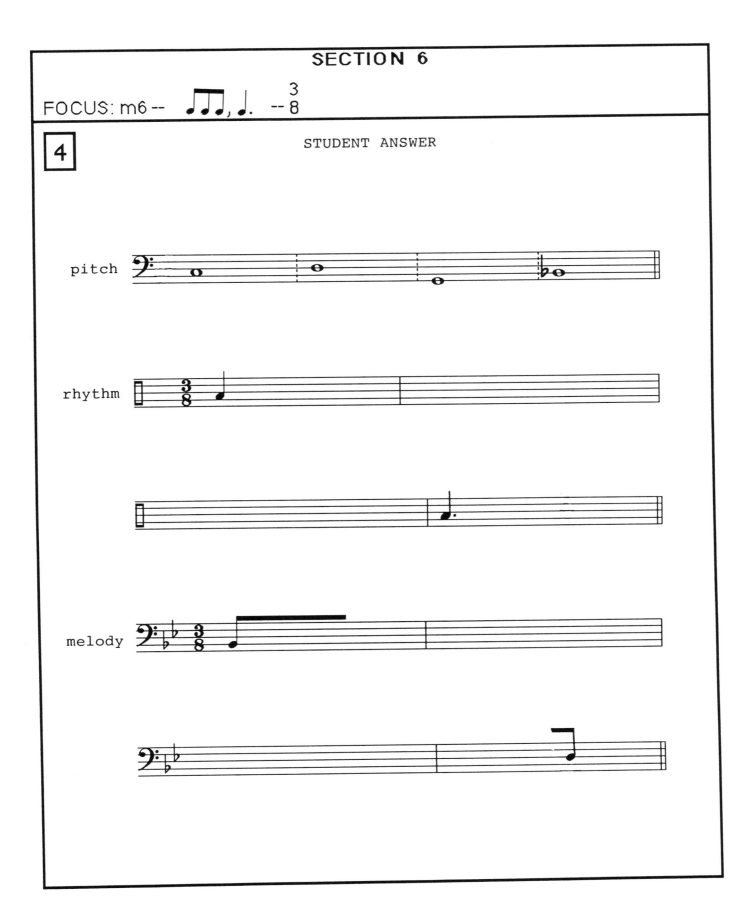

FOCUS: m6 -- ♫♪, ♩. -- $\frac{3}{8}$

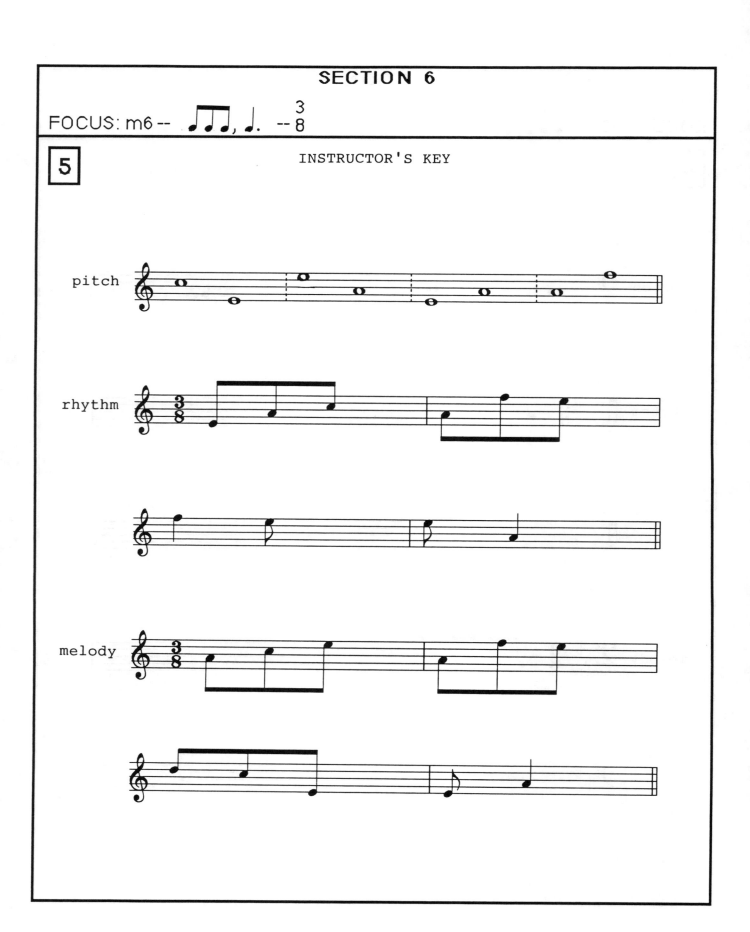

INSTRUCTOR'S KEY

# SECTION 6

FOCUS: m6 -- 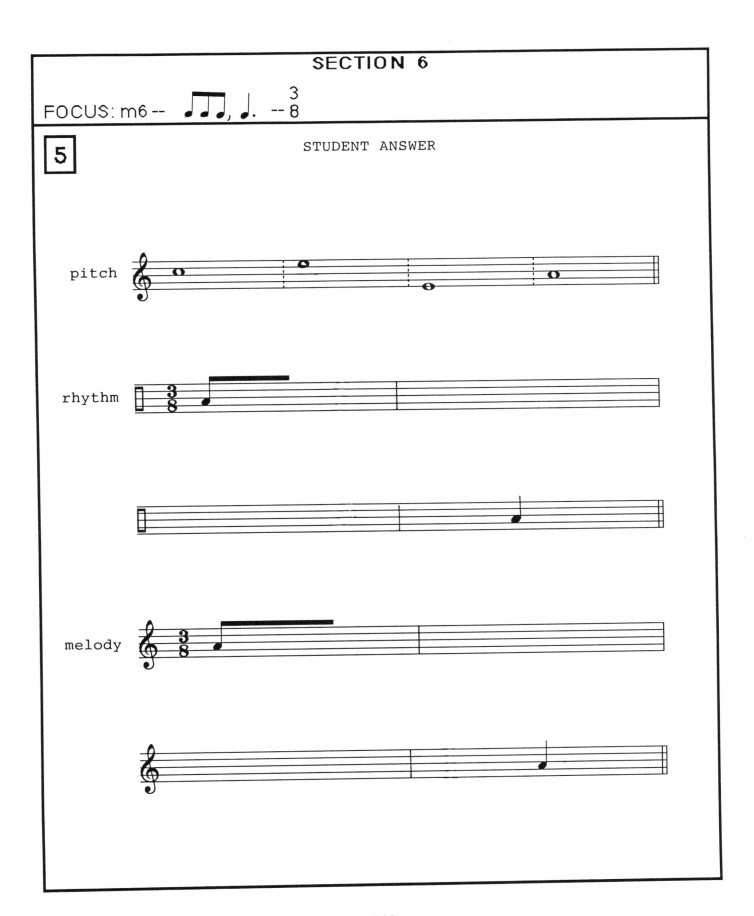 , -- 3/8

5  STUDENT ANSWER

pitch

rhythm

melody

# SECTION 6

FOCUS: m6 -- 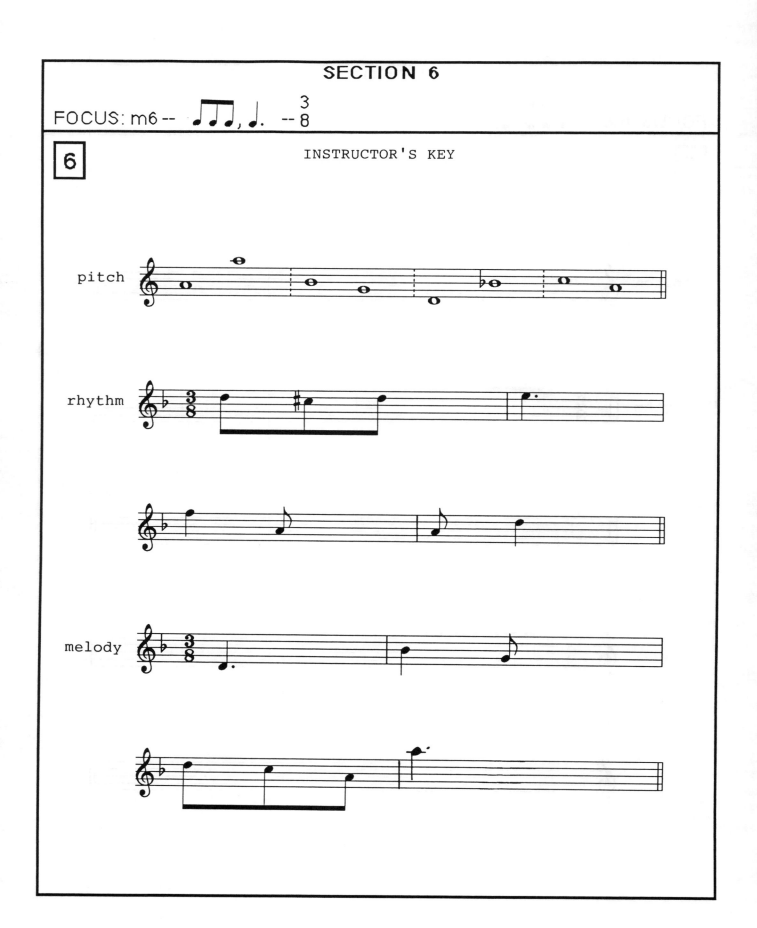 , ♩. -- 3/8

6    INSTRUCTOR'S KEY

pitch

rhythm

melody

112

# SECTION 6

FOCUS: m6 -- ♪♪♪ , ♩. -- 3/8

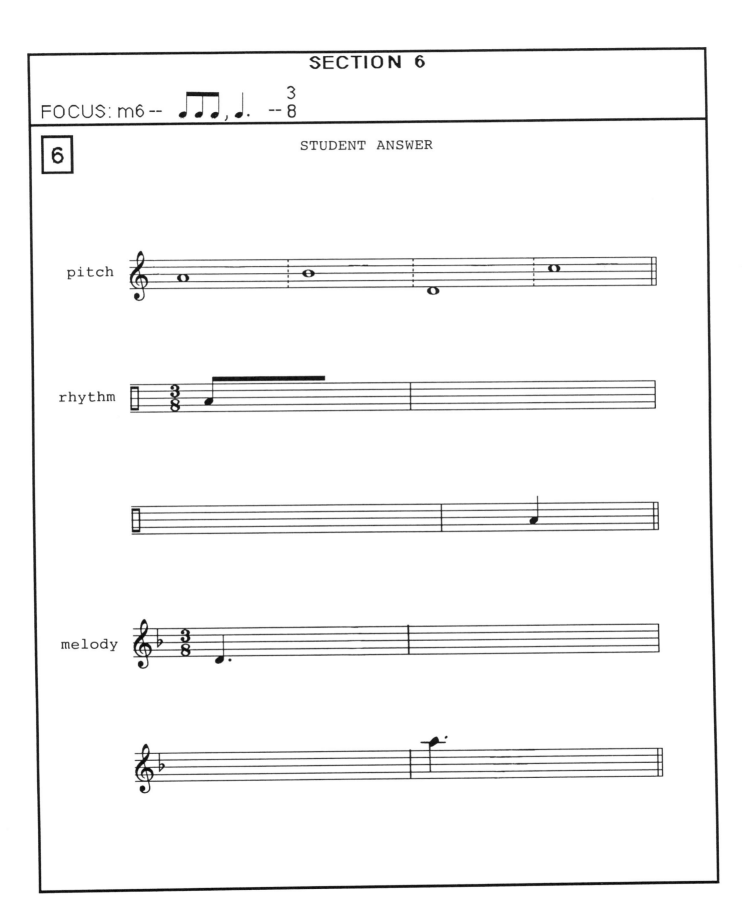

STUDENT ANSWER

6

pitch

rhythm

melody

FOCUS: m6 -- ♪♪♪, ♩. -- 3/8

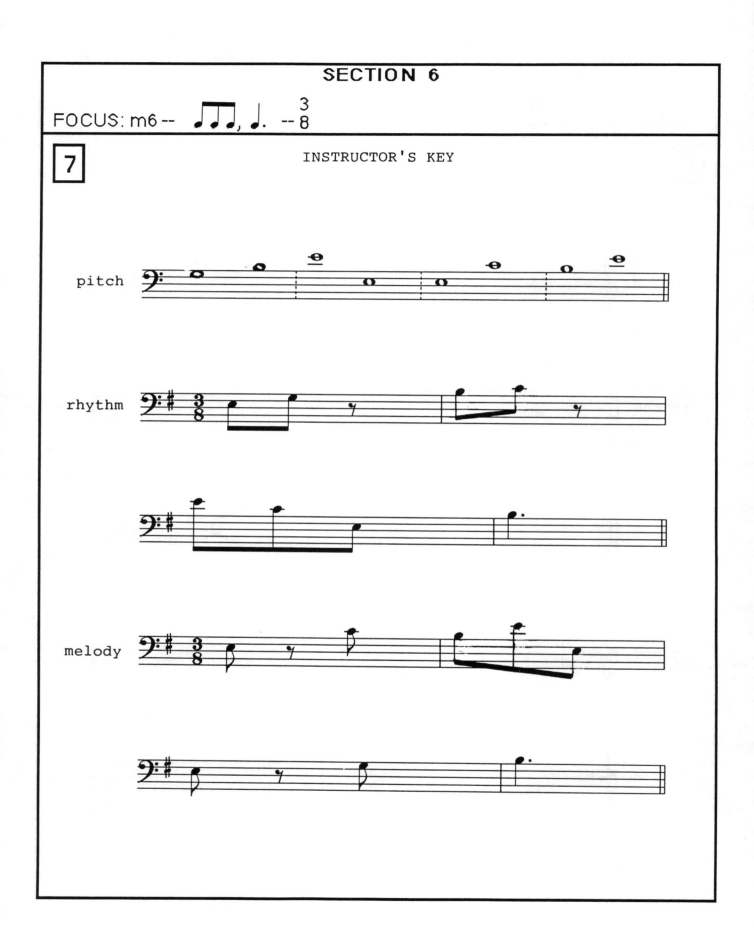

# SECTION 6

FOCUS: m6 -- 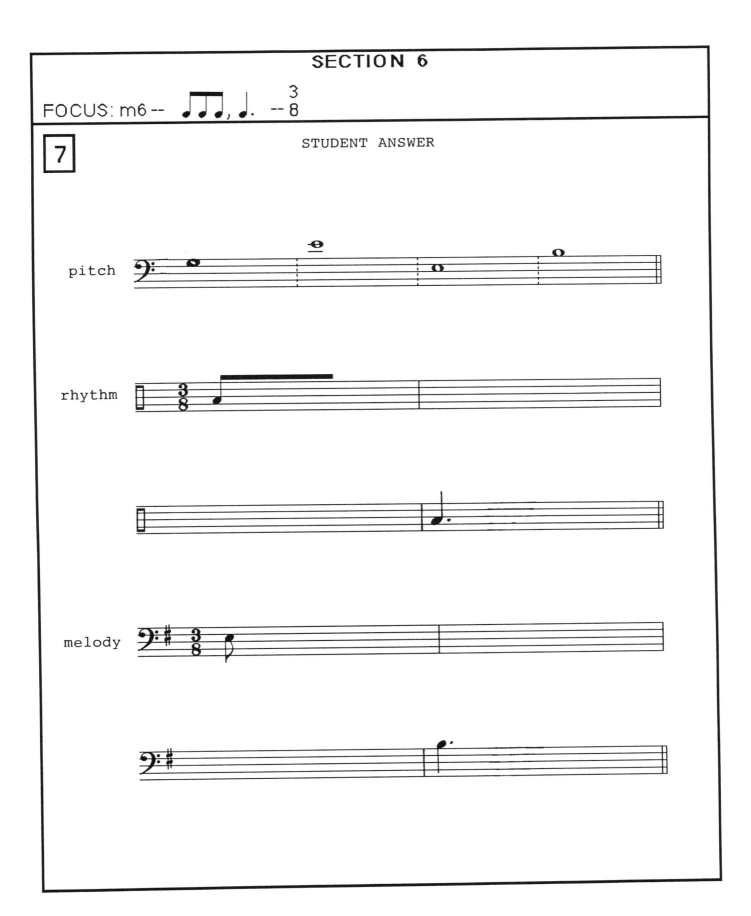 , ♩. -- 3/8

STUDENT ANSWER

7

pitch

rhythm

melody

# SECTION 6

FOCUS: m6 -- ♪♪♪ , ♩. -- 3/8

8 INSTRUCTOR'S KEY

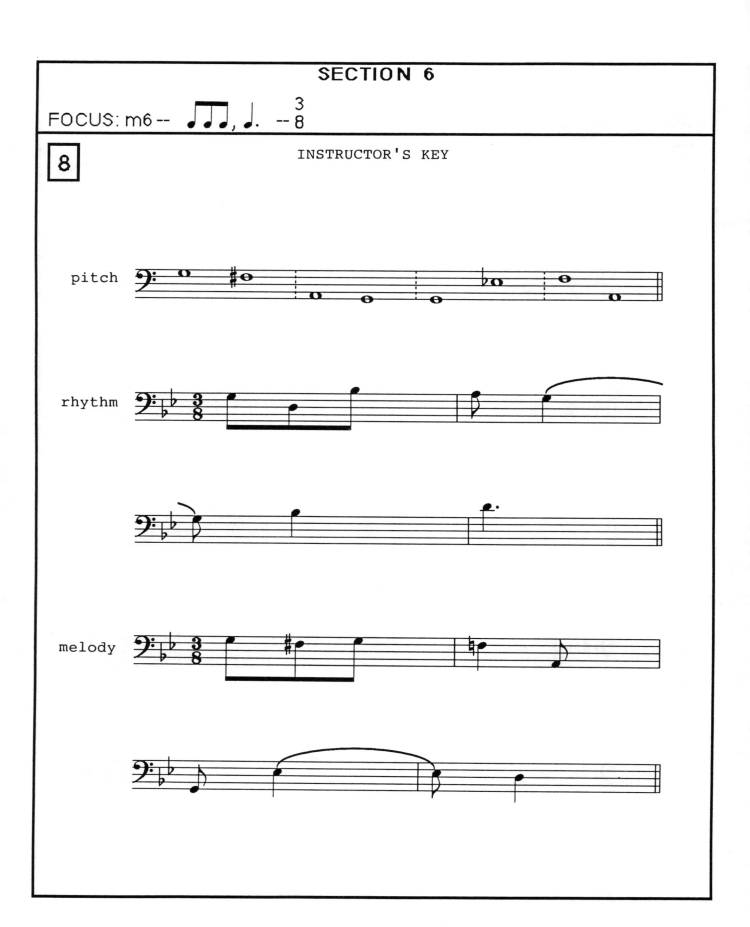

# SECTION 6

FOCUS: m6 -- ♪♪♪, ♩. -- $\frac{3}{8}$

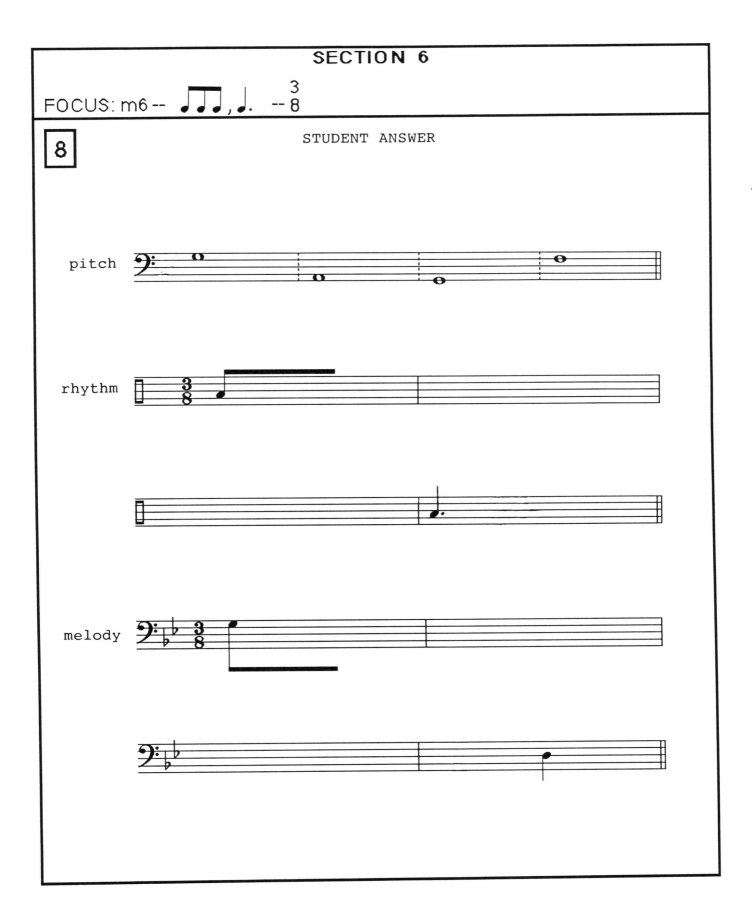

STUDENT ANSWER

**8**

pitch

rhythm

melody

# SECTION 6A

**FOCUS:** Primary Triads,
first inversion

| INSTRUCTOR'S KEY: | STUDENT ANSWER: |
|---|---|

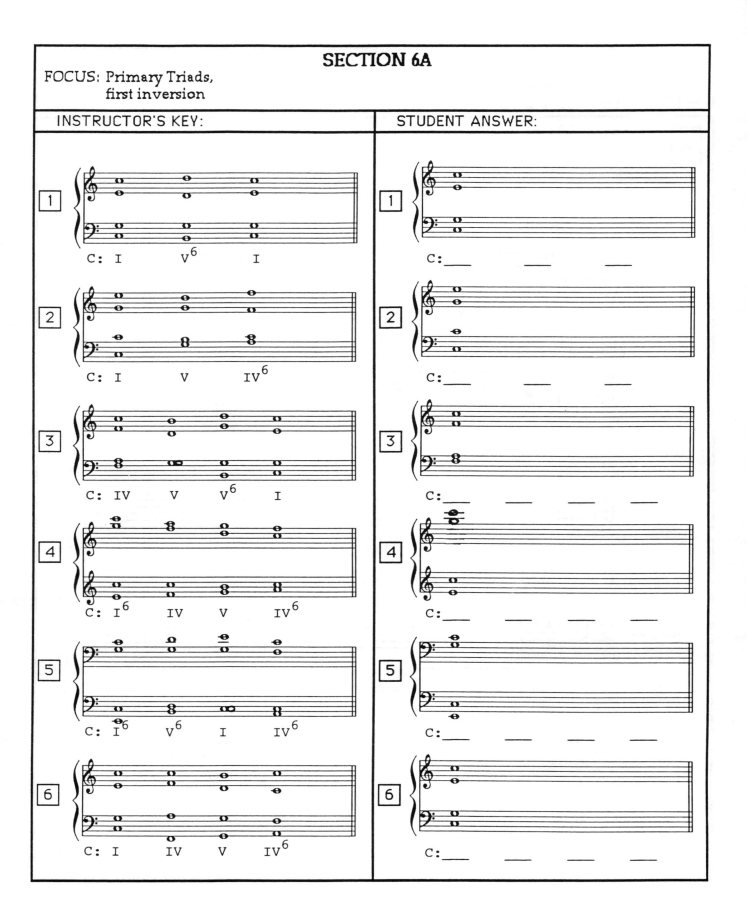

1  C: I  V⁶  I

2  C: I  V  IV⁶

3  C: IV  V  V⁶  I

4  C: I⁶  IV  V  IV⁶

5  C: I⁶  V⁶  I  IV⁶

6  C: I  IV  V  IV⁶

118

# SECTION 6A

FOCUS: Primary Triads,
first inversion

| INSTRUCTOR'S KEY | STUDENT ANSWER |
|---|---|

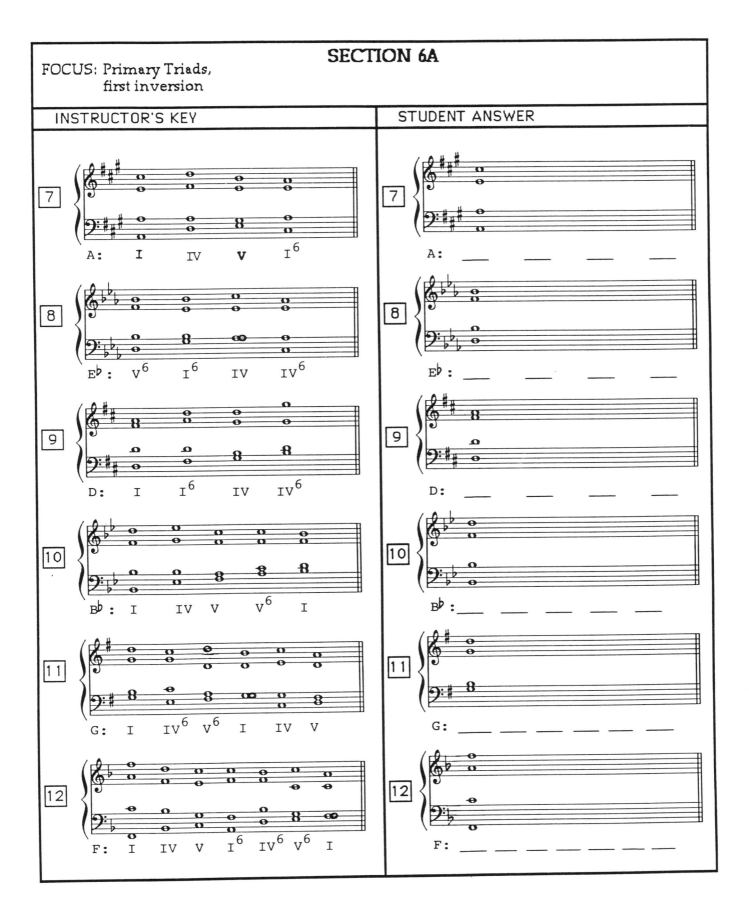

7  A:   I    IV    V    I⁶

8  E♭:   V⁶   I⁶   IV   IV⁶

9  D:   I    I⁶   IV   IV⁶

10  B♭:  I   IV   V   V⁶   I

11  G:   I   IV⁶  V⁶   I   IV   V

12  F:   I   IV   V   I⁶   IV⁶   V⁶   I

7  A: ___ ___ ___ ___

8  E♭: ___ ___ ___ ___

9  D: ___ ___ ___ ___

10  B♭: ___ ___ ___ ___ ___

11  G: ___ ___ ___ ___ ___ ___

12  F: ___ ___ ___ ___ ___ ___ ___

# SECTION 6B

**FOCUS:** Primary Triads,
first inversion

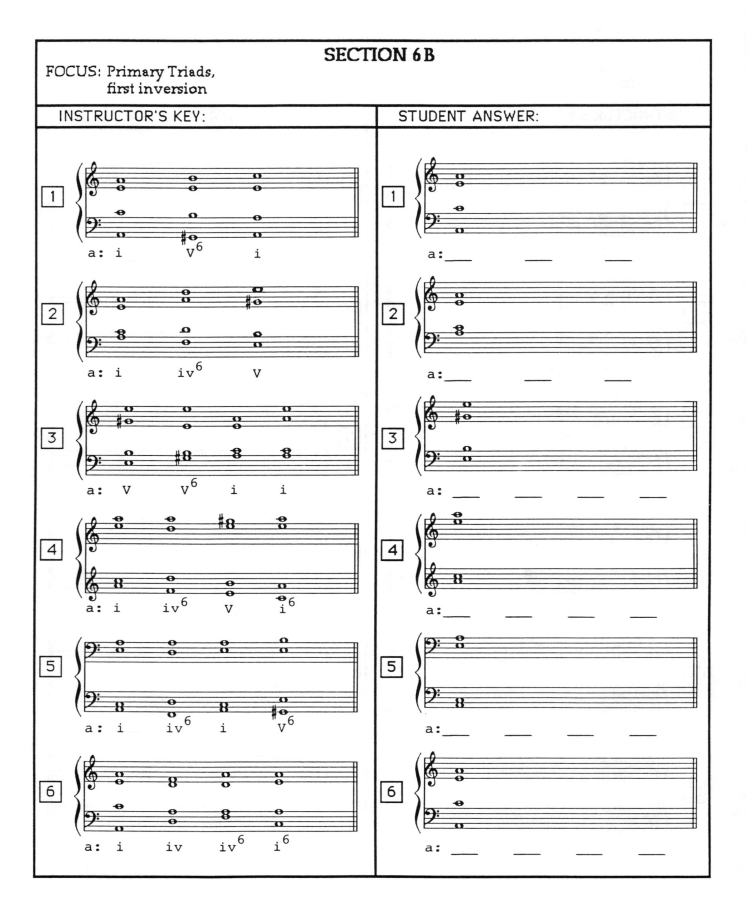

# SECTION 6B

**FOCUS:** Primary Triads,
first inversion

| INSTRUCTOR'S KEY | STUDENT ANSWER |
|---|---|

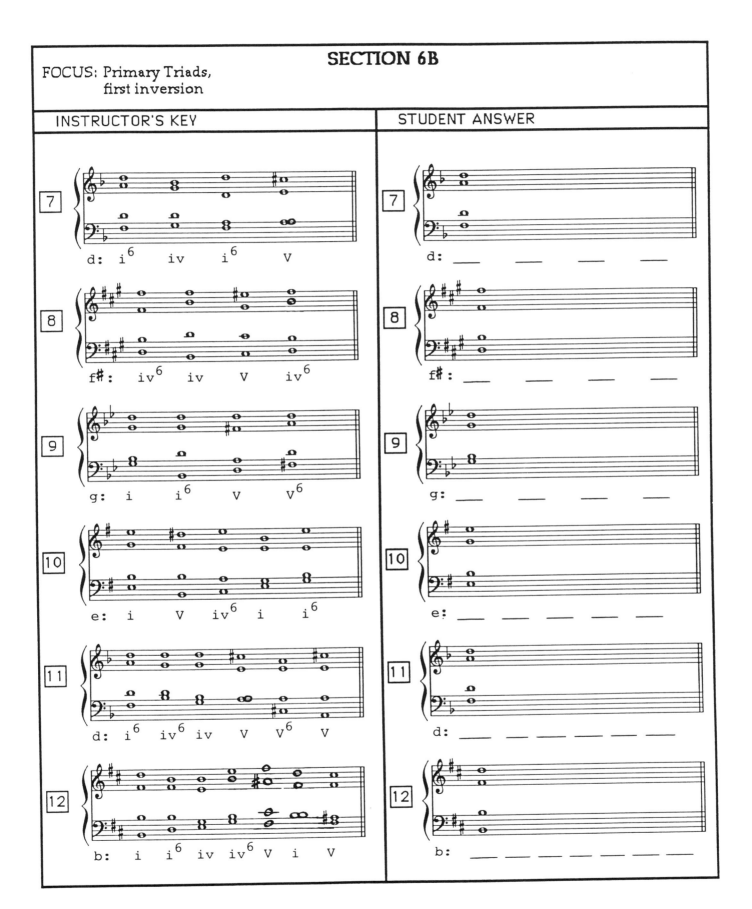

7
d: $i^6$   iv   $i^6$   V

7
d: ___  ___  ___  ___

8
f#: $iv^6$   iv   V   $iv^6$

8
f#: ___  ___  ___  ___

9
g: i   $i^6$   V   $V^6$

9
g: ___  ___  ___  ___

10
e: i   V   $iv^6$   i   $i^6$

10
e: ___  ___  ___  ___  ___

11
d: $i^6$   $iv^6$   iv   V   $V^6$   V

11
d: ___  ___  ___  ___  ___  ___

12
b: i   $i^6$   iv   $iv^6$   V   i   V

12
b: ___  ___  ___  ___  ___  ___  ___

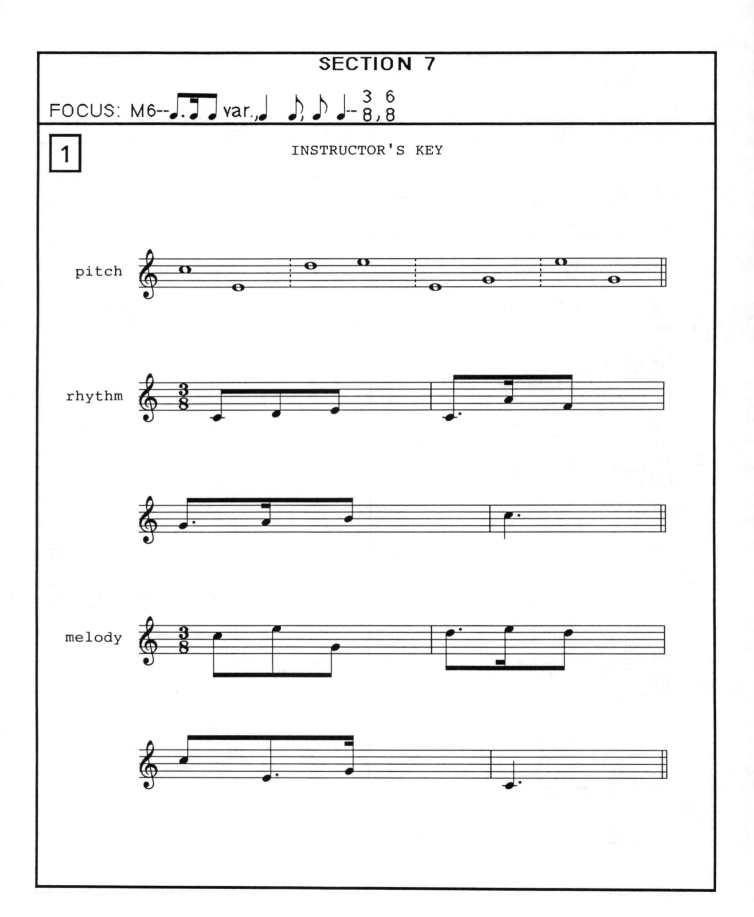

# SECTION 7

FOCUS: M6-- var., 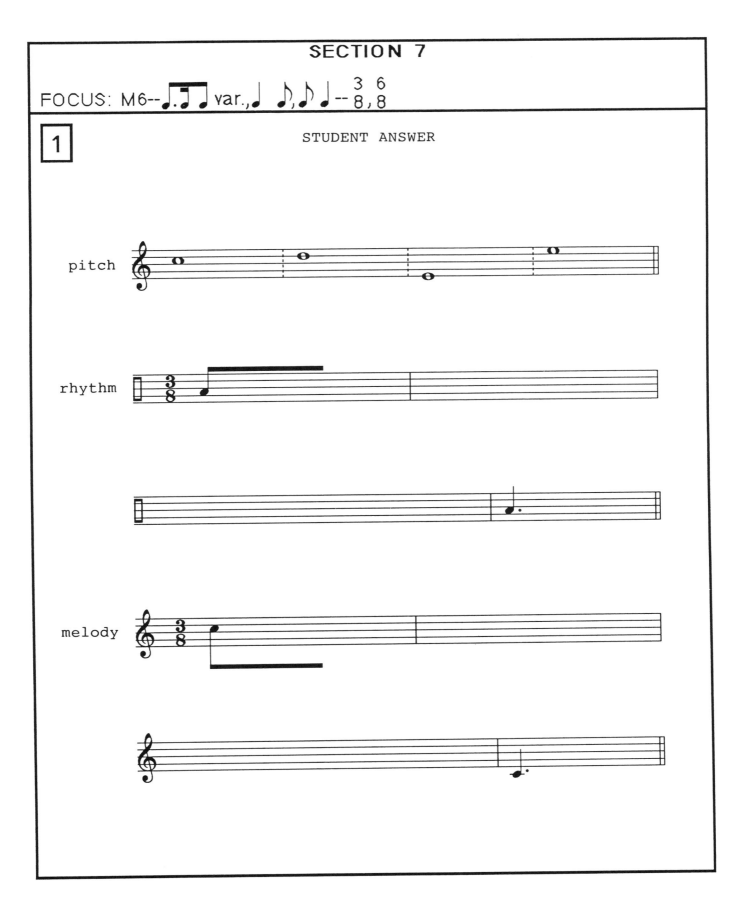 ♩ ♪,♪ ♩ -- 3 6 / 8,8

# SECTION 7

FOCUS: M6-- ♩.♩ ♩ var., ♩ ♪, ♪ ♩ -- 3/8, 6/8

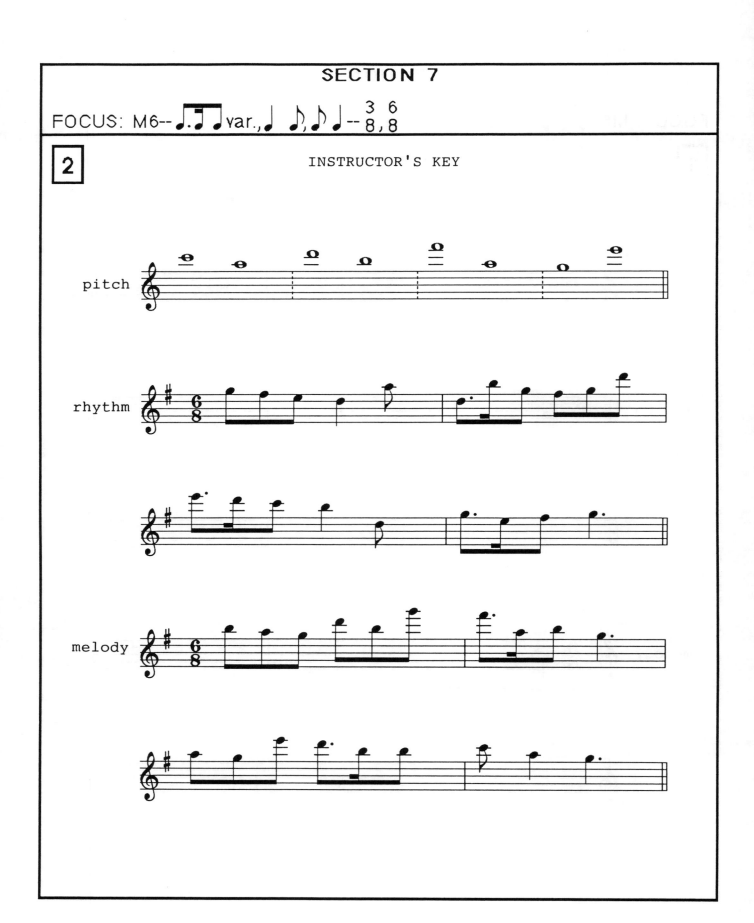

2    INSTRUCTOR'S KEY

pitch

rhythm

melody

# SECTION 7

FOCUS: M6-- 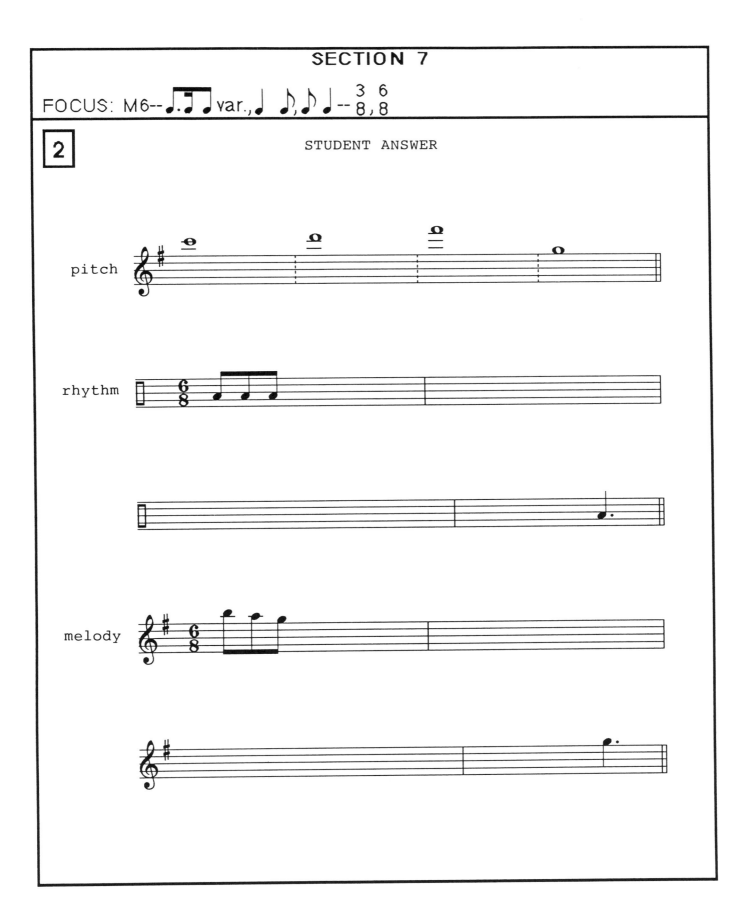var., 3 6 -- 8,8

2   STUDENT ANSWER

pitch

rhythm

melody

125

# SECTION 7

FOCUS: M6-- ♪.♫♩ var., ♩ ♪, ♪♩ -- $\frac{3}{8}, \frac{6}{8}$

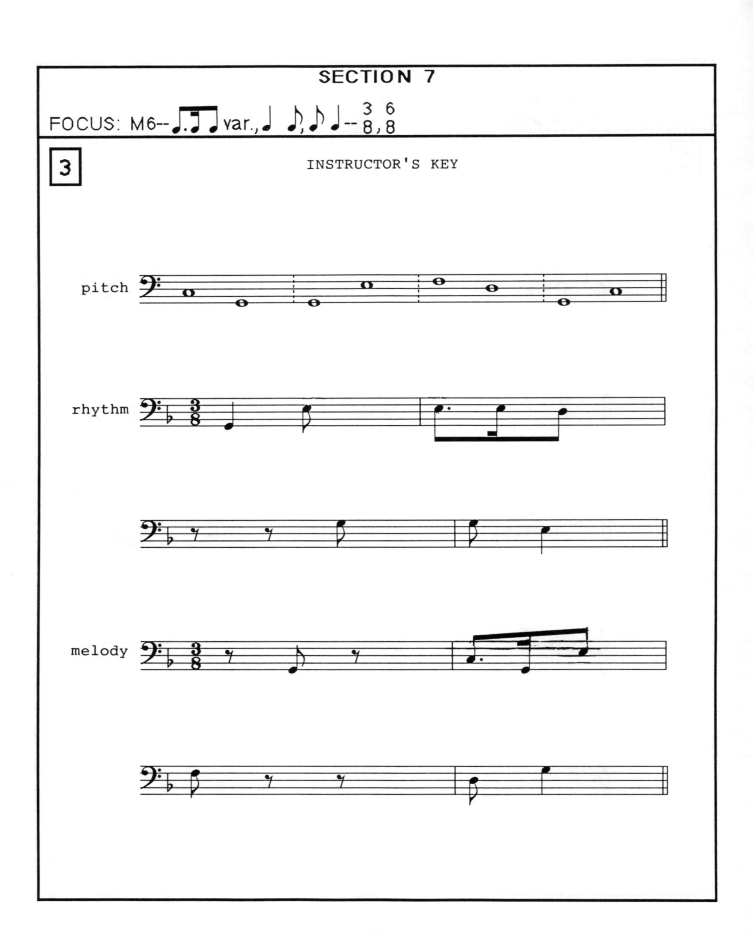

3

INSTRUCTOR'S KEY

# SECTION 7

FOCUS: M6-- 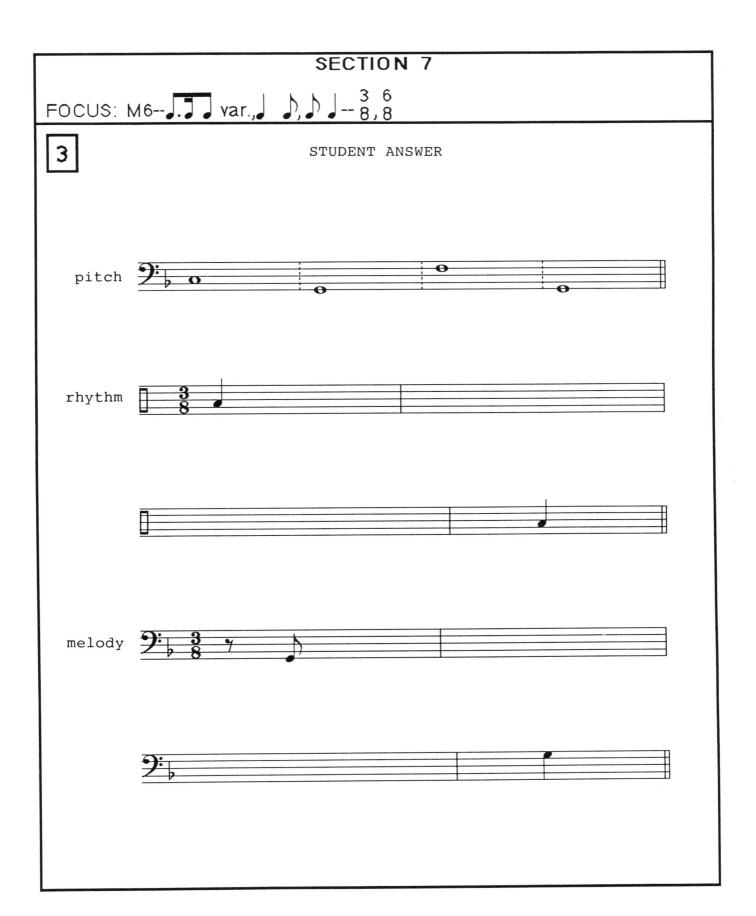 var., -- 3/8, 6/8

# SECTION 7

FOCUS: M6--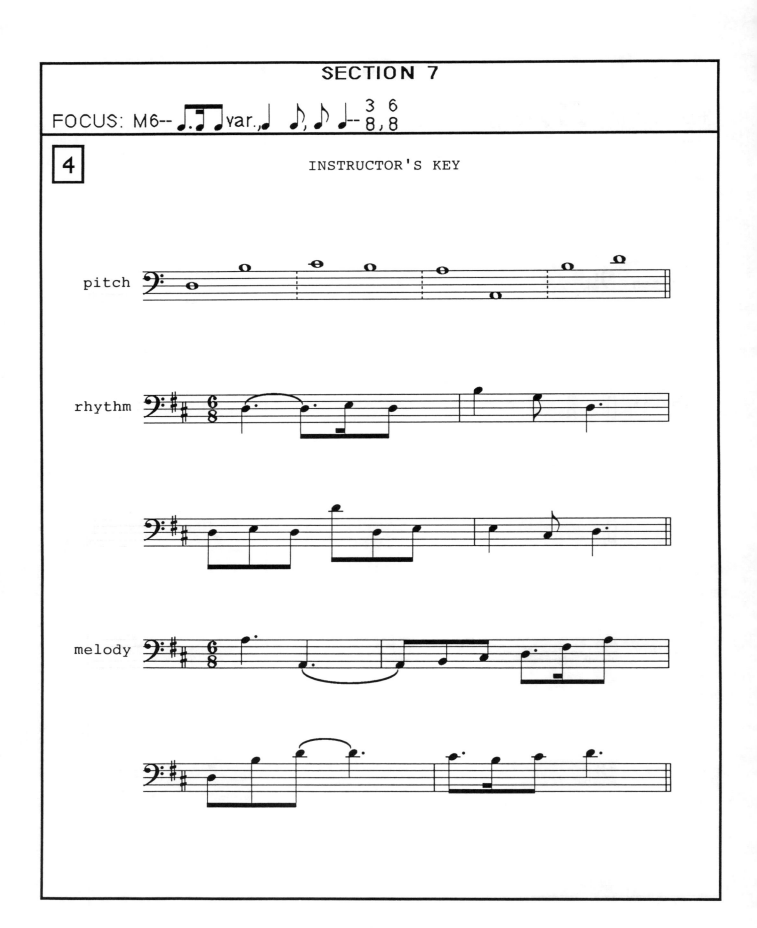

128

# SECTION 7

FOCUS: M6-- 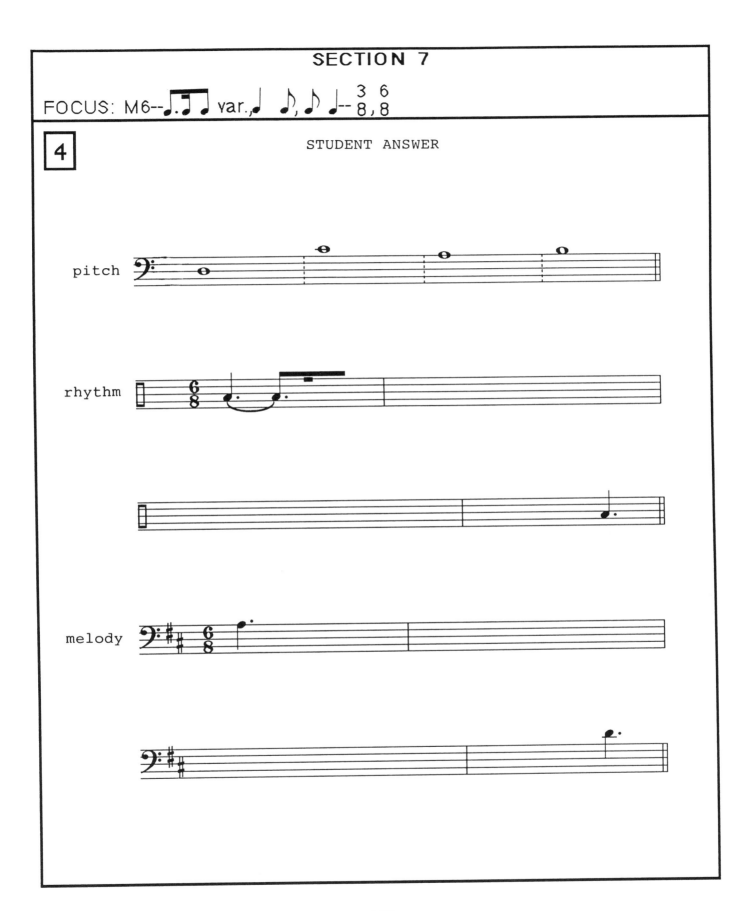 var., 3 6
8, 8

**4**

STUDENT ANSWER

pitch

rhythm

melody

FOCUS: M6-- ♩.♪♩ var.♩ ♪,♪ ♩-- $\frac{3}{8},\frac{6}{8}$

5            INSTRUCTOR'S KEY

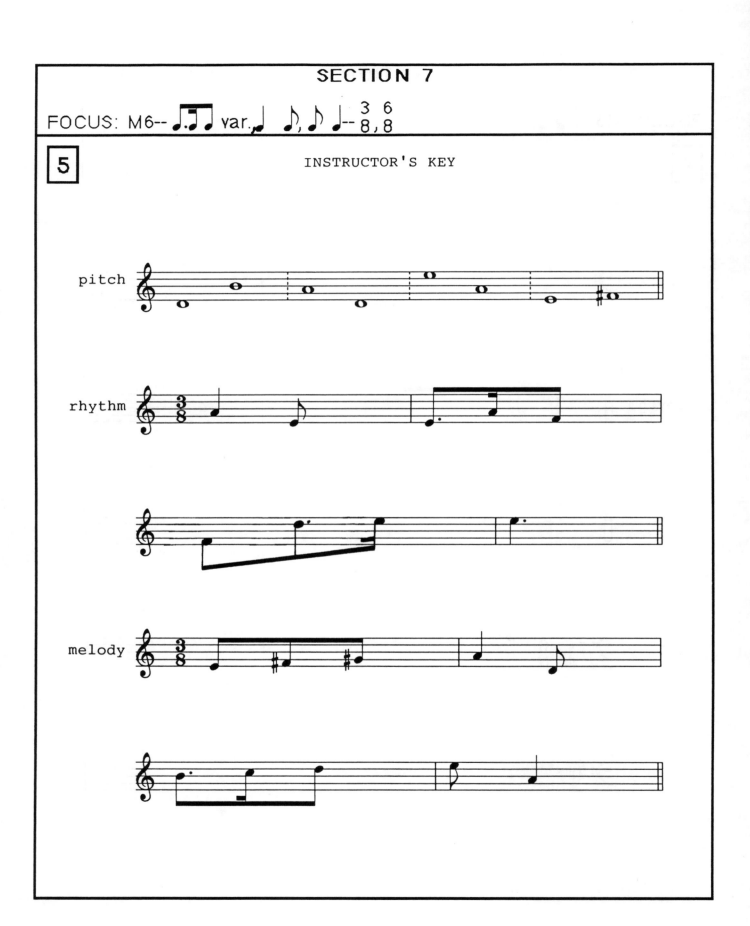

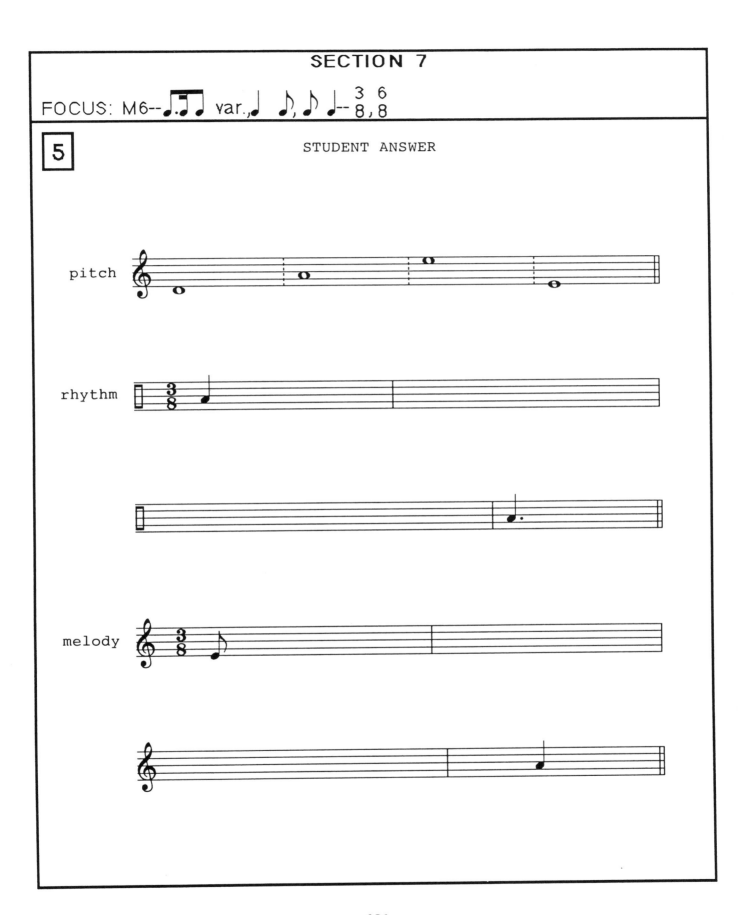

# SECTION 7

FOCUS: M6--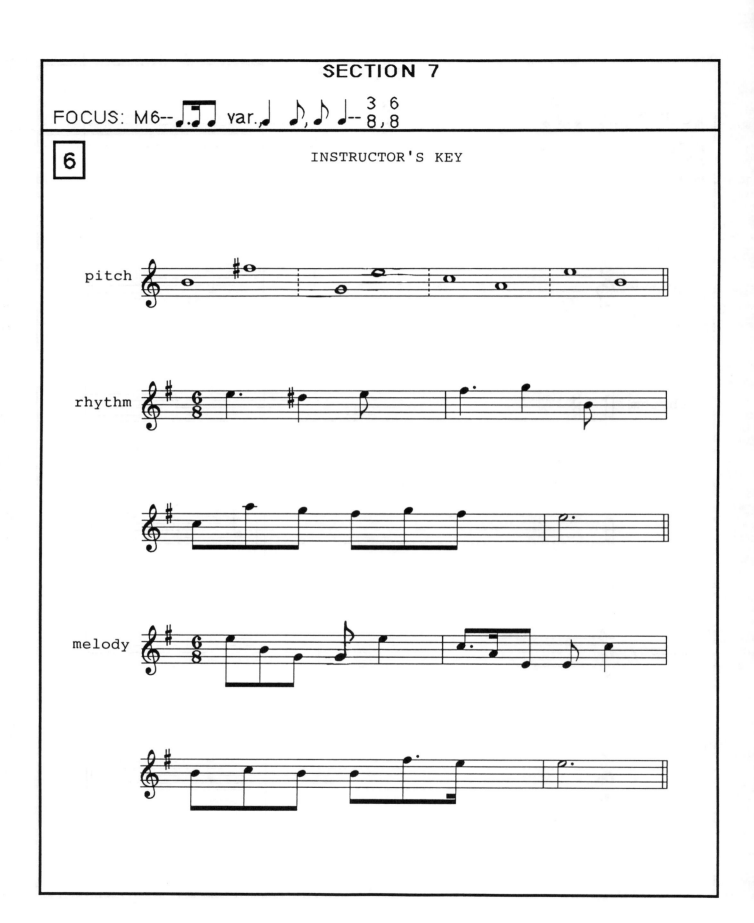

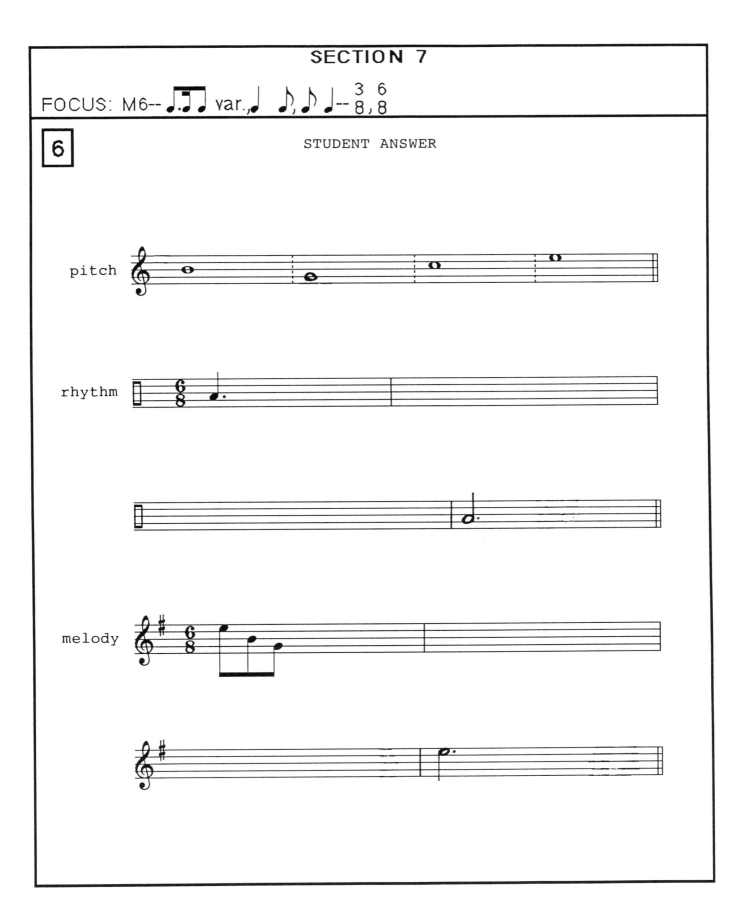

# SECTION 7

FOCUS: M6-- ♩.♪♩ var., ♩ ♪, ♪ ♩ -- 3/8, 6/8

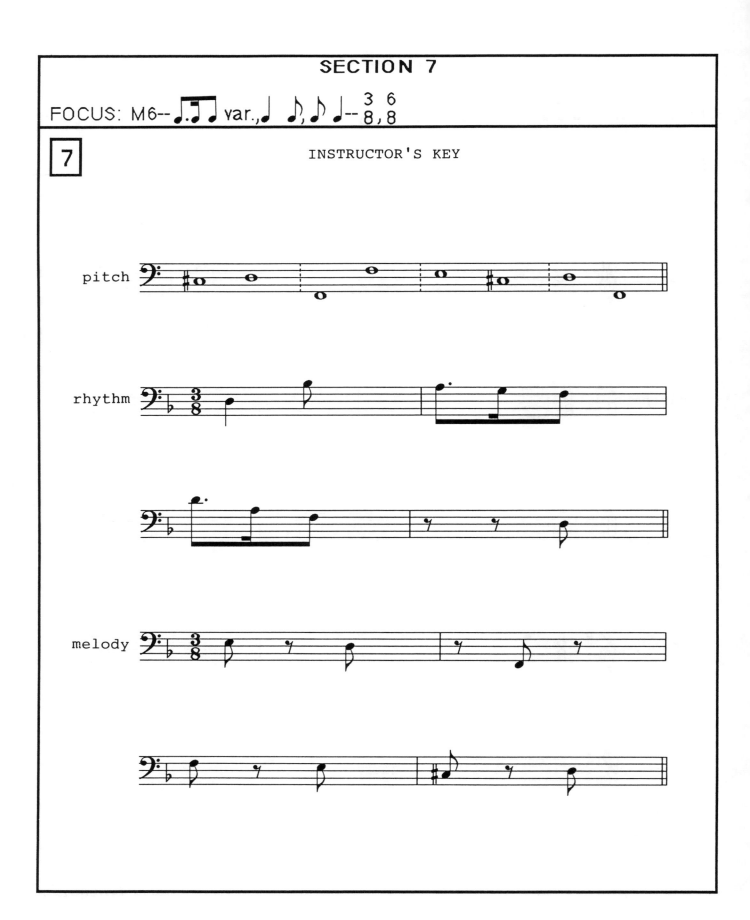

7    INSTRUCTOR'S KEY

pitch

rhythm

melody

# SECTION 7

FOCUS: M6-- 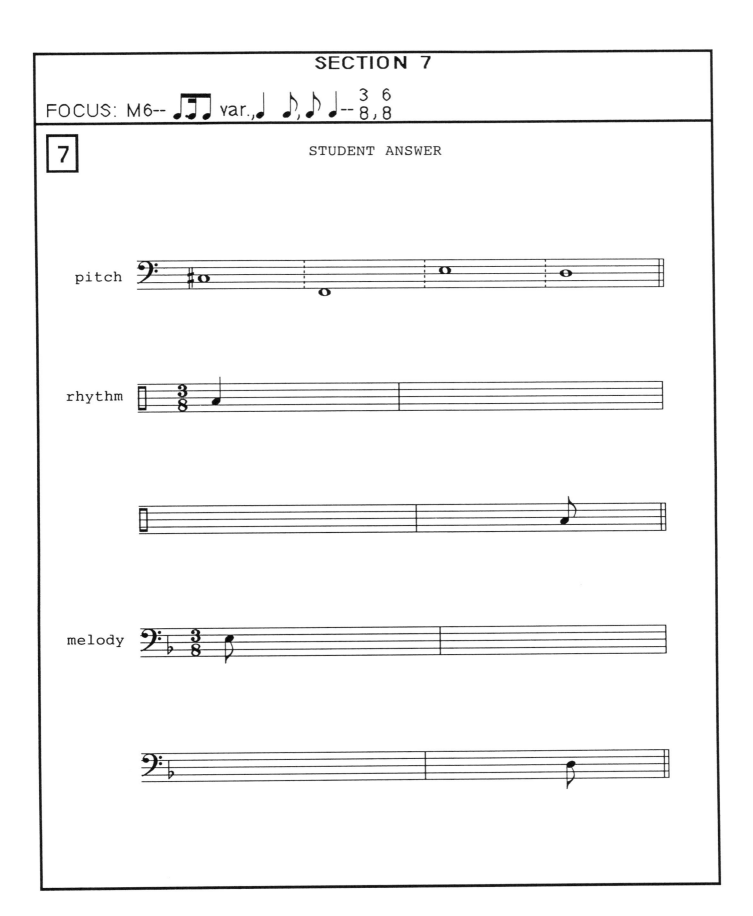 var., ♩ ♪,♪ ♩-- 3 6
8, 8

## 7    STUDENT ANSWER

pitch

rhythm

melody

135

# SECTION 7

FOCUS: M6--♩♪♩ var.,♩ ♪,♪ ♩--$\frac{3}{8}, \frac{6}{8}$

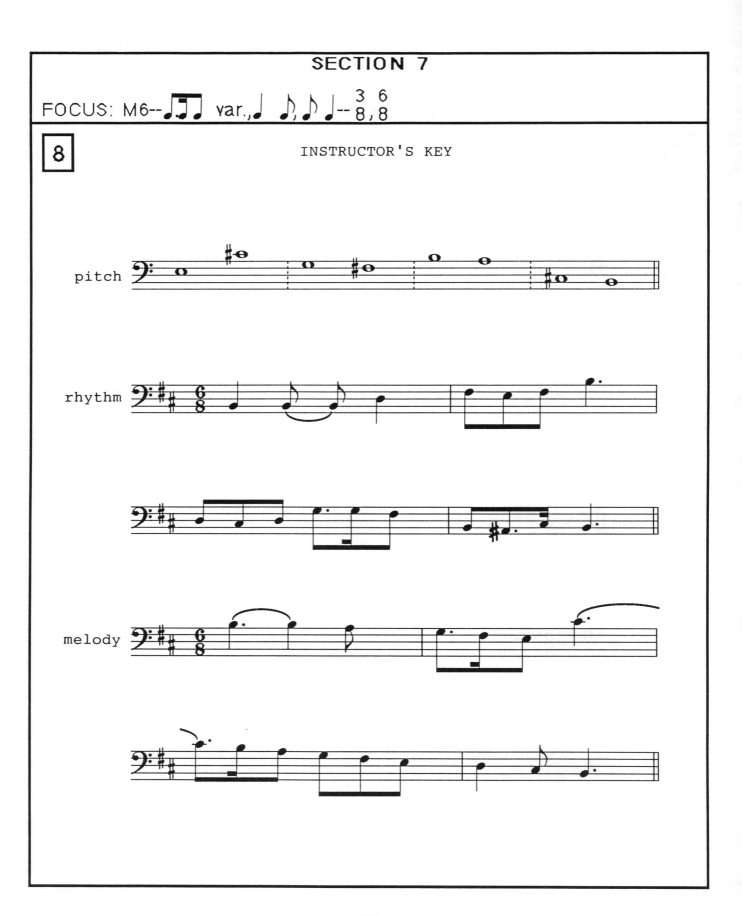

**8**  INSTRUCTOR'S KEY

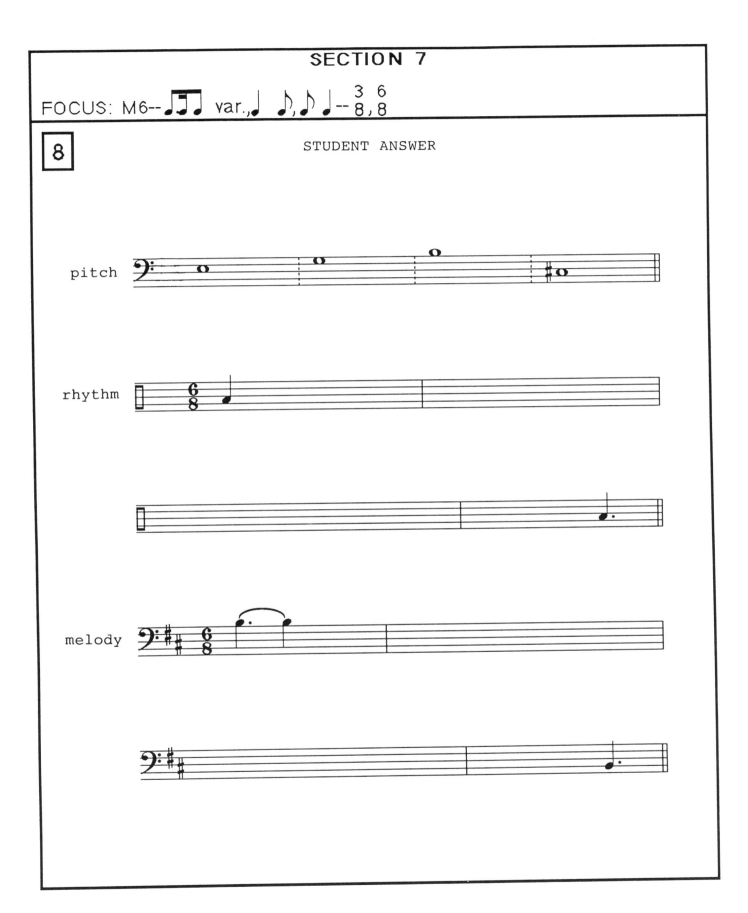

# SECTION 7A

**FOCUS:** Dominant Seventh, root postion and inversions

| INSTRUCTOR'S KEY: | STUDENT ANSWER: |
| --- | --- |

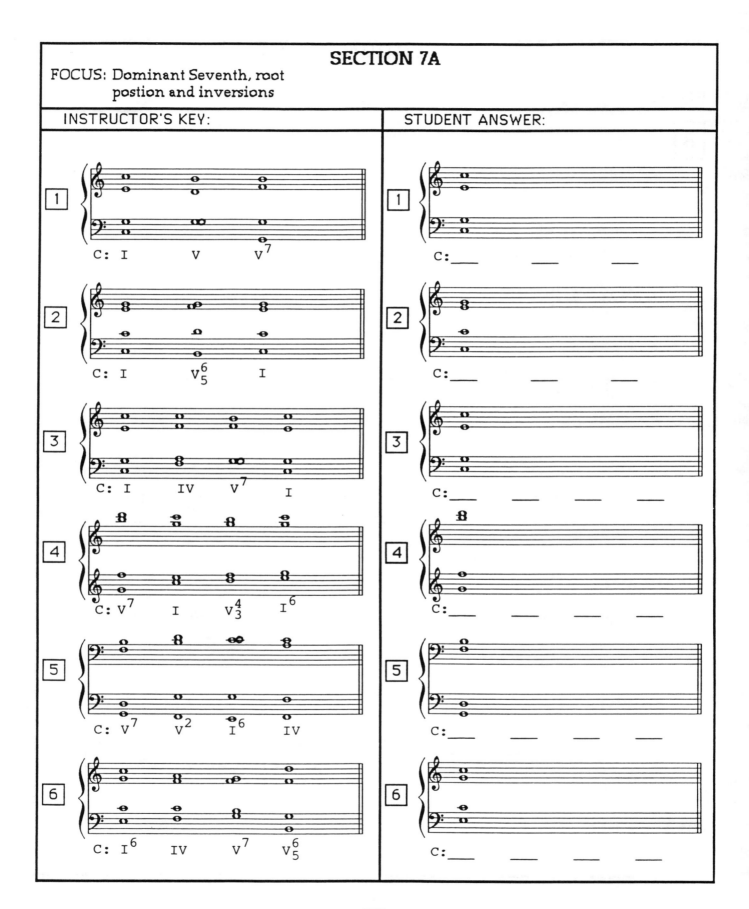

1. C: I  V  $V^7$

2. C: I  $V^6_5$  I

3. C: I  IV  $V^7$  I

4. C: $V^7$  I  $V^4_3$  $I^6$

5. C: $V^7$  $V^2$  $I^6$  IV

6. C: $I^6$  IV  $V^7$  $V^6_5$

# SECTION 7A

FOCUS: Dominant Seventh, root
position and inversions

| INSTRUCTOR'S KEY | STUDENT ANSWER |
|---|---|

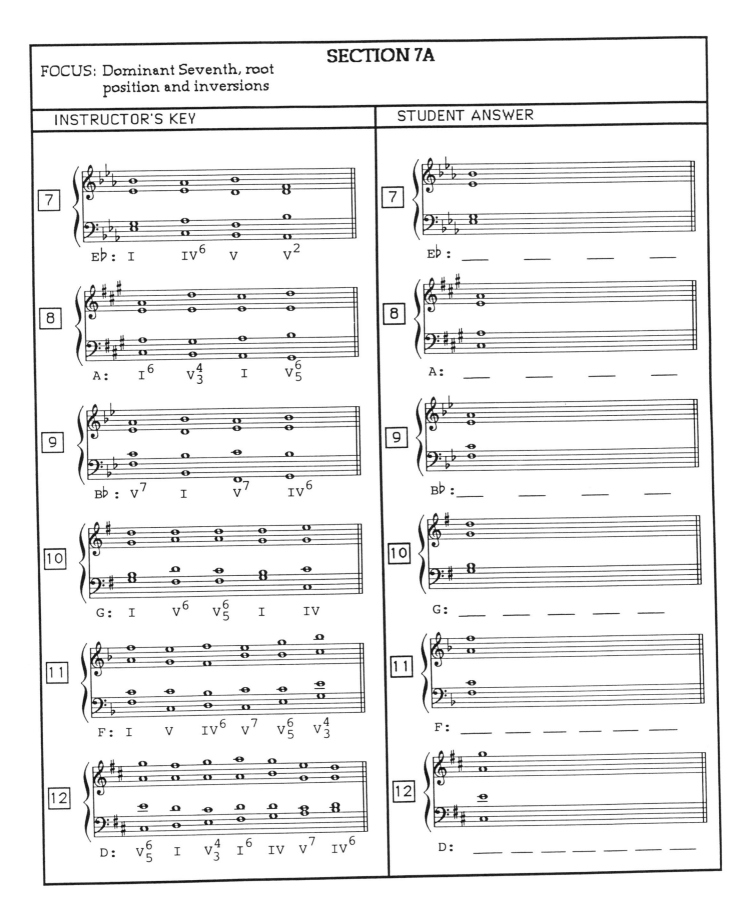

7
Eb: I  IV$^6$  V  V$^2$

Eb: ___  ___  ___  ___

8
A: I$^6$  V$^4_3$  I  V$^6_5$

A: ___  ___  ___  ___

9
Bb: V$^7$  I  V$^7$  IV$^6$

Bb: ___  ___  ___  ___

10
G: I  V$^6$  V$^6_5$  I  IV

G: ___  ___  ___  ___  ___

11
F: I  V  IV$^6$  V$^7$  V$^6_5$  V$^4_3$

F: ___  ___  ___  ___  ___  ___

12
D: V$^6_5$  I  V$^4_3$  I$^6$  IV  V$^7$  IV$^6$

D: ___  ___  ___  ___  ___  ___  ___

# SECTION 7 B

FOCUS: Dominant Seventh, root
postion and inversions

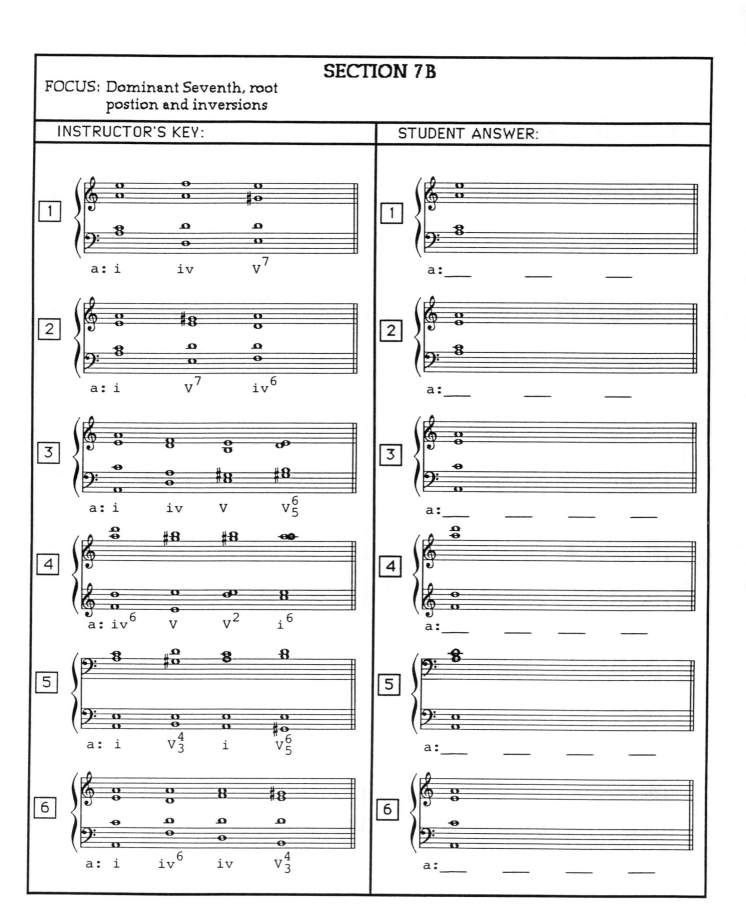

INSTRUCTOR'S KEY:

1. a: i    iv    V$^7$

2. a: i    V$^7$    iv$^6$

3. a: i    iv    V    V$^6_5$

4. a: iv$^6$    V    V$^2$    i$^6$

5. a: i    V$^4_3$    i    V$^6_5$

6. a: i    iv$^6$    iv    V$^4_3$

STUDENT ANSWER:

1. a:___    ___    ___

2. a:___    ___    ___

3. a:___    ___    ___    ___

4. a:___    ___    ___    ___

5. a:___    ___    ___    ___

6. a:___    ___    ___    ___

140

# SECTION 7 B

FOCUS: Dominant Seventh, root
position and inversions

| INSTRUCTOR'S KEY | STUDENT ANSWER |
|---|---|

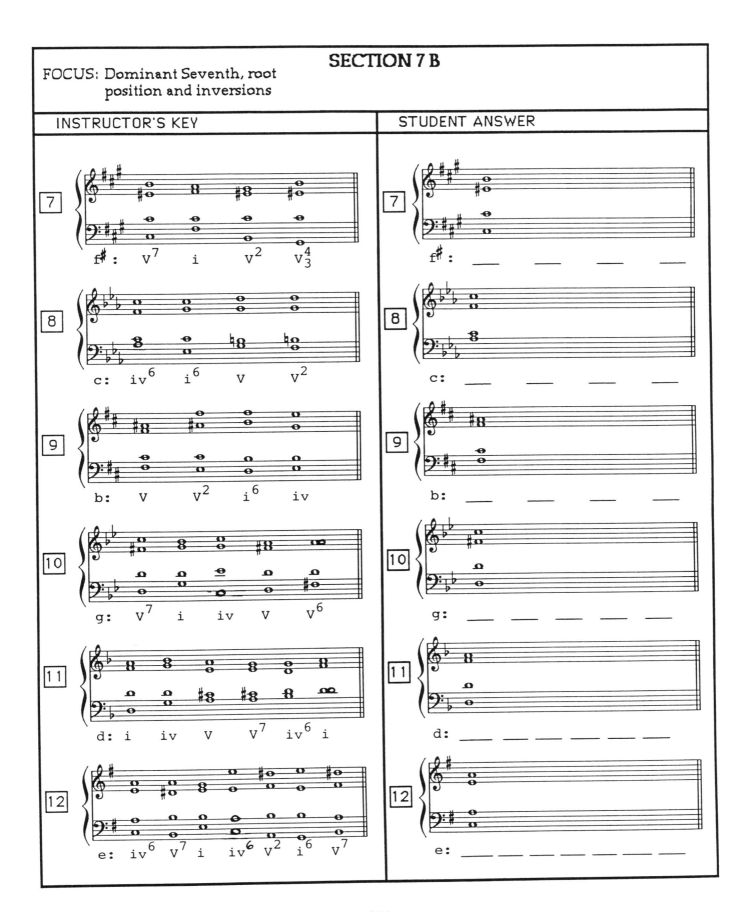

141

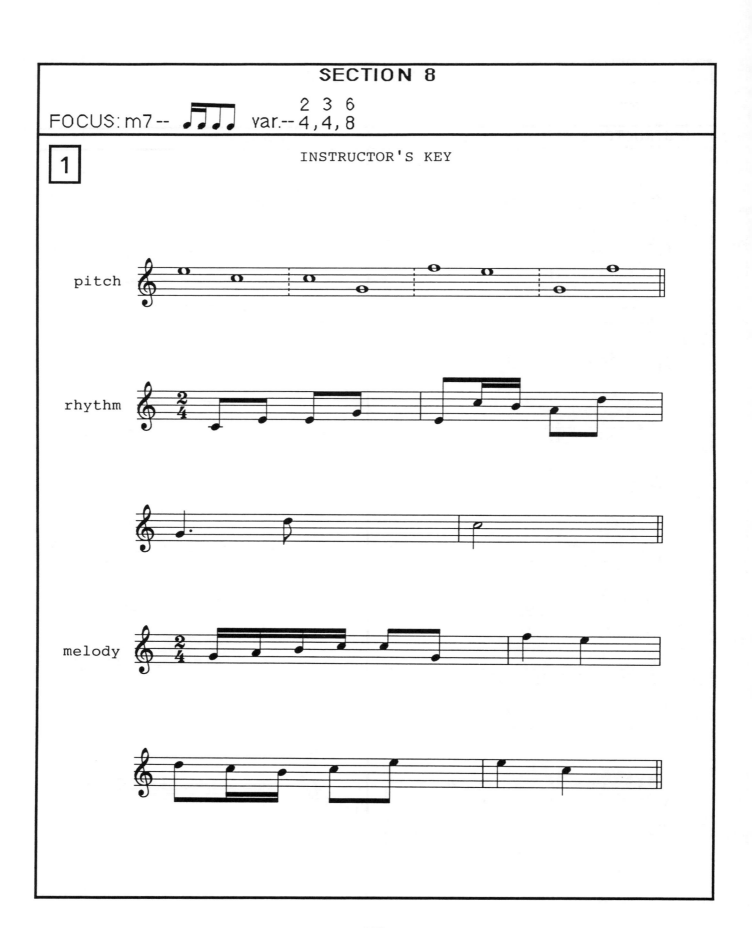

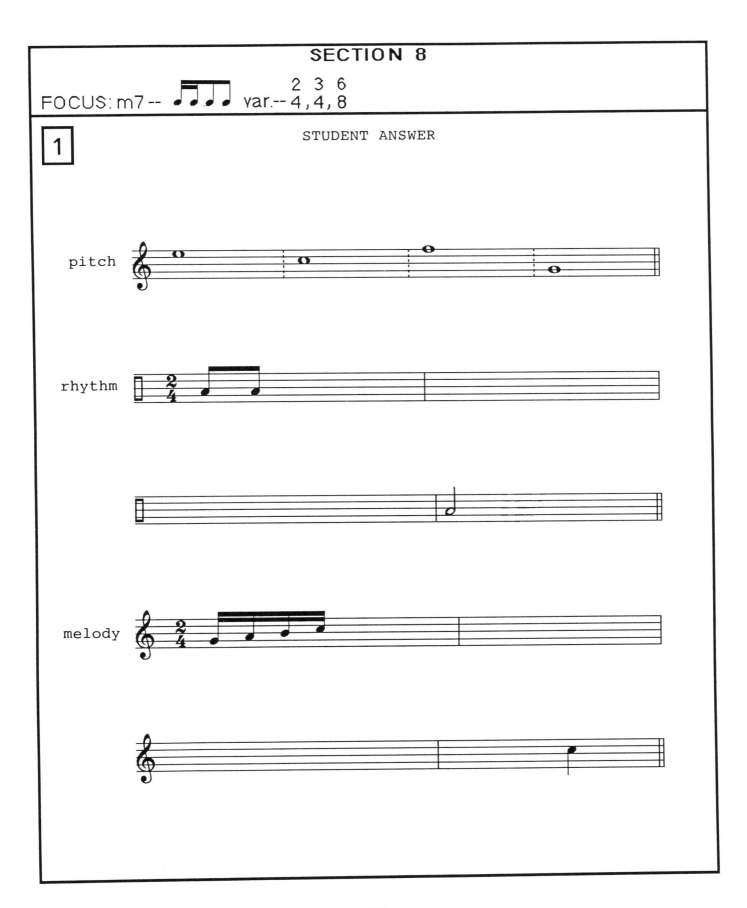

FOCUS: m7 -- ♪♪♪♪ var.-- 2 3 6 / 4,4,8

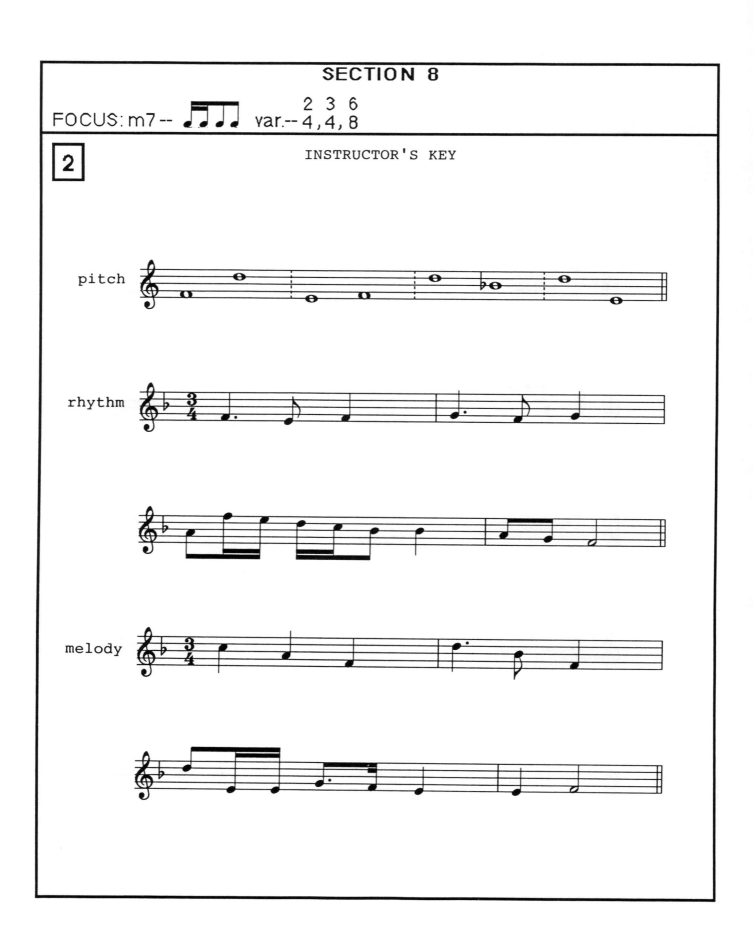

2  INSTRUCTOR'S KEY

pitch

rhythm

melody

# SECTION 8

FOCUS: m7 -- ♪♪♪♪ var.-- 2 3 6 / 4, 4, 8

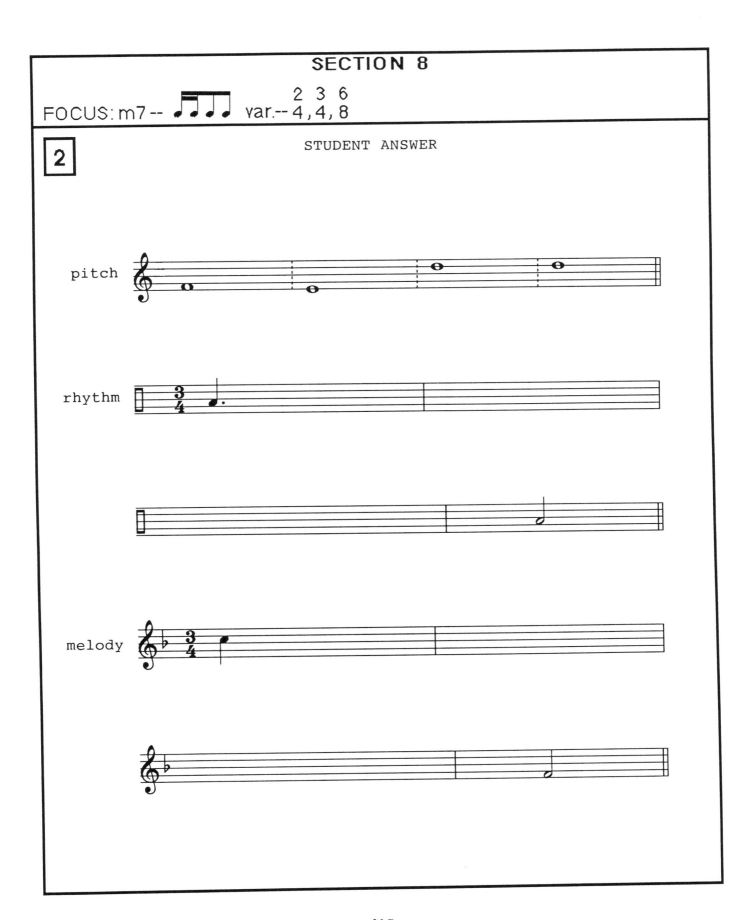

145

# SECTION 8

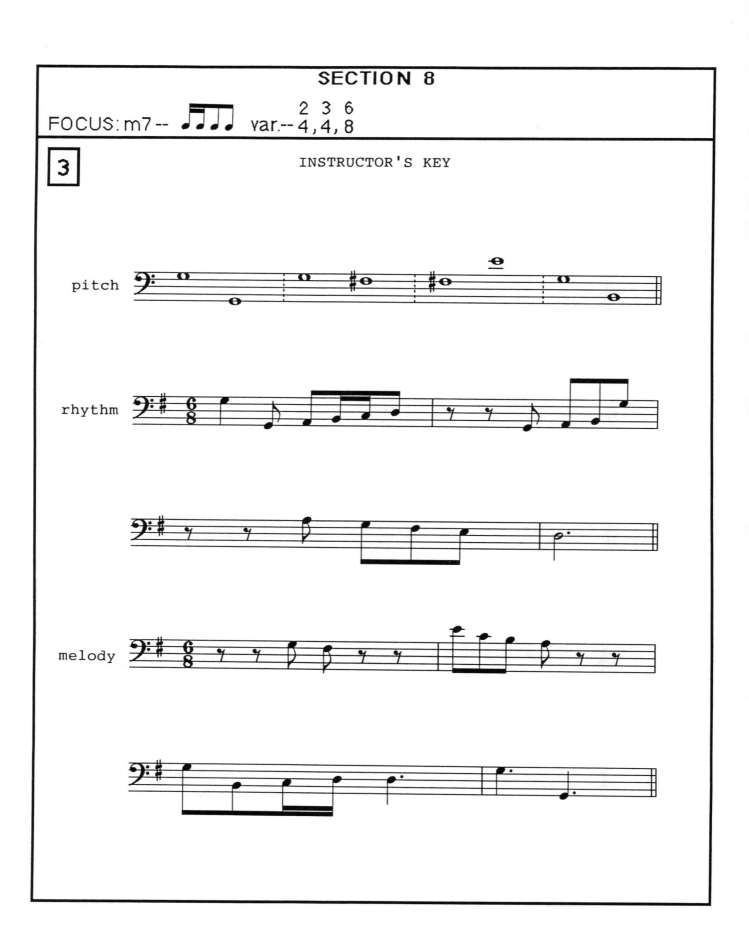

# SECTION 8

FOCUS: m7 -- ♪♪♪♪ var.-- $\frac{2}{4}, \frac{3}{4}, \frac{6}{8}$

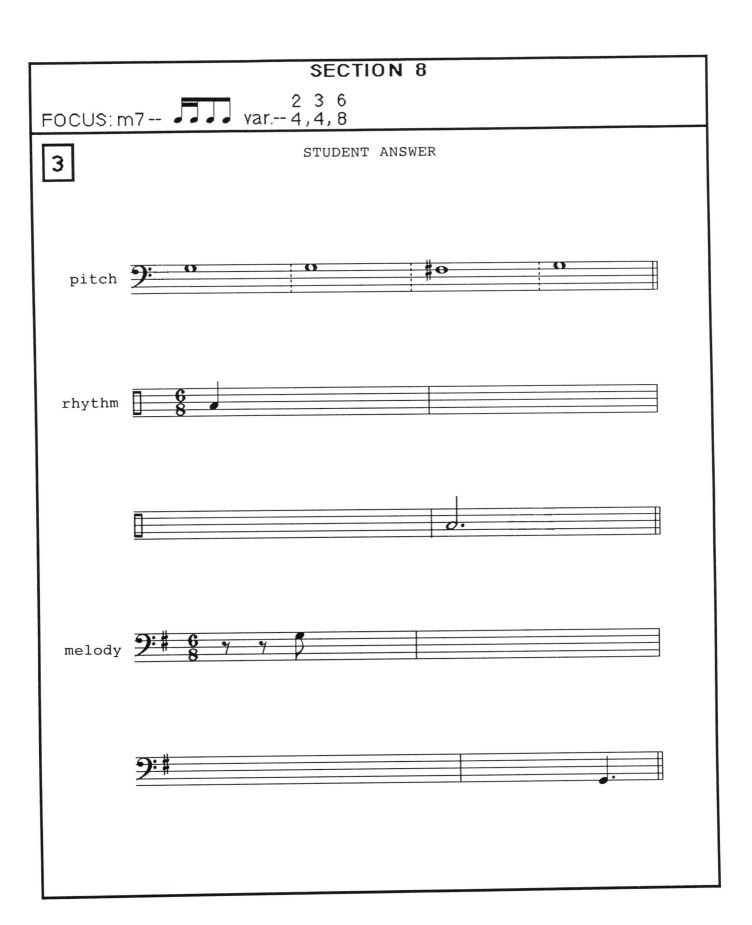

STUDENT ANSWER

**3**

pitch

rhythm

melody

FOCUS: m7-- ♪♫♫ var.-- 2 3 6 / 4,4,8

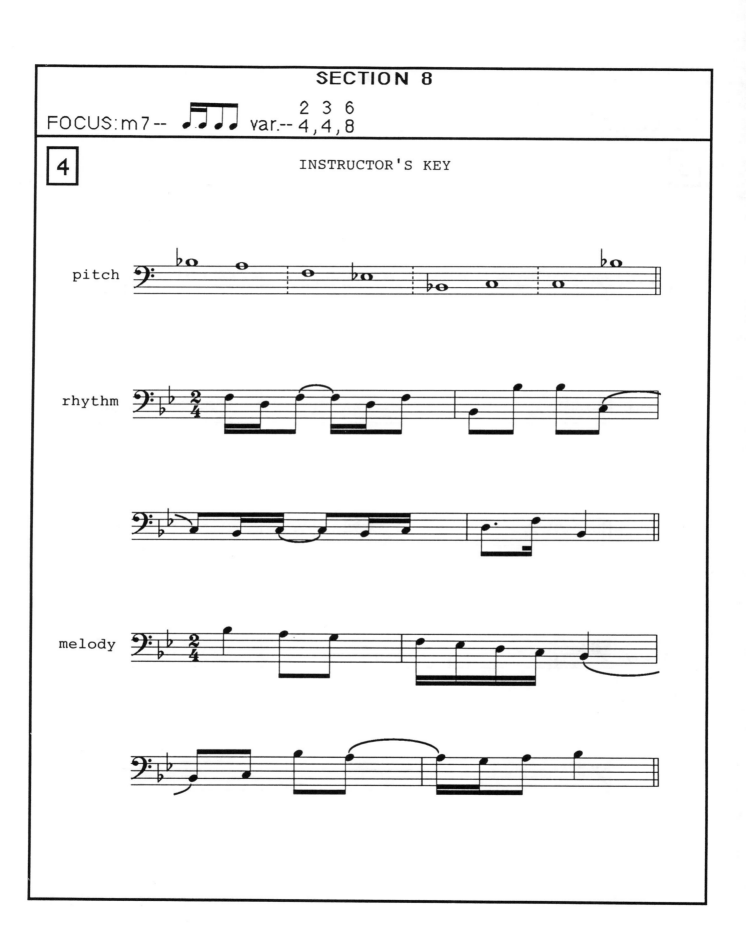

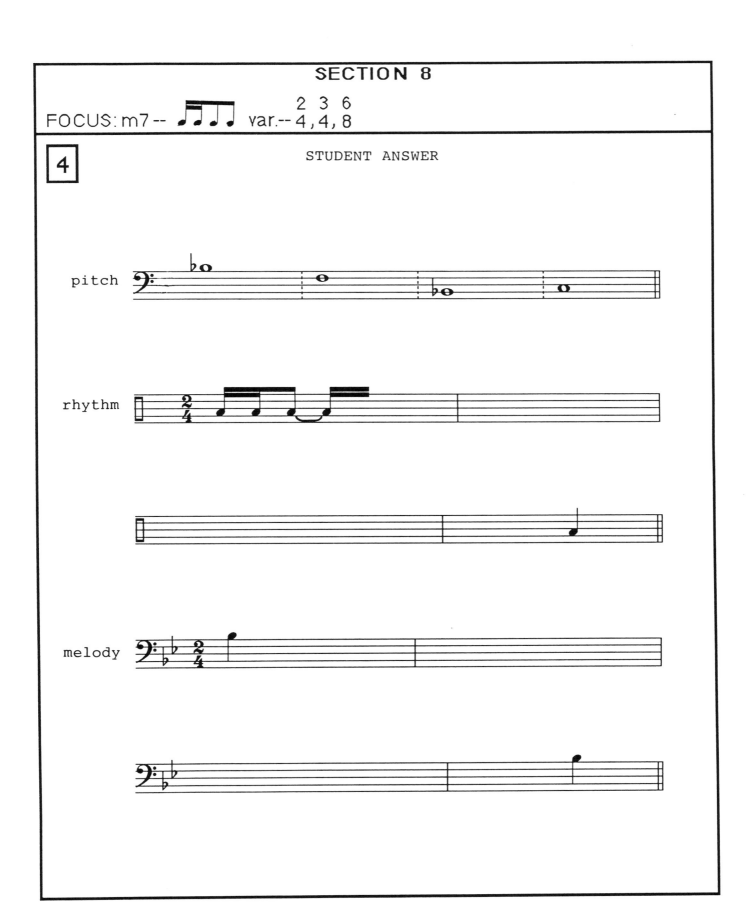

# SECTION 8

FOCUS: m7 -- ♪♪♫ var.-- $\begin{smallmatrix}2&3&6\\4&4&8\end{smallmatrix}$

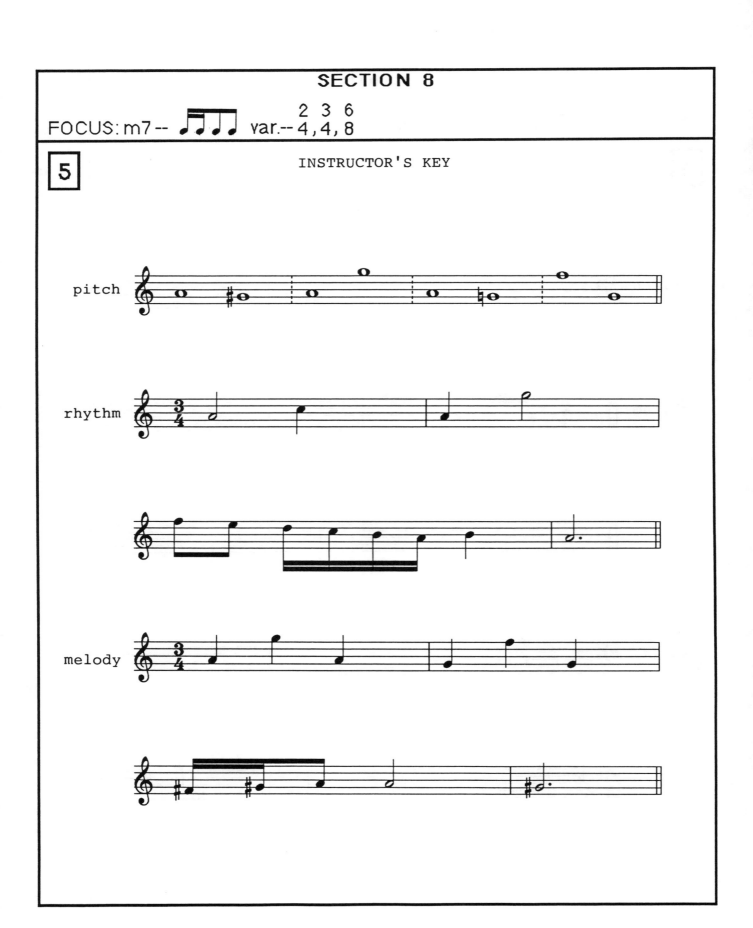

5

INSTRUCTOR'S KEY

pitch

rhythm

melody

150

# SECTION 8

FOCUS: m7 -- ♪♪♪♪ var. -- 2 3 6 / 4 , 4 , 8

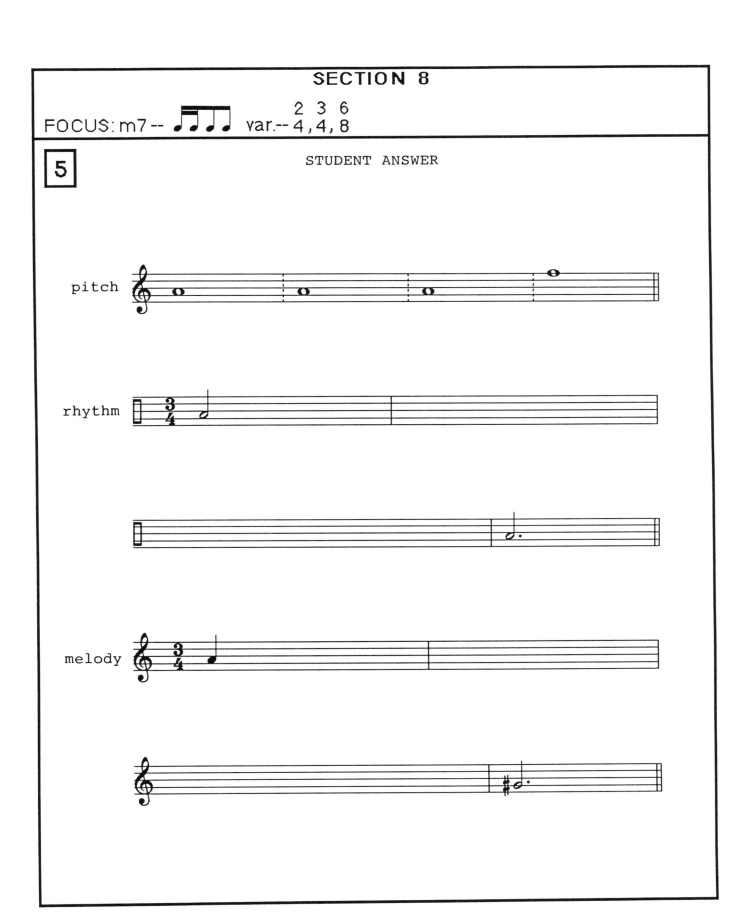

STUDENT ANSWER

5

pitch

rhythm

melody

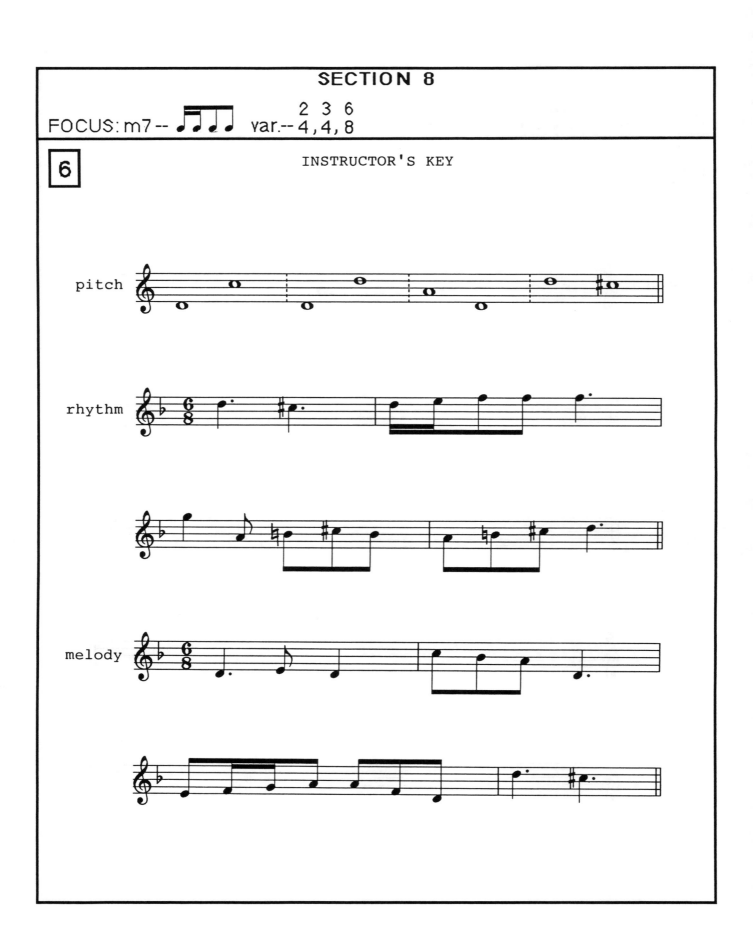

# SECTION 8

FOCUS: m7 -- ♪♪♪♪ var.-- 2 3 6
                        4,4,8

6  STUDENT ANSWER

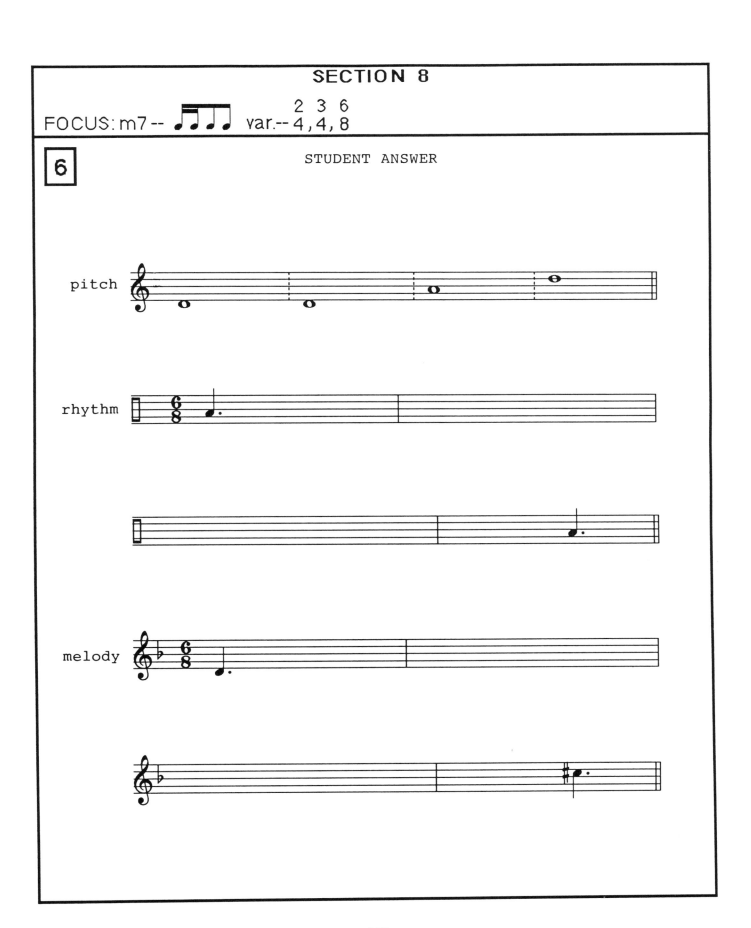

FOCUS: m7 -- ♪♪♪♪ var.-- 2 3 6 / 4,4,8

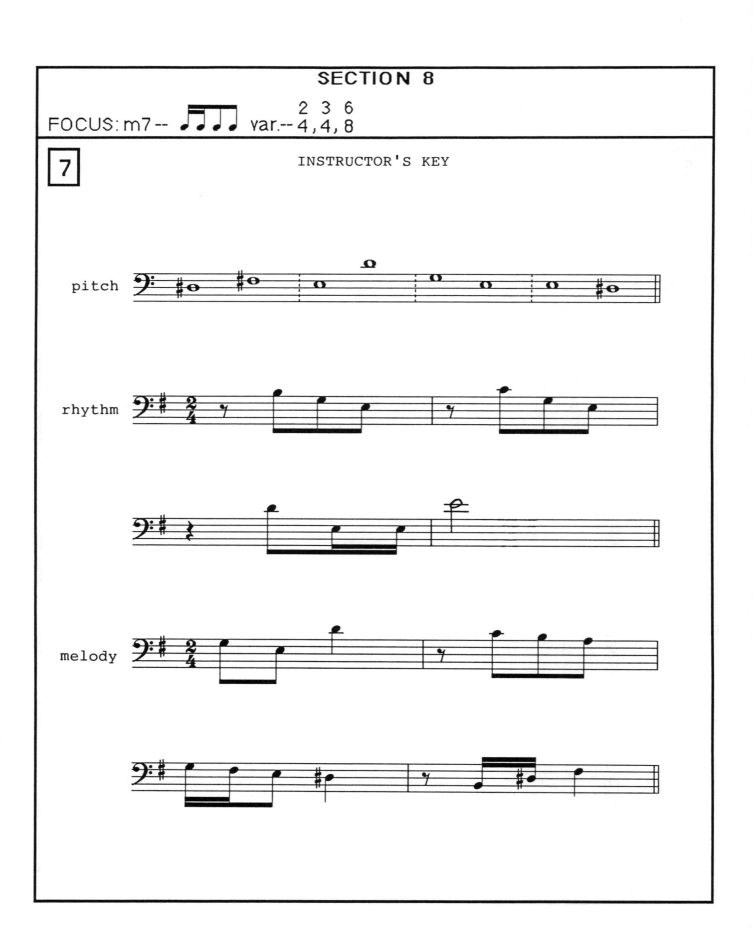

7

INSTRUCTOR'S KEY

pitch

rhythm

melody

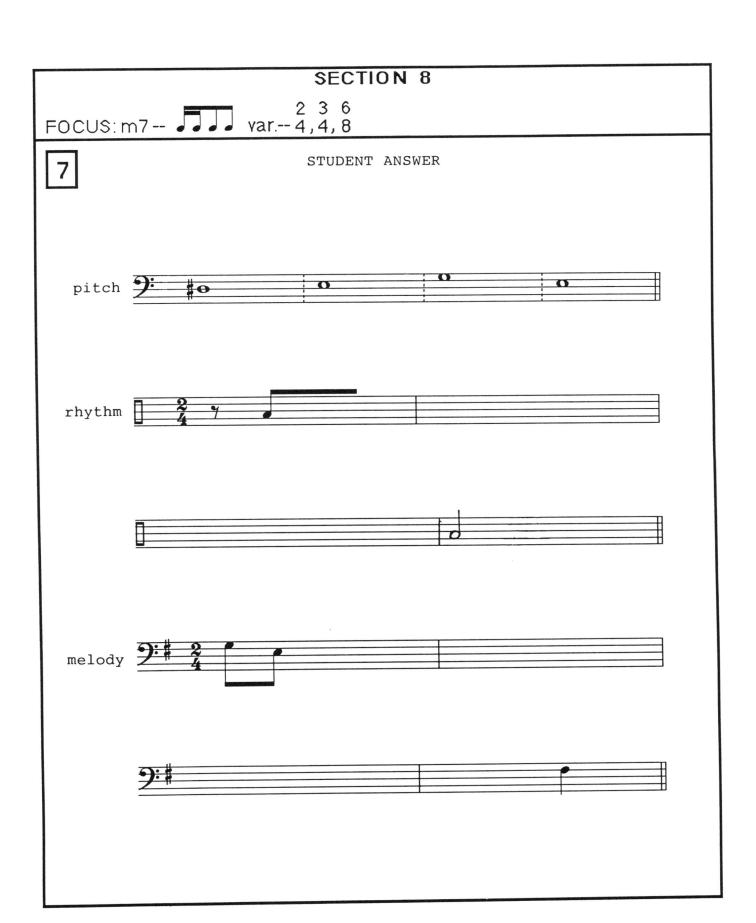

# SECTION 8

FOCUS: m7 -- ♩♩♩♩ var.-- 2 3 6 / 4,4,8

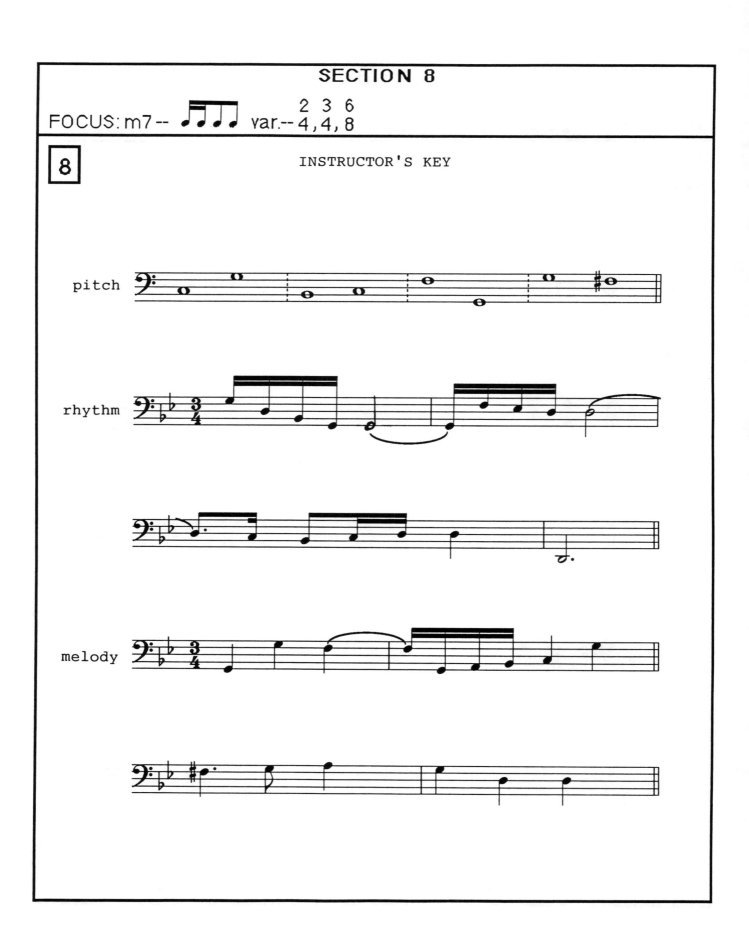

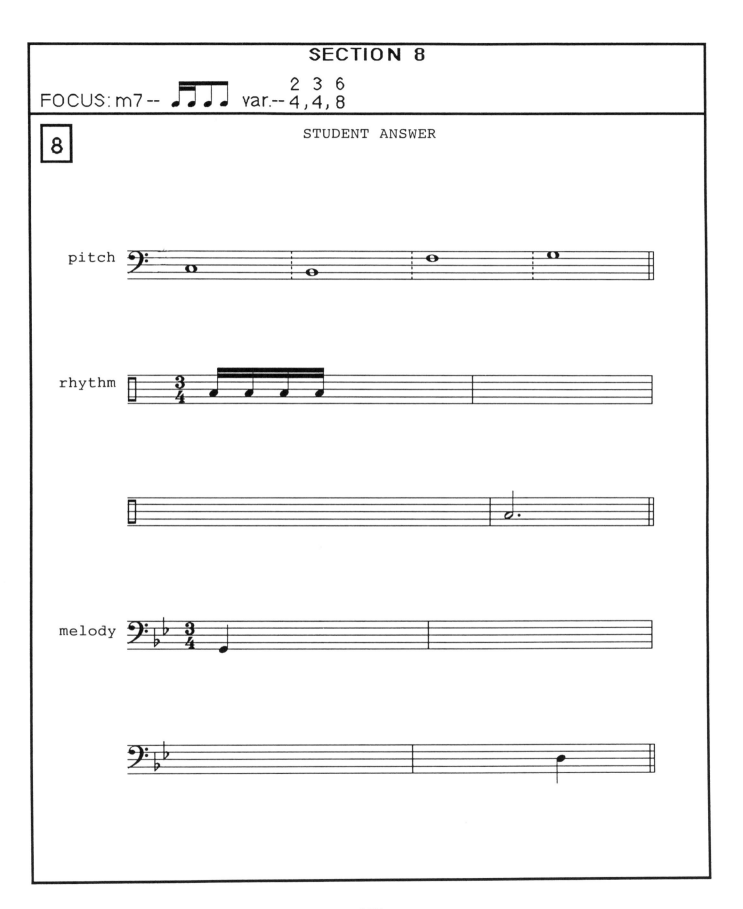

# SECTION 8A

FOCUS: Tonic Six-Four

INSTRUCTOR'S KEY:

STUDENT ANSWER:

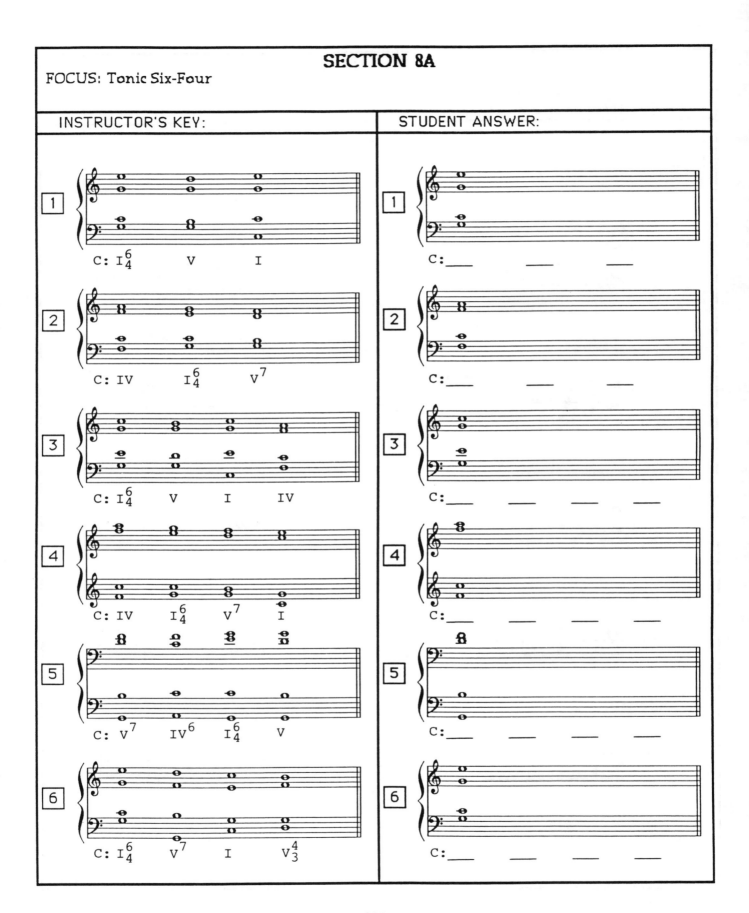

FOCUS: Tonic Six-Four

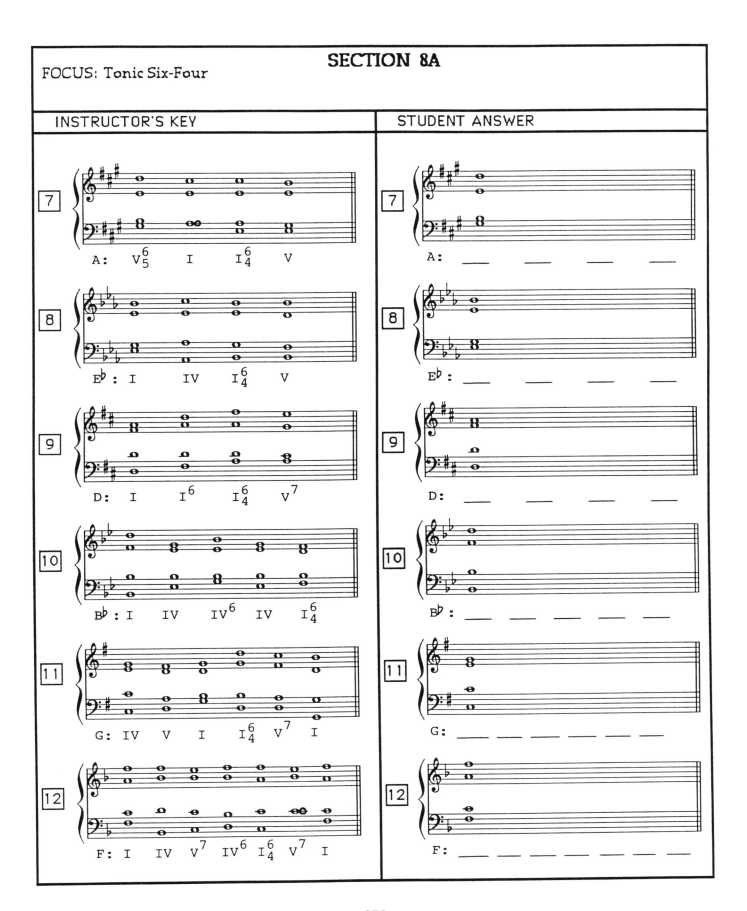

# SECTION 8B

**FOCUS:** Tonic Six-Four

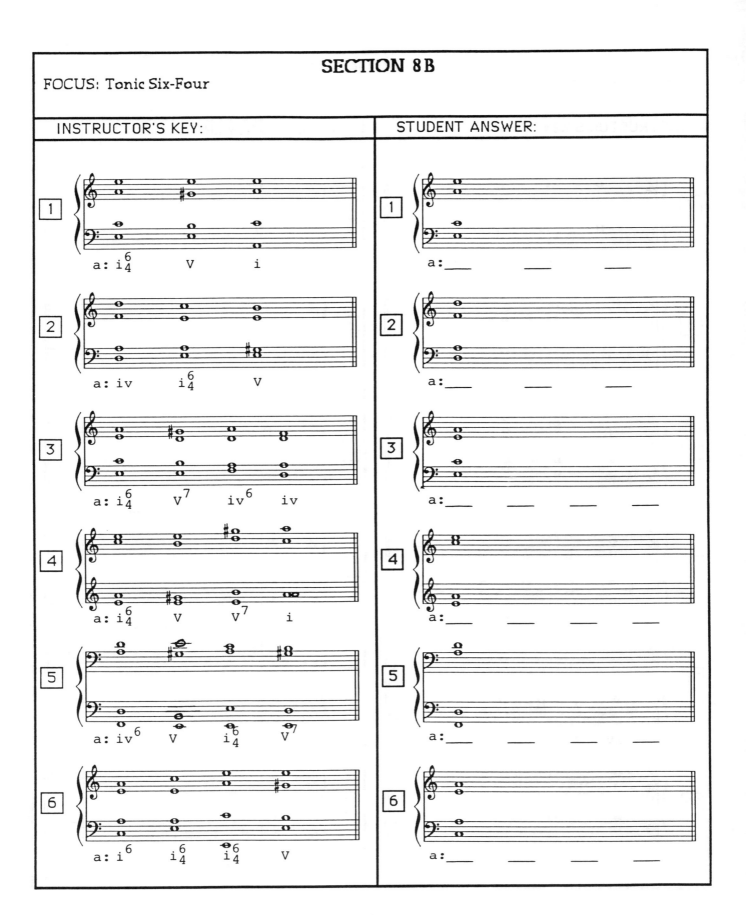

INSTRUCTOR'S KEY:

1. a: $i_4^6$   V   i
2. a: iv   $i_4^6$   V
3. a: $i_4^6$   $V^7$   $iv^6$   iv
4. a: $i_4^6$   V   $V^7$   i
5. a: $iv^6$   V   $i_4^6$   $V^7$
6. a: $i^6$   $i_4^6$   $i_4^6$   V

STUDENT ANSWER:

1. a:___ ___ ___
2. a:___ ___ ___
3. a:___ ___ ___ ___
4. a:___ ___ ___ ___
5. a:___ ___ ___ ___
6. a:___ ___ ___ ___

160

# SECTION 8B

FOCUS: Tonic Six-Four

| INSTRUCTOR'S KEY | STUDENT ANSWER |
|---|---|

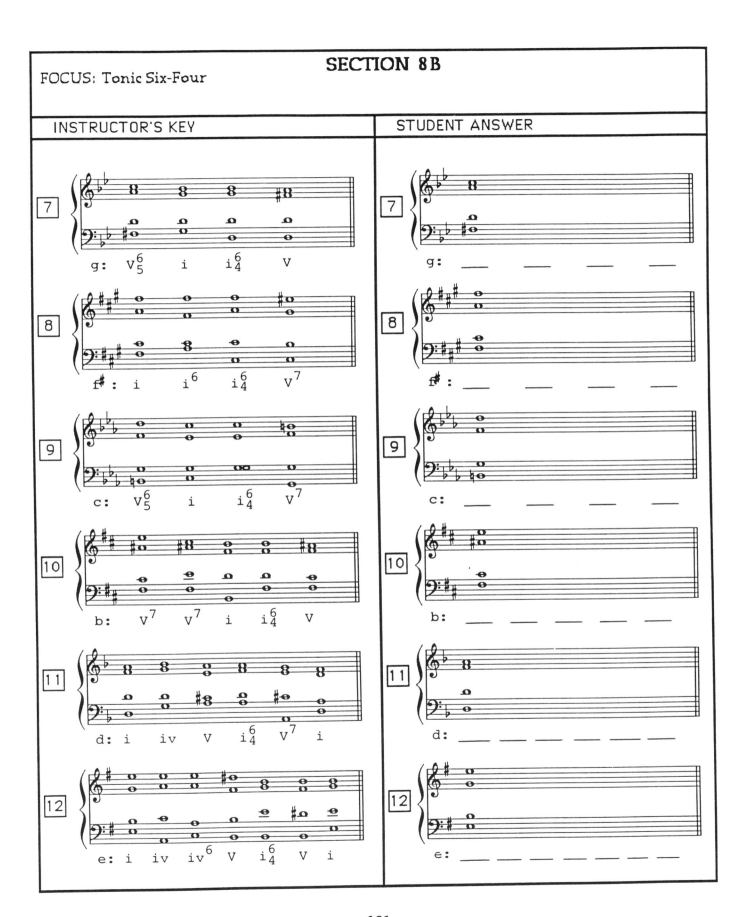

7  g:  $V^6_5$   i   $i^6_4$   V

8  f#:  i   $i^6$   $i^6_4$   $V^7$

9  c:  $V^6_5$   i   $i^6_4$   $V^7$

10  b:  $V^7$   $V^7$   i   $i^6_4$   V

11  d:  i   iv   V   $i^6_4$   $V^7$   i

12  e:  i   iv   $iv^6$   V   $i^6_4$   V   i

Student answers:

7  g: ___  ___  ___  ___

8  f#: ___  ___  ___  ___

9  c: ___  ___  ___  ___

10  b: ___  ___  ___  ___  ___

11  d: ___  ___  ___  ___  ___  ___

12  e: ___  ___  ___  ___  ___  ___  ___

161

# SECTION 9

FOCUS: M7- 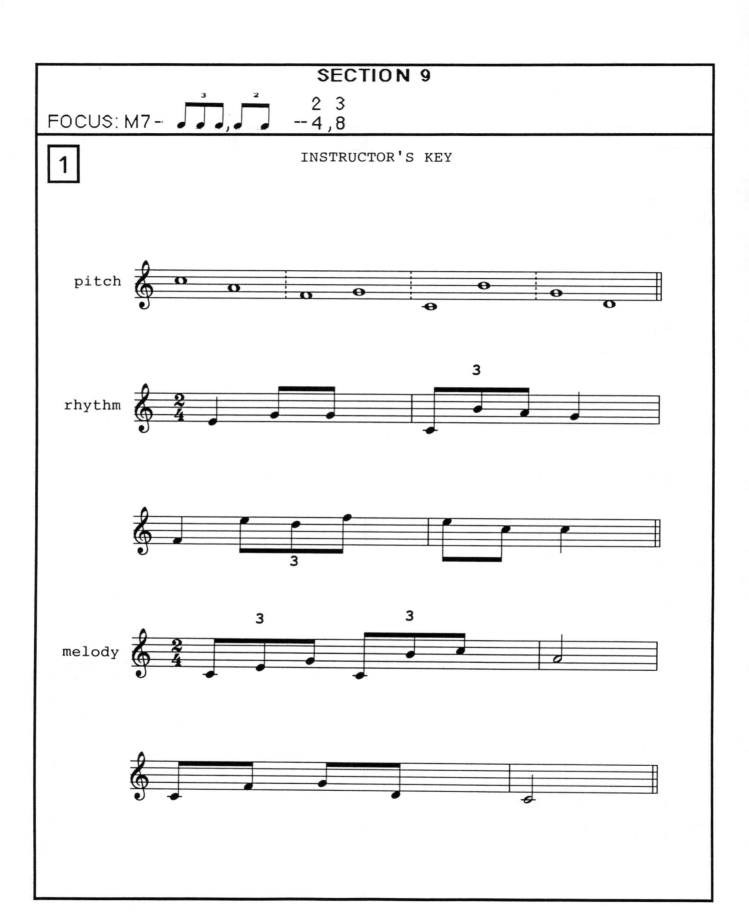 2 3
          -- 4,8

1  INSTRUCTOR'S KEY

pitch

rhythm

melody

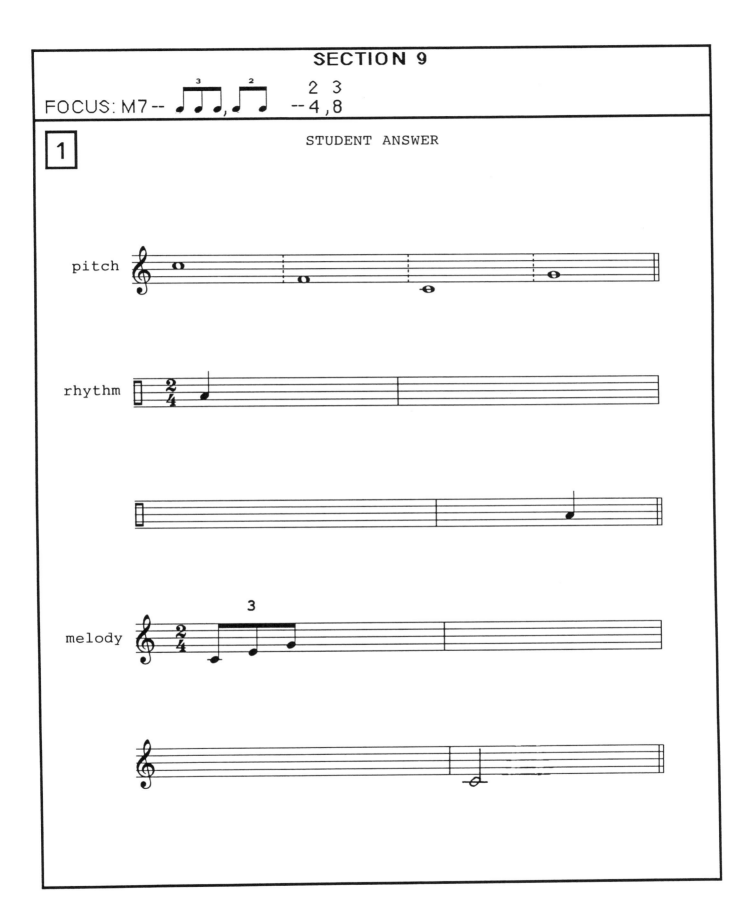

# SECTION 9

FOCUS: M7 -- ♩♩♩ , ♩♩ -- $\frac{2}{4}, \frac{3}{8}$

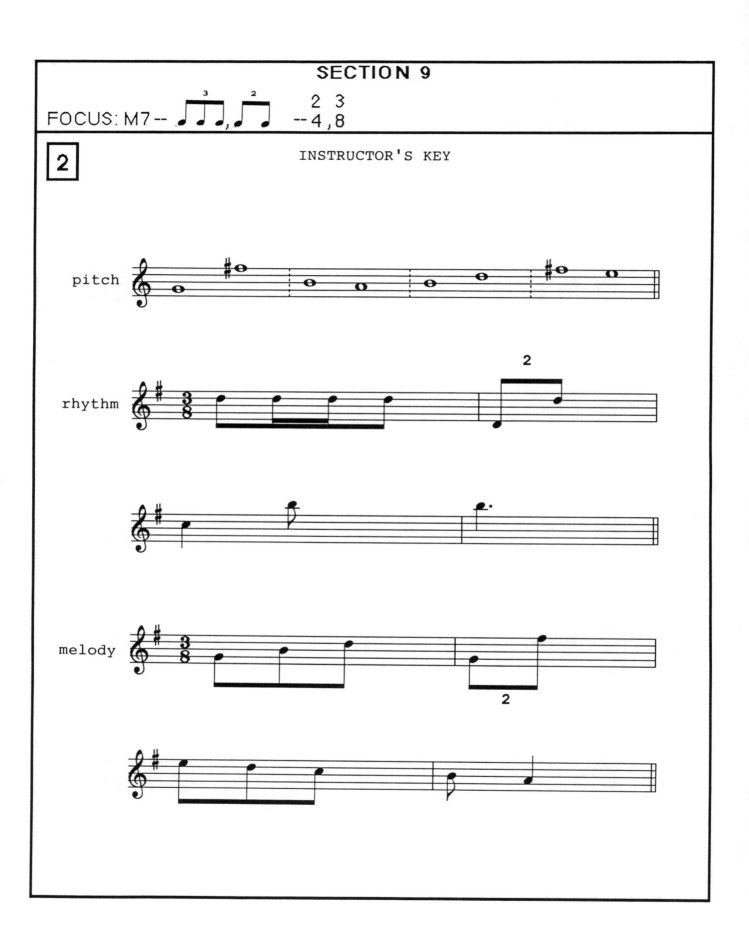

INSTRUCTOR'S KEY

pitch

rhythm

melody

# SECTION 9

FOCUS: M7 --

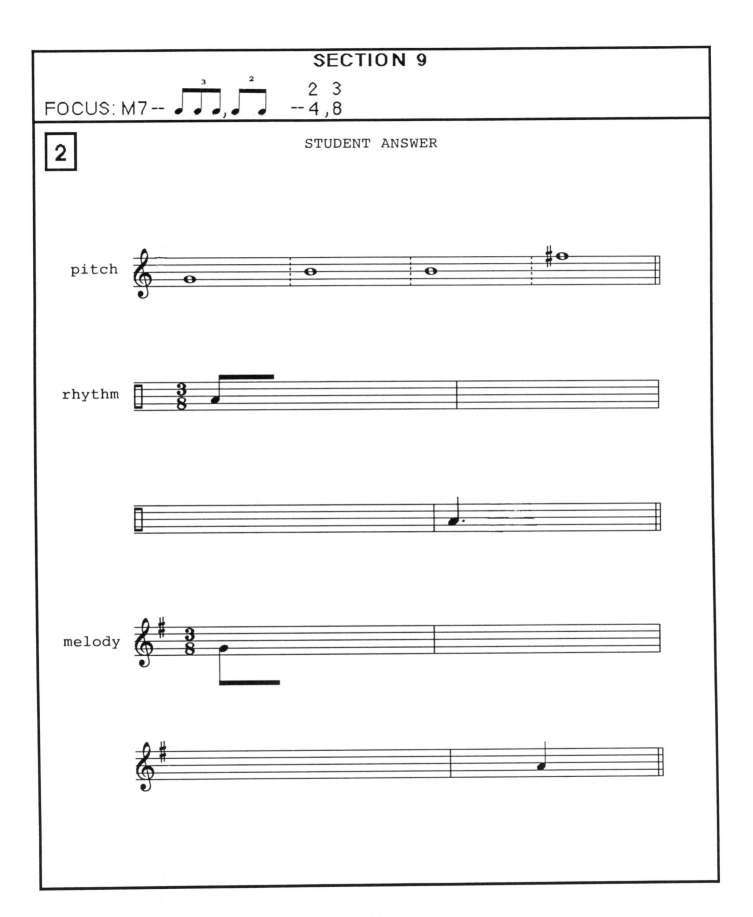

165

# SECTION 9

FOCUS: M7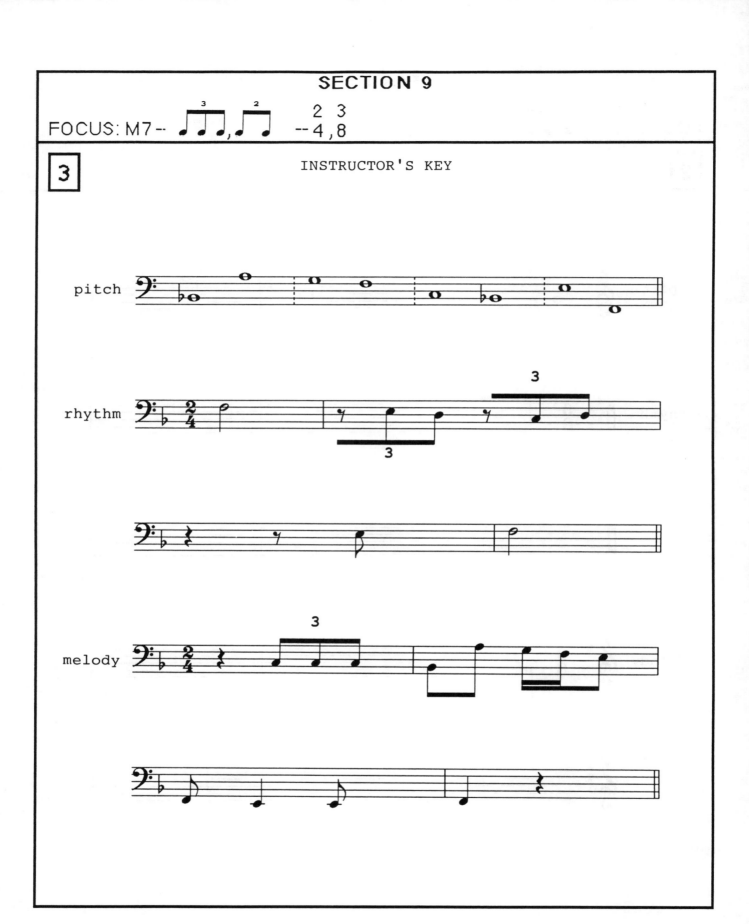

INSTRUCTOR'S KEY

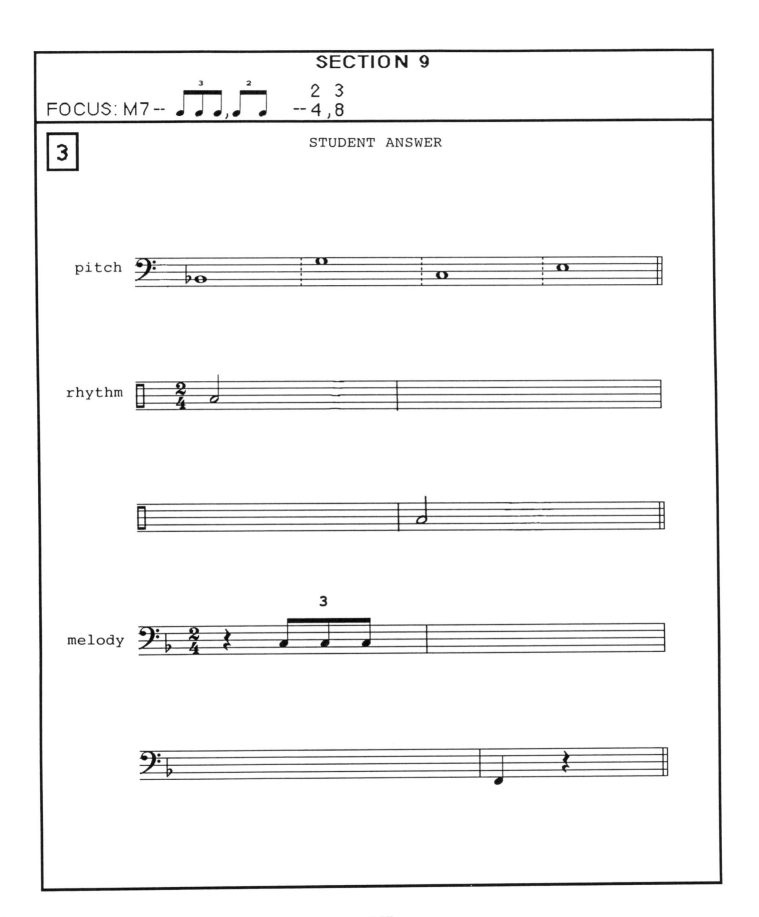

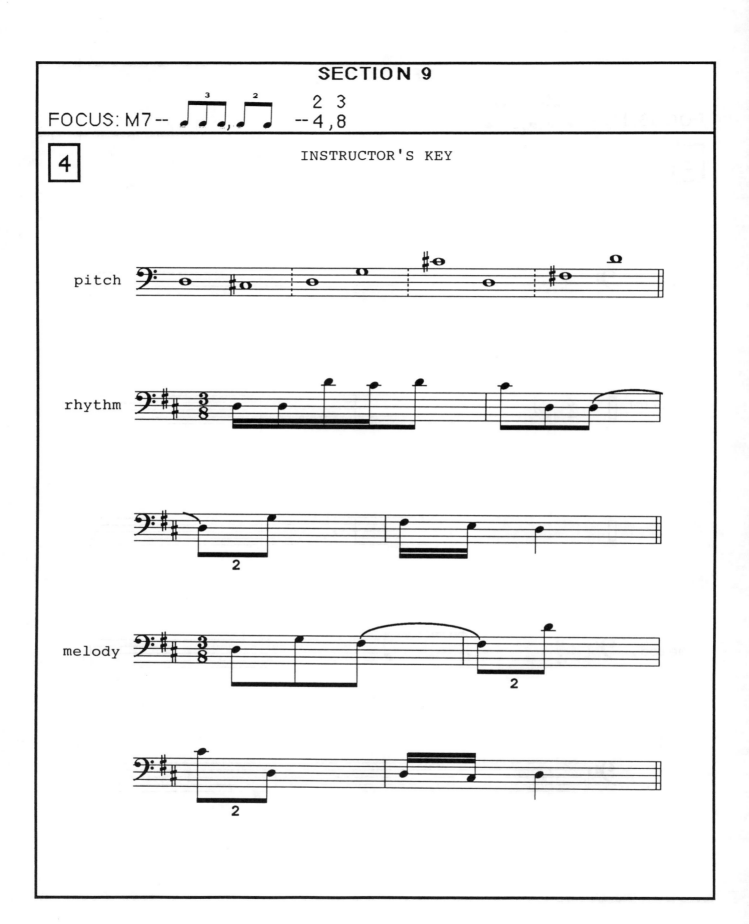

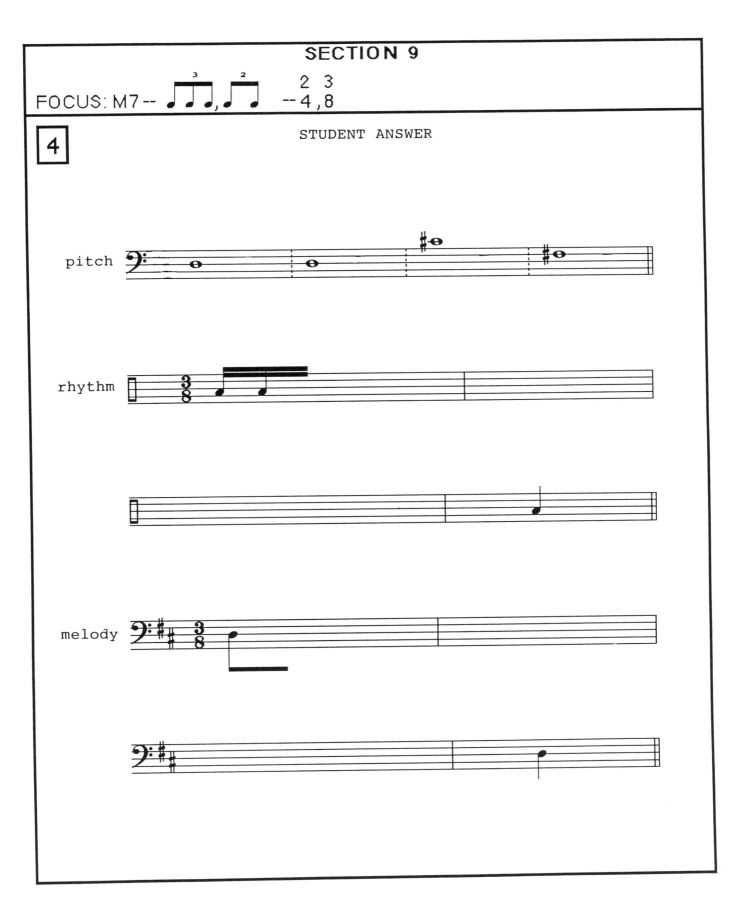

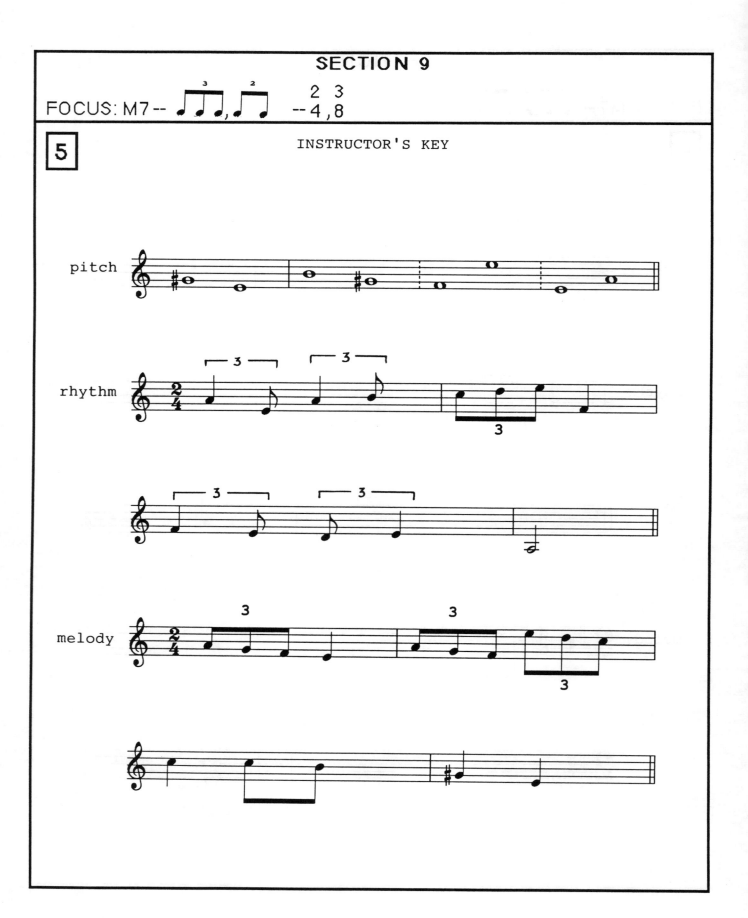

170

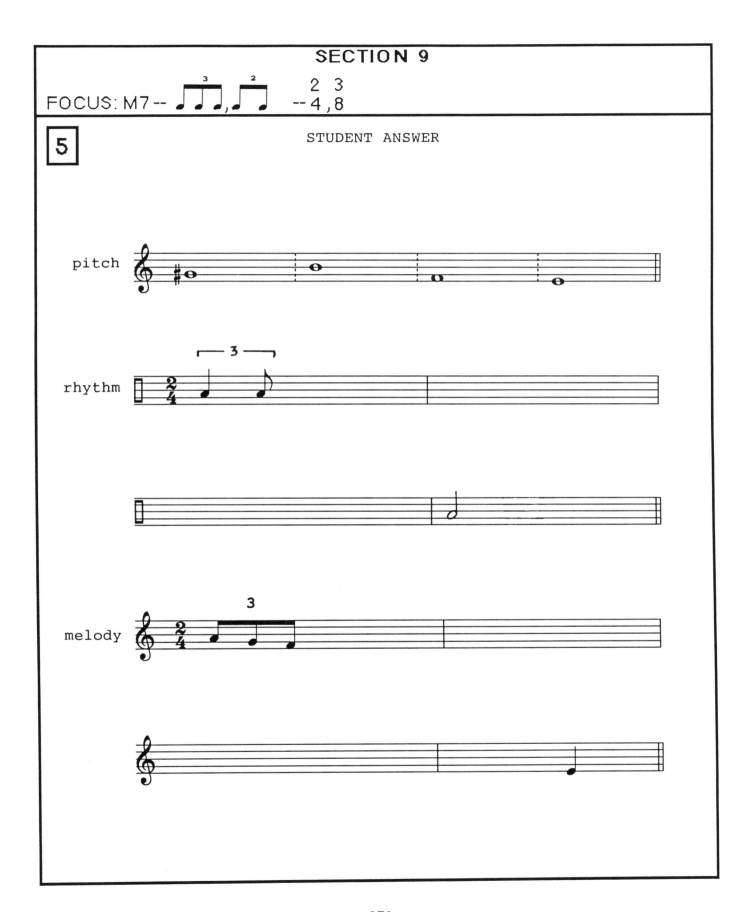

# SECTION 9

FOCUS: M7 -- [musical notation: two beamed note groups labeled 3 and 2]  -- $\frac{2}{4}$, $\frac{3}{8}$

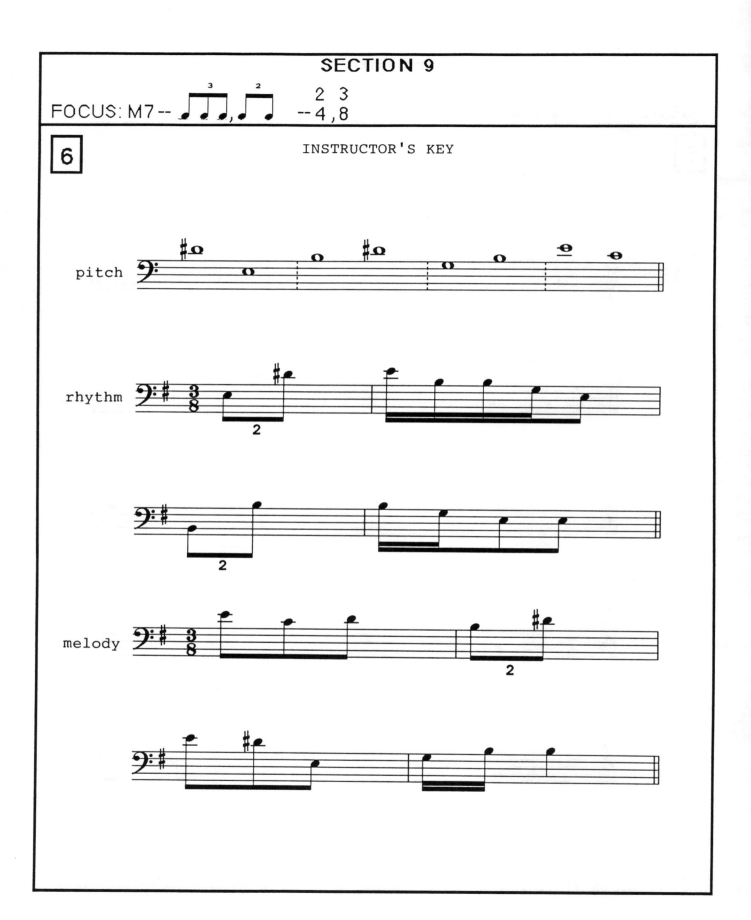

INSTRUCTOR'S KEY

6

pitch

rhythm

melody

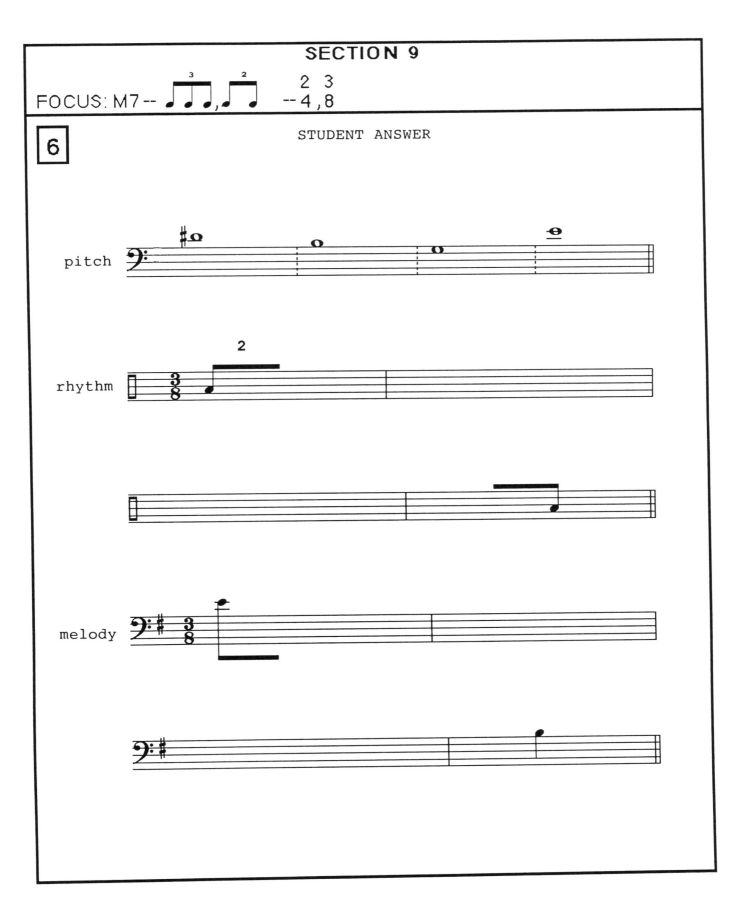

FOCUS: M7 -- ♪♪♪, ♪♪ -- 2 3
4, 8

7  INSTRUCTOR'S KEY

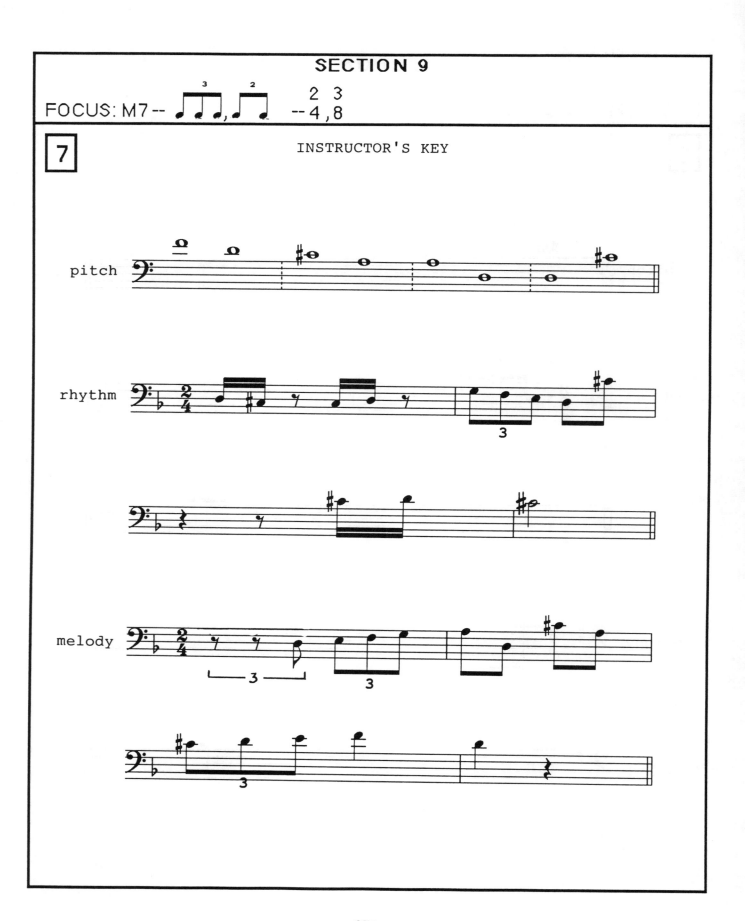

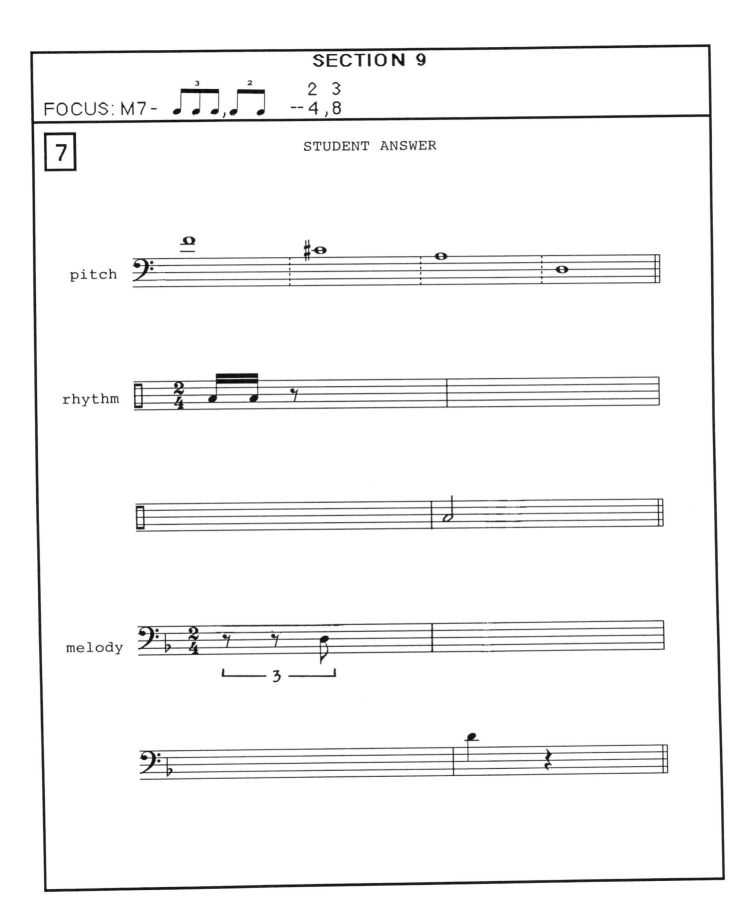

# SECTION 9

FOCUS: M7--

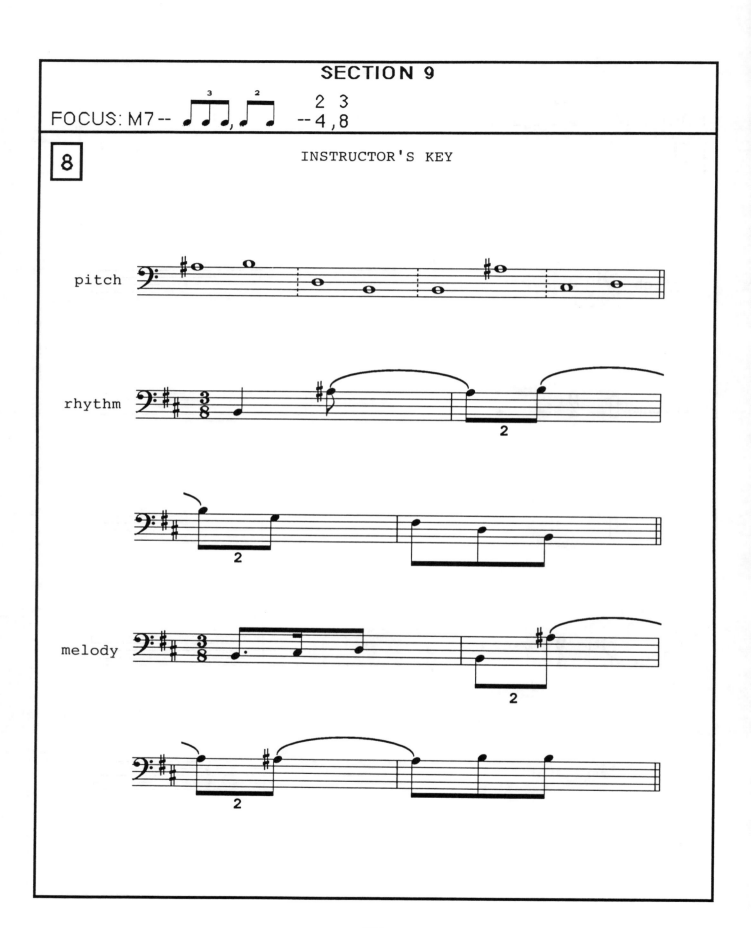

INSTRUCTOR'S KEY

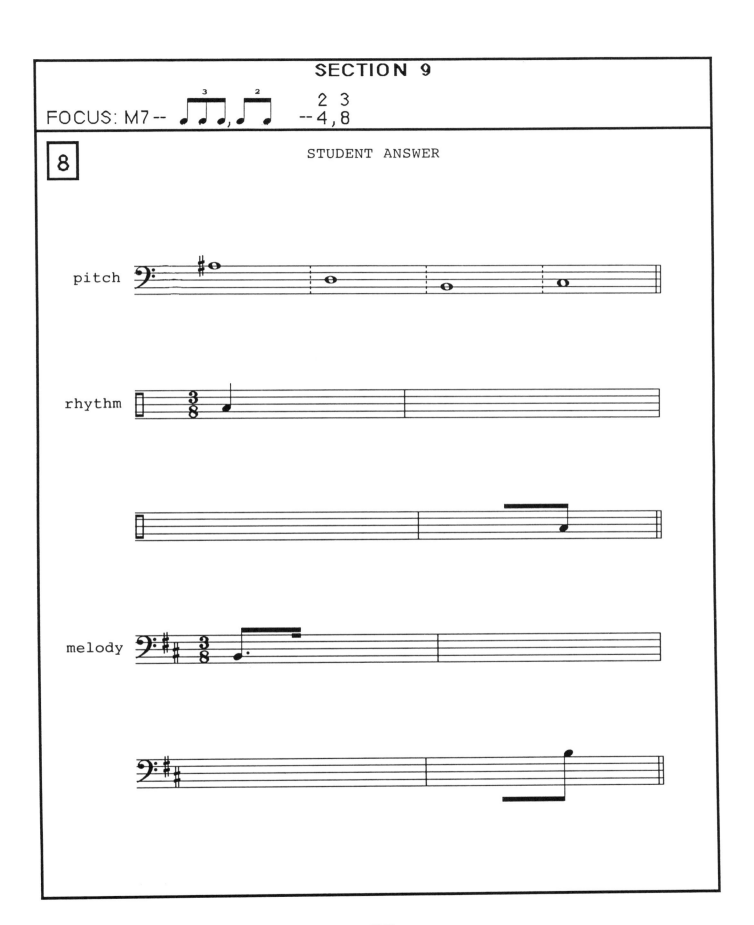

# SECTION 9A

FOCUS: Primary Triads,
second inversion

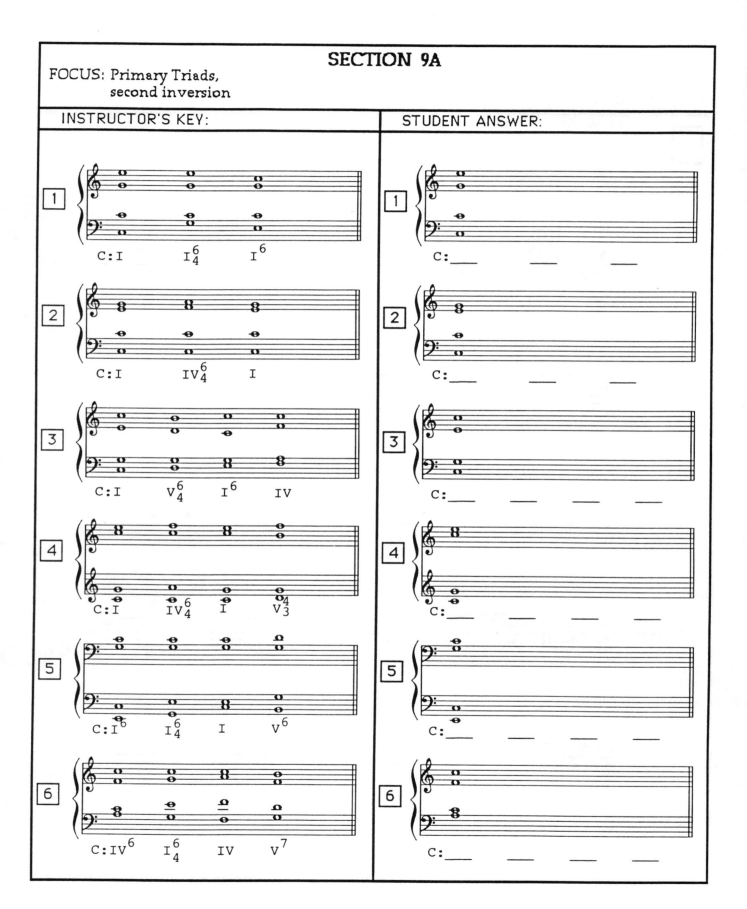

INSTRUCTOR'S KEY:

1. C:I  I$^6_4$  I$^6$

2. C:I  IV$^6_4$  I

3. C:I  V$^6_4$  I$^6$  IV

4. C:I  IV$^6_4$  I  V$^4_3$

5. C:I$^6$  I$^6_4$  I  V$^6$

6. C:IV$^6$  I$^6_4$  IV  V$^7$

STUDENT ANSWER:

1. C:___  ___  ___

2. C:___

3. C:___  ___  ___  ___

4. C:___

5. C:___  ___  ___  ___

6. C:___  ___  ___  ___

178

# SECTION 9A

FOCUS: Primary Triads,
        second inversion

| INSTRUCTOR'S KEY | STUDENT ANSWER |
|---|---|

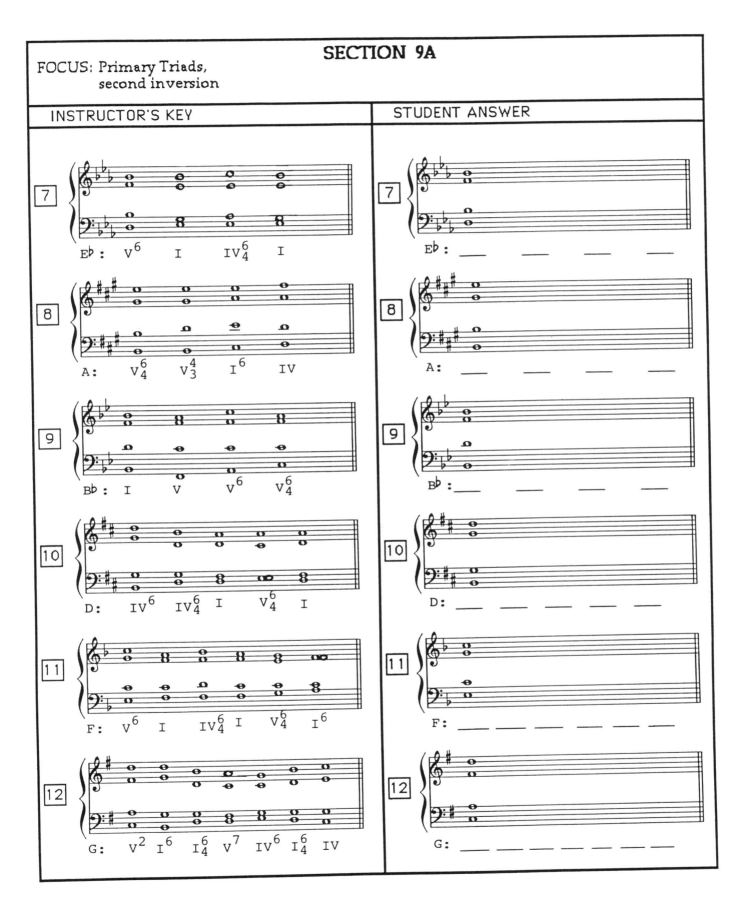

7  $E\flat$:  $V^6$  I  $IV^6_4$  I

8  A:  $V^6_4$  $V^4_3$  $I^6$  IV

9  $B\flat$:  I  V  $V^6$  $V^6_4$

10  D:  $IV^6$  $IV^6_4$  I  $V^6_4$  I

11  F:  $V^6$  I  $IV^6_4$  I  $V^6_4$  $I^6$

12  G:  $V^2$  $I^6$  $I^6_4$  $V^7$  $IV^6$  $I^6_4$  IV

7  $E\flat$: ___ ___ ___ ___

8  A: ___ ___ ___ ___

9  $B\flat$: ___ ___ ___ ___

10  D: ___ ___ ___ ___ ___

11  F: ___ ___ ___ ___ ___ ___

12  G: ___ ___ ___ ___ ___ ___ ___

179

# SECTION 9B

**FOCUS:** Primary Triads,
second inversion

INSTRUCTOR'S KEY: | STUDENT ANSWER:

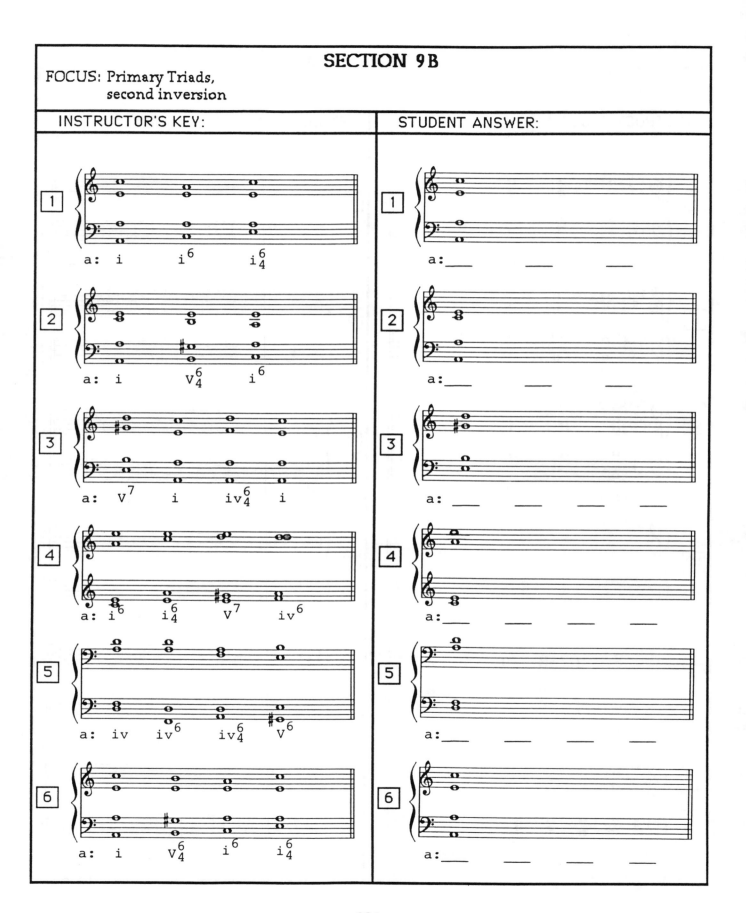

# SECTION 9B

FOCUS: Primary Triads,
second inversion

| INSTRUCTOR'S KEY | STUDENT ANSWER |
|---|---|

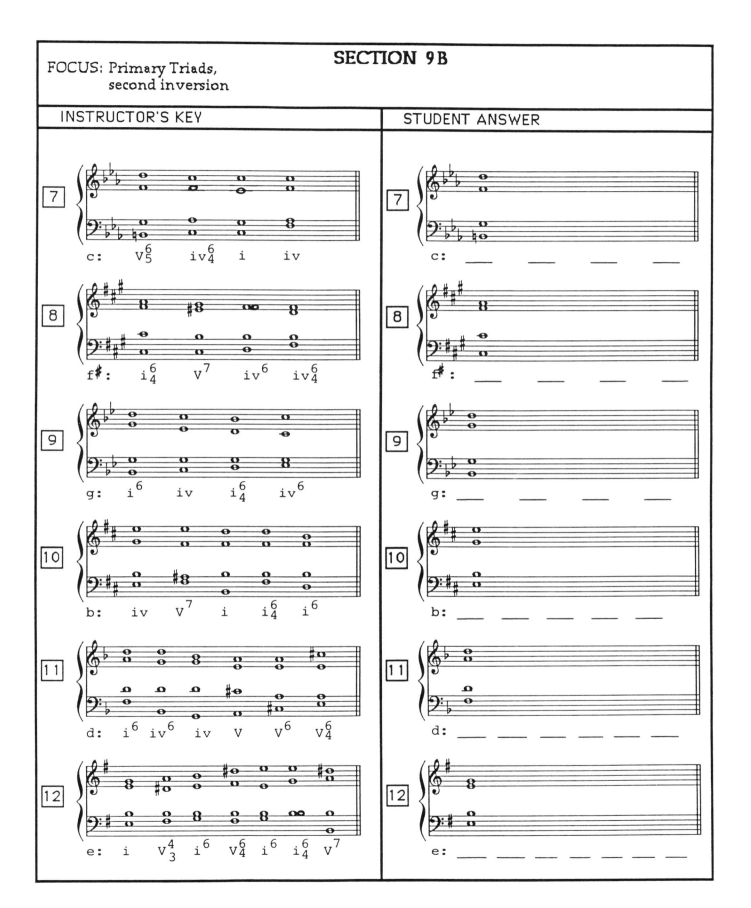

7  c:  $V_5^6$   $iv_4^6$   $i$   $iv$

7  c: ___  ___  ___  ___

8  f#:  $i_4^6$   $V^7$   $iv^6$   $iv_4^6$

8  f#: ___  ___  ___  ___

9  g:  $i^6$   $iv$   $i_4^6$   $iv^6$

9  g: ___  ___  ___  ___

10  b:  $iv$   $V^7$   $i$   $i_4^6$   $i^6$

10  b: ___  ___  ___  ___  ___

11  d:  $i^6$   $iv^6$   $iv$   $V$   $V^6$   $V_4^6$

11  d: ___  ___  ___  ___  ___  ___

12  e:  $i$   $V_3^4$   $i^6$   $V_4^6$   $i^6$   $i_4^6$   $V^7$

12  e: ___  ___  ___  ___  ___  ___  ___

181

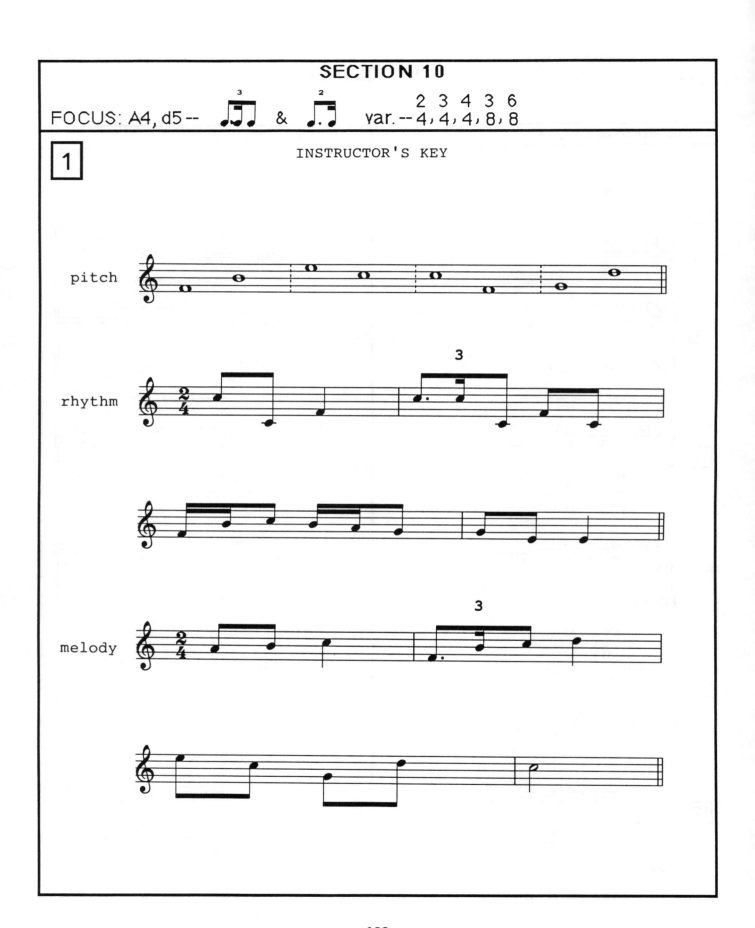

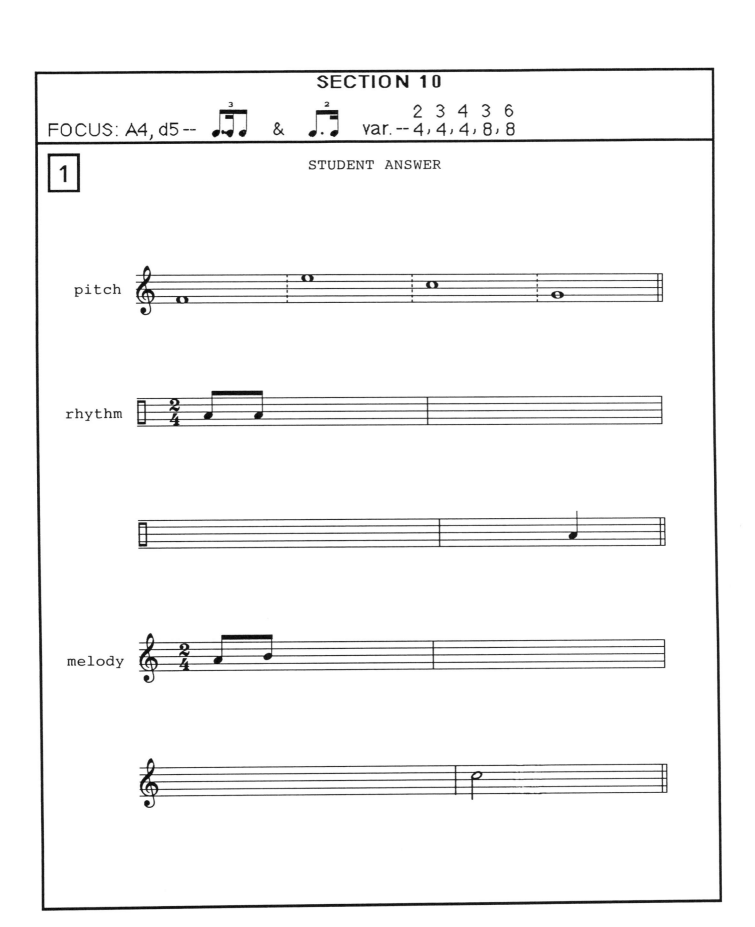

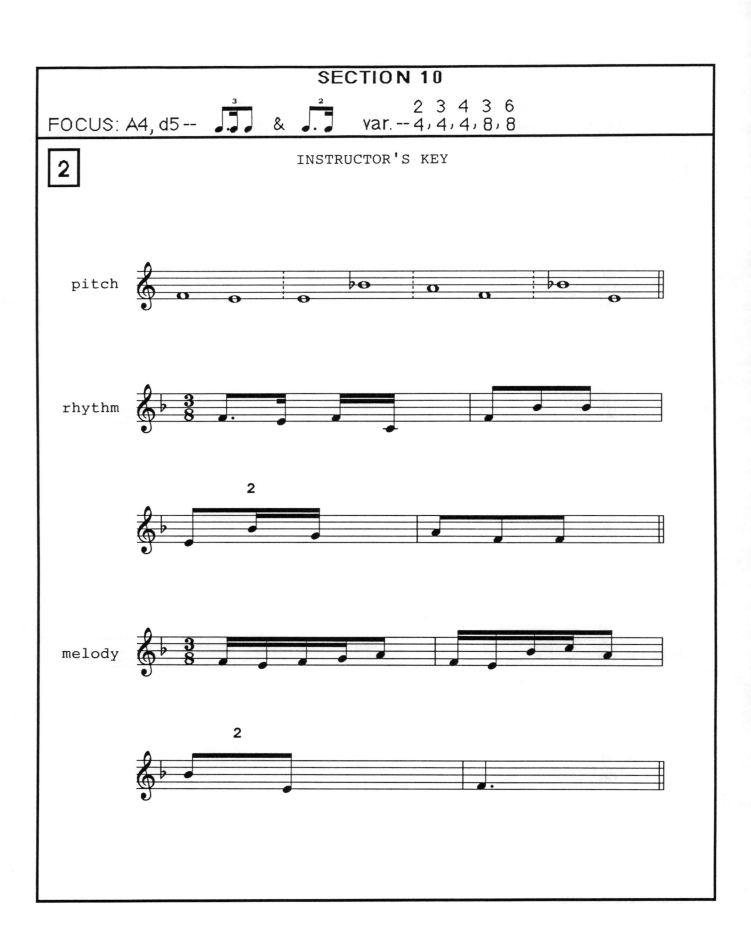

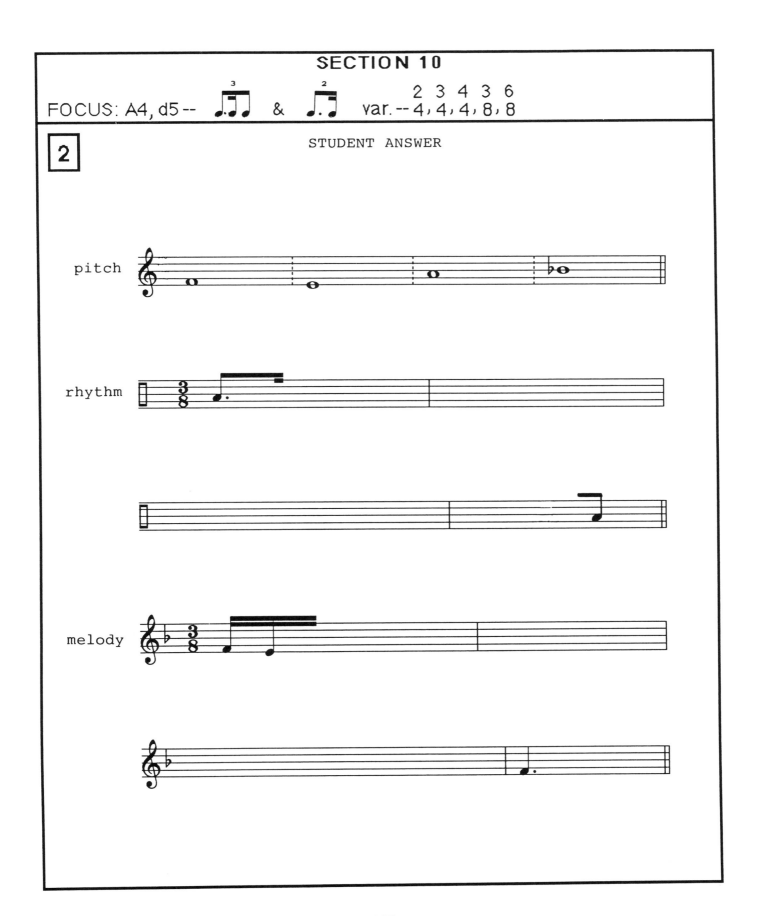

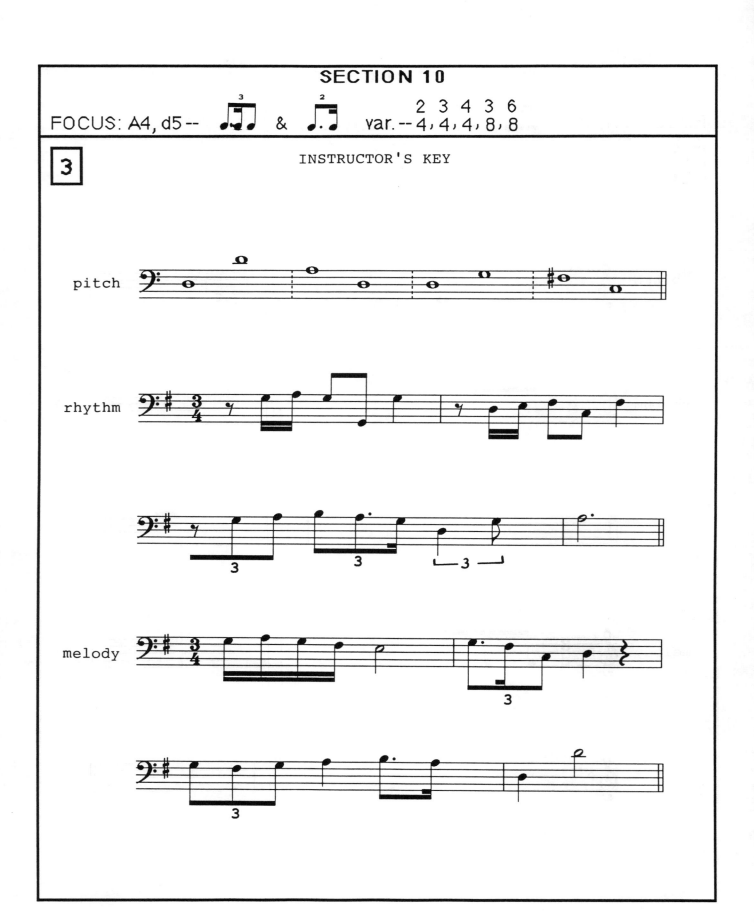

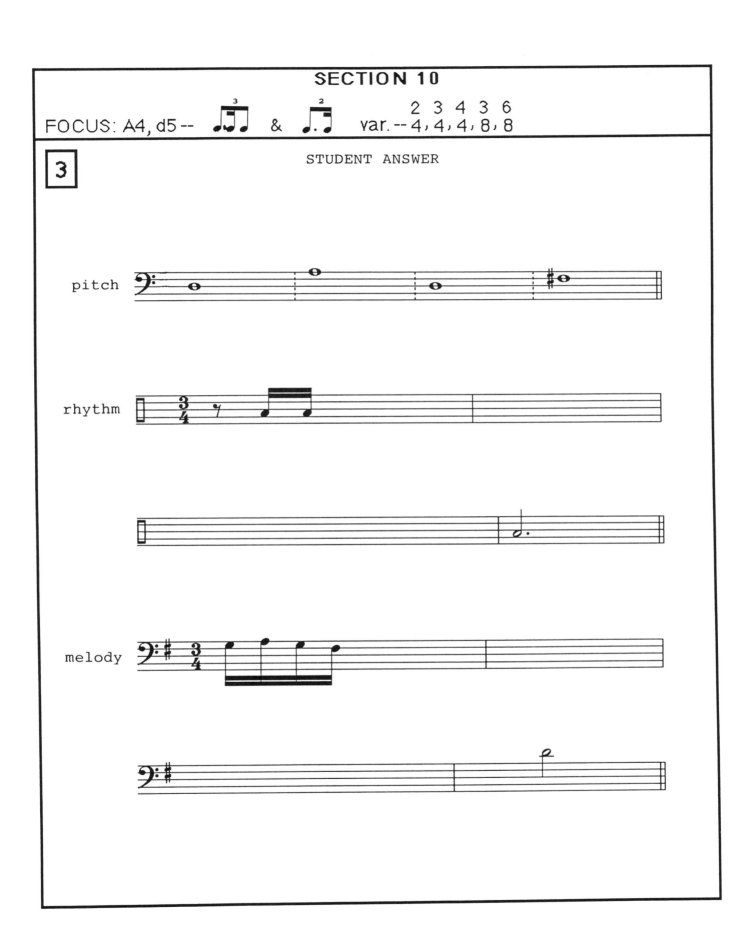

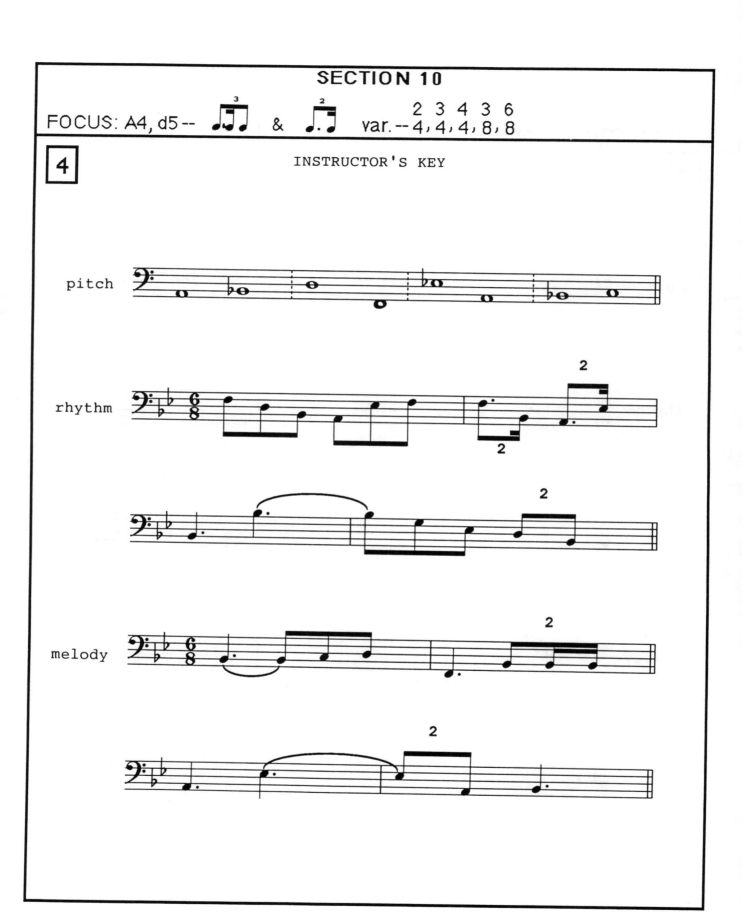

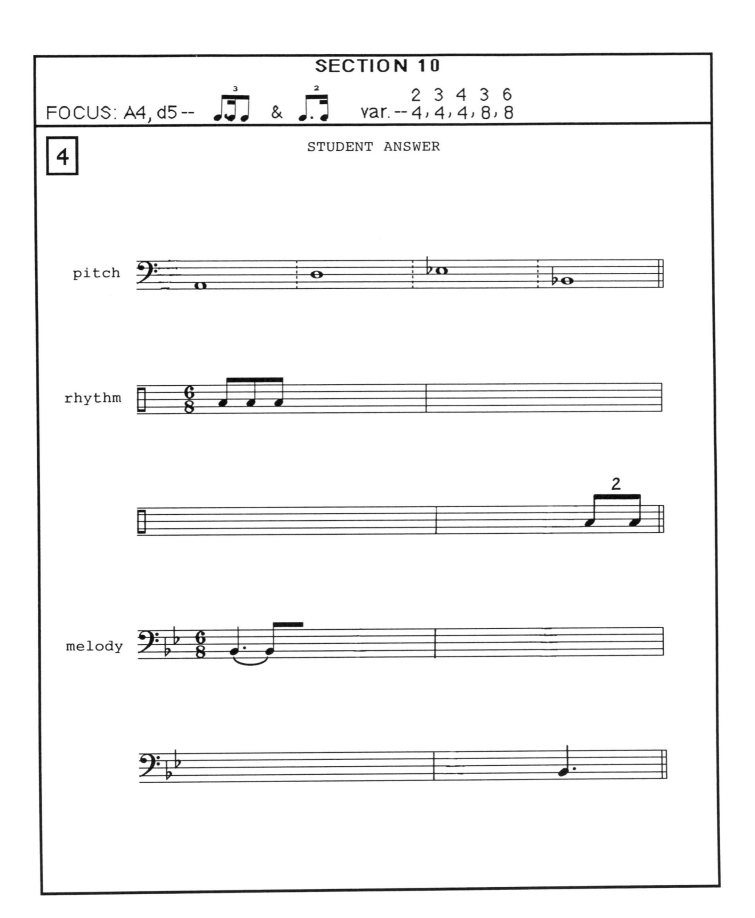

189

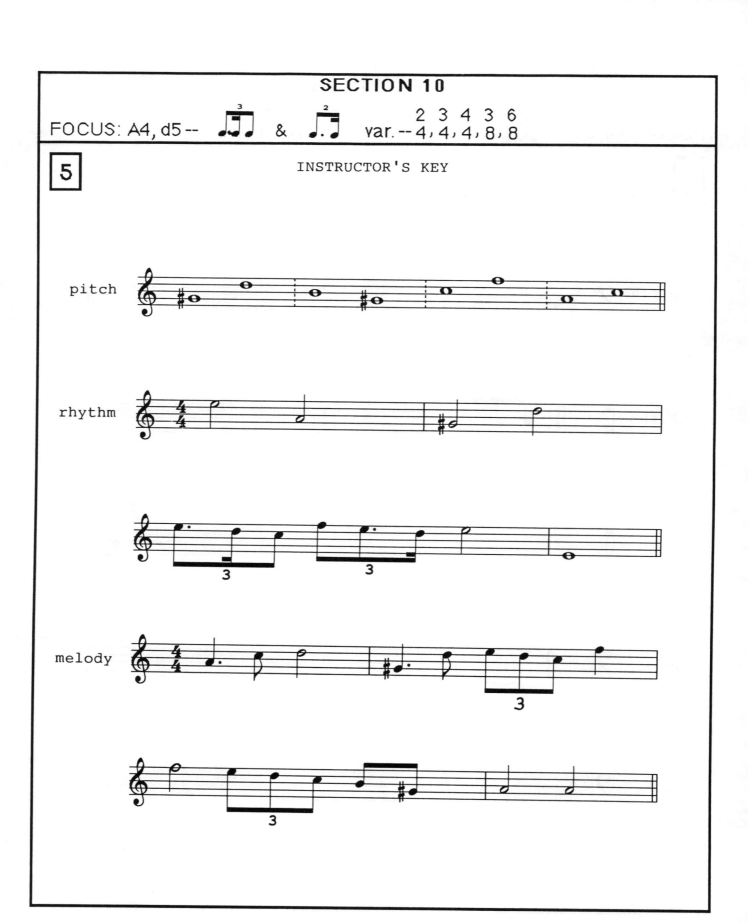

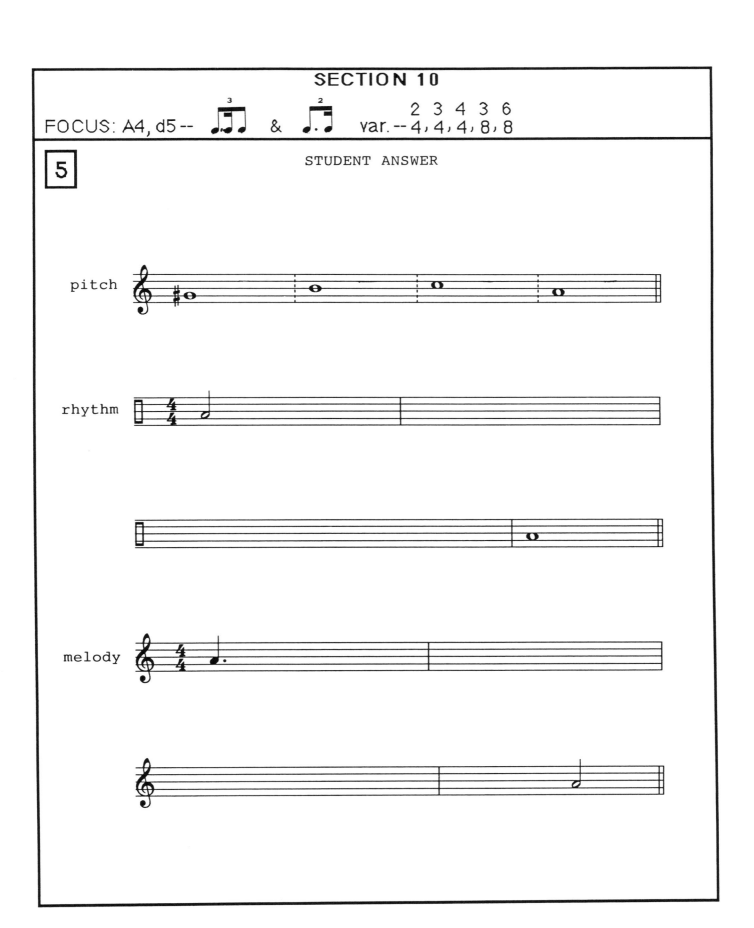

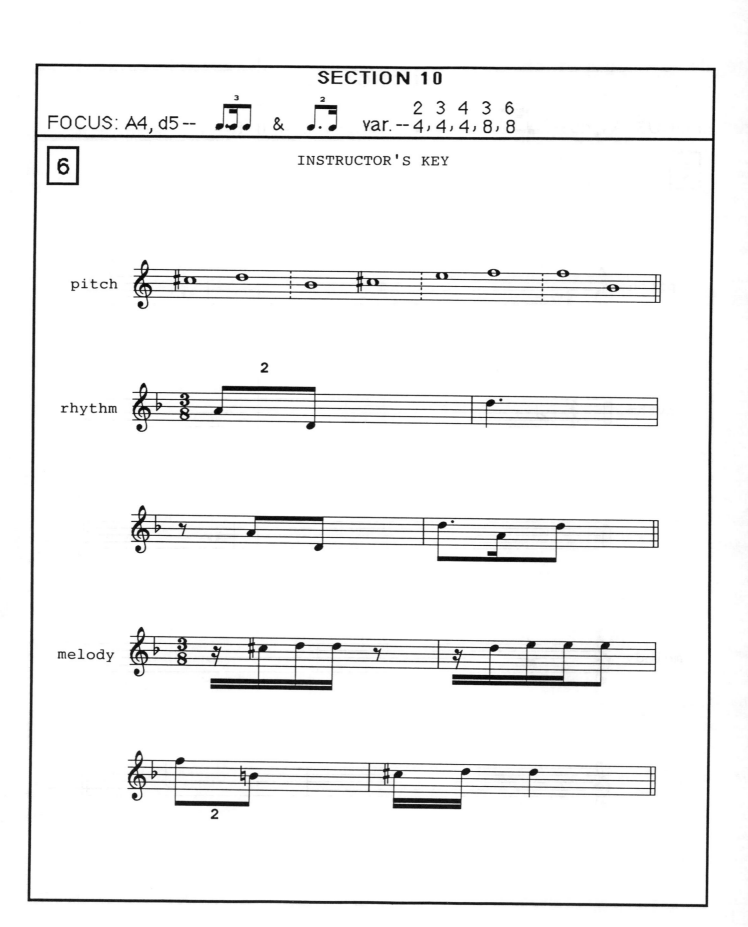

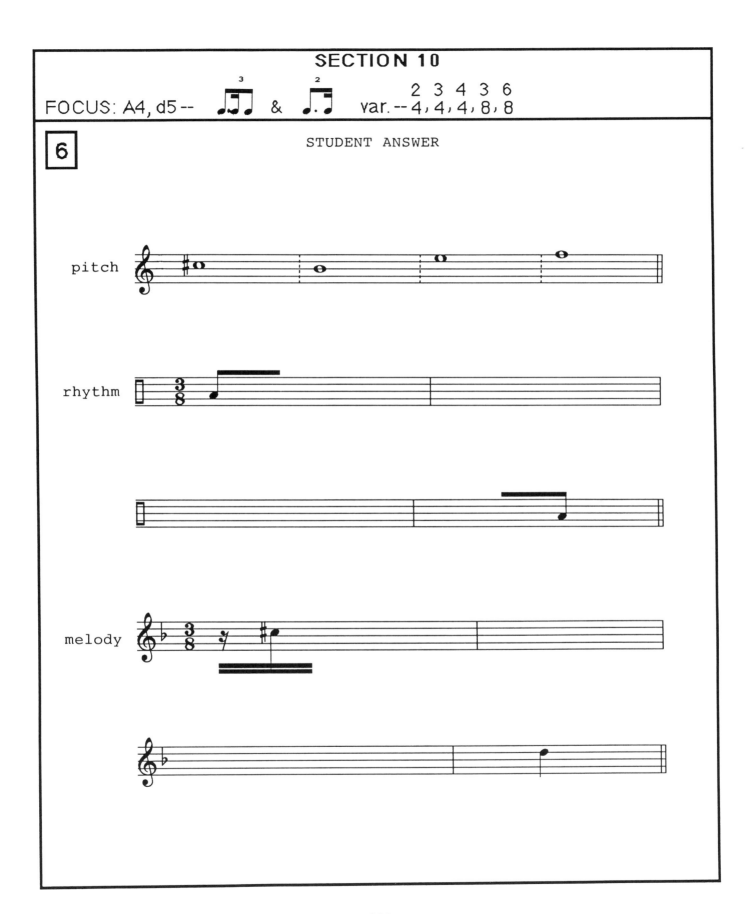

FOCUS: A4, d5 -- ♩♩ ³ & ♩.♩ ²  var. -- $\frac{2}{4}, \frac{3}{4}, \frac{4}{4}, \frac{3}{8}, \frac{6}{8}$

7    INSTRUCTOR'S KEY

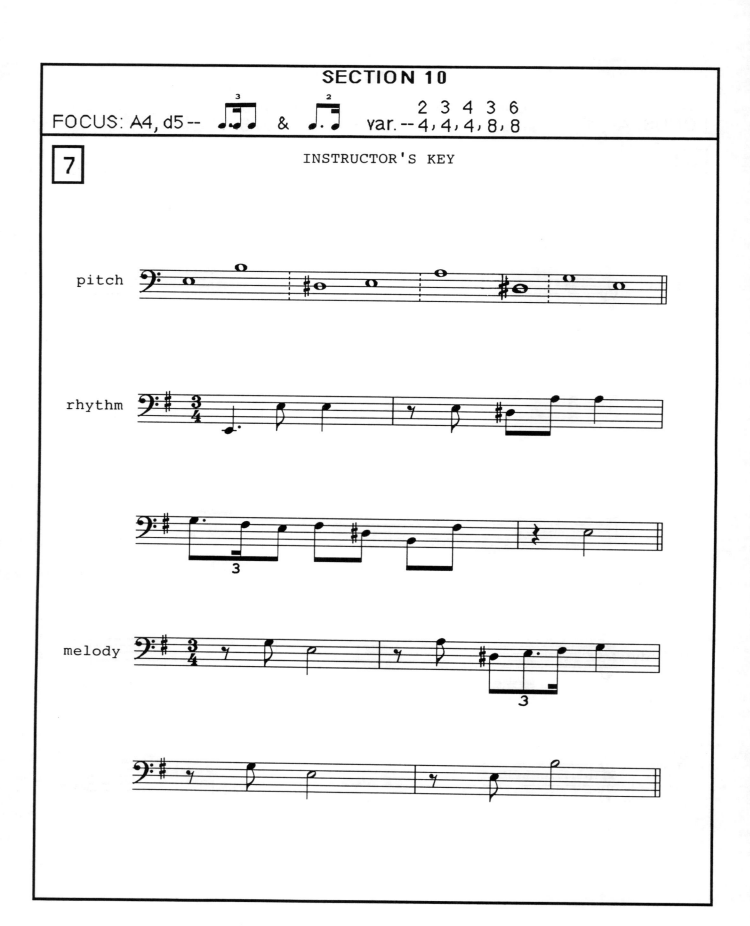

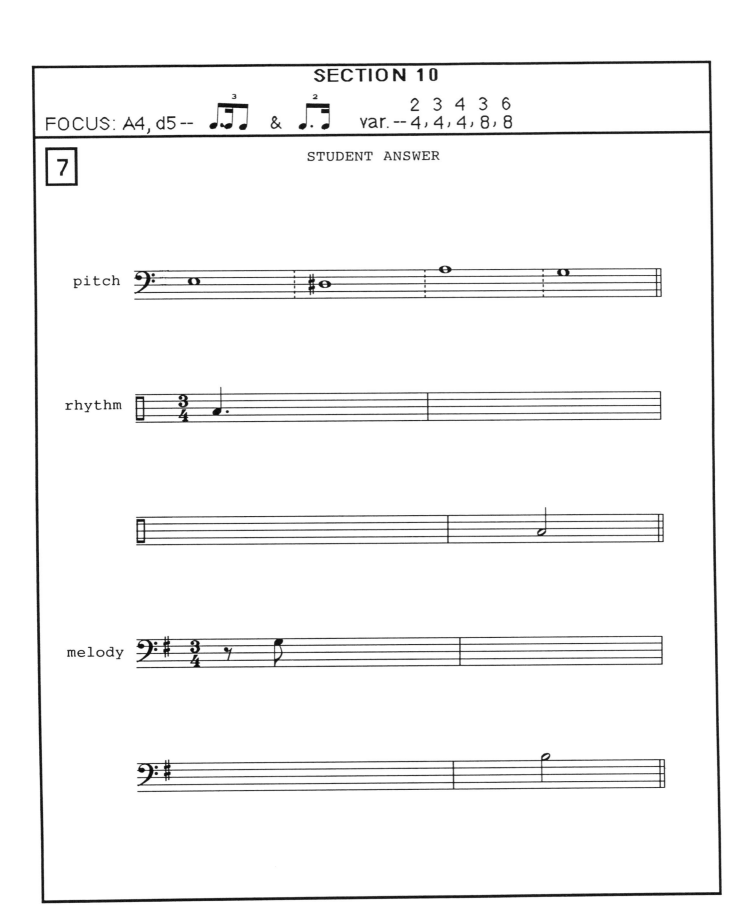

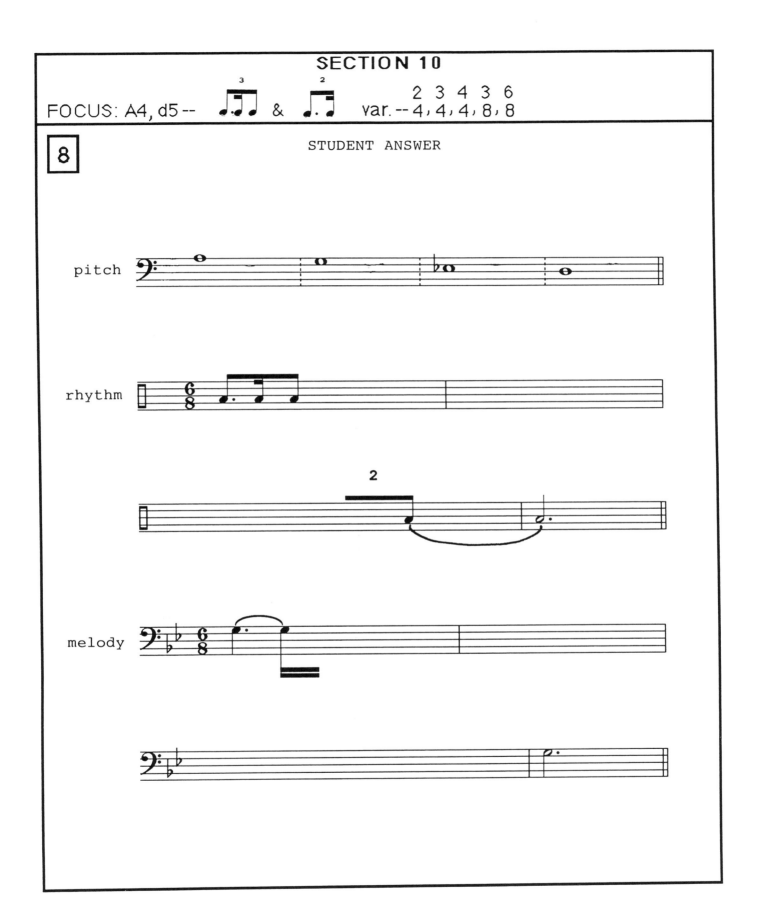

# SECTION 10A

FOCUS: Tonic, Subdominant Sevenths,
root position, first inversion

INSTRUCTOR'S KEY:

STUDENT ANSWER:

**1**

C: I      $I^7$     $I^6_5$

**1**

C: ___   ___   ___

**2**

C: I     IV    $IV^7$

**2**

C: ___   ___   ___

**3**

C: I   $IV^7$   IV   $IV^6_5$

**3**

C: ___   ___   ___

**4**

C: $V^7$   I   $IV^7$   V

**4**

C: ___   ___   ___   ___

**5**

C: $I^6$   $IV^7$   $IV^6_5$   V

**5**

C: ___   ___   ___   ___

**6**

C: I   $V^6_4$   $I^6$   $I^6_5$

**6**

C: ___   ___   ___   ___

198

# SECTION 10A

FOCUS: Tonic, Subdominant Sevenths,
root position, first inversion

| INSTRUCTOR'S KEY | STUDENT ANSWER |
| --- | --- |

7  E♭:  V     V$^7$     IV$^6$     IV$^6_5$

7  E♭: ___  ___  ___  ___

8  A:  I     I$^7$     IV     IV$^7$

8  A: ___  ___  ___  ___

9  B♭:  IV$^7$     I$^7$     V$^7$     IV$^6$

9  B♭: ___  ___  ___  ___

10  D:  IV     V     I     I$^6_5$     IV

10  D: ___  ___  ___  ___  ___

11  F:  I$^7$     V$^7$     IV$^6$     IV$^6$     V     I

11  F: ___  ___  ___  ___  ___  ___

12  G:  IV$^6_5$     V$^6$     I     I$^6$     I$^6_5$     IV     IV$^7$

12  G: ___  ___  ___  ___  ___  ___  ___

199

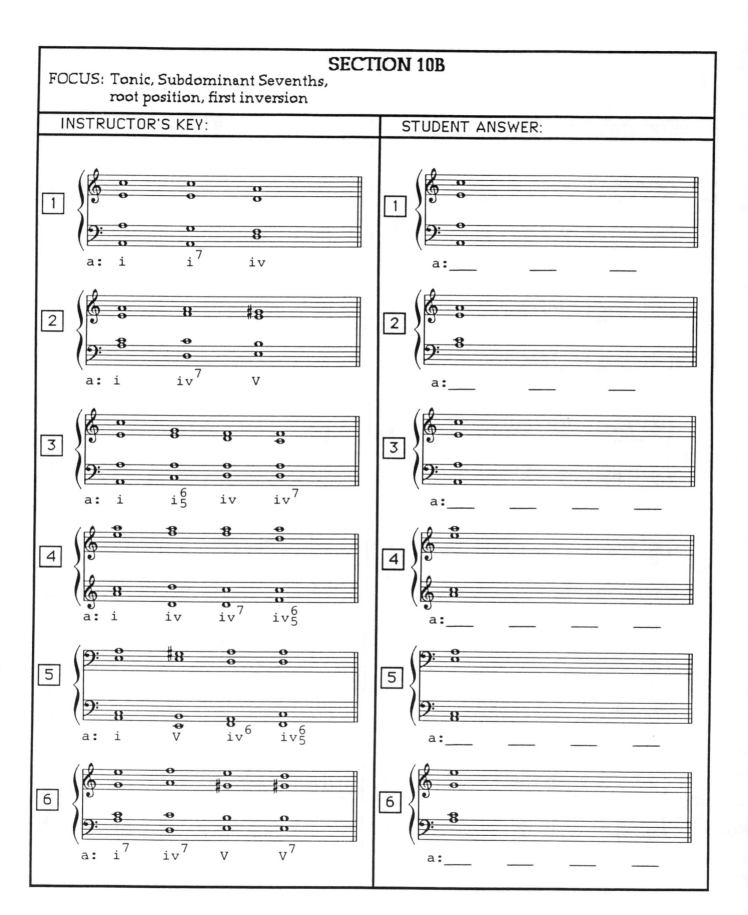

# SECTION 10B

FOCUS: Tonic, Subdominant Sevenths,
root position, first inversion

| INSTRUCTOR'S KEY | STUDENT ANSWER |
|---|---|

# UNIT 2

# DIATONIC
# TONAL DICTATION

# SECTION 1

FOCUS: m2, M2, A2-- ♩ ♩-- 2/4

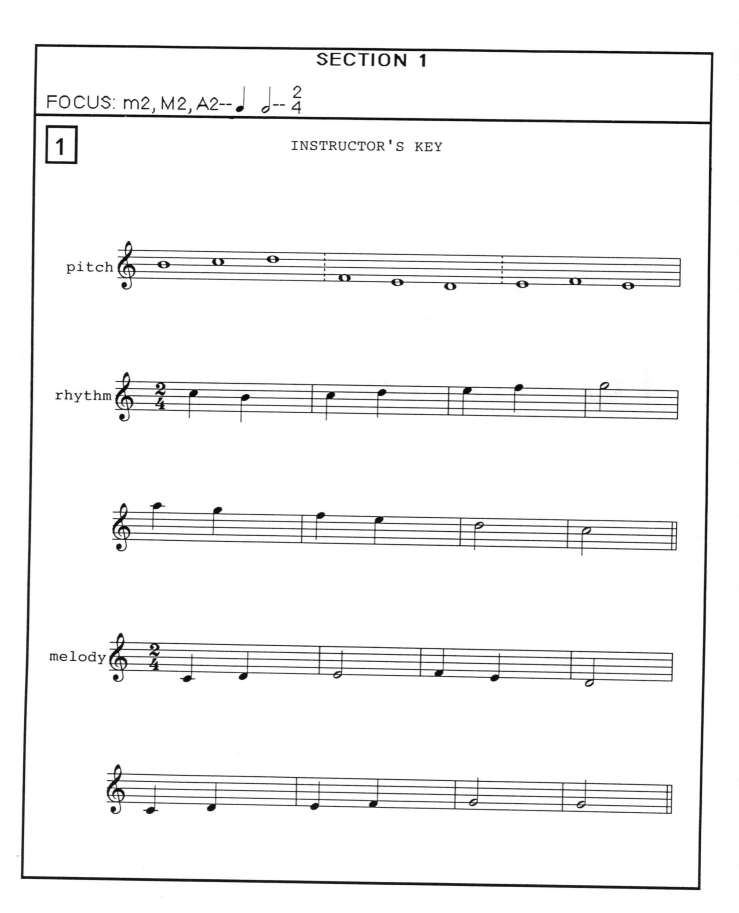

1  INSTRUCTOR'S KEY

# SECTION 1

FOCUS: m2, M2, A2-- ♩ ♩ -- 2/4

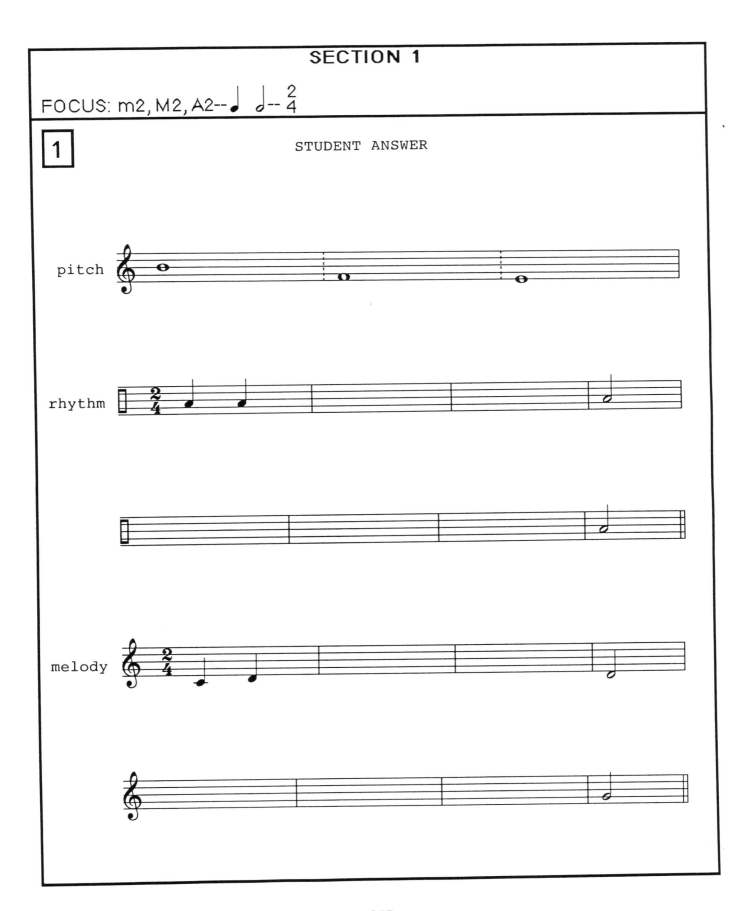

1

STUDENT ANSWER

pitch

rhythm

melody

# SECTION 1

**FOCUS: m2, M2, A2--** ♩ ♩-- 2/4

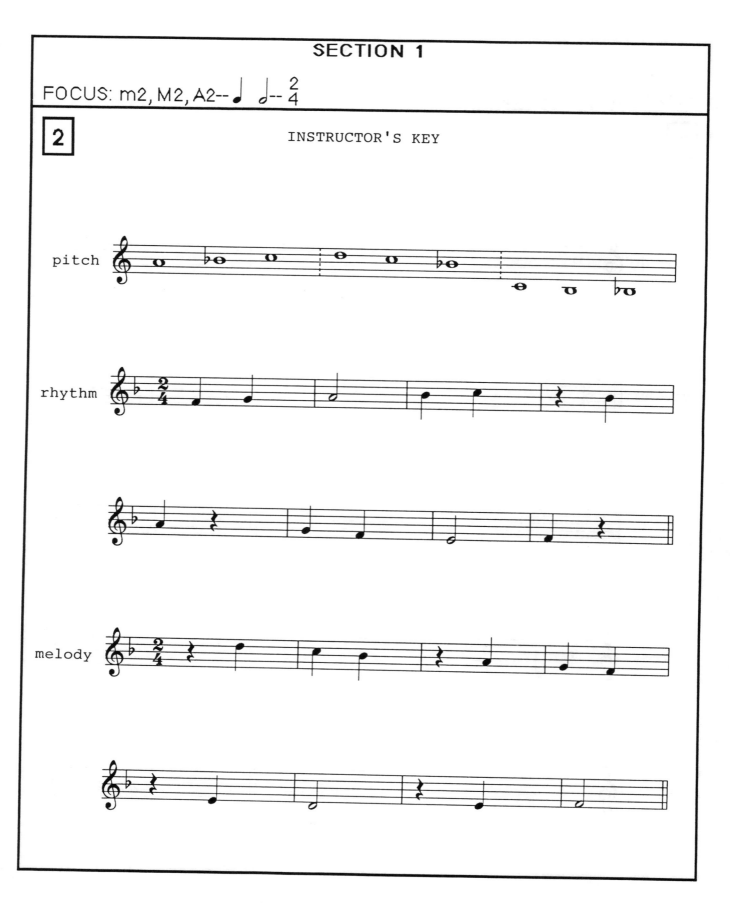

INSTRUCTOR'S KEY

pitch

rhythm

melody

# SECTION 1

FOCUS: m2, M2, A2-- ♩ ♩-- 2/4

2    STUDENT ANSWER

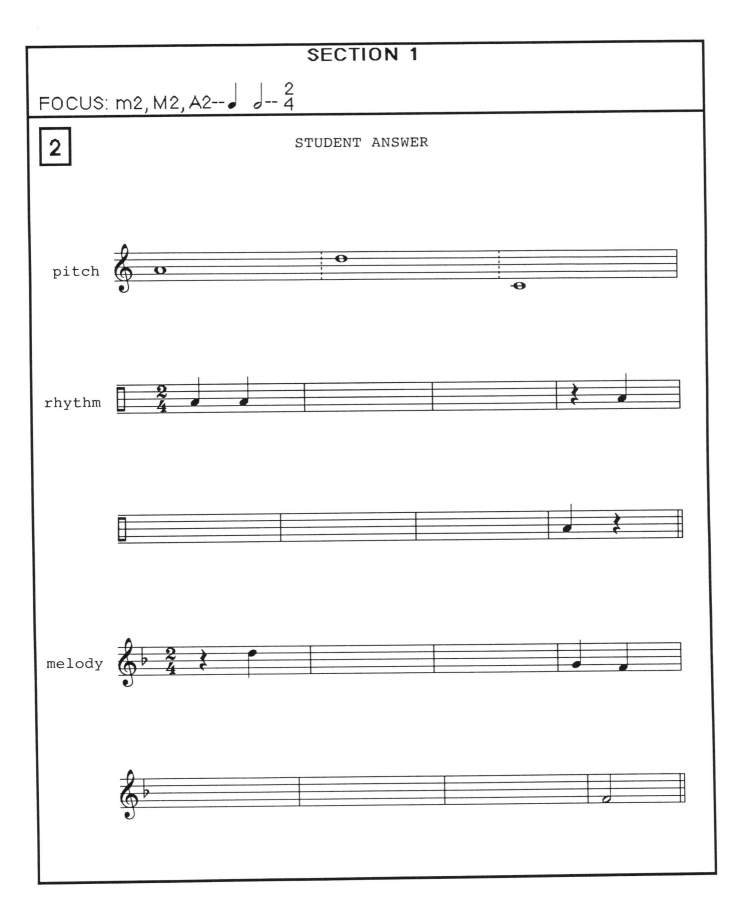

pitch

rhythm

melody

# SECTION 1

FOCUS: m2, M2, A2 -- ♩ ♩ -- $\frac{2}{4}$

3    INSTRUCTOR'S KEY

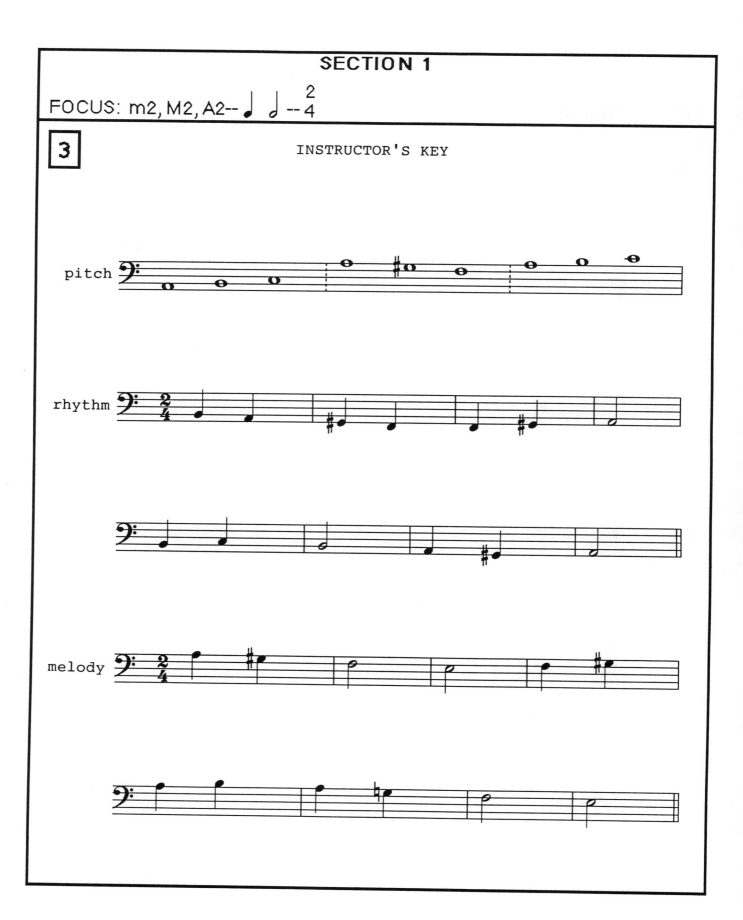

# SECTION 1

FOCUS: m2, M2, A2 -- ♩ ♩ -- $\frac{2}{4}$

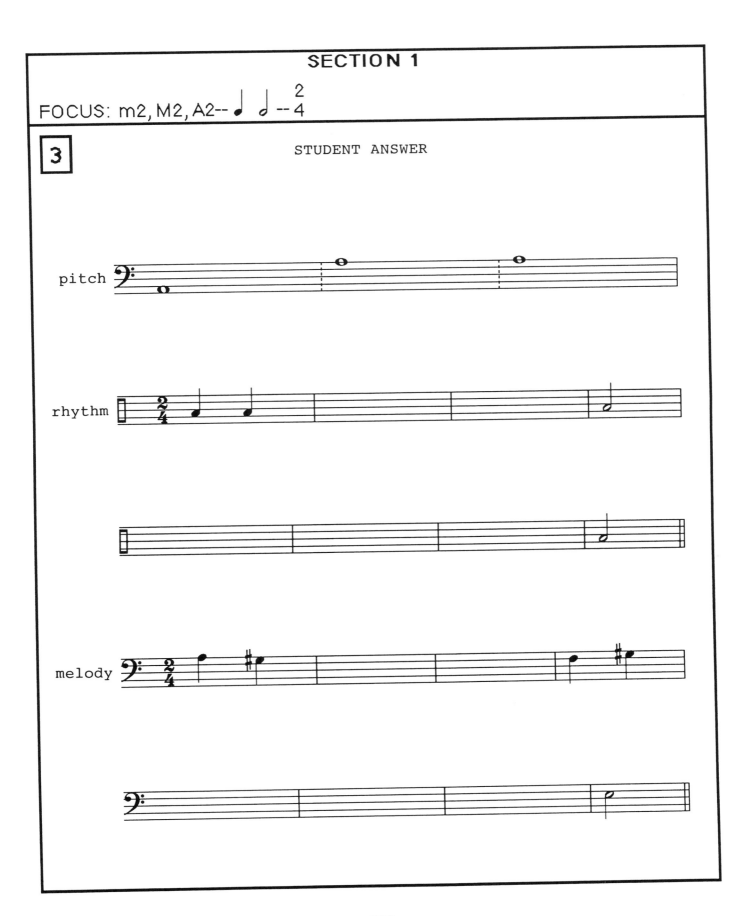

3

STUDENT ANSWER

# SECTION 1

FOCUS: m2, M2, A2 -- ♩ ♩ -- $\frac{2}{4}$

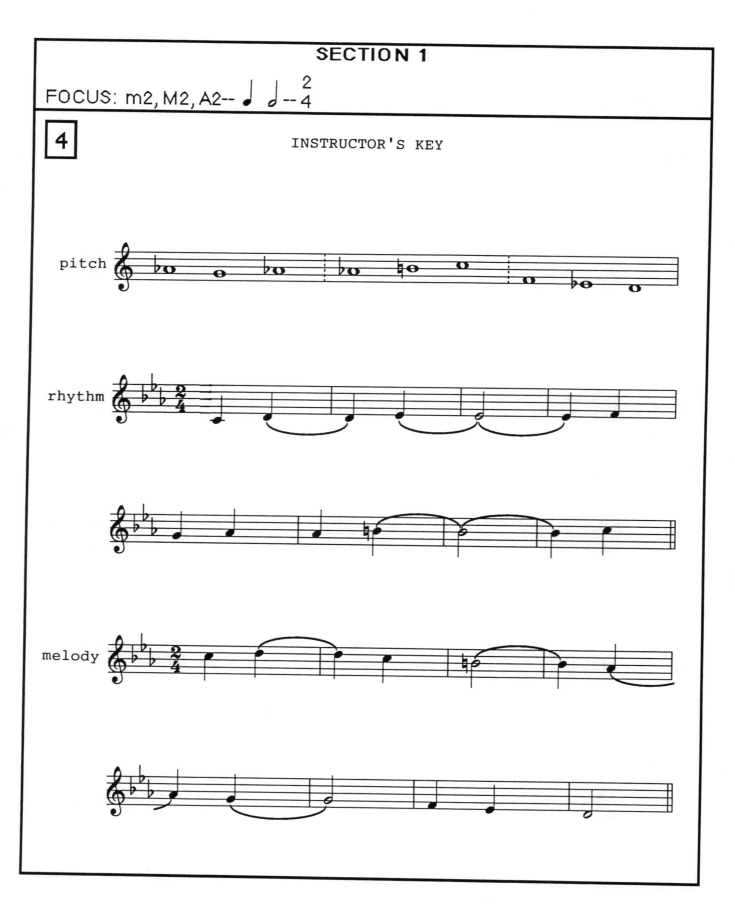

4    INSTRUCTOR'S KEY

# SECTION 1

FOCUS: m2, M2, A2-- ♩ ♩ -- 2/4

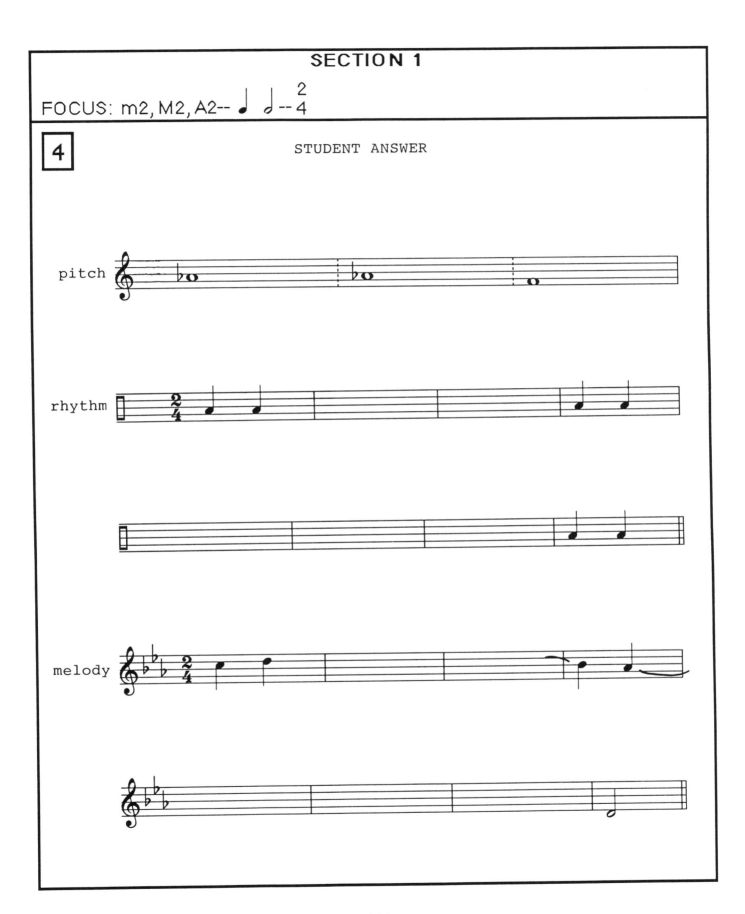

# SECTION 1A

**FOCUS:** Supertonic, root position, first inversion

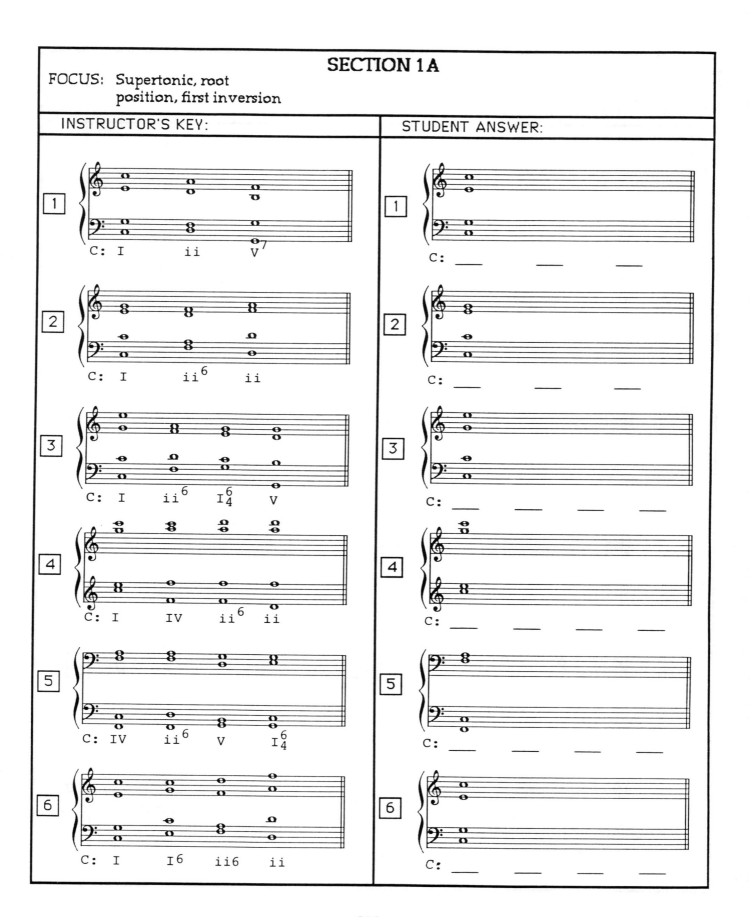

INSTRUCTOR'S KEY:

STUDENT ANSWER:

1.    C: I    ii    V$^7$

1.    C: ___ ___ ___

2.    C: I    ii$^6$    ii

2.    C: ___ ___ ___

3.    C: I    ii$^6$    I$^6_4$    V

3.    C: ___ ___ ___ ___

4.    C: I    IV    ii$^6$    ii

4.    C: ___ ___ ___ ___

5.    C: IV    ii$^6$    V    I$^6_4$

5.    C: ___ ___ ___ ___

6.    C: I    I$^6$    ii6    ii

6.    C: ___ ___ ___ ___

212

# SECTION 1A

FOCUS:  Supertonic, root
        position, first inversion

| INSTRUCTOR'S KEY | STUDENT ANSWER |
|---|---|

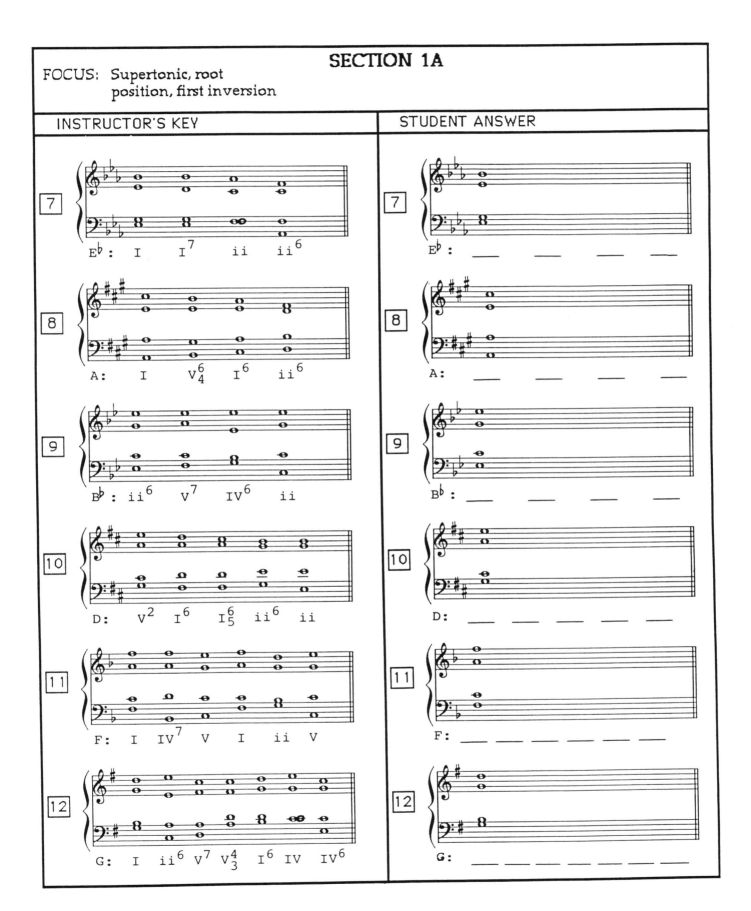

7  E♭: I   I⁷   ii   ii⁶

8  A: I   V⁶₄   I⁶   ii⁶

9  B♭: ii⁶   V⁷   IV⁶   ii

10  D: V²   I⁶   I⁶₅   ii⁶   ii

11  F: I   IV⁷   V   I   ii   V

12  G: I   ii⁶   V⁷   V⁴₃   I⁶   IV   IV⁶

7  E♭: ___ ___ ___ ___

8  A: ___ ___ ___ ___

9  B♭: ___ ___ ___ ___

10  D: ___ ___ ___ ___ ___

11  F: ___ ___ ___ ___ ___ ___

12  G: ___ ___ ___ ___ ___ ___ ___

213

# SECTION 1 B

**FOCUS:** Supertonic, root position, first inversion

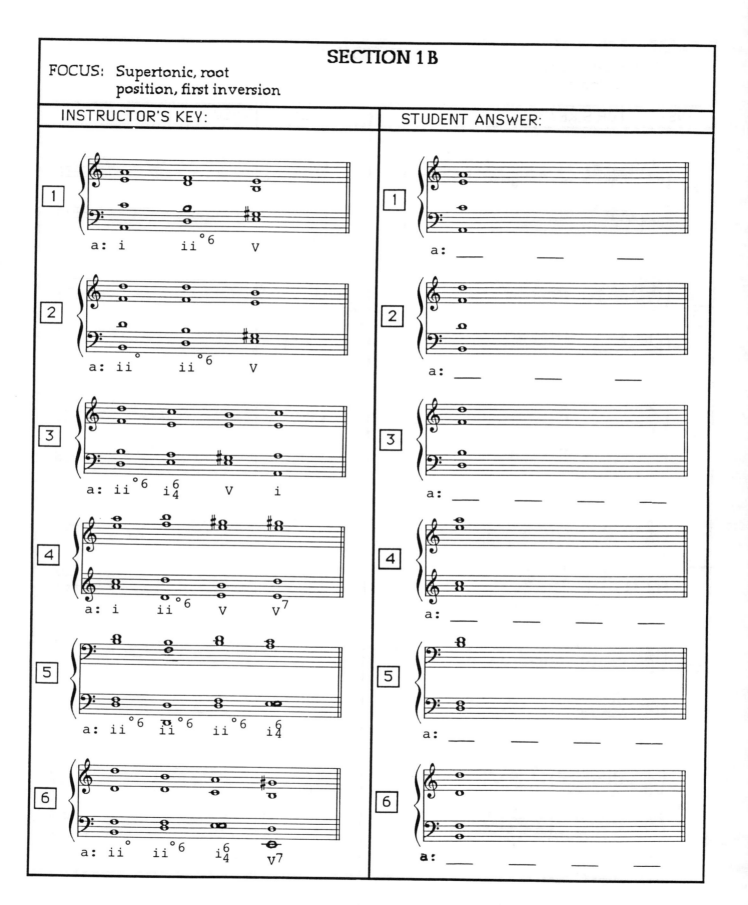

INSTRUCTOR'S KEY:

1  a: i  ii°6  V

2  a: ii°  ii°6  V

3  a: ii°6  i6/4  V  i

4  a: i  ii°6  V  V7

5  a: ii°6  ii°6  ii°6  i6/4

6  a: ii°  ii°6  i6/4  V7

STUDENT ANSWER:

1  a: ___  ___  ___

2  a: ___

3  a: ___  ___  ___  ___

4  a: ___

5  a: ___  ___  ___

6  a: ___  ___  ___

214

# SECTION 1B

FOCUS: Supertonic, root
position, first inversion

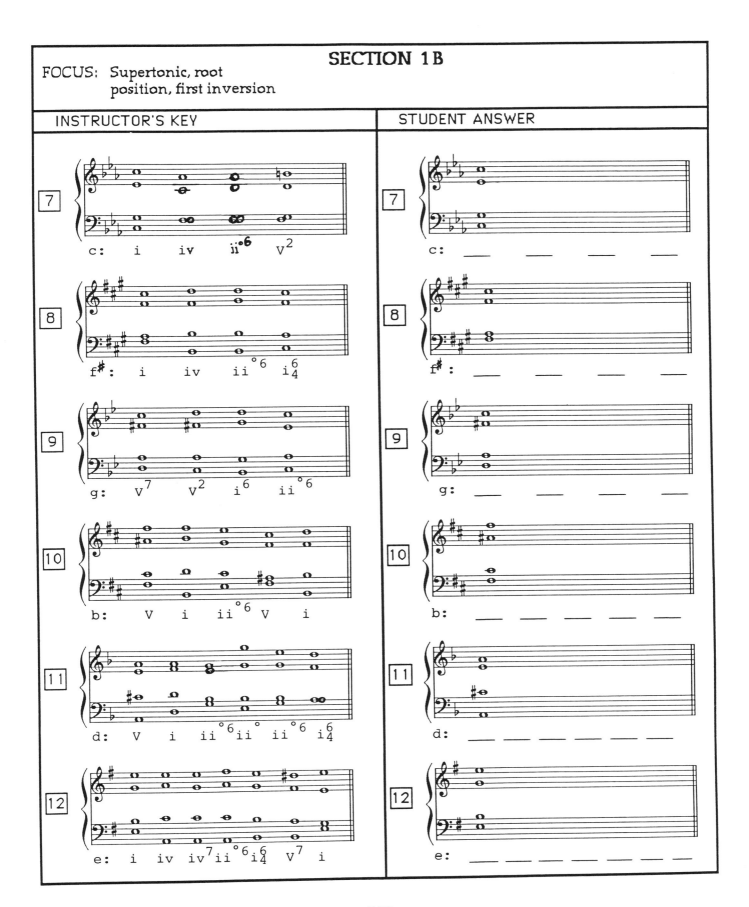

INSTRUCTOR'S KEY

STUDENT ANSWER

215

FOCUS: m3, M3-- ♩. -- 3/4

INSTRUCTOR'S KEY

pitch

rhythm

melody

# SECTION 2

FOCUS: m3, M3-- ♩. -- 3/4

STUDENT ANSWER

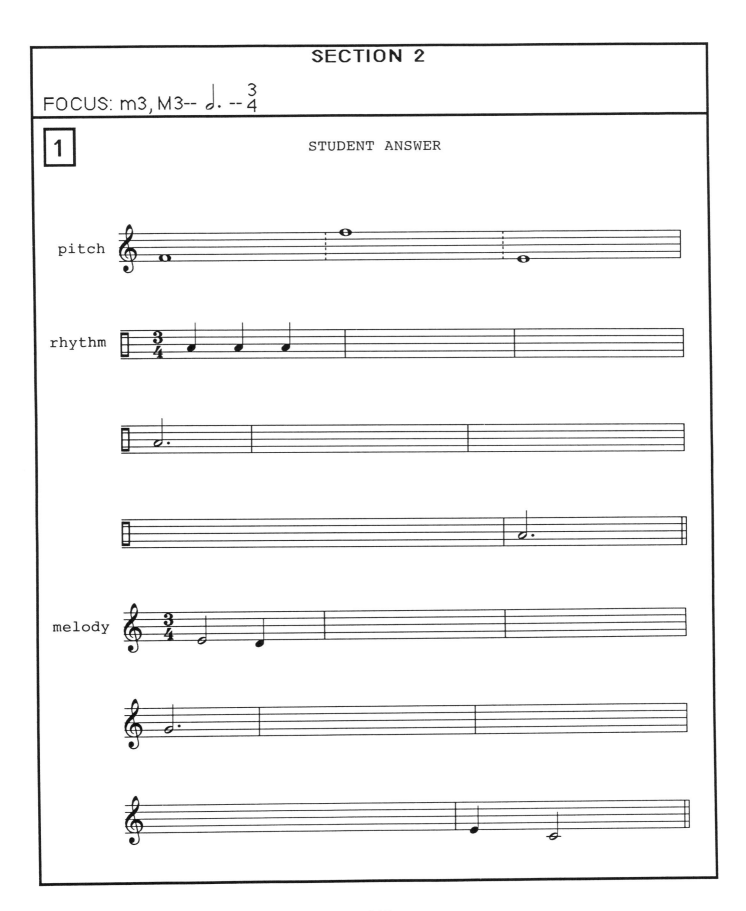

pitch

rhythm

melody

217

# SECTION 2

FOCUS: m3, M3 -- ♩. -- 3/4

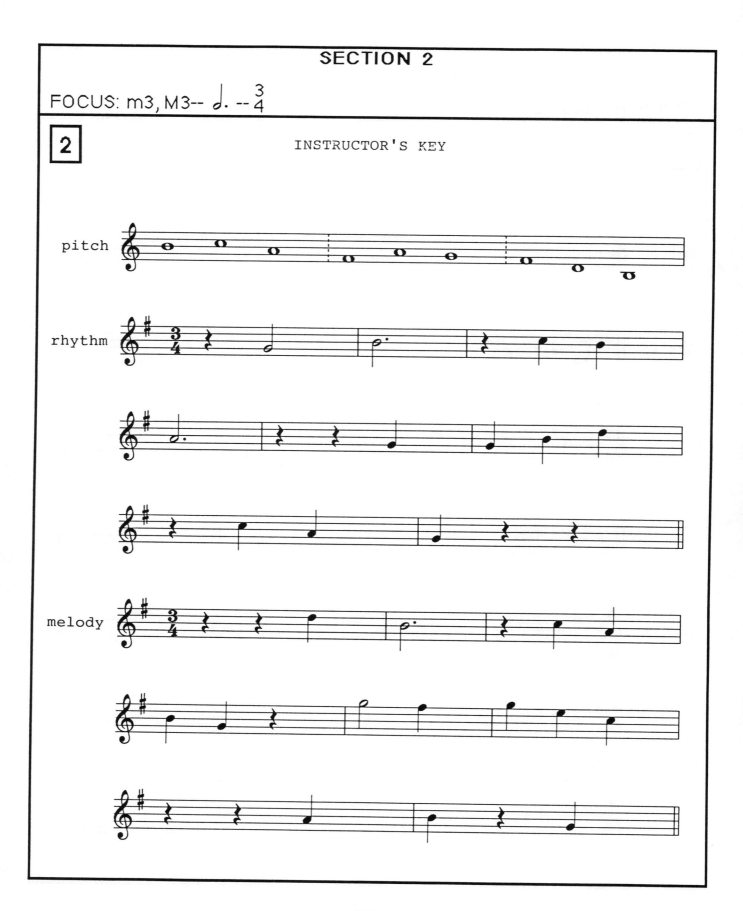

218

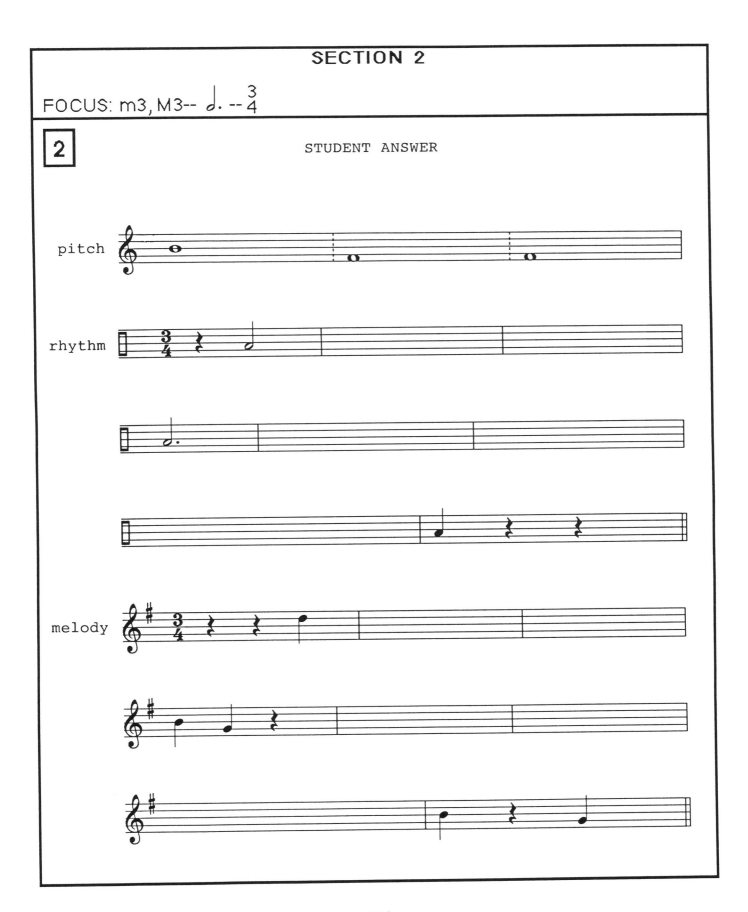

# SECTION 2

FOCUS: m3, M3 -- ♩. -- $\frac{3}{4}$

# SECTION 2

FOCUS: m3, M3 -- ♩. -- 3/4

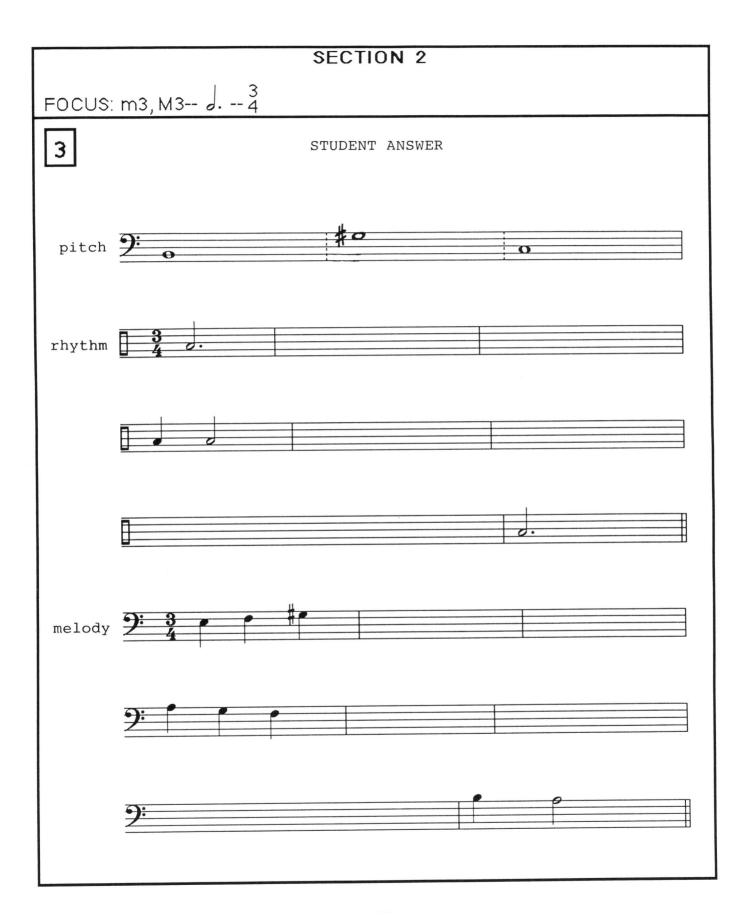

# SECTION 2

FOCUS: m3, M3 -- ♩. -- 3/4

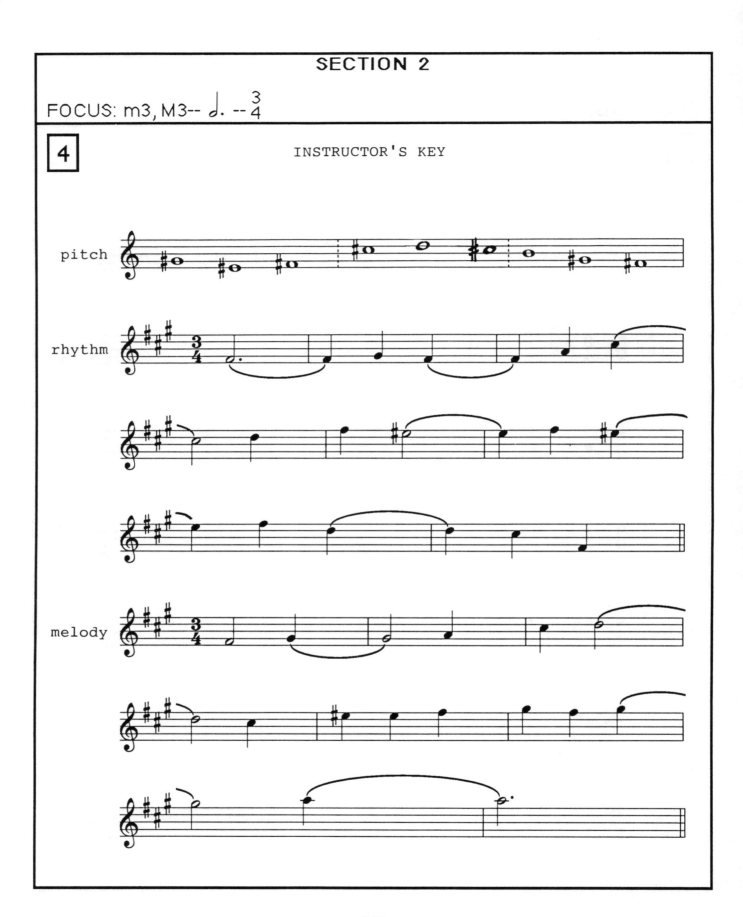

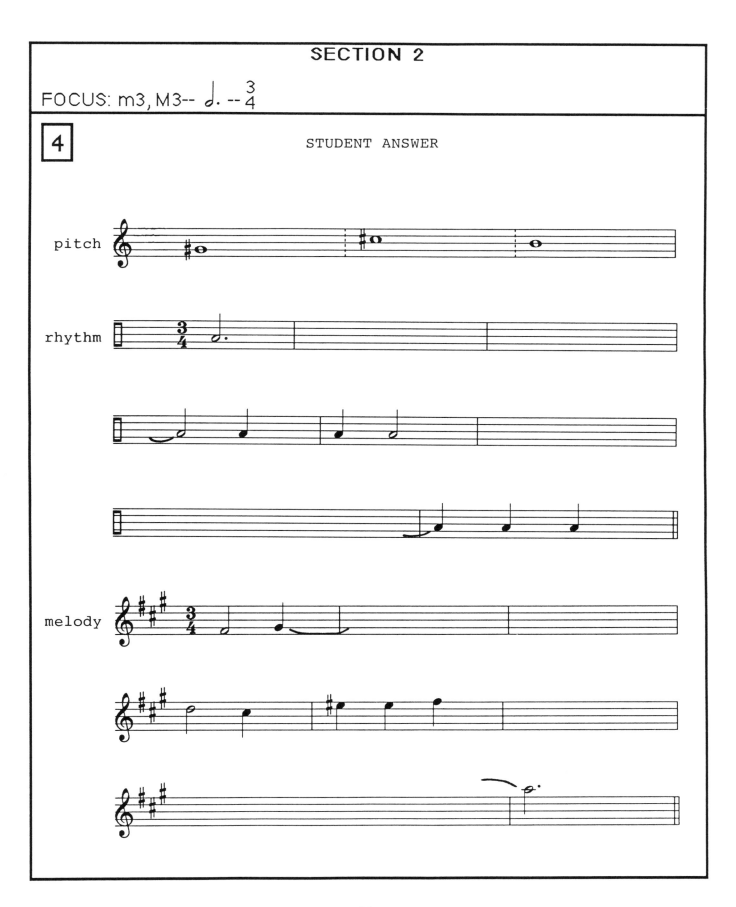

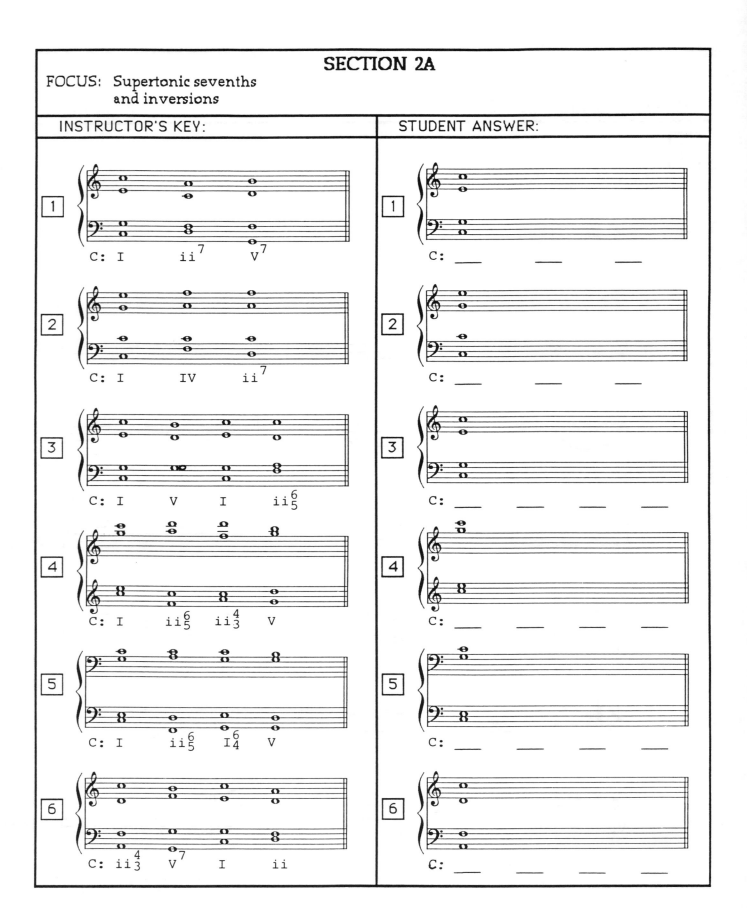

# SECTION 2A

FOCUS: Supertonic sevenths
and inversions

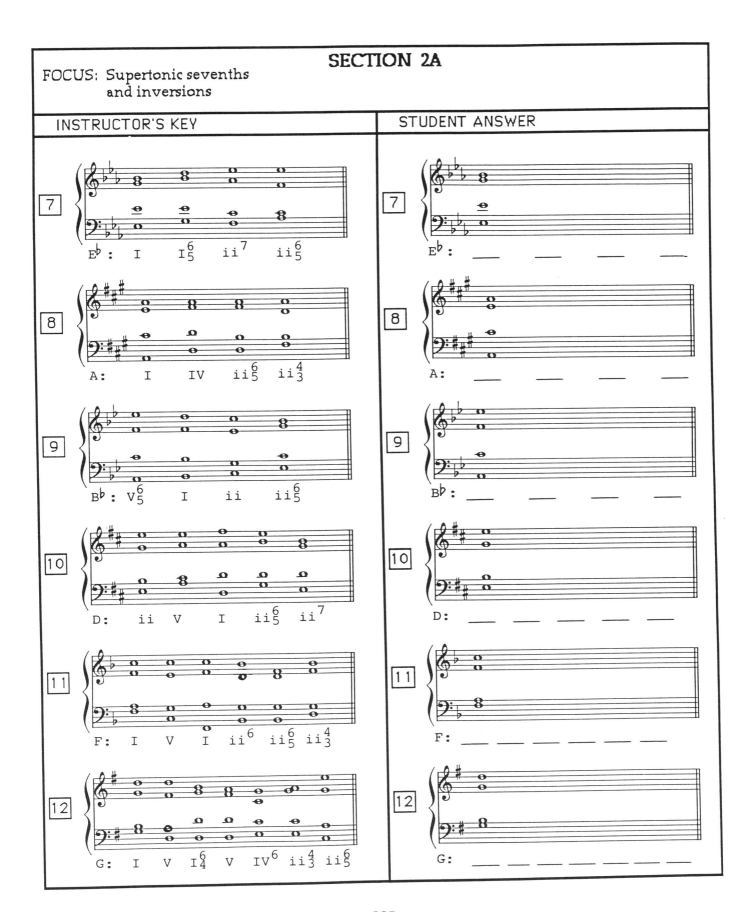

INSTRUCTOR'S KEY

STUDENT ANSWER

7   E♭:  I    I$^6_5$   ii$^7$   ii$^6_5$

7   E♭: ___ ___ ___ ___

8   A:   I    IV   ii$^6_5$   ii$^4_3$

8   A: ___ ___ ___ ___

9   B♭:  V$^6_5$   I    ii   ii$^6_5$

9   B♭: ___ ___ ___ ___

10  D:  ii   V    I   ii$^6_5$   ii$^7$

10  D: ___ ___ ___ ___ ___

11  F:  I   V   I   ii$^6$   ii$^6_5$   ii$^4_3$

11  F: ___ ___ ___ ___ ___ ___

12  G:  I   V   I$^6_4$   V   IV$^6$   ii$^4_3$   ii$^6_5$

12  G: ___ ___ ___ ___ ___ ___ ___

# SECTION 2B

**FOCUS:** Supertonic sevenths
and inversions

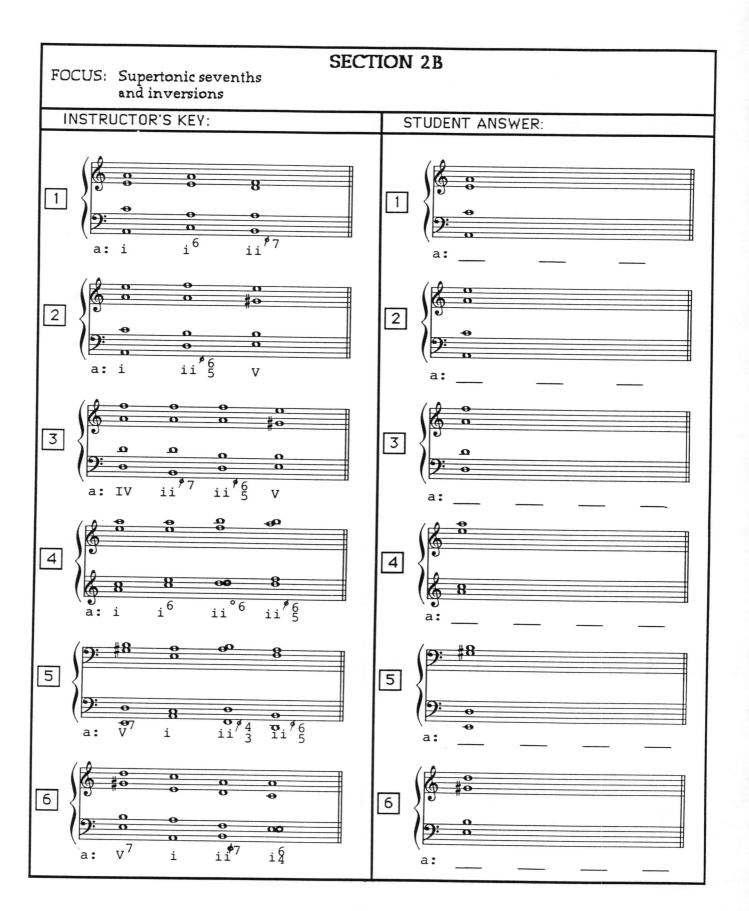

# SECTION 2B

FOCUS: Supertonic sevenths
and inversions

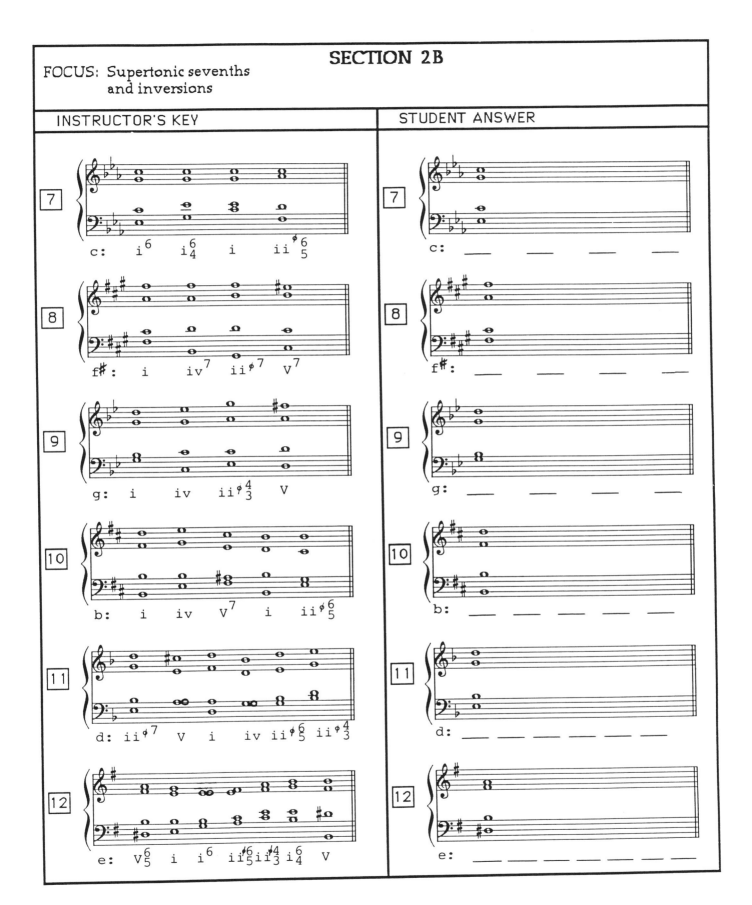

# SECTION 3

FOCUS: P8-- ♩♩ -- $\frac{2}{4}, \frac{3}{4}$

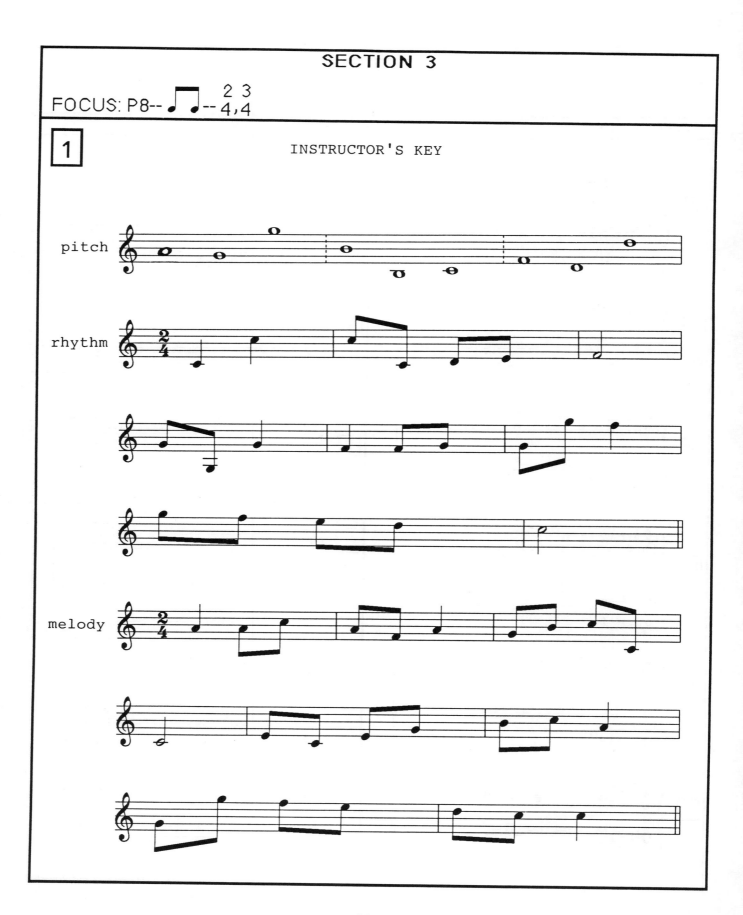

**1**          INSTRUCTOR'S KEY

# SECTION 3

FOCUS: P8-- ♩♩ -- $\frac{2}{4}, \frac{3}{4}$

## 1

STUDENT ANSWER

229

# SECTION 3

FOCUS: P8-- ♪♪ -- 2 3 / 4,4

# SECTION 3

FOCUS: P8-- ♩♩ -- 2 3 / 4,4

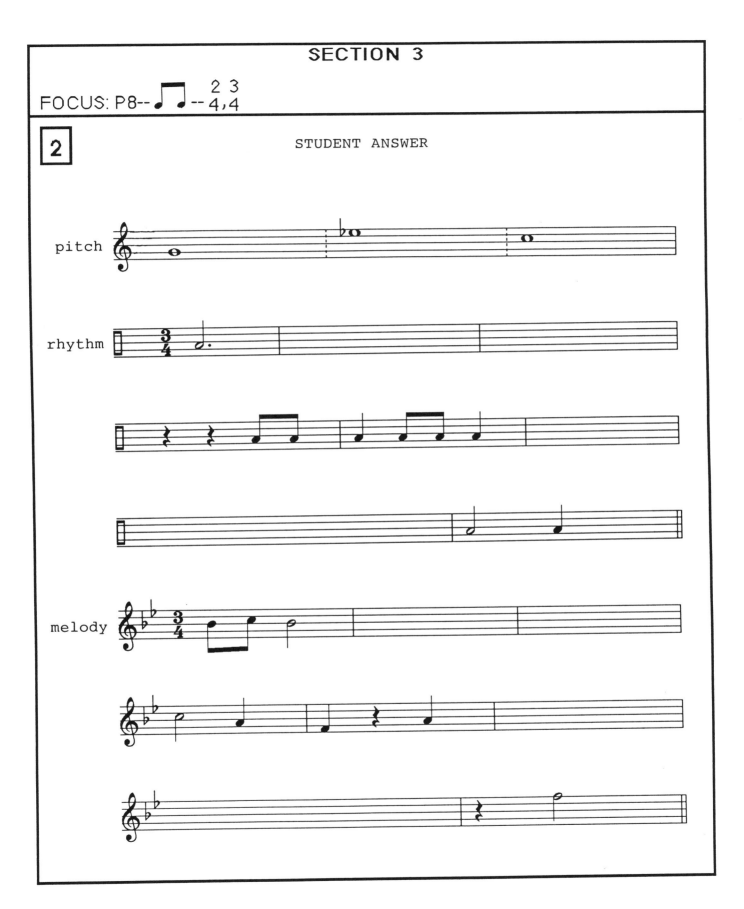

FOCUS: P8-- ♩♩ -- 2 3 / 4,4

**3** INSTRUCTOR'S KEY

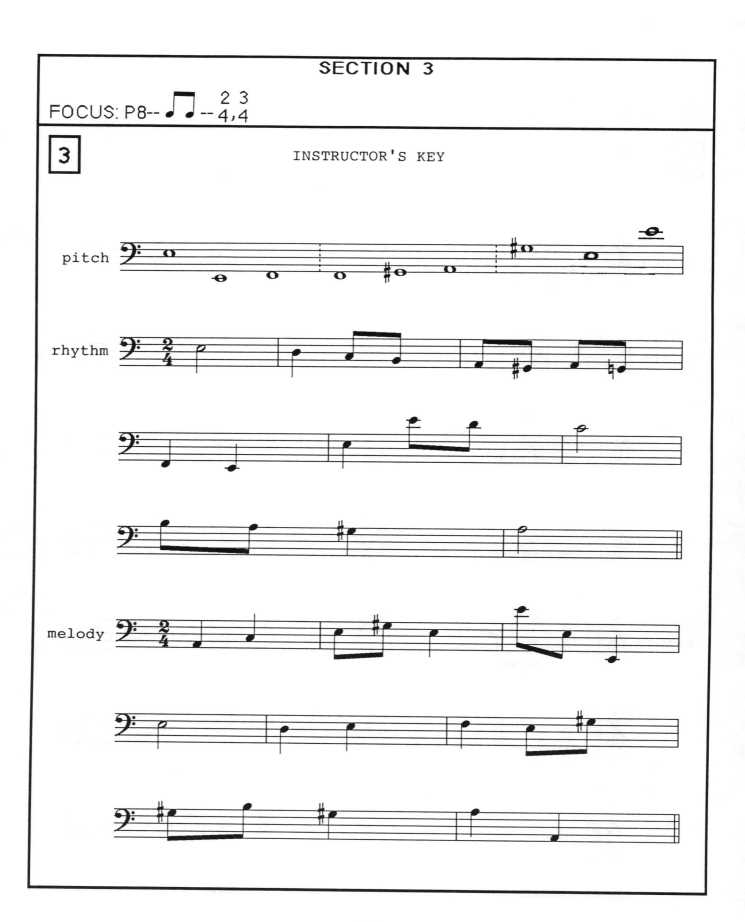

# SECTION 3

FOCUS: P8-- ♩♩ -- 2 3/4,4

STUDENT ANSWER

233

# SECTION 3

FOCUS: P8-- ♩♩ -- 2 3 / 4,4

4

INSTRUCTOR'S KEY

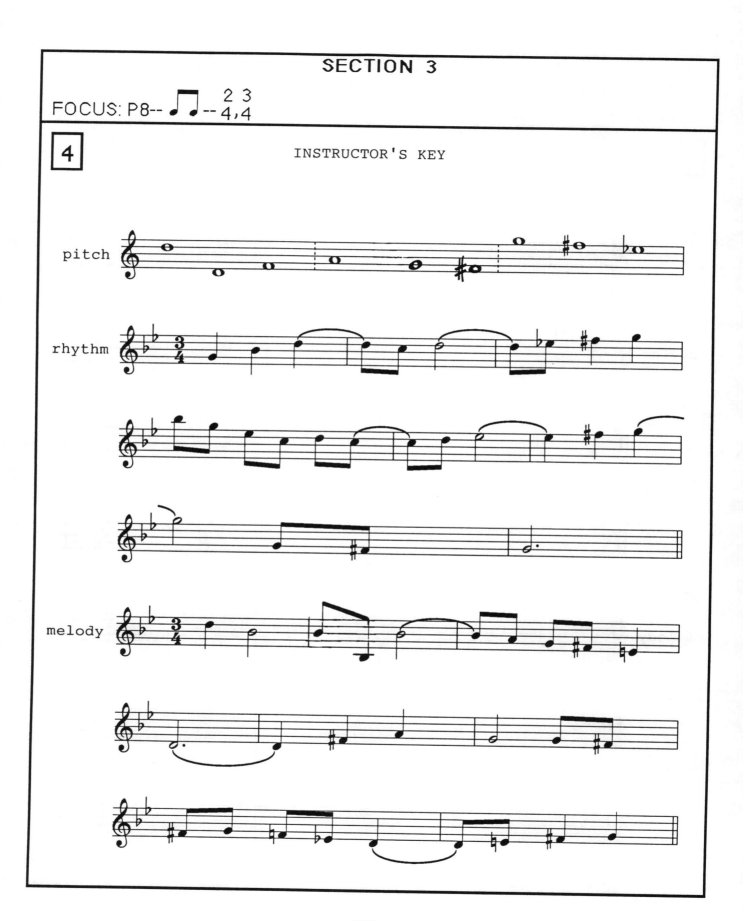

234

# SECTION 3A

FOCUS: Mediant

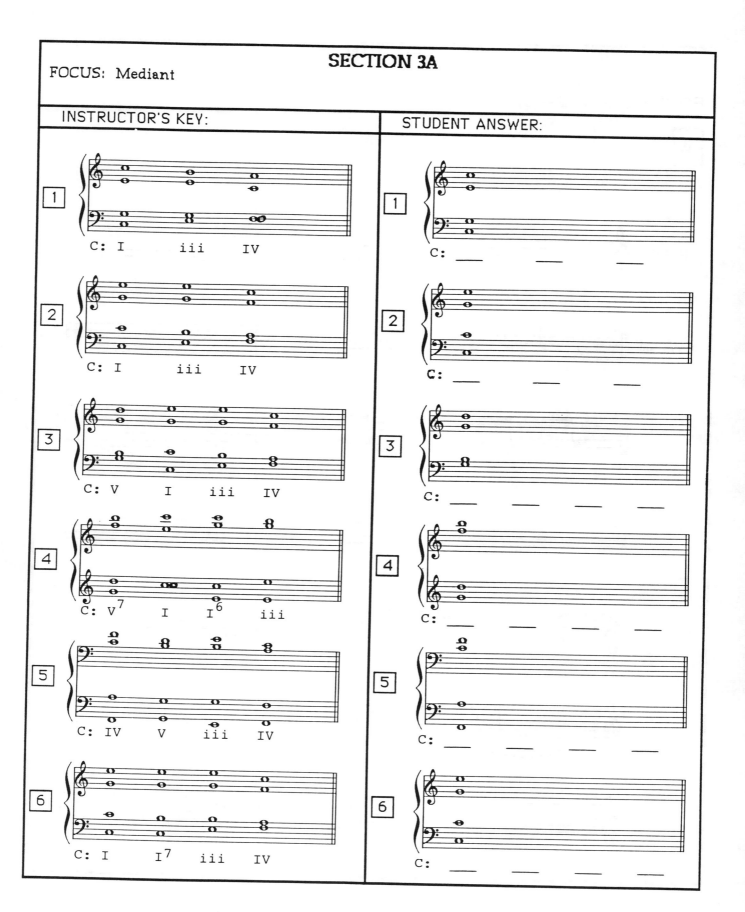

| INSTRUCTOR'S KEY: | STUDENT ANSWER: |

# SECTION 3A

FOCUS: Mediant

| INSTRUCTOR'S KEY | STUDENT ANSWER |
|---|---|

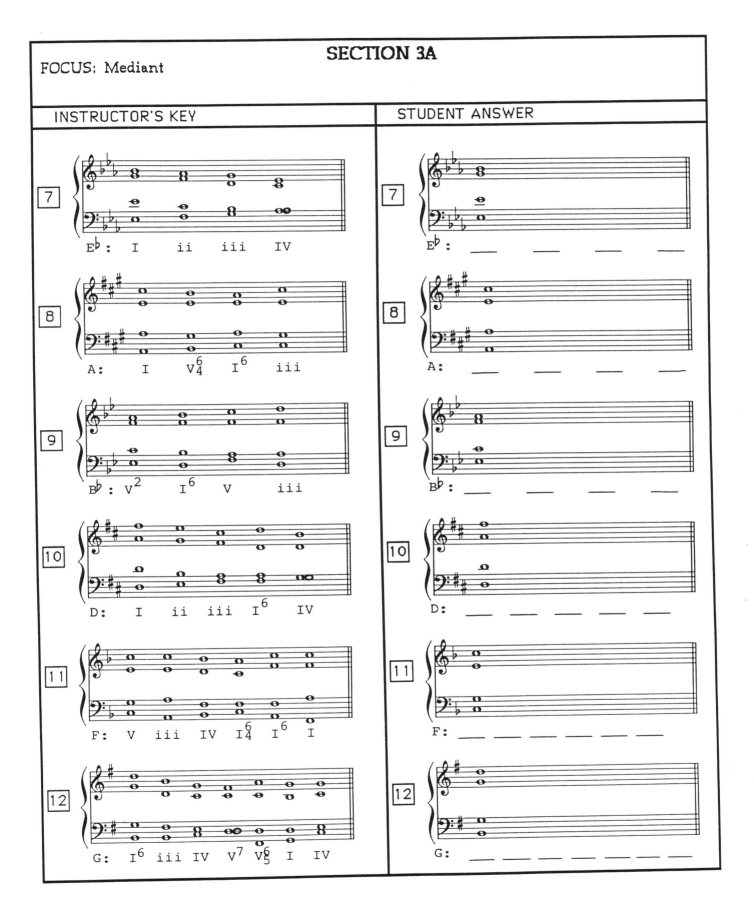

7  Eb: I   ii   iii   IV

8  A:   I   V$^6_4$   I$^6$   iii

9  Bb: V$^2$   I$^6$   V   iii

10  D:   I   ii   iii   I$^6$   IV

11  F:   V   iii   IV   I$^6_4$   I$^6$   I

12  G:   I$^6$   iii   IV   V$^7$   V$^6_5$   I   IV

7  Eb: ___ ___ ___ ___

8  A:  ___ ___ ___ ___

9  Bb: ___ ___ ___ ___

10  D:  ___ ___ ___ ___ ___

11  F:  ___ ___ ___ ___ ___ ___

12  G:  ___ ___ ___ ___ ___ ___ ___

237

# SECTION 3B

**FOCUS:** Mediant

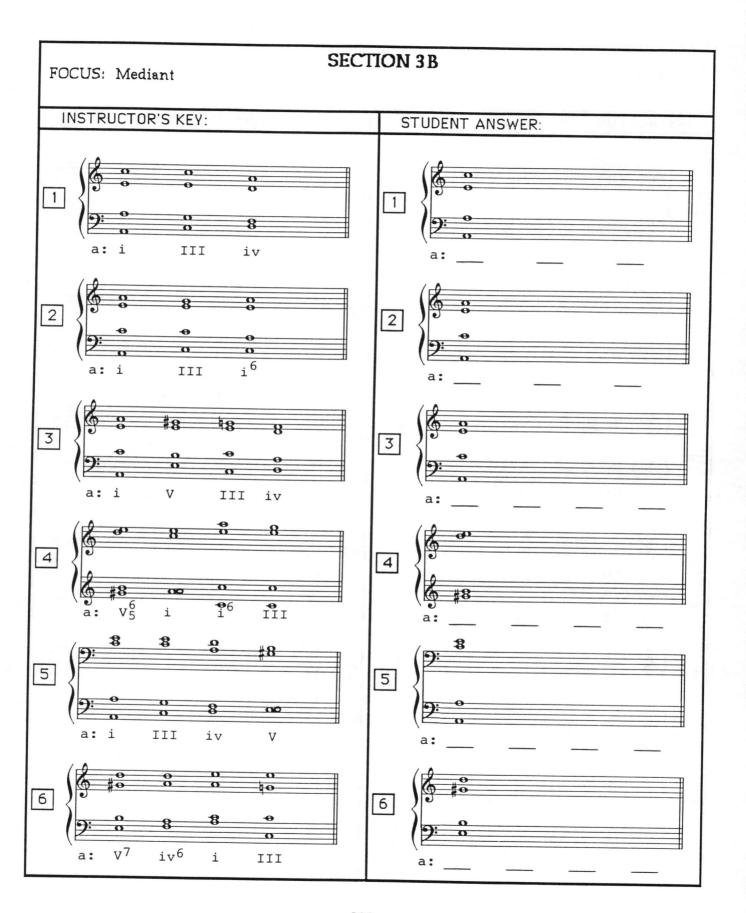

INSTRUCTOR'S KEY:

1. a: i     III     iv

2. a: i     III     i$^6$

3. a: i     V     III    iv

4. a: V$^6_5$    i    i$^6$    III

5. a: i     III    iv    V

6. a: V$^7$    iv$^6$    i    III

STUDENT ANSWER:

1. a: ___    ___    ___

2. a: ___    ___    ___

3. a: ___    ___    ___

4. a: ___    ___    ___    ___

5. a: ___    ___    ___    ___

6. a: ___    ___    ___    ___

238

# SECTION 3B

FOCUS: Mediant

| INSTRUCTOR'S KEY | STUDENT ANSWER |
|---|---|

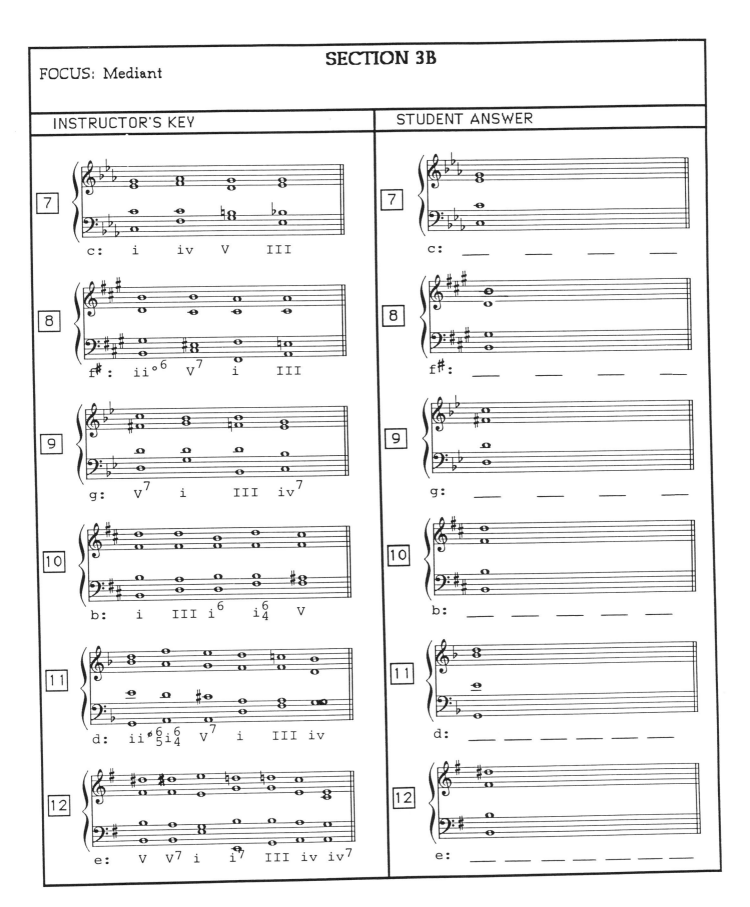

7  c:  i    iv    V    III

7  c: ___  ___  ___  ___

8  f#:  ii°$^6$   V$^7$   i    III

8  f#: ___  ___  ___  ___

9  g:  V$^7$   i    III   iv$^7$

9  g: ___  ___  ___  ___

10  b:  i    III   i$^6$   i$^6_4$   V

10  b: ___  ___  ___  ___  ___

11  d:  ii$^{ø6}_5$i$^6_4$   V$^7$   i    III   iv

11  d: ___  ___  ___  ___  ___

12  e:  V    V$^7$   i    i$^7$   III   iv   iv$^7$

12  e: ___  ___  ___  ___  ___  ___  ___

239

# SECTION 4

FOCUS: P5, d5-- ♩. ♪, ♩. -- 4/4

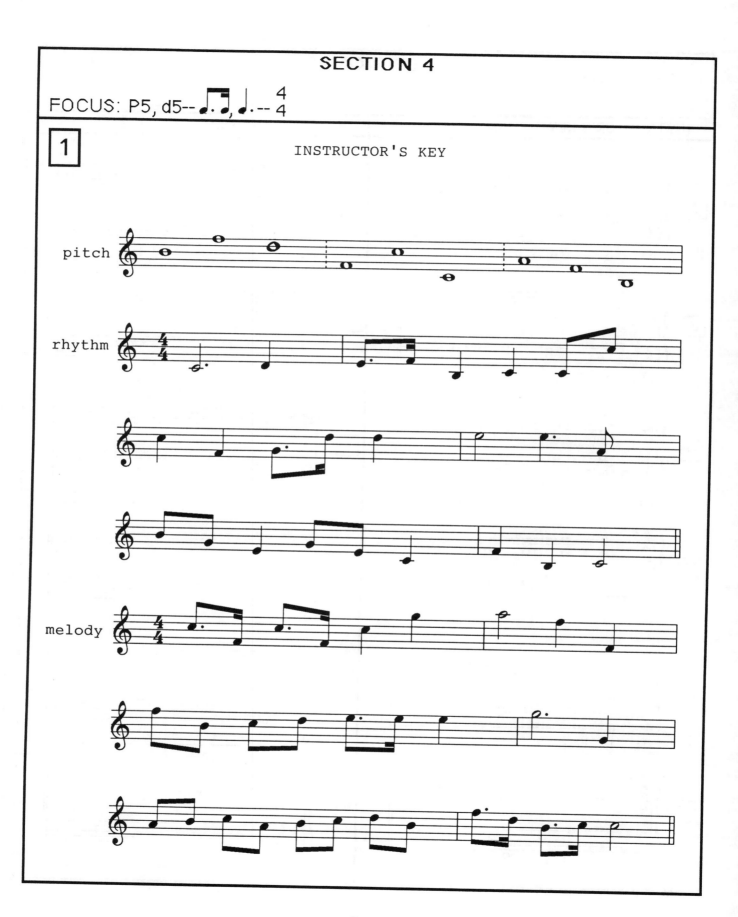

1. INSTRUCTOR'S KEY

pitch

rhythm

melody

# SECTION 4

FOCUS: P5, d5--  𝅘𝅥𝅮. 𝅘𝅥𝅯, 𝅘𝅥. -- 4/4

**1** STUDENT ANSWER

pitch

rhythm

melody

241

# SECTION 4

FOCUS: P5, d5

INSTRUCTOR'S KEY

pitch

rhythm

melody

# SECTION 4

FOCUS: P5, d5 --

243

# SECTION 4

FOCUS: P5, d5-- ♪.♪, ♩. -- 4/4

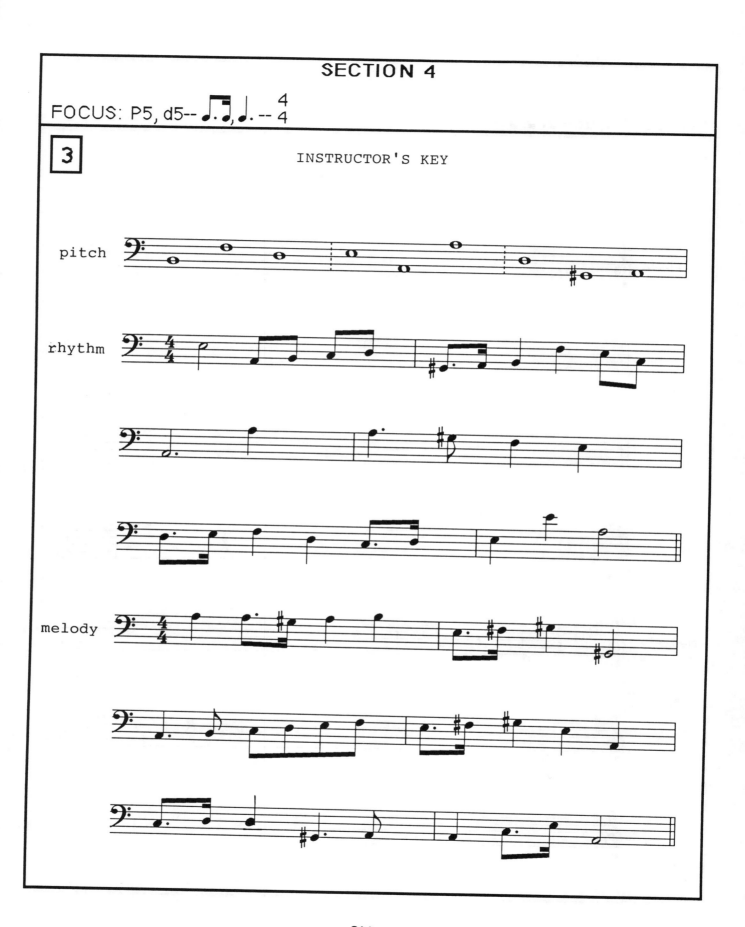

3

INSTRUCTOR'S KEY

pitch

rhythm

melody

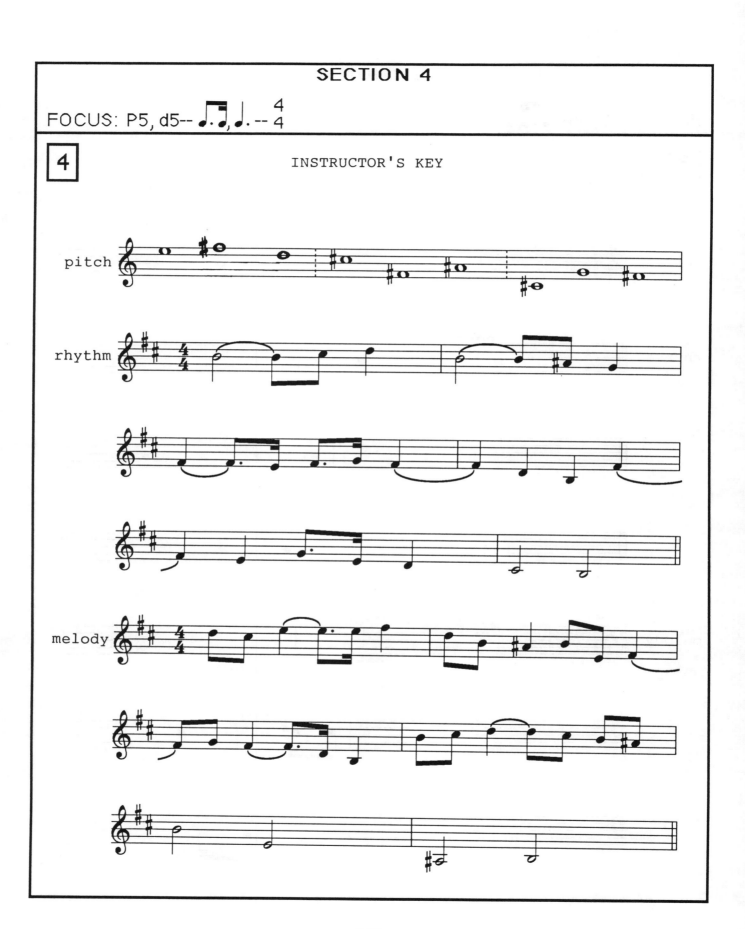

# SECTION 4

FOCUS: P5, d5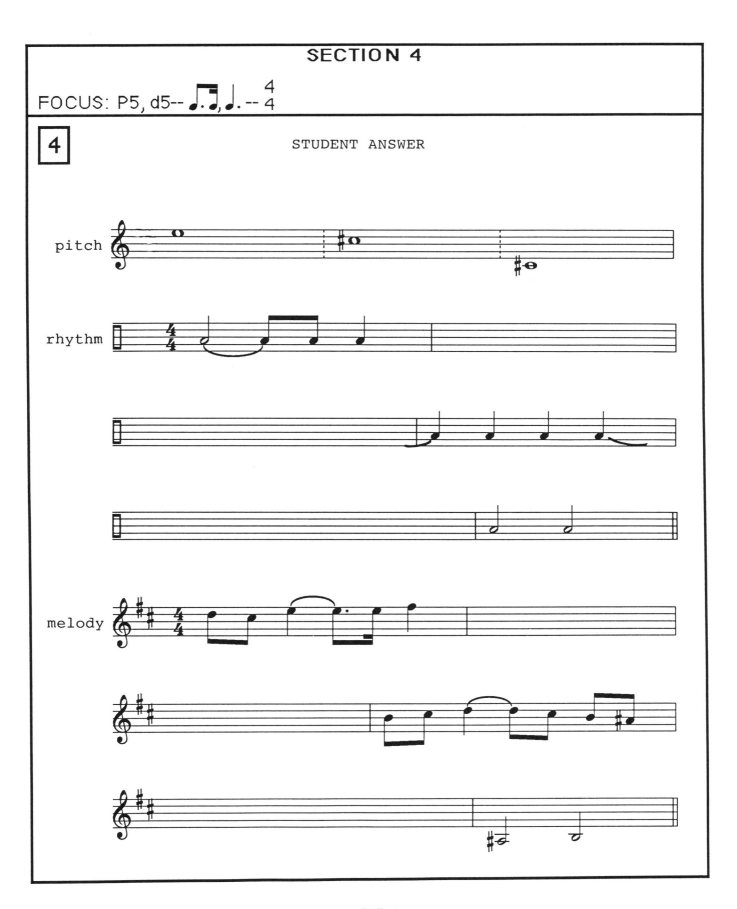

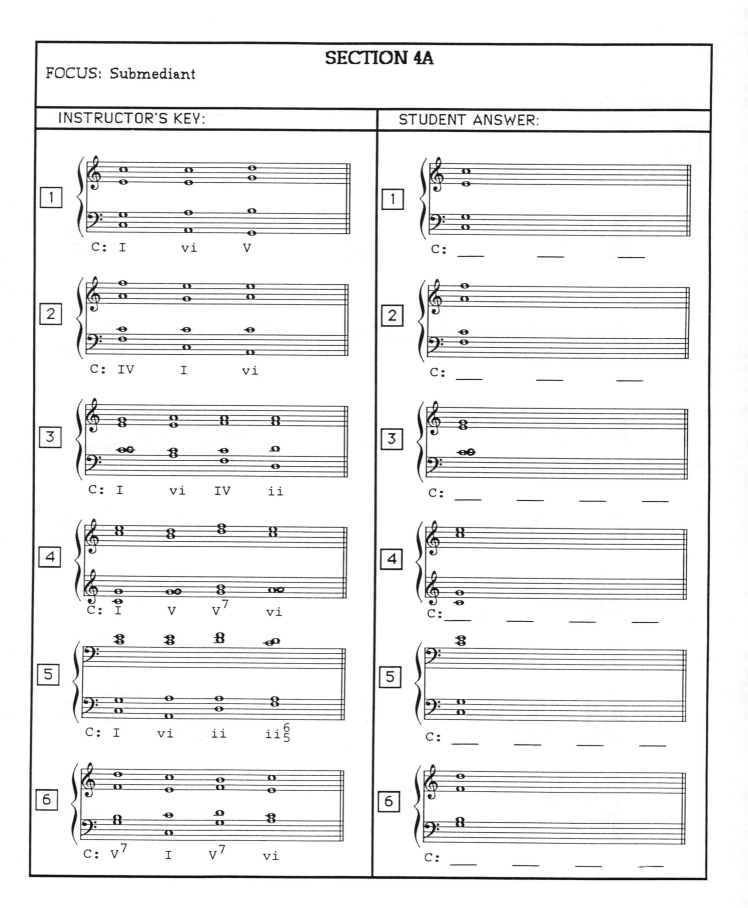

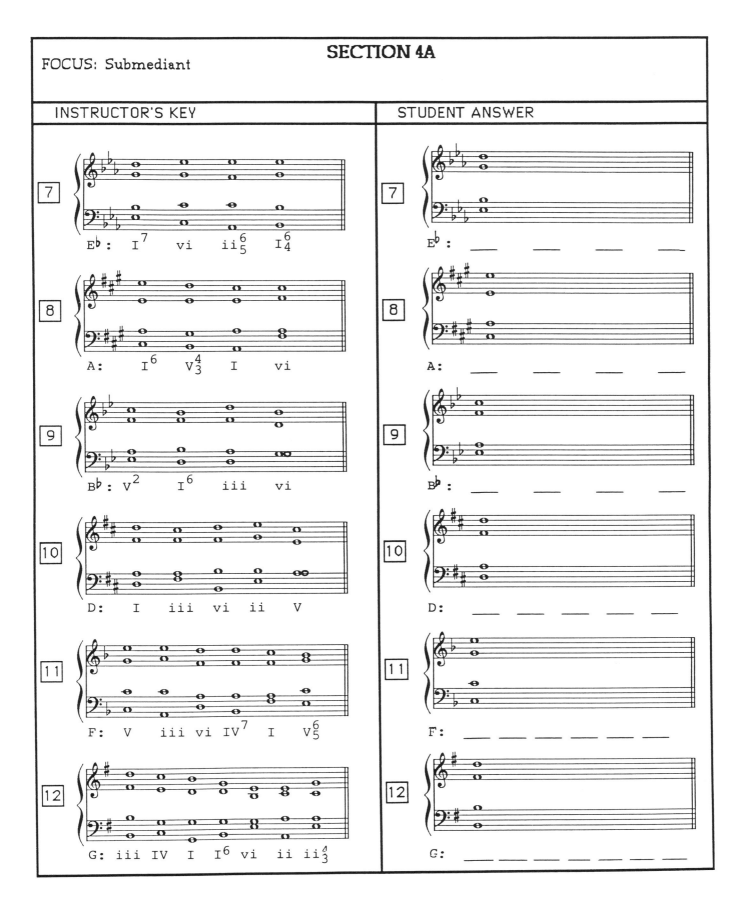

SECTION 4A

FOCUS: Submediant

INSTRUCTOR'S KEY                                  STUDENT ANSWER

7   E♭:  I⁷   vi   ii⁶₅   I⁶₄          7   E♭: ___ ___ ___ ___

8   A:   I⁶   V⁴₃   I   vi             8   A: ___ ___ ___ ___

9   B♭:  V²   I⁶   iii   vi            9   B♭: ___ ___ ___ ___

10  D:   I   iii   vi   ii   V         10  D: ___ ___ ___ ___ ___

11  F:   V   iii  vi  IV⁷  I  V⁶₅      11  F: ___ ___ ___ ___ ___ ___

12  G:  iii  IV  I  I⁶  vi  ii  ii⁴₃   12  G: ___ ___ ___ ___ ___ ___ ___

249

# SECTION 4 B

FOCUS: Submediant

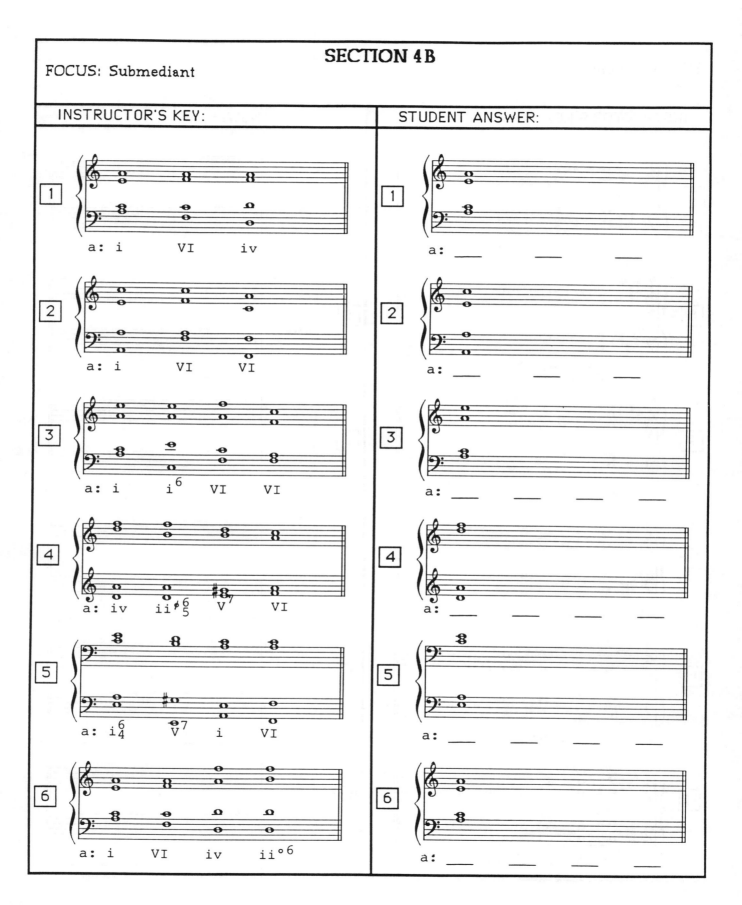

INSTRUCTOR'S KEY:

1. a: i    VI    iv

2. a: i    VI    VI

3. a: i    i⁶    VI    VI

4. a: iv    ii♯⁶₅    V⁷    VI

5. a: i⁶₄    V⁷    i    VI

6. a: i    VI    iv    ii°⁶

STUDENT ANSWER:

1. a: __    __    __

2. a: __    __    __

3. a: __    __    __    __

4. a: __    __    __    __

5. a: __    __    __    __

6. a: __    __    __    __

250

# SECTION 4B

FOCUS: Submediant

| INSTRUCTOR'S KEY | STUDENT ANSWER |
|---|---|

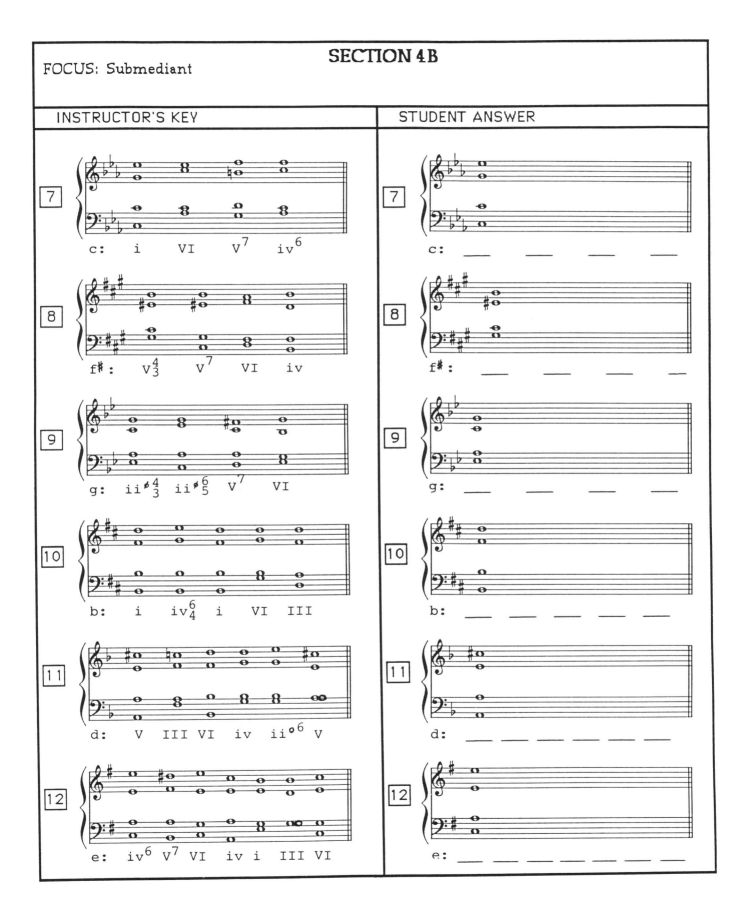

c:  i    VI    V⁷    iv⁶

c: ___  ___  ___  ___

f♯ :  v⁴₃    v⁷    VI    iv

f♯ : ___  ___  ___  ___

g:  ii⌀⁴₃    ii⌀⁶₅    v⁷    VI

g: ___  ___  ___  ___

b:  i    iv⁶₄    i    VI    III

b: ___  ___  ___  ___  ___

d:  V    III   VI    iv    ii°⁶    V

d: ___  ___  ___  ___  ___  ___

e:  iv⁶    v⁷   VI    iv    i    III   VI

e: ___  ___  ___  ___  ___  ___  ___

251

# SECTION 5

FOCUS: P4, A4-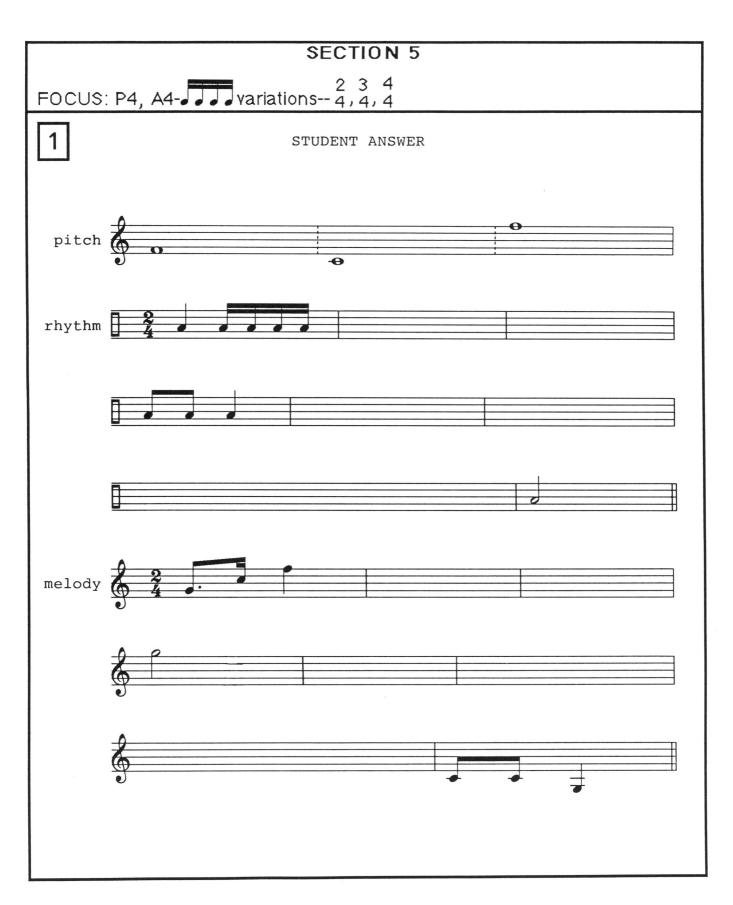variations-- $\frac{2}{4}$, $\frac{3}{4}$, $\frac{4}{4}$

1

STUDENT ANSWER

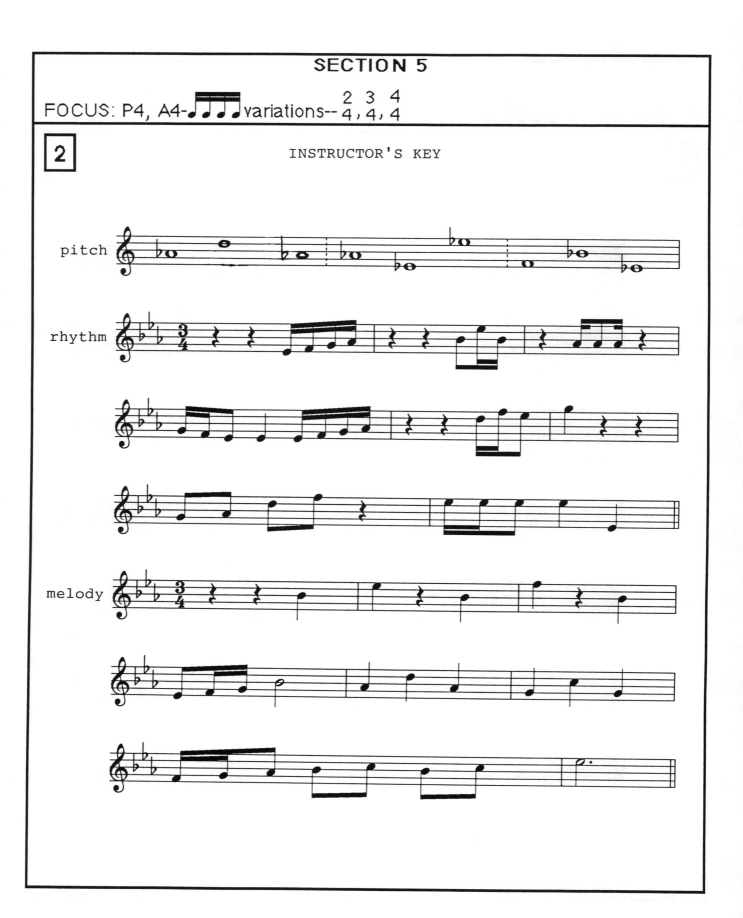

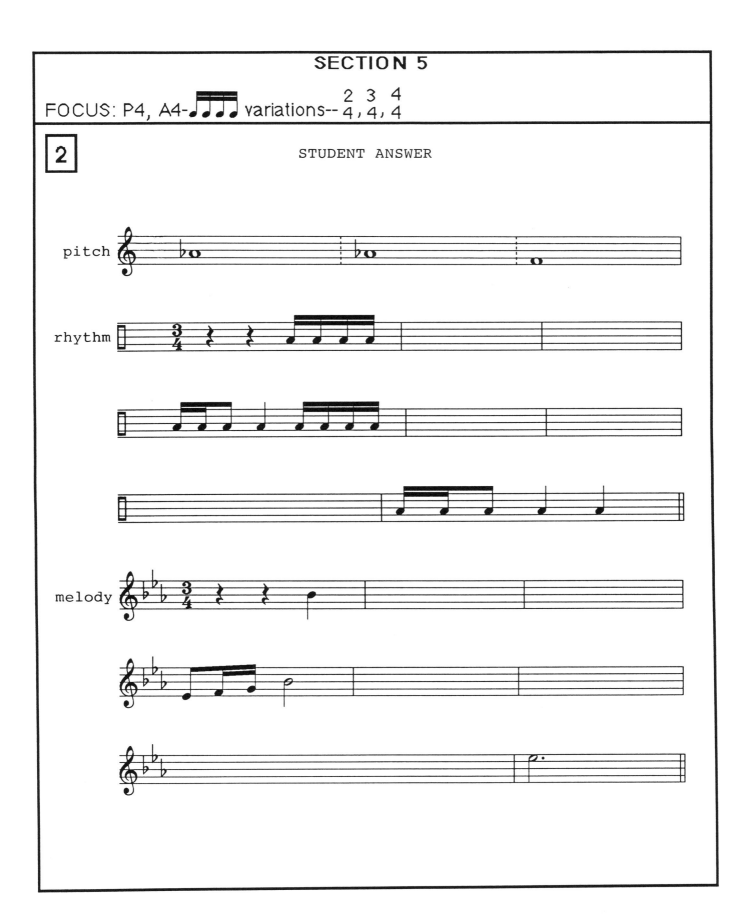

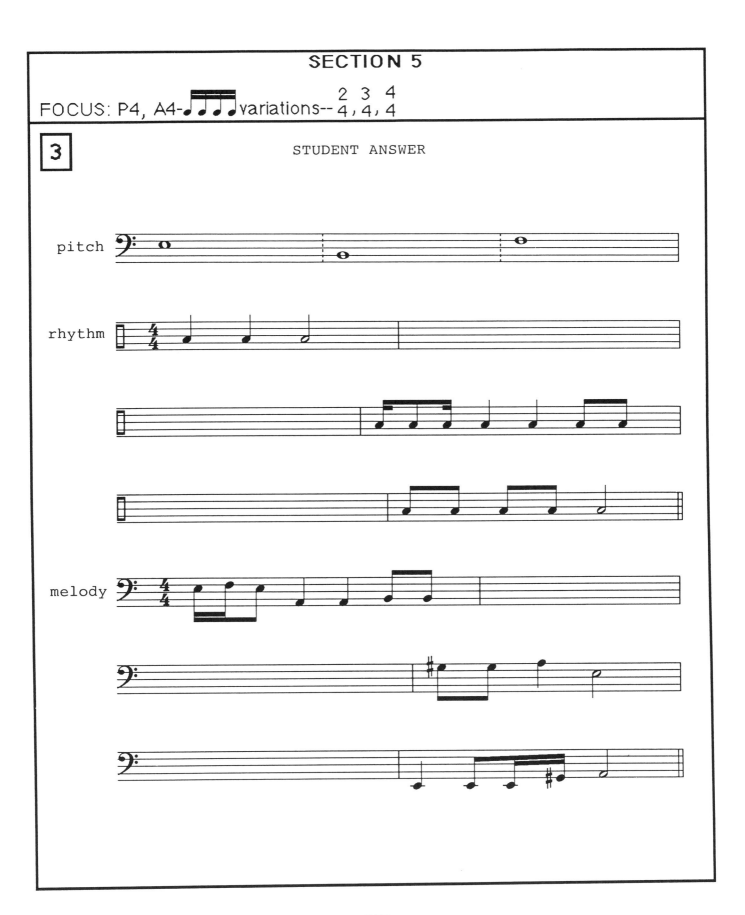

257

# SECTION 5

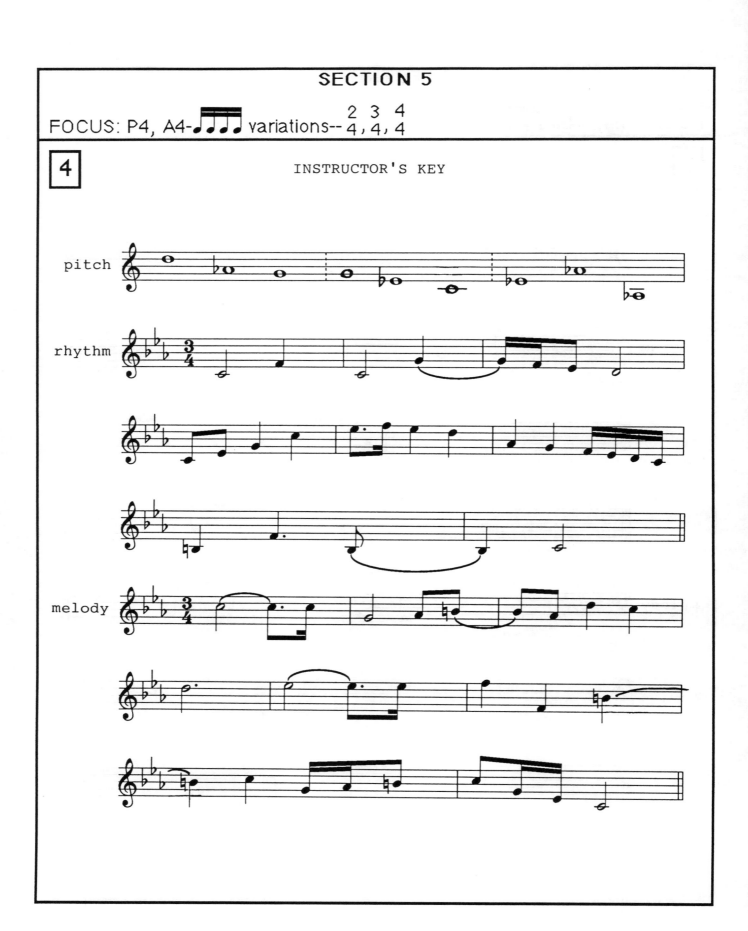

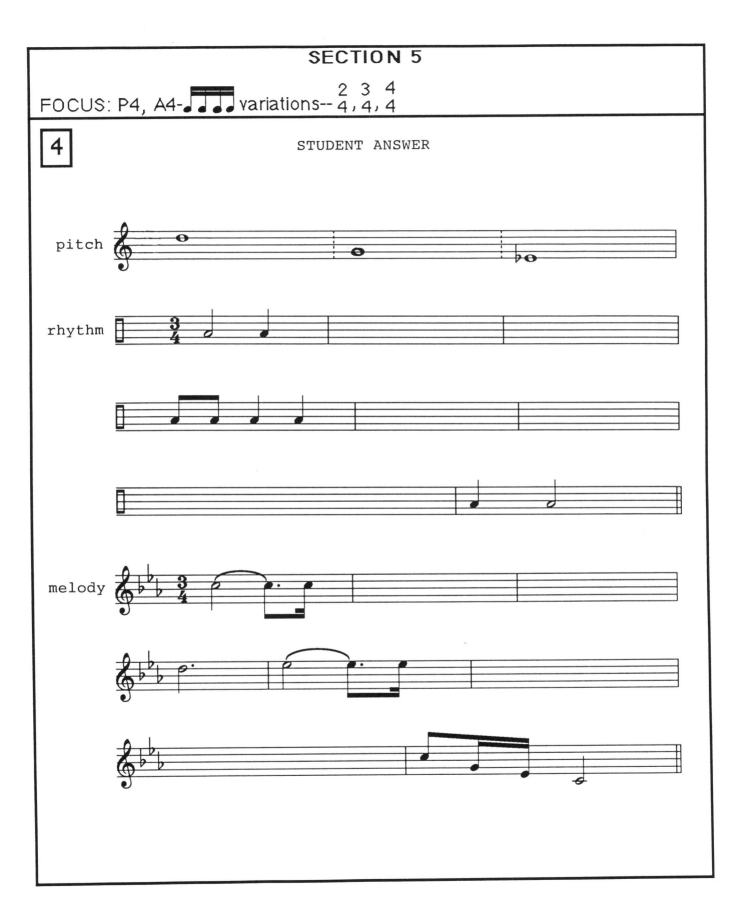

# SECTION 5A

FOCUS: Leading Tone Triad, root
position, first inversion

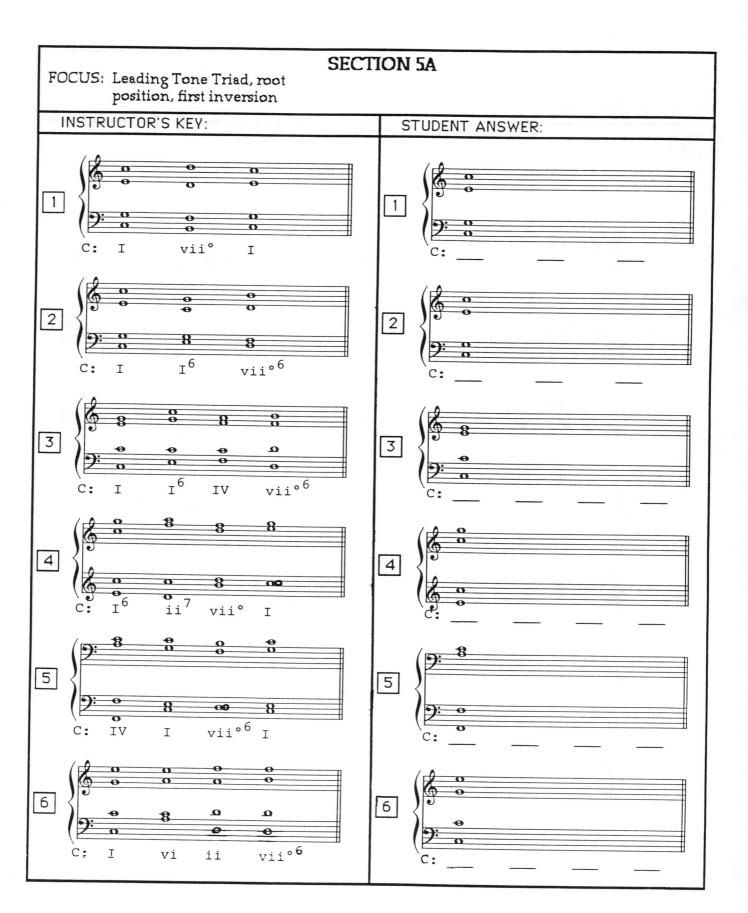

INSTRUCTOR'S KEY:

1   C:  I       vii°    I

2   C:  I       I⁶      vii°⁶

3   C:  I       I⁶      IV      vii°⁶

4   C:  I⁶      ii⁷     vii°    I

5   C:  IV      I       vii°⁶   I

6   C:  I       vi      ii      vii°⁶

STUDENT ANSWER:

1   C:  ___     ___     ___

2   C:  ___     ___     ___

3   C:  ___     ___     ___     ___

4   C:  ___     ___     ___     ___

5   C:  ___     ___     ___     ___

6   C:  ___     ___     ___     ___

260

FOCUS: Leading Tone Triad, root
position, first inversion

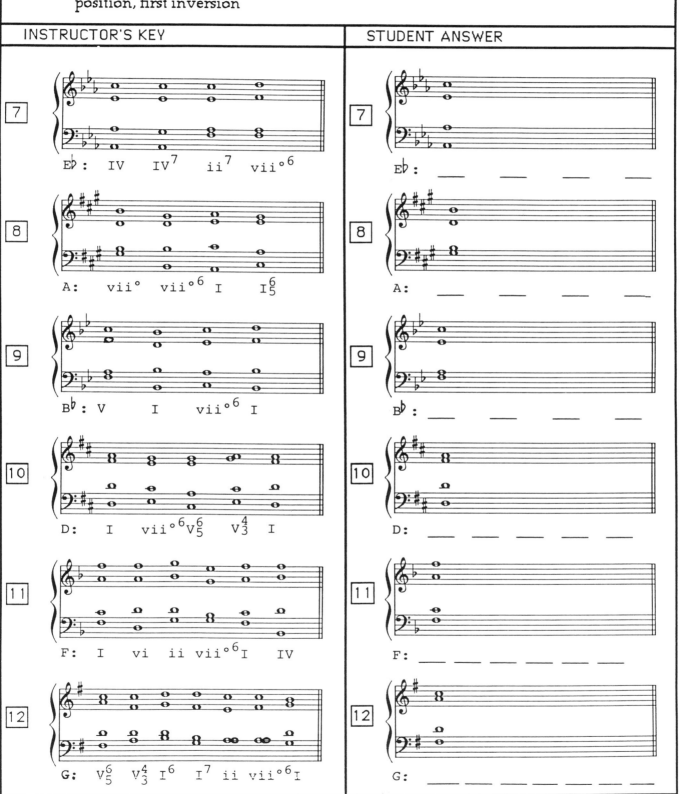

# SECTION 5B

FOCUS: Leading Tone Triad, root
        position, first inversion

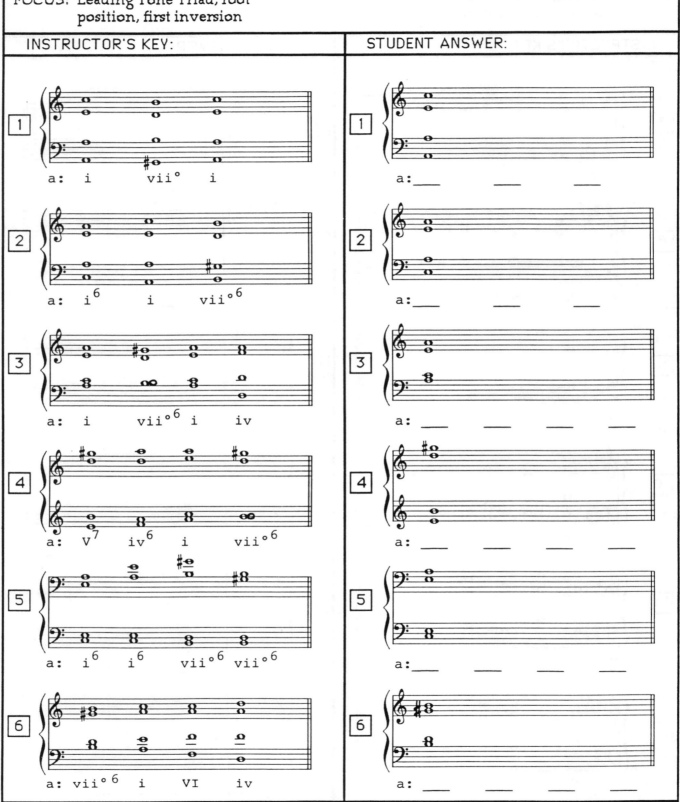

262

# SECTION 5B

FOCUS: Leading Tone Triad, root
position, first inversion

INSTRUCTOR'S KEY

STUDENT ANSWER

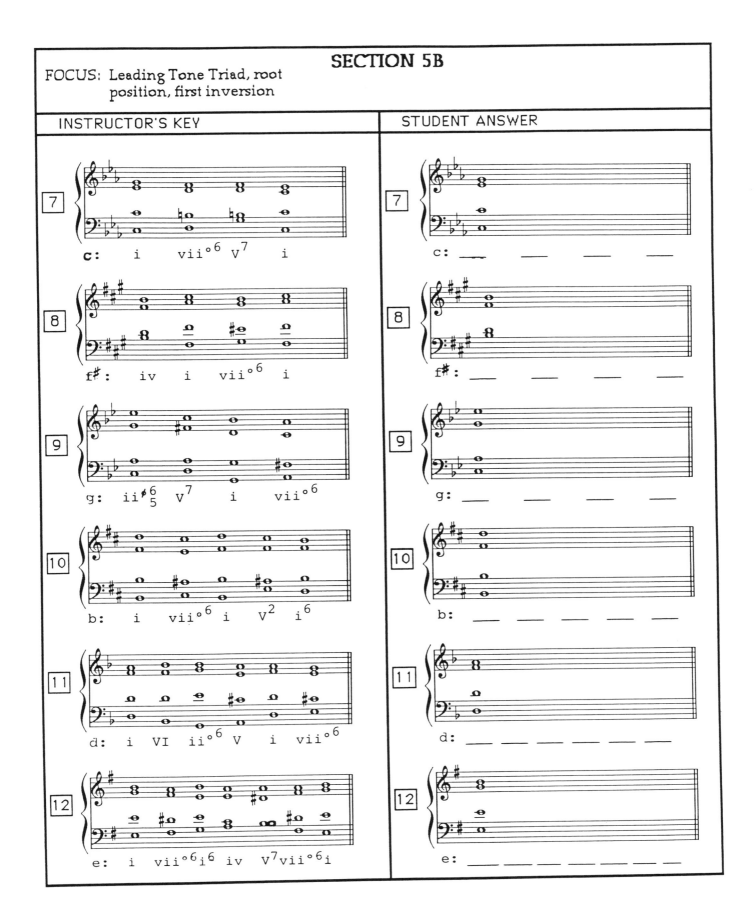

7  c:    i    vii°⁶  V⁷    i

7  c: ___ ___ ___ ___

8  f#:   iv    i   vii°⁶   i

8  f# : ___ ___ ___ ___

9  g:  ii⌀⁶₅  V⁷    i   vii°⁶

9  g: ___ ___ ___ ___

10  b:   i  vii°⁶  i   V²  i⁶

10  b: ___ ___ ___ ___ ___

11  d:  i  VI  ii°⁶  V   i  vii°⁶

11  d: ___ ___ ___ ___ ___ ___

12  e:  i  vii°⁶ i⁶  iv  V⁷ vii°⁶ i

12  e: ___ ___ ___ ___ ___ ___ ___

263

# SECTION 6

FOCUS: m6-- ♩., ♫♫, ♩ ♪ - 3/8

1  INSTRUCTOR'S KEY

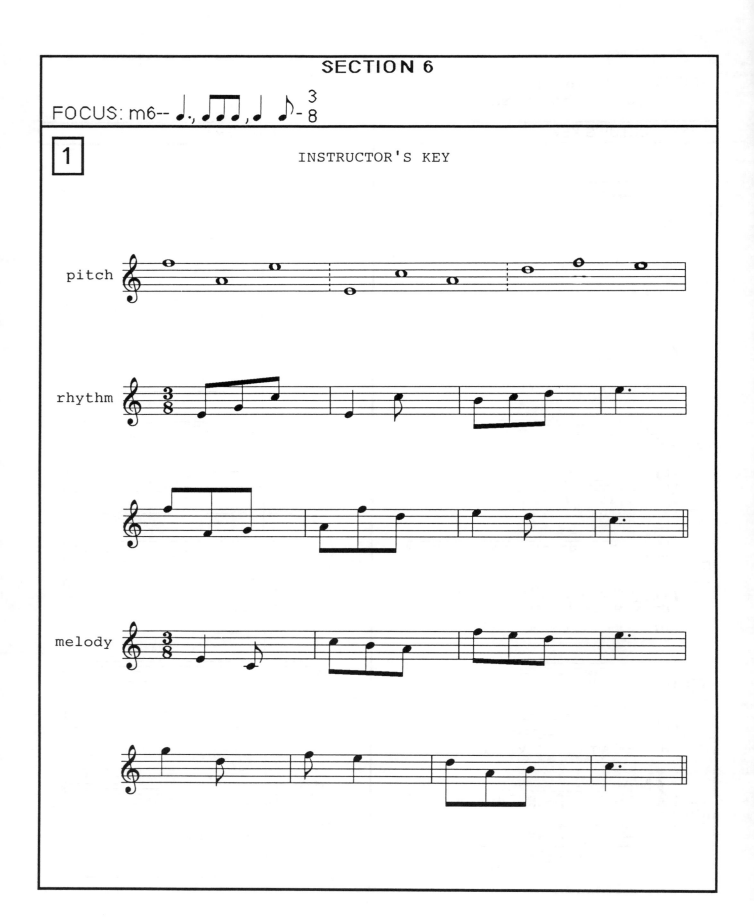

# SECTION 6

FOCUS: m6-- ♩. , ♫♪ , ♩ ♪ -- 3/8

1

STUDENT ANSWER

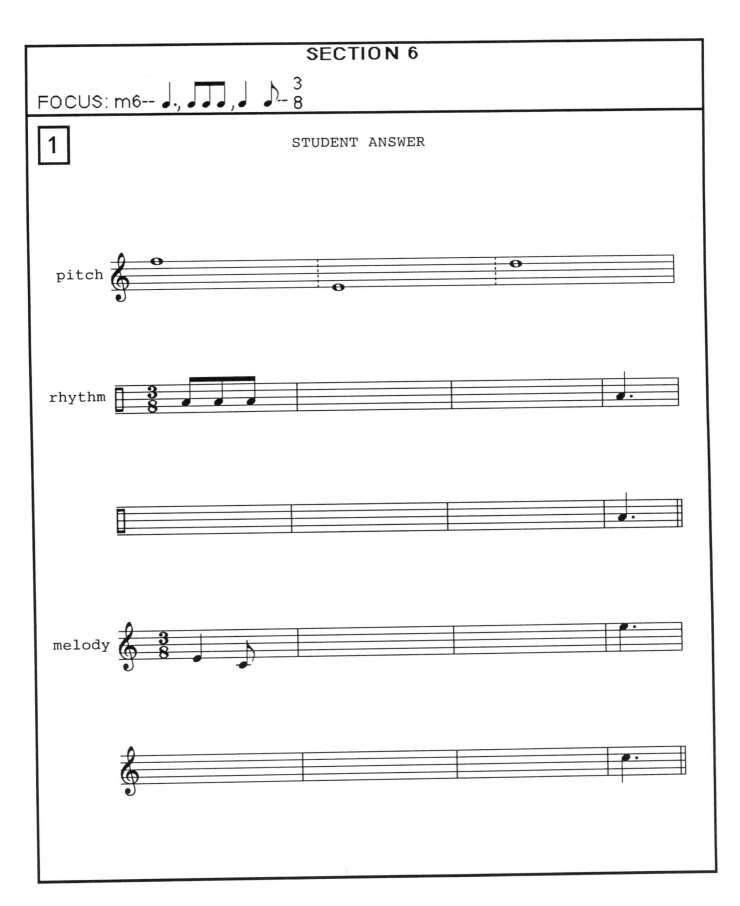

# SECTION 6

FOCUS: m6-- ♩., ♫♫, ♩ ♪- 3/8

## 2            INSTRUCTOR'S KEY

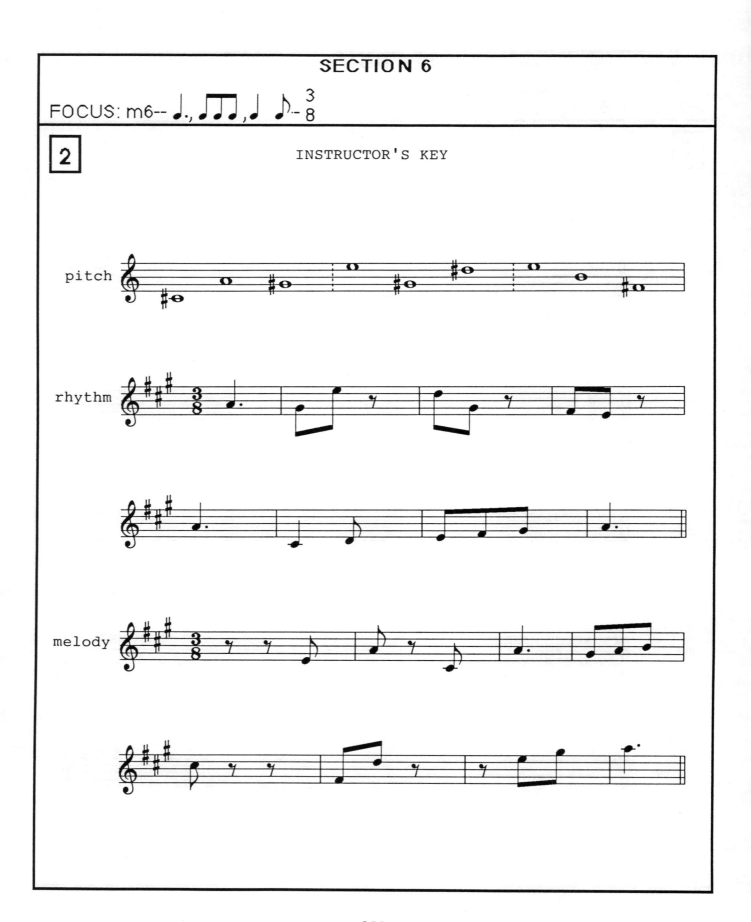

FOCUS: m6-- ♩. , ♫♩ , ♩ ♪ - 3/8

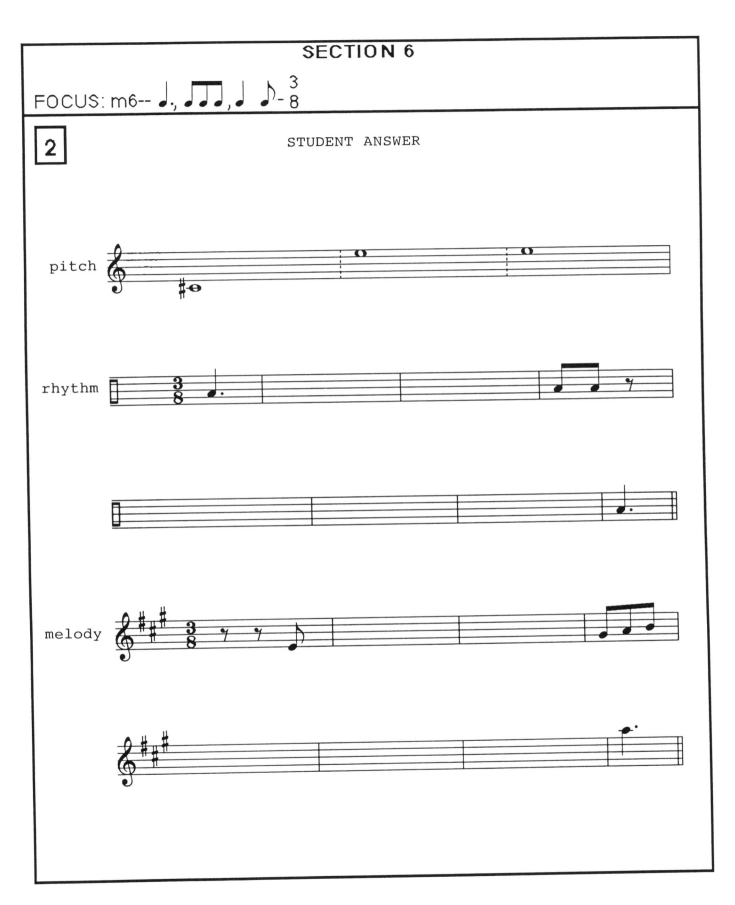

STUDENT ANSWER

pitch

rhythm

melody

FOCUS: m6-- ♩., ♩♩♩, ♩ ♪- 3/8

3  INSTRUCTOR'S KEY

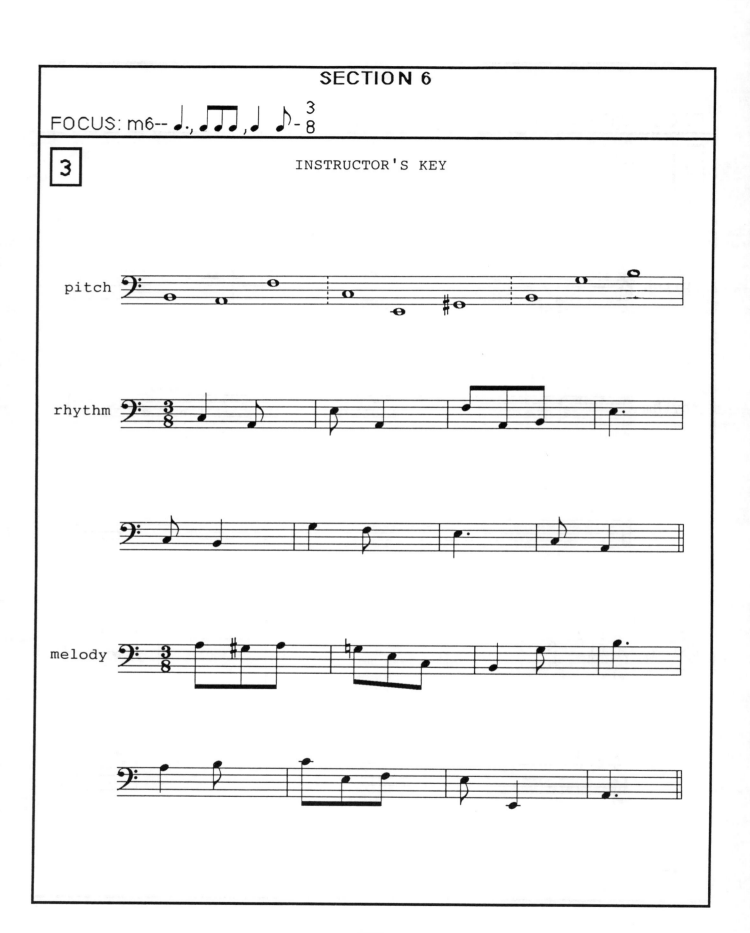

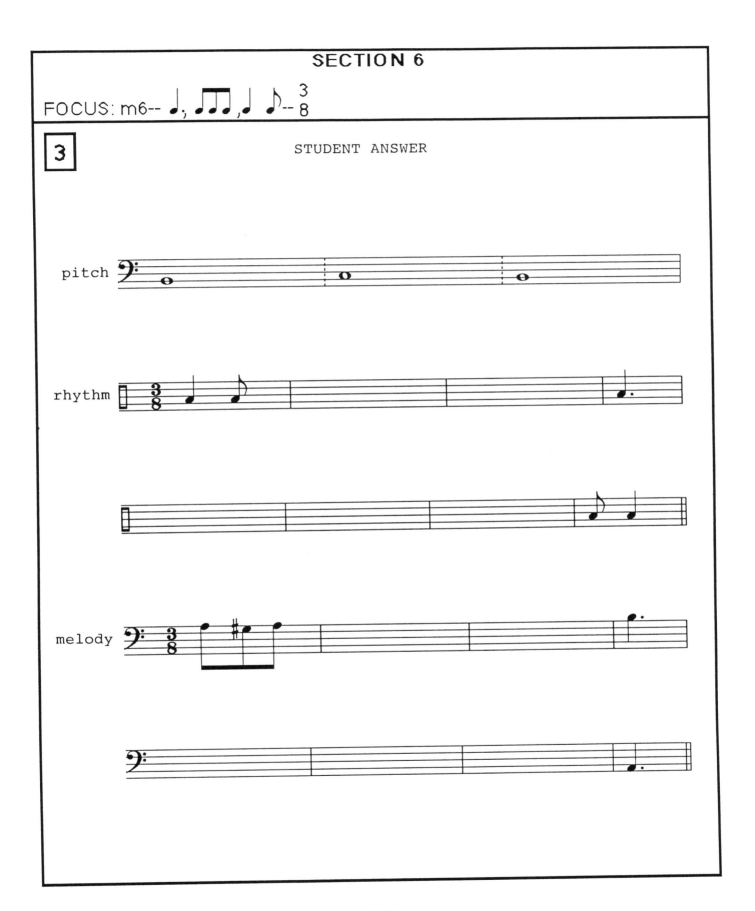

# SECTION 6

FOCUS: m6-- ♩., ♫♫, ♩ ♪ - 3/8

**4** INSTRUCTOR'S KEY

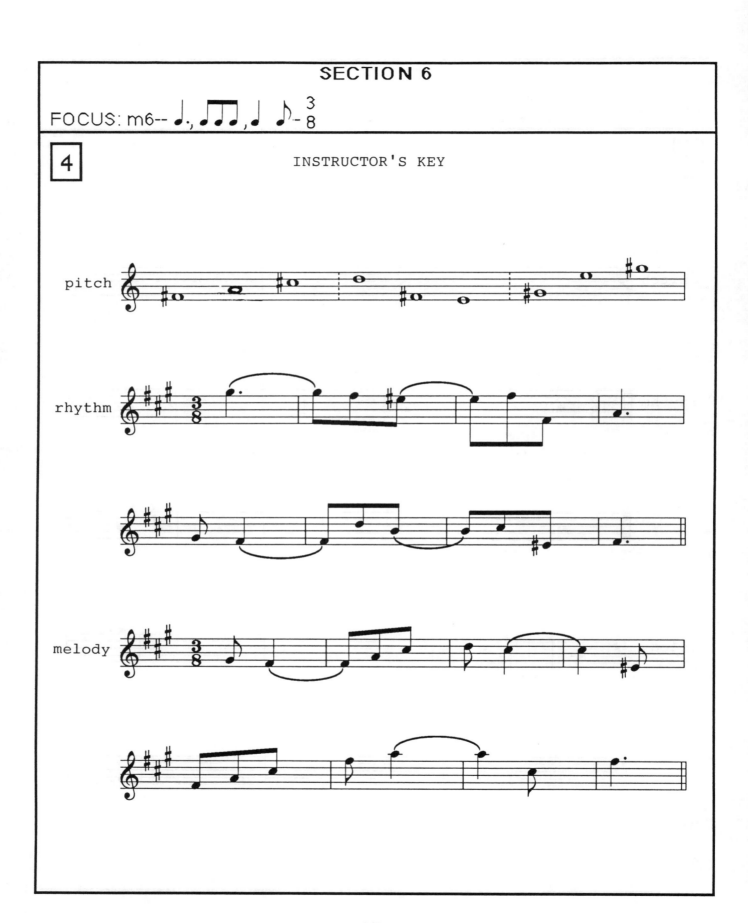

# SECTION 6

FOCUS: m6-- ♩., ♫♪ , ♩ ♪ -- 3/8

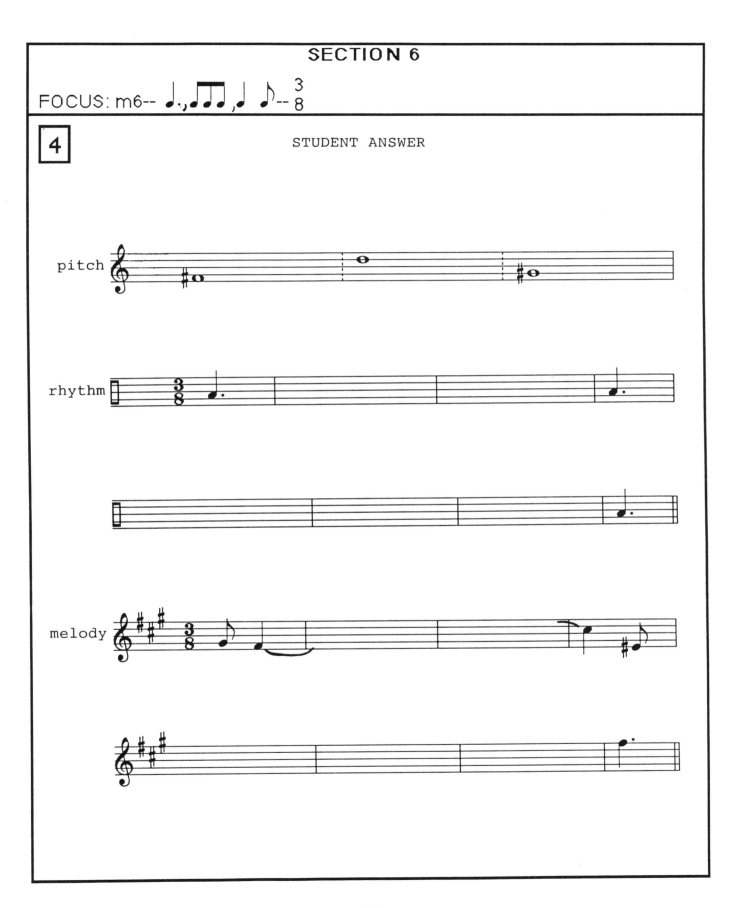

STUDENT ANSWER

pitch

rhythm

melody

271

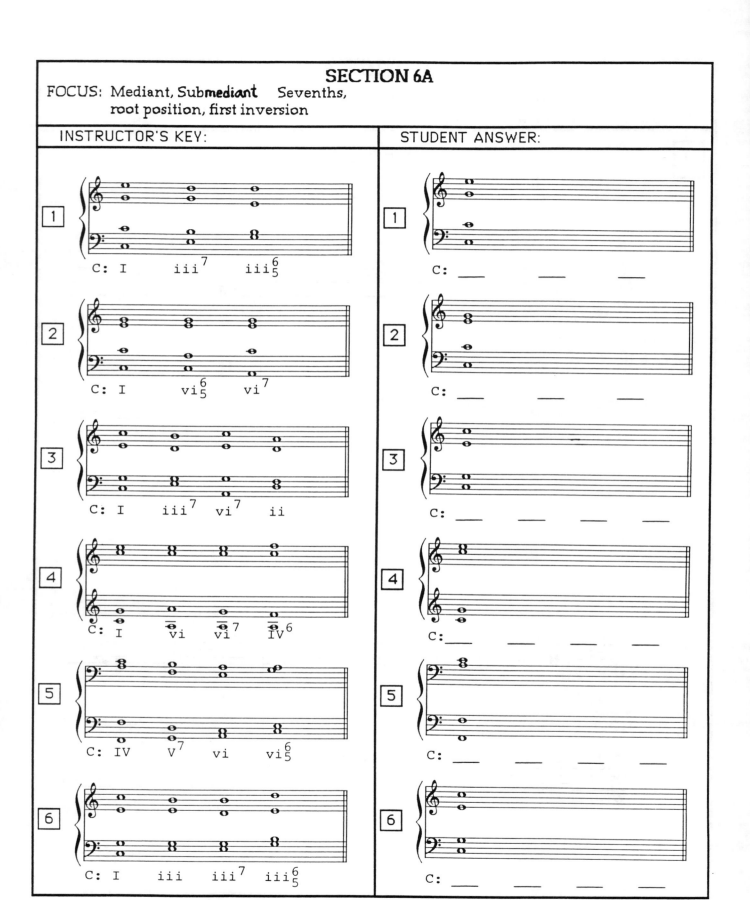

FOCUS: Mediant, Submediant Sevenths,
root position, first inversion

| INSTRUCTOR'S KEY | STUDENT ANSWER |
|---|---|

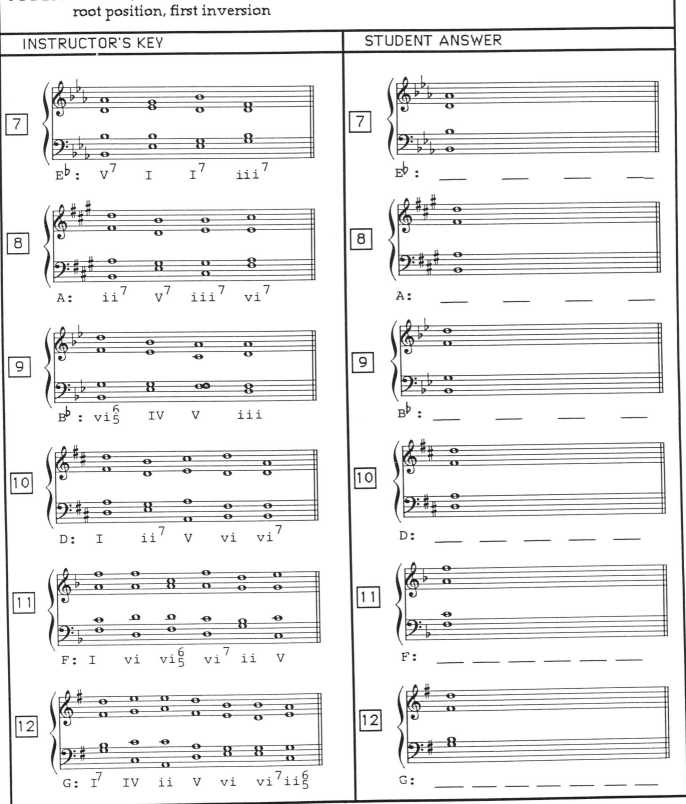

7  E♭:  V⁷  I  I⁷  iii⁷

8  A:  ii⁷  V⁷  iii⁷  vi⁷

9  B♭:  vi⁶₅  IV  V  iii

10  D:  I  ii⁷  V  vi  vi⁷

11  F:  I  vi  vi⁶₅  vi⁷  ii  V

12  G:  I⁷  IV  ii  V  vi  vi⁷ii⁶₅

7  E♭: ___ ___ ___ ___

8  A: ___ ___ ___ ___

9  B♭: ___ ___ ___ ___

10  D: ___ ___ ___ ___ ___

11  F: ___ ___ ___ ___ ___ ___

12  G: ___ ___ ___ ___ ___ ___ ___

# SECTION 6B

FOCUS: Mediant, Submediant Sevenths,
root position, first inversion

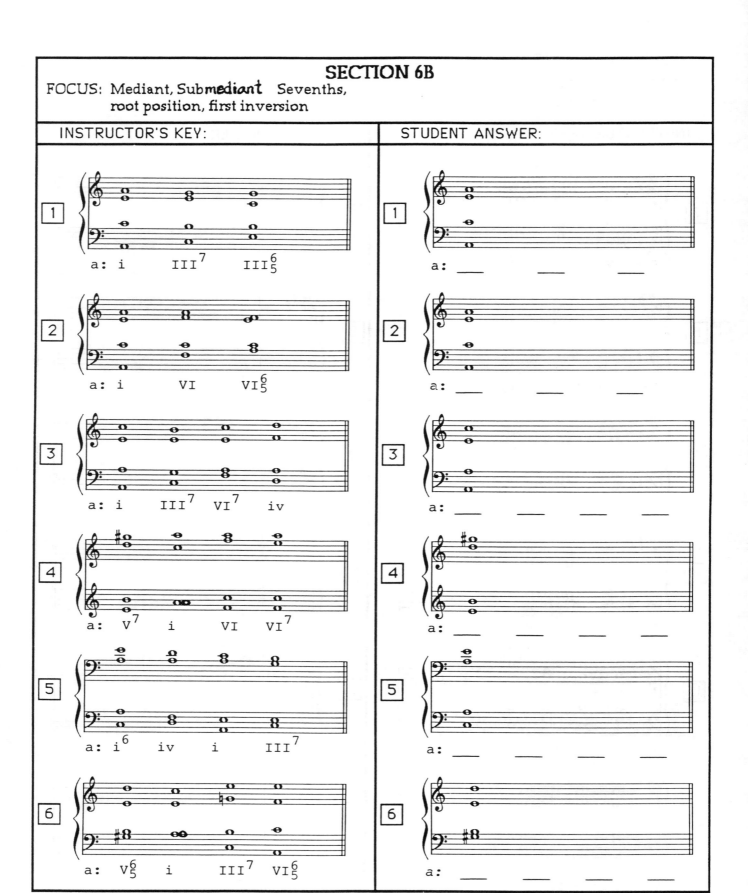

INSTRUCTOR'S KEY:

1. a: i    III⁷    III⁶₅

2. a: i    VI    VI⁶₅

3. a: i    III⁷    VI⁷    iv

4. a: V⁷    i    VI    VI⁷

5. a: i⁶    iv    i    III⁷

6. a: V⁶₅    i    III⁷    VI⁶₅

STUDENT ANSWER:

1. a: ___  ___  ___

2. a: ___  ___  ___

3. a: ___  ___  ___  ___

4. a: ___  ___  ___  ___

5. a: ___  ___  ___  ___

6. a: ___  ___  ___  ___

# SECTION 6B

FOCUS: Mediant, Submediant Sevenths,
root position, first inversion

| INSTRUCTOR'S KEY | STUDENT ANSWER |
|---|---|

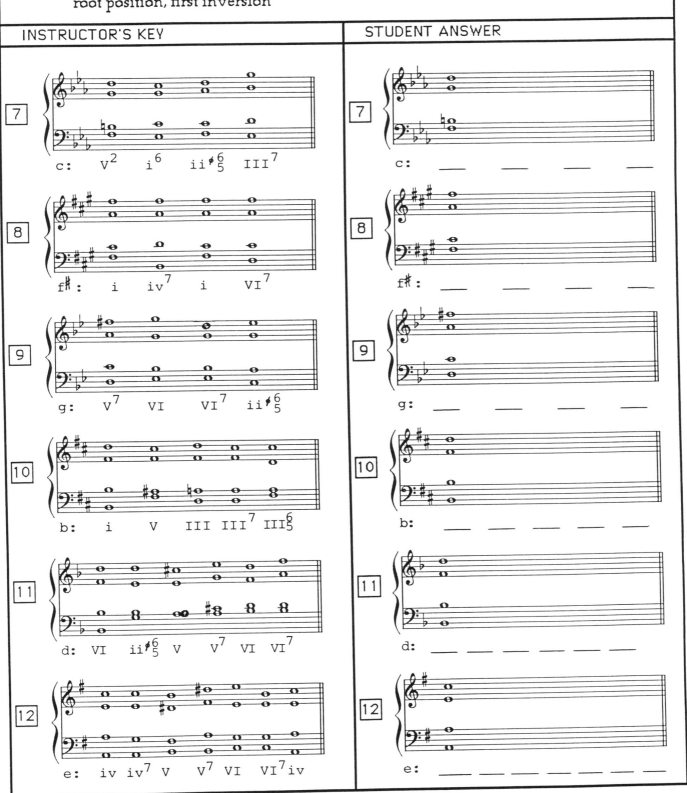

7  c:  V² i⁶ ii∅⁶₅ III⁷

7  c: ___ ___ ___ ___

8  f♯: i iv⁷ i VI⁷

8  f♯: ___ ___ ___ ___

9  g: V⁷ VI VI⁷ ii∅⁶₅

9  g: ___ ___ ___ ___

10  b: i V III III⁷ III⁶₅

10  b: ___ ___ ___ ___ ___

11  d: VI ii∅⁶₅ V V⁷ VI VI⁷

11  d: ___ ___ ___ ___ ___ ___

12  e: iv iv⁷ V V⁷ VI VI⁷ iv

12  e: ___ ___ ___ ___ ___ ___ ___

# SECTION 7

FOCUS: M6-- ♩.♫ variations-- $\frac{3}{8}, \frac{6}{8}$

1  INSTRUCTOR'S KEY

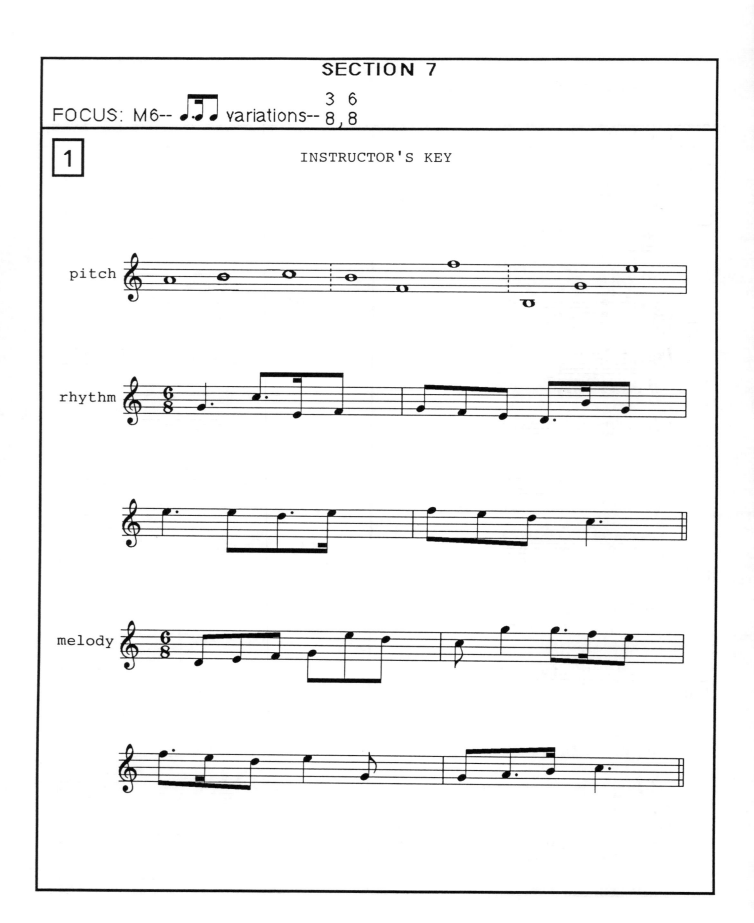

# SECTION 7

FOCUS: M6-- ♪♫♪ variations-- $\frac{3}{8}$, $\frac{6}{8}$

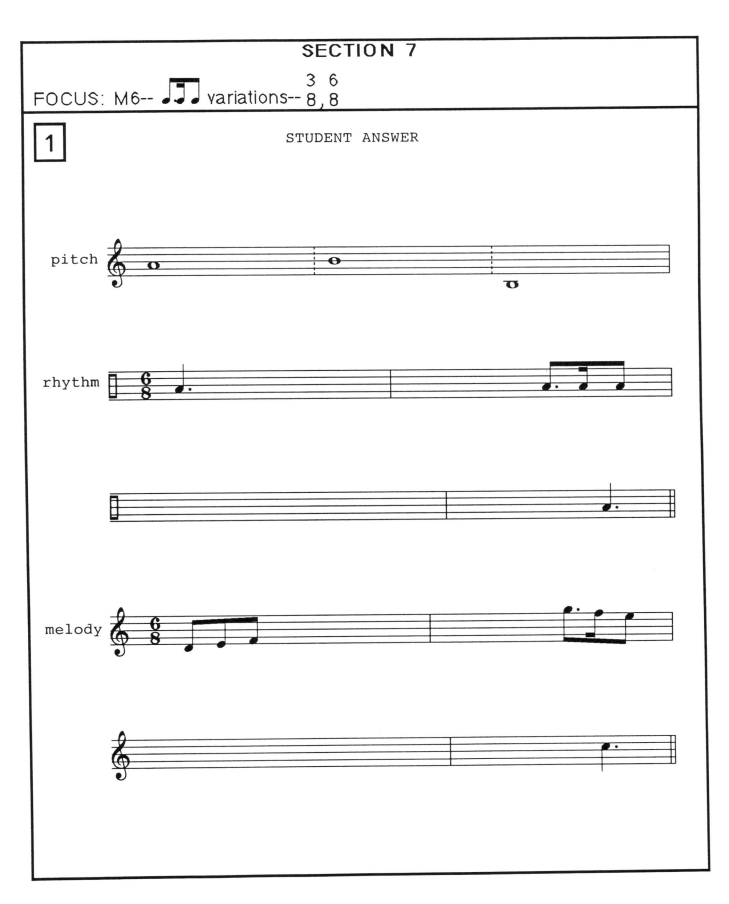

1  STUDENT ANSWER

pitch

rhythm

melody

# SECTION 7

FOCUS: M6-- ♩♫♩ variations-- $\frac{3}{8}, \frac{6}{8}$

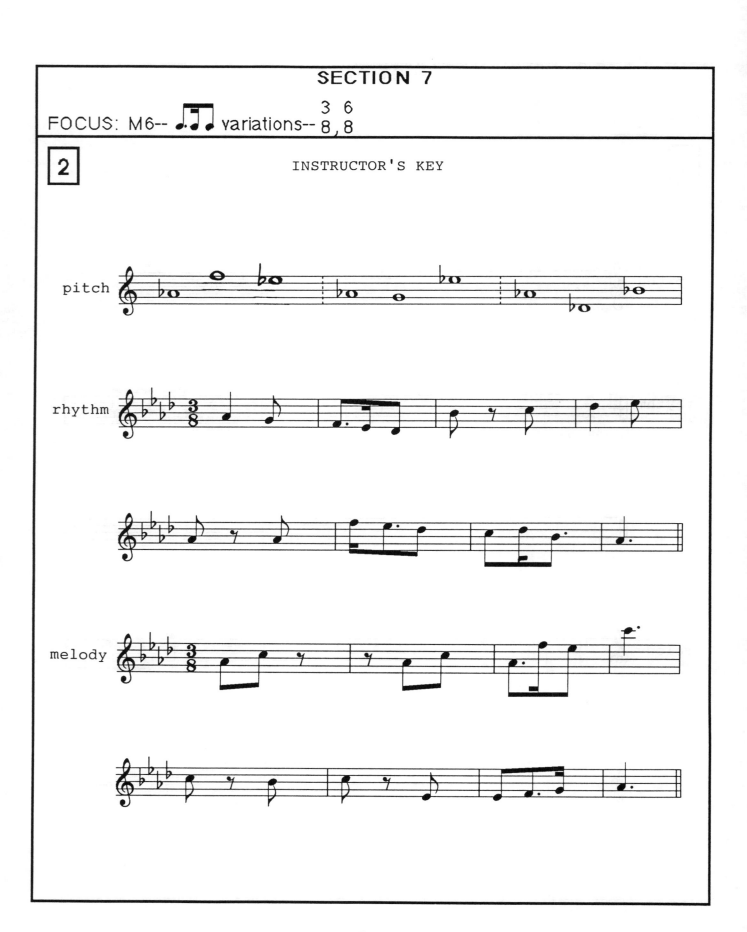

2

INSTRUCTOR'S KEY

pitch

rhythm

melody

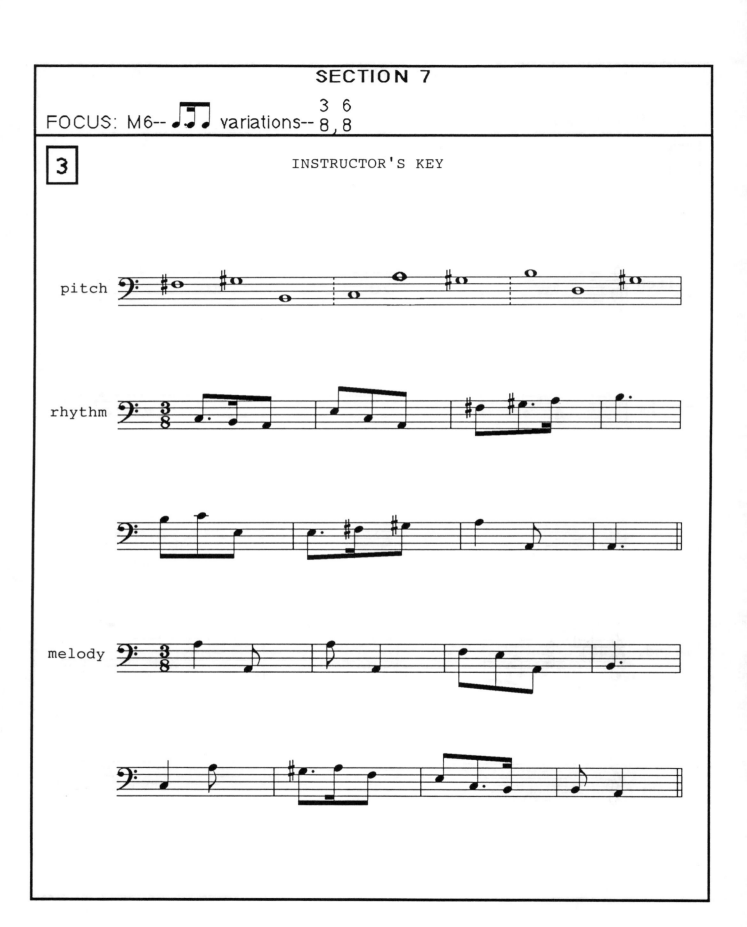

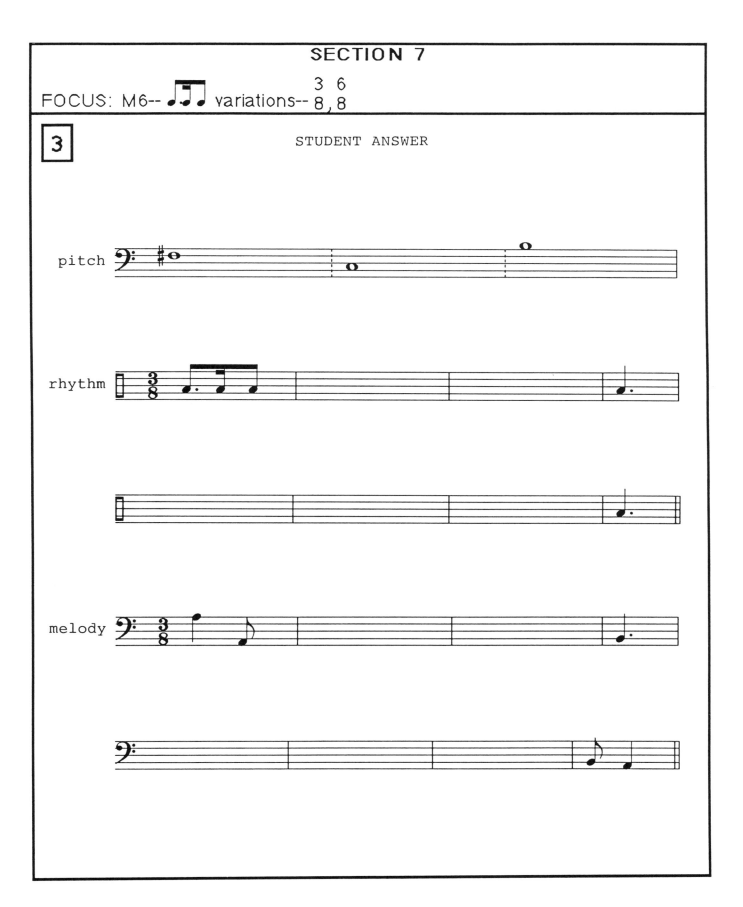

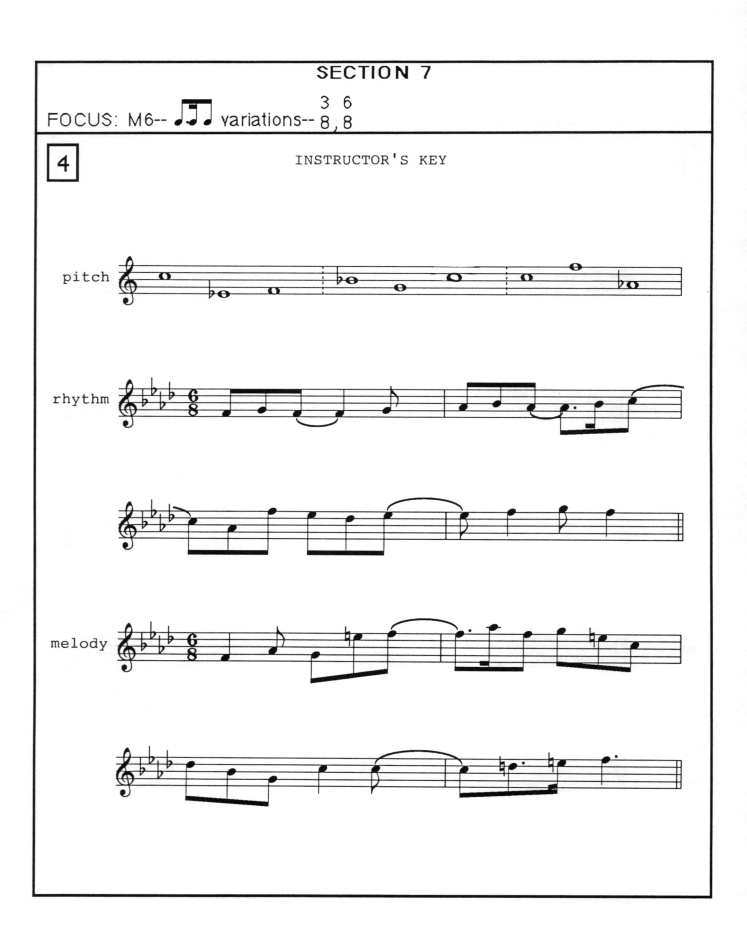

# SECTION 7

FOCUS: M6-- 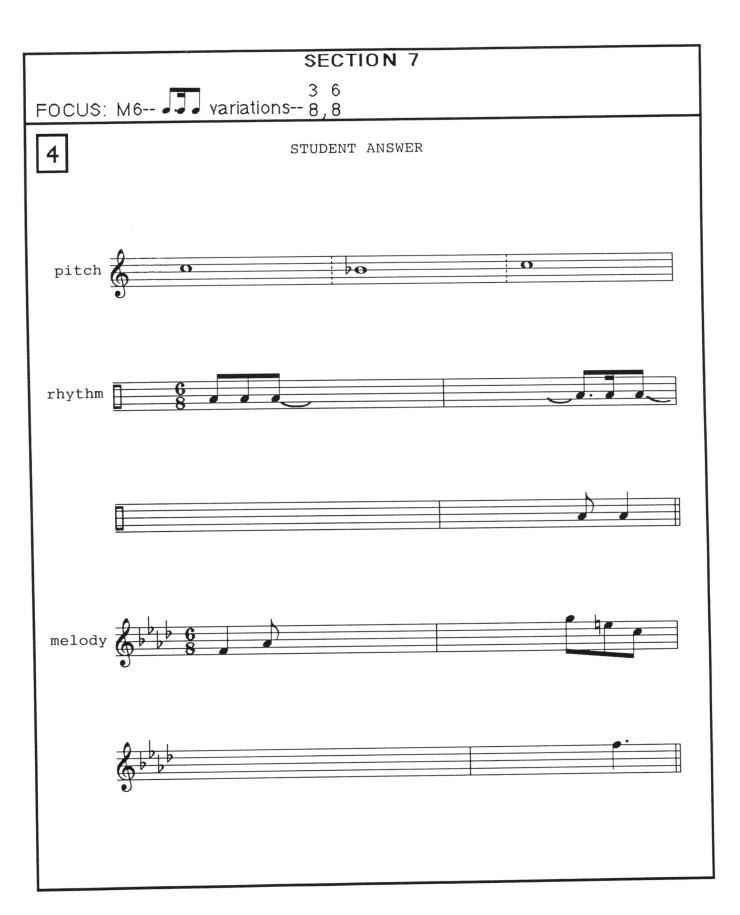 variations-- $\frac{3}{8}, \frac{6}{8}$

STUDENT ANSWER

# SECTION 7A

**FOCUS:** Borrowed Mediant,
Submediant, Subtonic

INSTRUCTOR'S KEY:

STUDENT ANSWER:

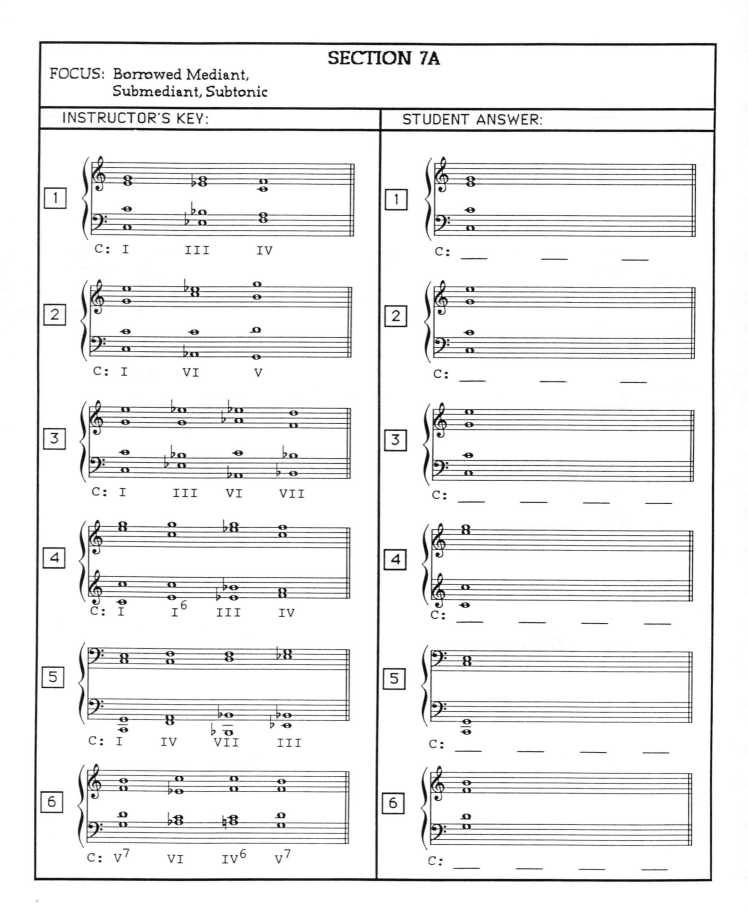

# SECTION 7A

FOCUS: Borrowed Mediant,
Submediant, Subtonic

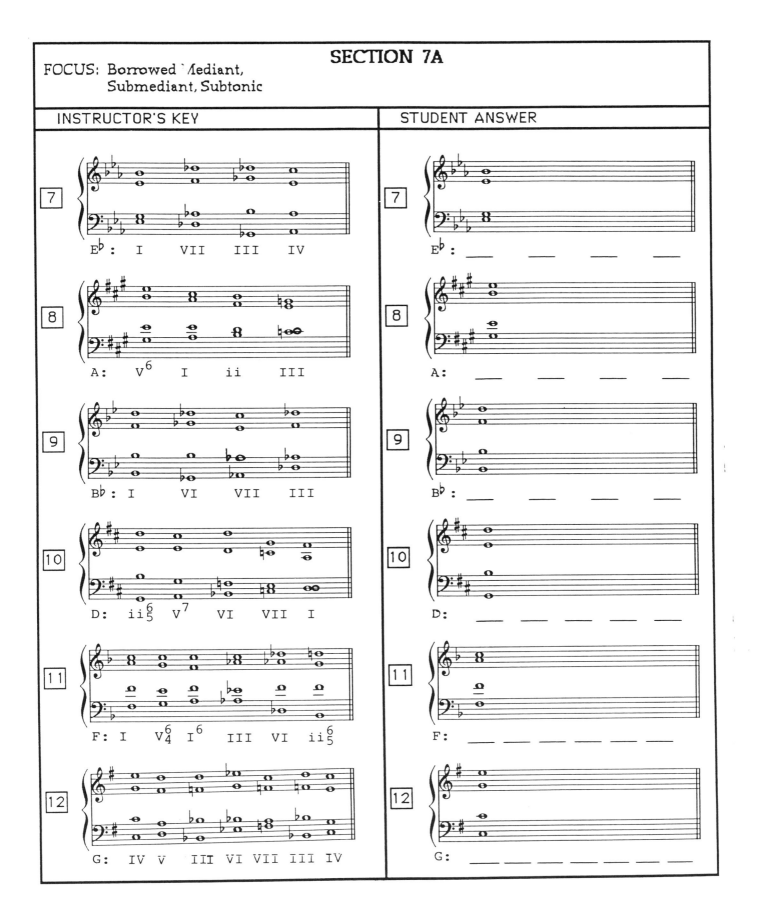

# SECTION 7B

FOCUS: Borrowed Submediant,
Subtonic, and Tonic

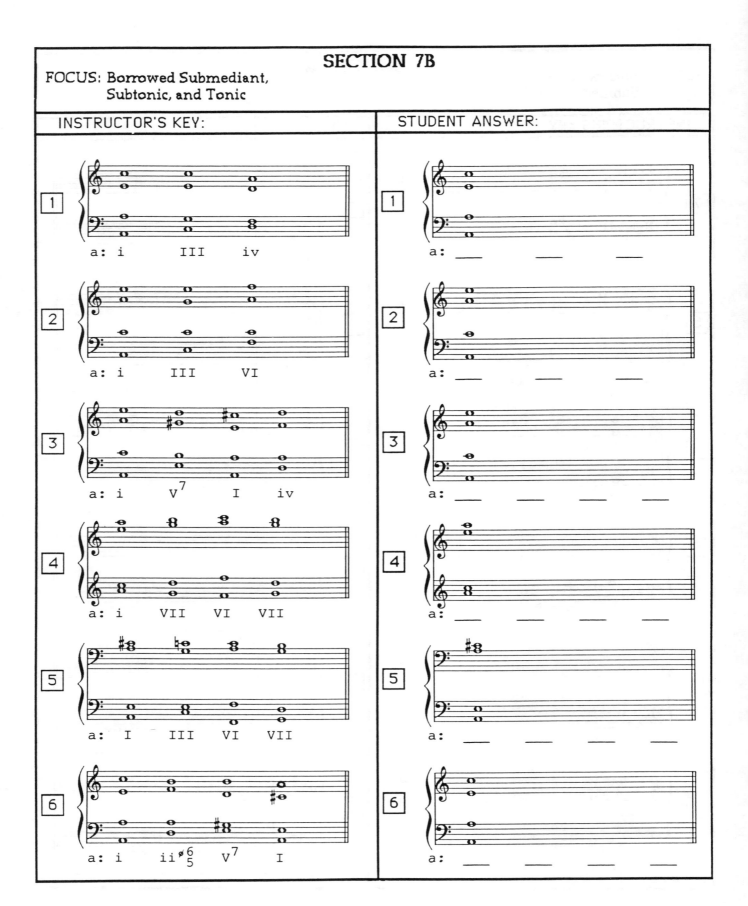

INSTRUCTOR'S KEY:

1. a: i III iv
2. a: i III VI
3. a: i V⁷ I iv
4. a: i VII VI VII
5. a: I III VI VII
6. a: i ii°⁶₅ V⁷ I

STUDENT ANSWER:

1. a: ___ ___ ___
2. a: ___ ___ ___
3. a: ___ ___ ___
4. a: ___ ___ ___ ___
5. a: ___ ___ ___ ___
6. a: ___ ___ ___ ___

# SECTION 7B

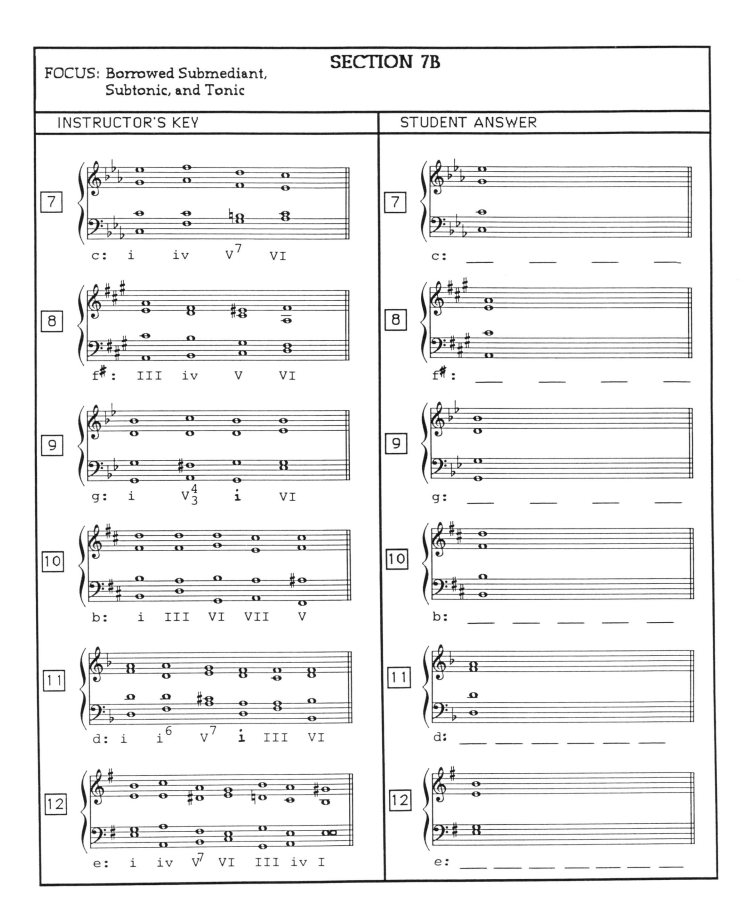

287

FOCUS: m7-- ♪♪♪♪ variations-- $\frac{3}{8}$, $\frac{6}{8}$

1

INSTRUCTOR'S KEY

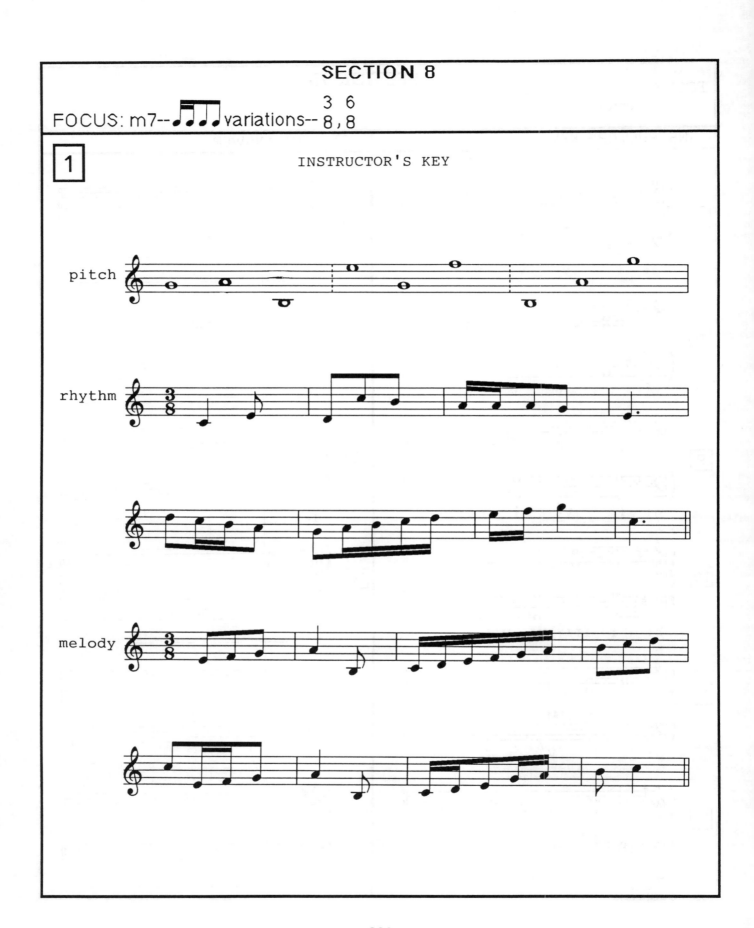

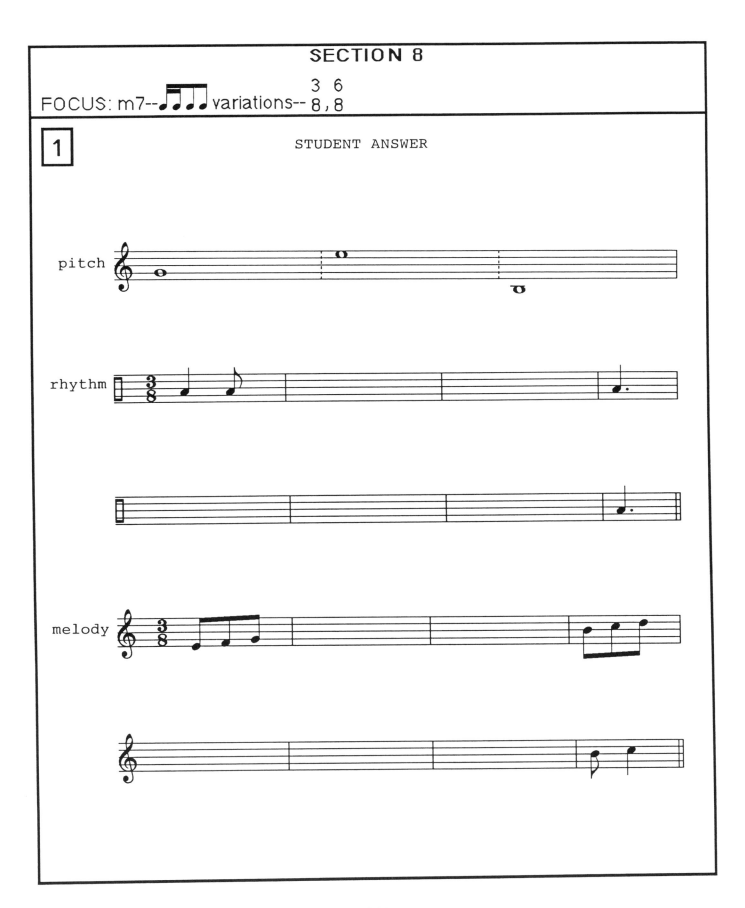

# SECTION 8

FOCUS: m7-- ♫♫ variations-- $\frac{3}{8}$, $\frac{6}{8}$

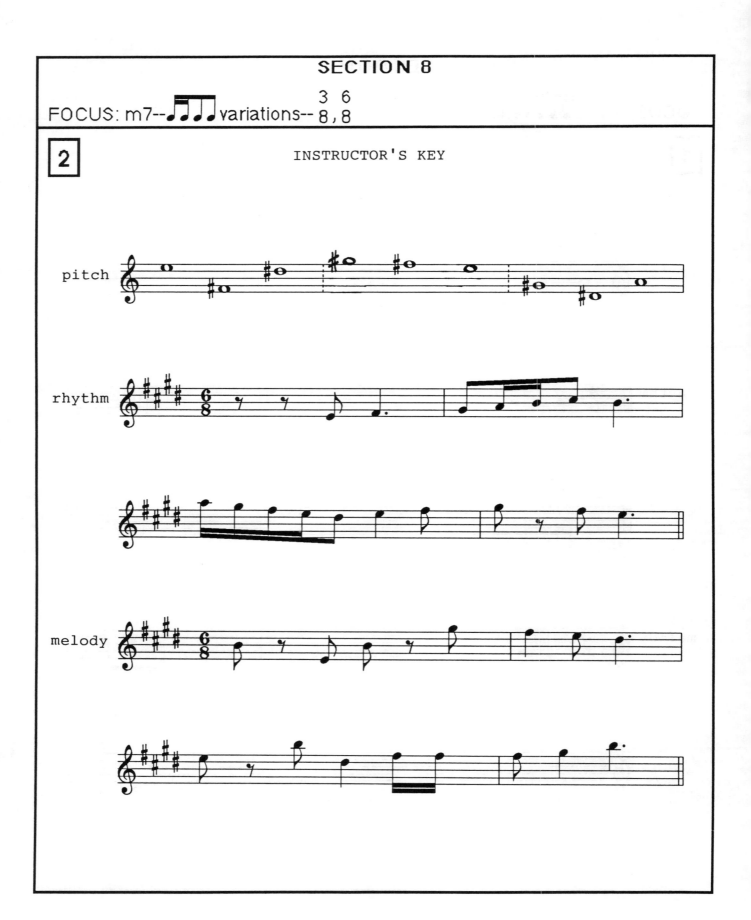

INSTRUCTOR'S KEY

# SECTION 8

FOCUS: m7-- ♩♪♪♩ variations-- $\frac{3}{8}, \frac{6}{8}$

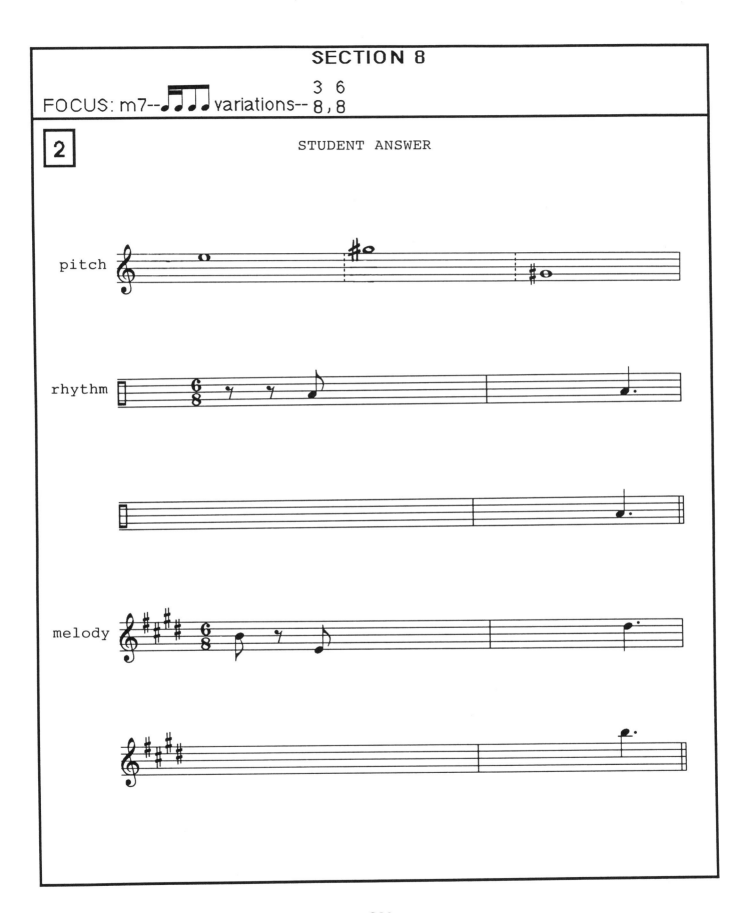

STUDENT ANSWER

pitch

rhythm

melody

291

FOCUS: m7--♪♪♪♪variations-- $\frac{3}{8}, \frac{6}{8}$

3    INSTRUCTOR'S KEY

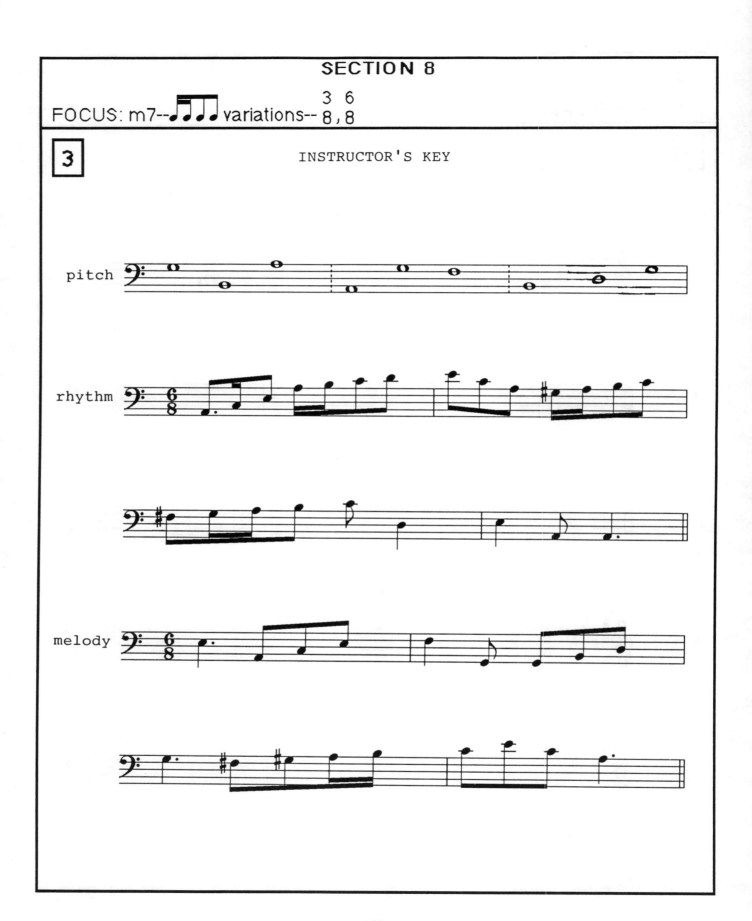

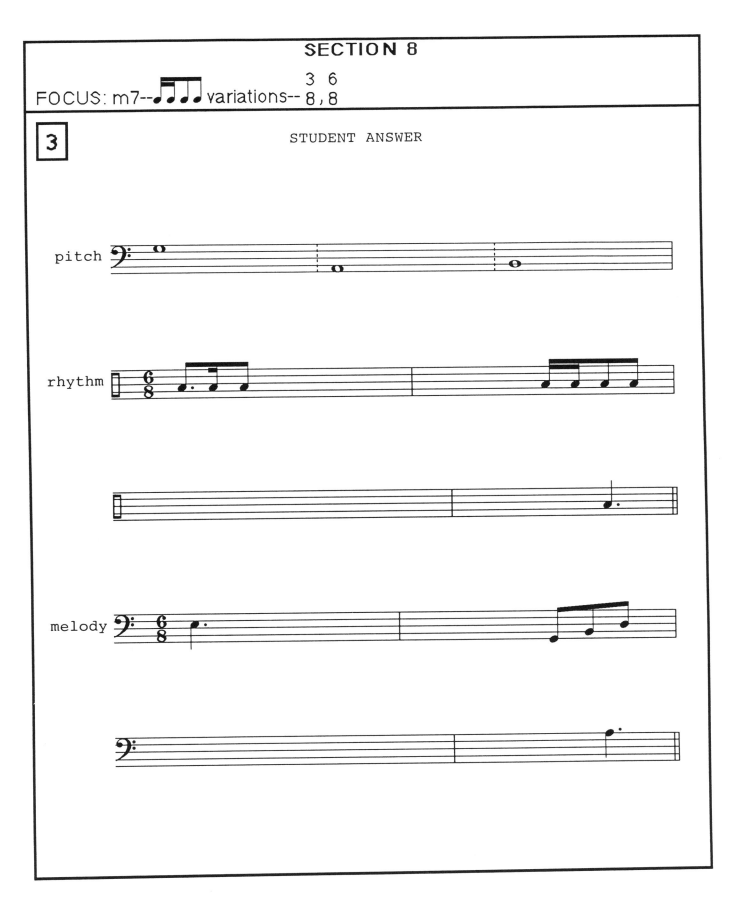

FOCUS: m7--♩♫♫♩ variations-- $\frac{3}{8}, \frac{6}{8}$

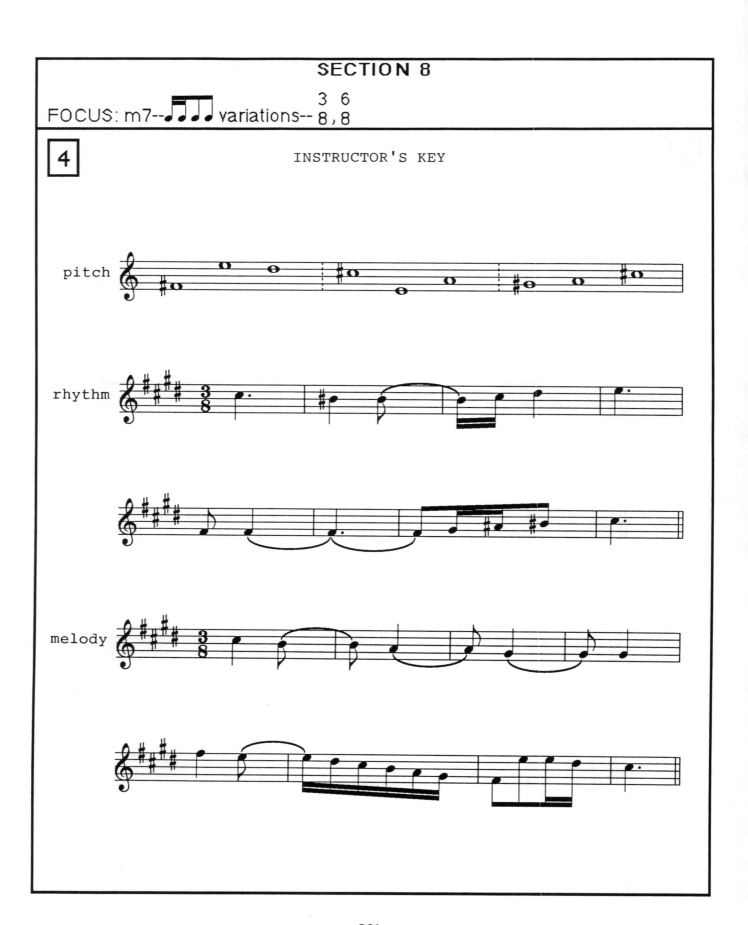

INSTRUCTOR'S KEY

FOCUS: m7--♪♪♪♪ variations-- $\frac{3}{8}$, $\frac{6}{8}$

| 4 | STUDENT ANSWER |
|---|---|

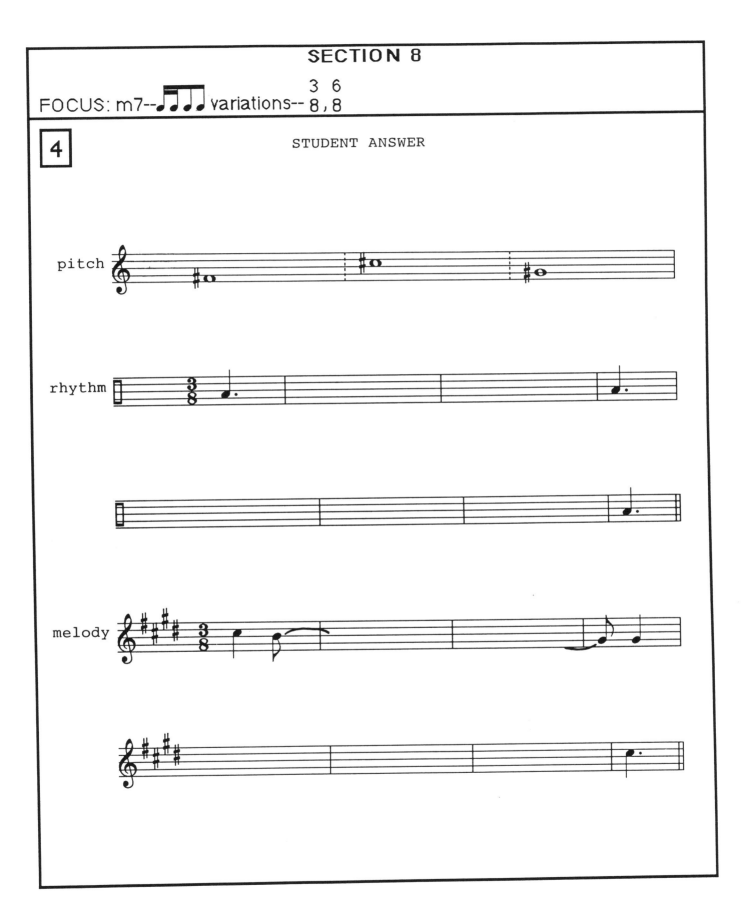

pitch

rhythm

melody

# SECTION 8A

**FOCUS:** Borrowed Supertonic-six,
         Minor Subdominant

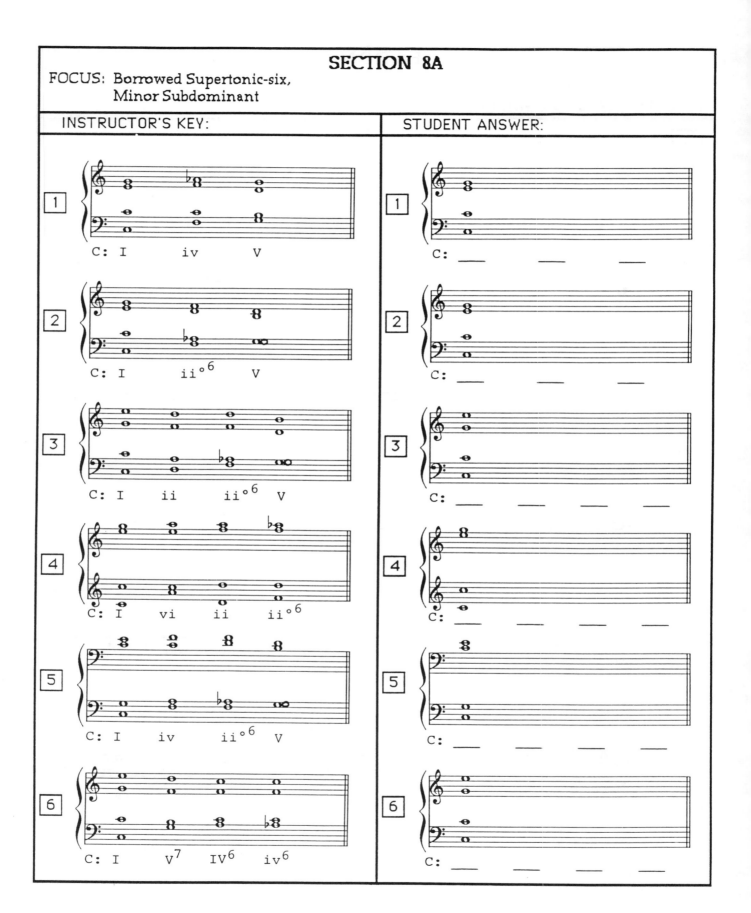

INSTRUCTOR'S KEY:

1  C: I    iv    V

2  C: I    ii°⁶    V

3  C: I    ii    ii°⁶    V

4  C: I    vi    ii    ii°⁶

5  C: I    iv    ii°⁶    V

6  C: I    V⁷    IV⁶    iv⁶

STUDENT ANSWER:

1  C: ___  ___  ___

2  C: ___  ___  ___

3  C: ___  ___  ___  ___

4  C: ___  ___  ___  ___

5  C: ___  ___  ___  ___

6  C: ___  ___  ___  ___

# SECTION 8A

FOCUS: Borrowed Supertonic-six,
Minor Subdominant

| INSTRUCTOR'S KEY | STUDENT ANSWER |
|---|---|

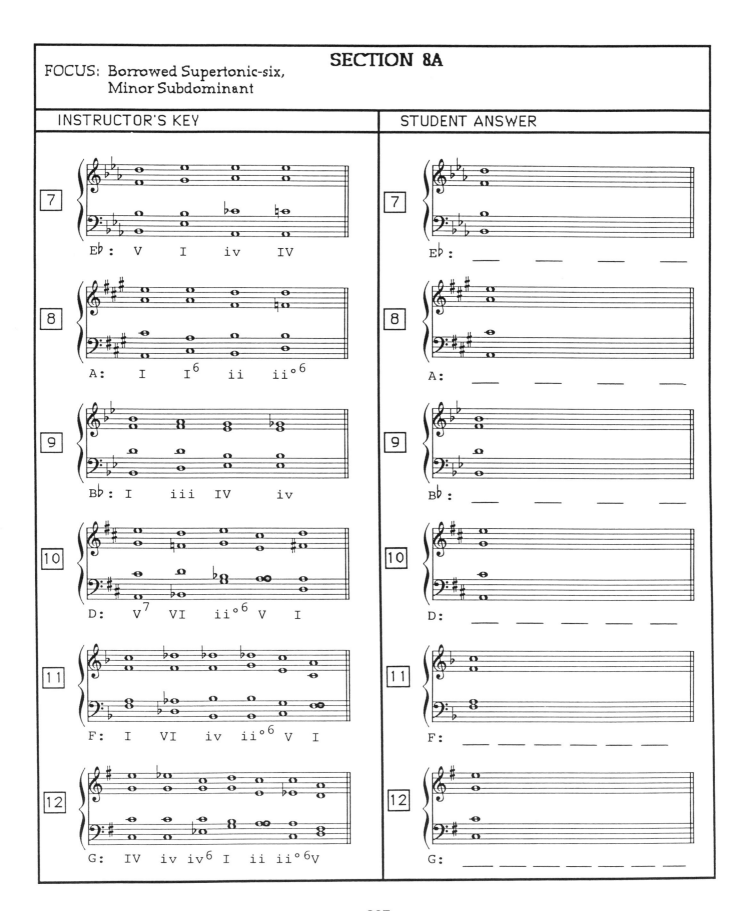

7  E♭:  V   I   iv   IV

8  A:  I   I⁶   ii   ii°⁶

9  B♭:  I   iii   IV   iv

10  D:  V⁷   VI   ii°⁶   V   I

11  F:  I   VI   iv   ii°⁶   V   I

12  G:  IV   iv   iv⁶   I   ii   ii°⁶   V

7  E♭: ___ ___ ___ ___

8  A: ___ ___ ___ ___

9  B♭: ___ ___ ___ ___

10  D: ___ ___ ___ ___ ___

11  F: ___ ___ ___ ___ ___ ___

12  G: ___ ___ ___ ___ ___ ___ ___

**FOCUS:** Tonic with picardy third, Subtonic

INSTRUCTOR'S KEY:  STUDENT ANSWER:

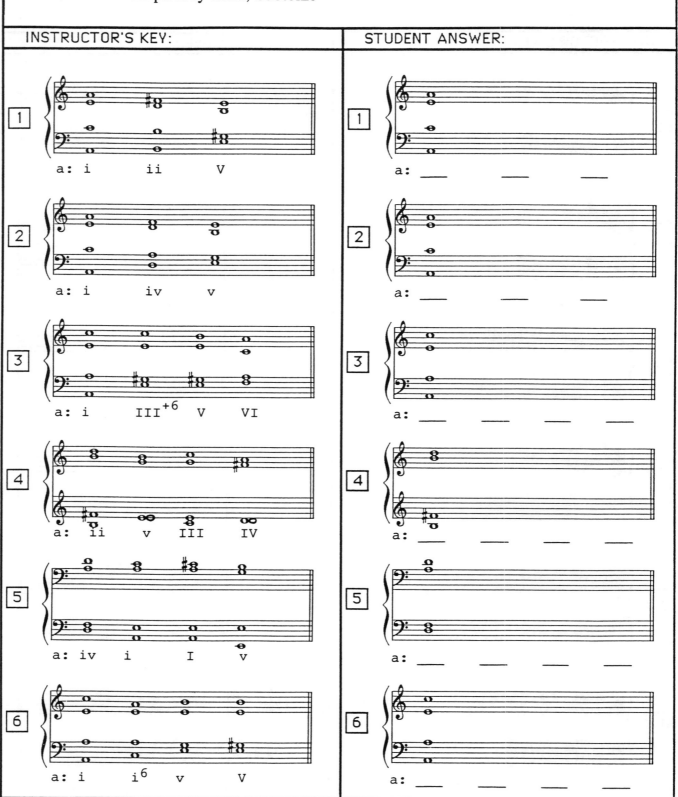

1  a: i   ii   V

2  a: i   iv   v

3  a: i   III$^{+6}$   V   VI

4  a: ii   v   III   IV

5  a: iv   i   I   v

6  a: i   i$^6$   v   V

# SECTION 8B

FOCUS: Tonic with picardy third, Subtonic

| INSTRUCTOR'S KEY | STUDENT ANSWER |
|---|---|

**7**

c:  i    ii    V    v

c: ___  ___  ___  ___

**8**

f#:  V    i    III$^{+6}$  V

f#: ___  ___  ___  ___

**9**

g:  I    ii°    ii    V    VI

g: ___  ___  ___  ___  ___

**10**

b:  i    I    iv    IV    V

b: ___  ___  ___  ___  ___

**11**

d:  i  III$^{+6}$  V    III  iv  ii

d: ___  ___  ___  ___  ___  ___

**12**

e:  i  iv  IV  IV$^6$  ii  ii°$^6$ii$^{ø6}_5$

e: ___  ___  ___  ___  ___  ___

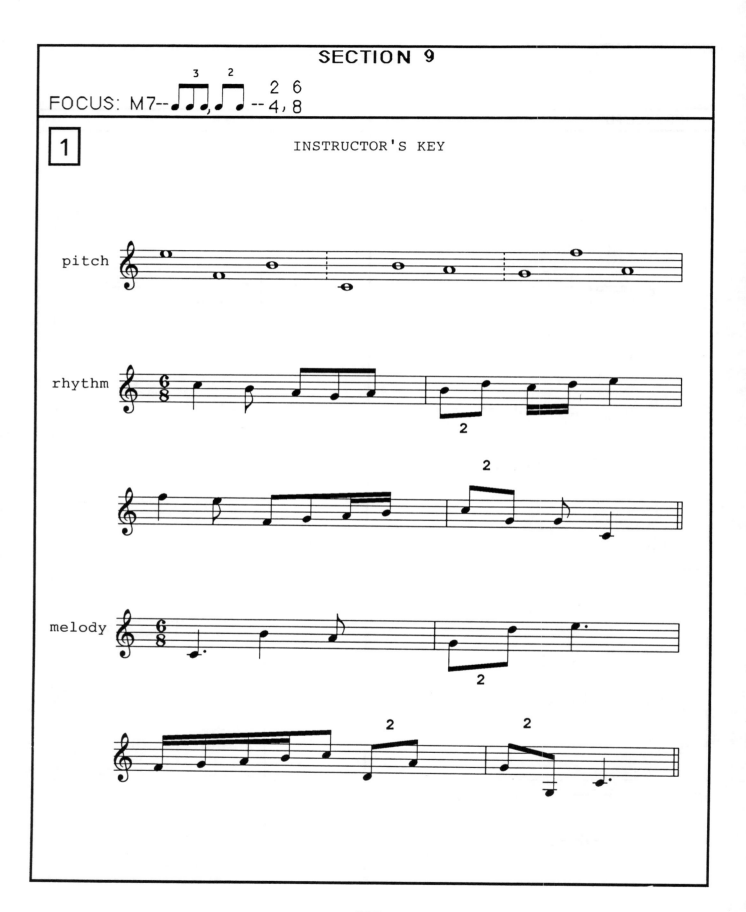

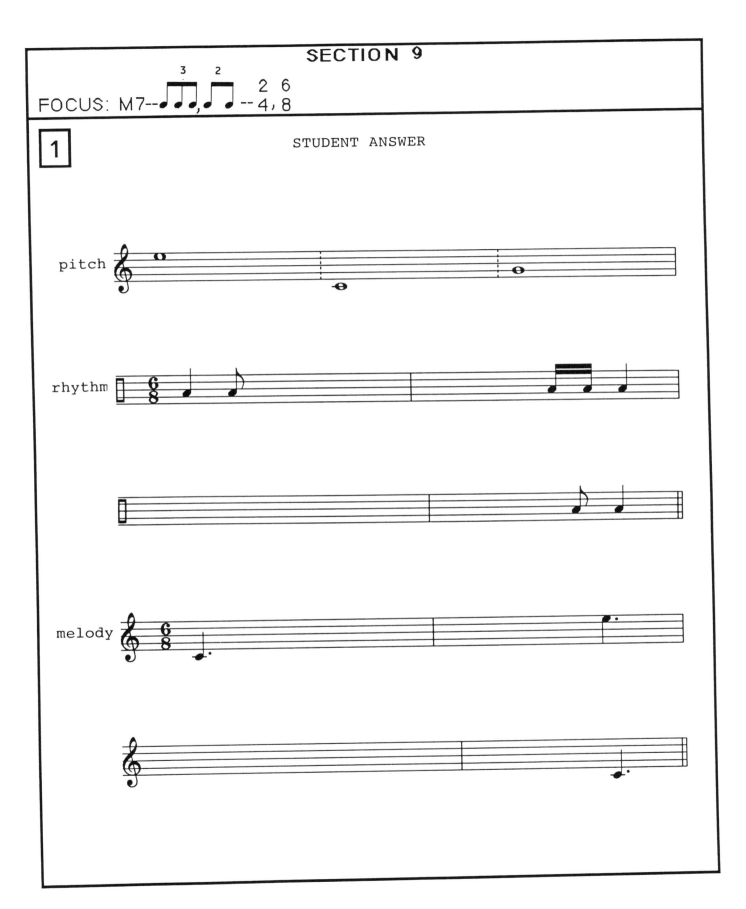

301

# SECTION 9

FOCUS: M7-- ♩♩♩,♩♩ --2 6 4,8

2          INSTRUCTOR'S KEY

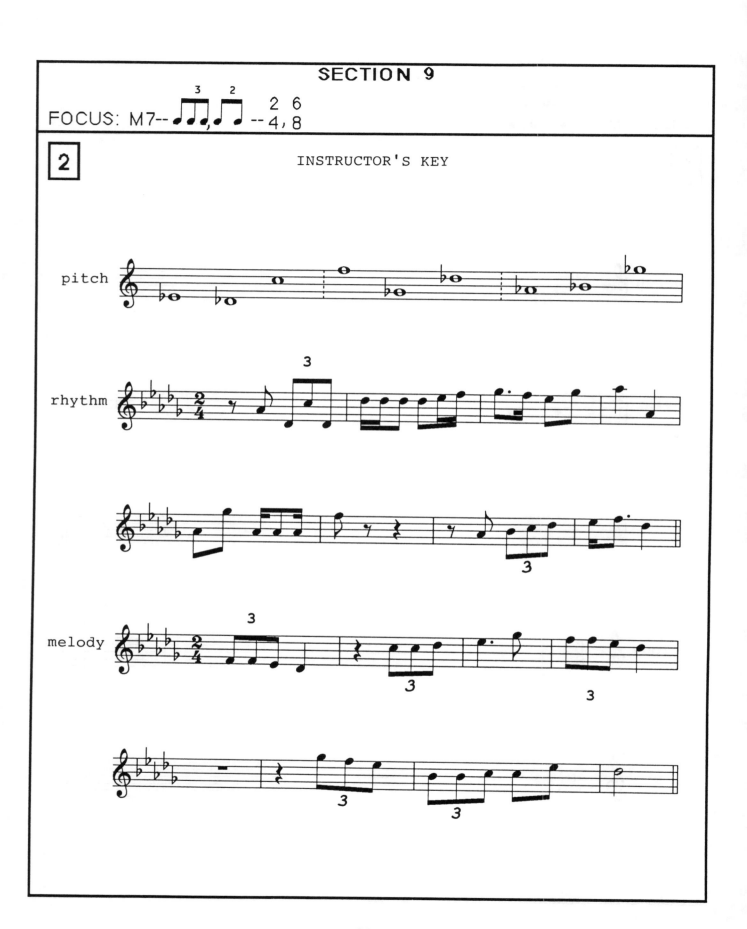

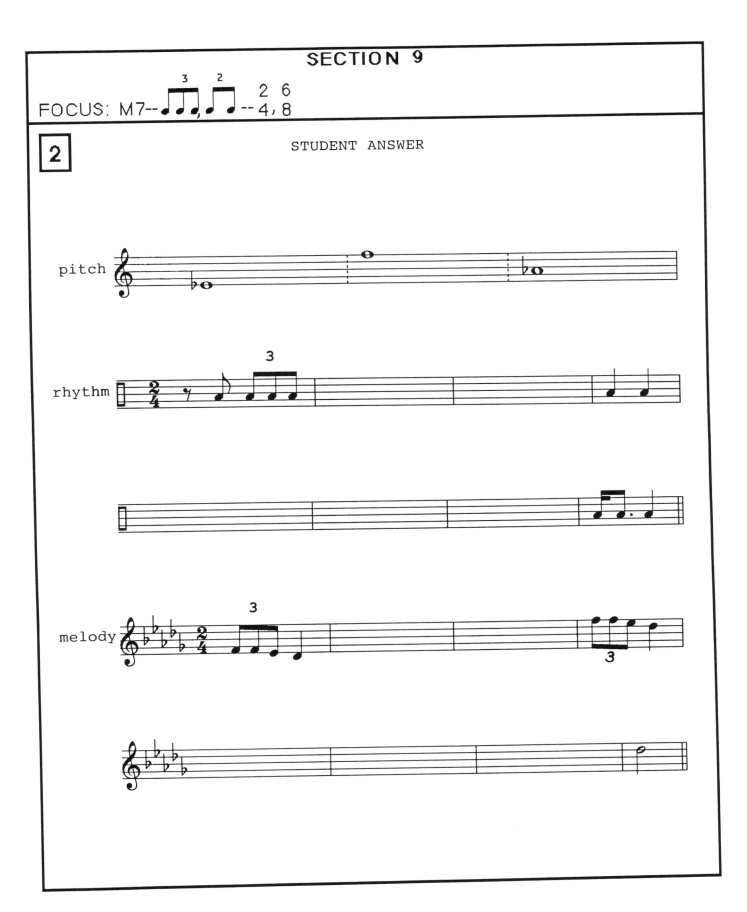

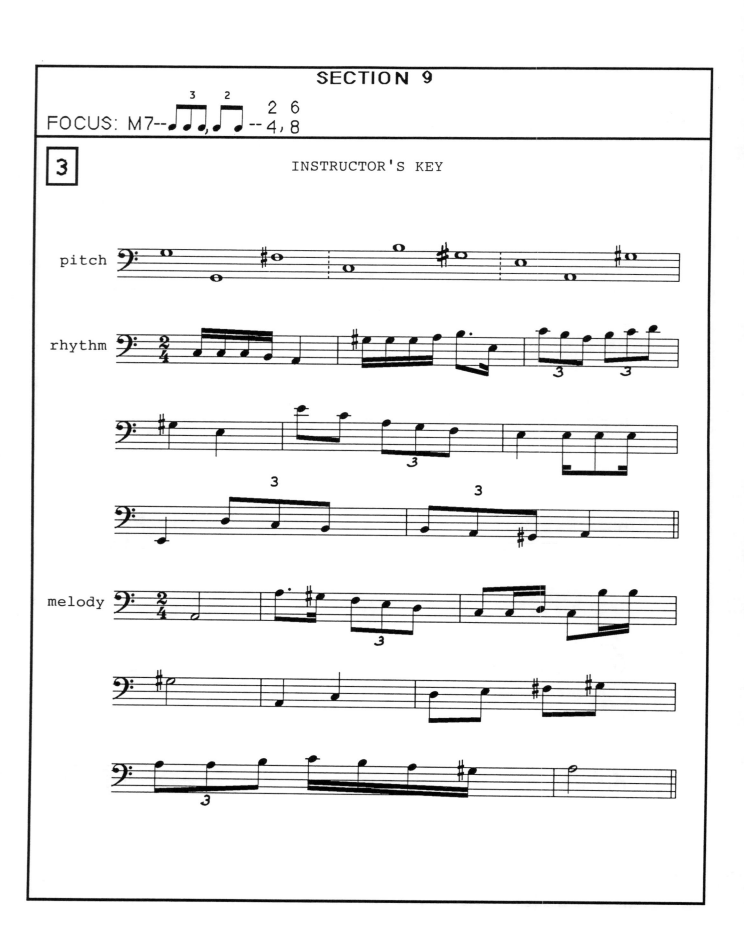

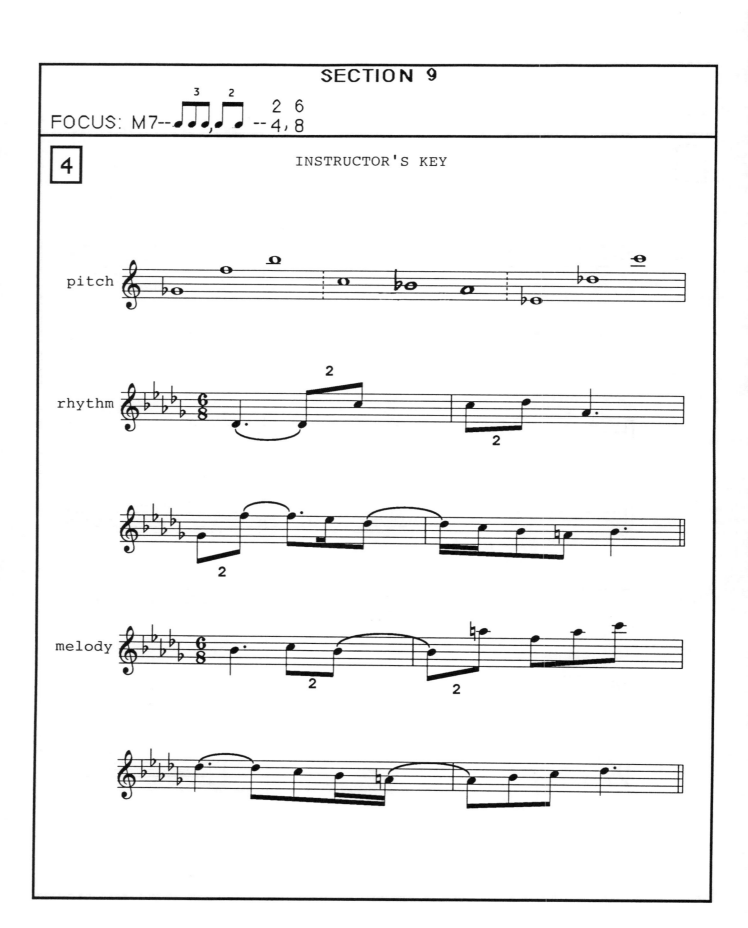

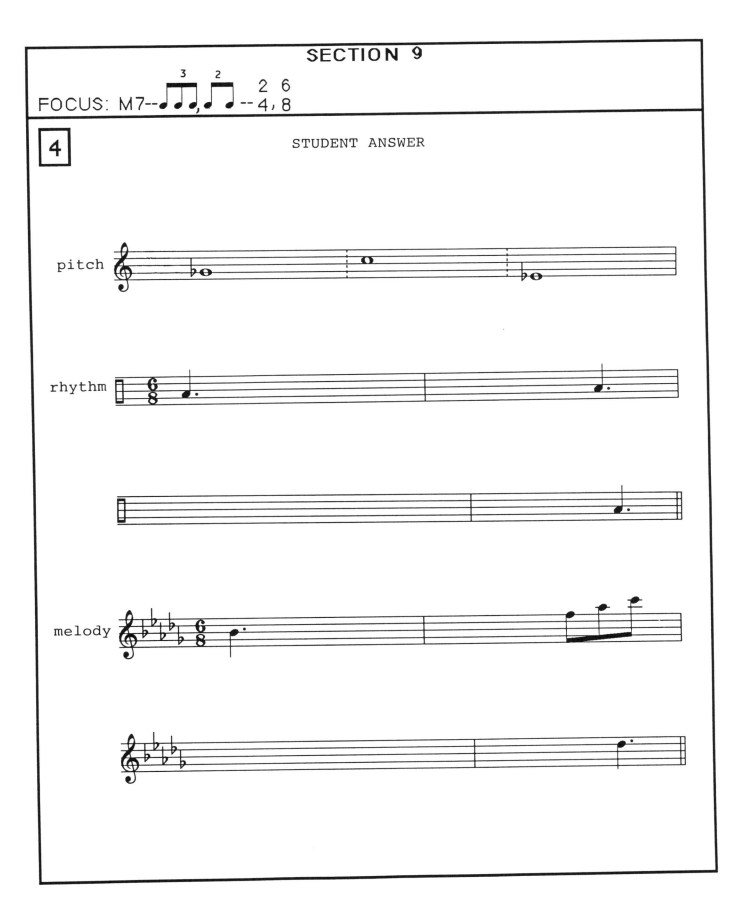

# SECTION 9A

**FOCUS:** Half-Diminished and Fully-
Diminished Sevenths

| INSTRUCTOR'S KEY: | STUDENT ANSWER: |
|---|---|

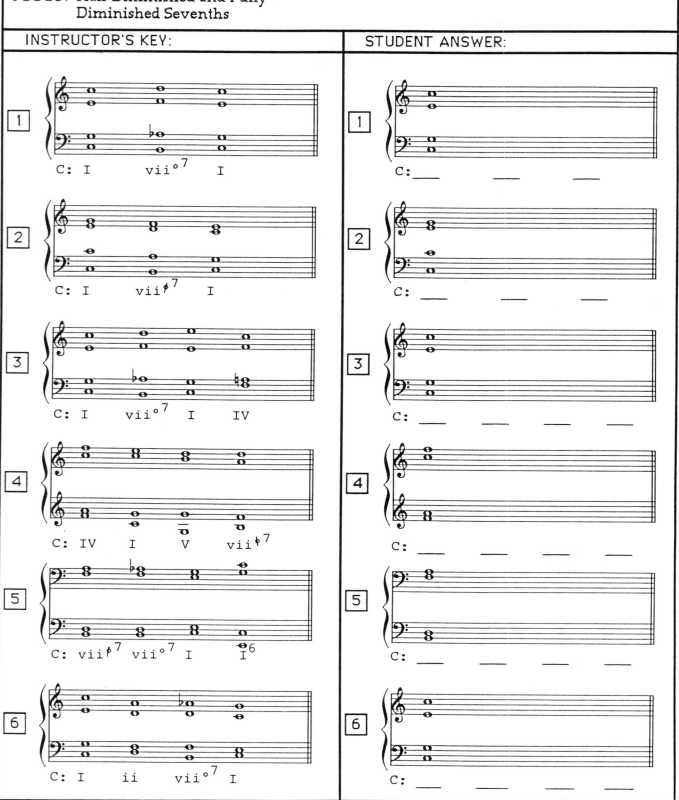

1  C: I   vii°⁷  I

2  C: I   viiᴓ⁷  I

3  C: I   vii°⁷  I   IV

4  C: IV   I   V   viiᴓ⁷

5  C: viiᴓ⁷  vii°⁷  I   I⁶

6  C: I   ii   vii°⁷  I

1  C: ___  ___  ___

2  C: ___  ___  ___

3  C: ___  ___  ___  ___

4  C: ___  ___  ___  ___

5  C: ___  ___  ___  ___

6  C: ___  ___  ___  ___

# SECTION 9A

FOCUS: Half-Diminished and Full-Diminished sevenths

| INSTRUCTOR'S KEY | STUDENT ANSWER |
|---|---|

**7**  E♭: I   vii°⁶   vii∅⁷   I

**7**  E♭: ___  ___  ___  ___

**8**  A:   I   V⁶₅   vii°⁷   I

**8**  A: ___  ___  ___  ___

**9**  B♭: I   iii   vii°⁷   I

**9**  B♭: ___  ___  ___  ___

**10**  D: I   I⁶   vii°⁷   vii°⁷   I

**10**  D: ___  ___  ___  ___

**11**  F: I vi  IV  ii  vii°⁷  I

**11**  F: ___  ___  ___  ___  ___

**12**  G: V⁷  V⁶₅  vii°⁷  I   ii  vii∅⁷  I

**12**  G: ___  ___  ___  ___  ___

309

# SECTION 9B

FOCUS: Fully-Diminished Sevenths

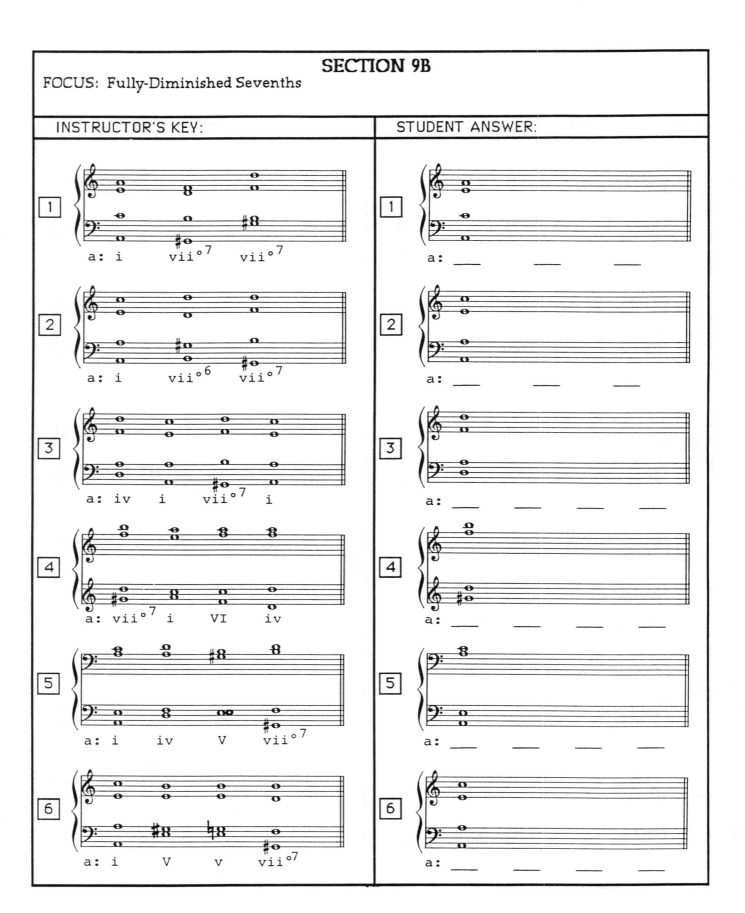

INSTRUCTOR'S KEY:

1. a: i    vii°⁷    vii°⁷

2. a: i    vii°⁶    vii°⁷

3. a: iv    i    vii°⁷    i

4. a: vii°⁷    i    VI    iv

5. a: i    iv    V    vii°⁷

6. a: i    V    v    vii°⁷

STUDENT ANSWER:

1. a: ___    ___    ___

2. a: ___    ___    ___

3. a: ___    ___    ___    ___

4. a: ___    ___    ___    ___

5. a: ___    ___    ___    ___

6. a: ___    ___    ___    ___

310

# SECTION 9B

FOCUS: Fully-Diminished Sevenths

| INSTRUCTOR'S KEY | STUDENT ANSWER |
|---|---|

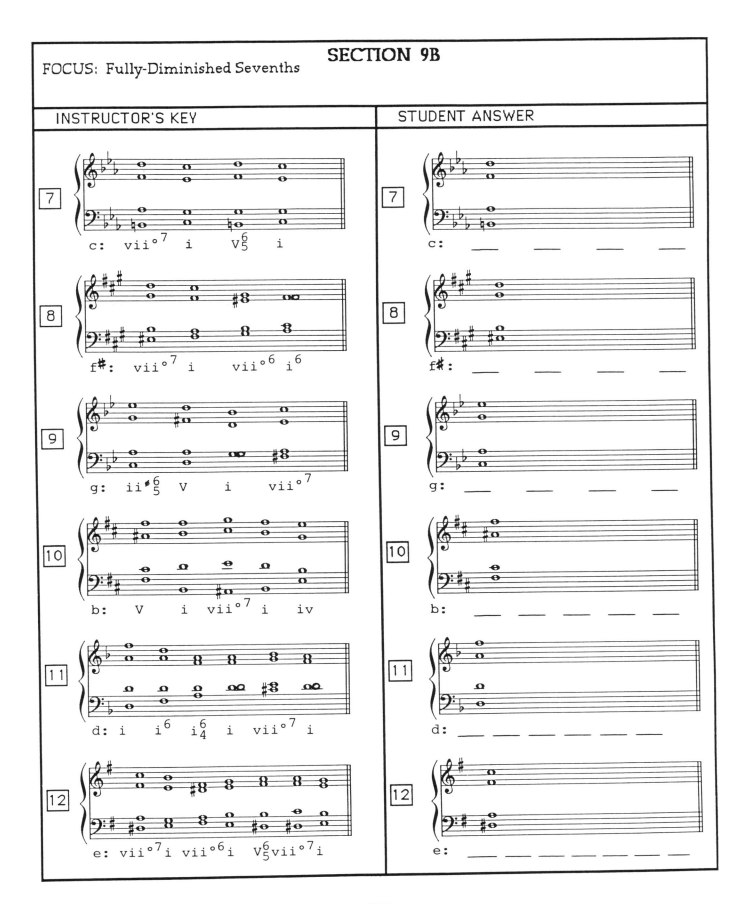

7  c:  vii°⁷  i  V⁶₅  i

7  c: ___  ___  ___  ___

8  f♯:  vii°⁷  i  vii°⁶  i⁶

8  f♯: ___  ___  ___  ___

9  g:  ii∅⁶₅  V  i  vii°⁷

9  g: ___  ___  ___  ___

10  b:  V  i  vii°⁷  i  iv

10  b: ___  ___  ___  ___  ___

11  d:  i  i⁶  i⁶₄  i  vii°⁷  i

11  d: ___  ___  ___  ___  ___  ___

12  e:  vii°⁷ i  vii°⁶ i  V⁶₅ vii°⁷ i

12  e: ___  ___  ___  ___  ___

311

# SECTION 10

FOCUS: dim 7-- 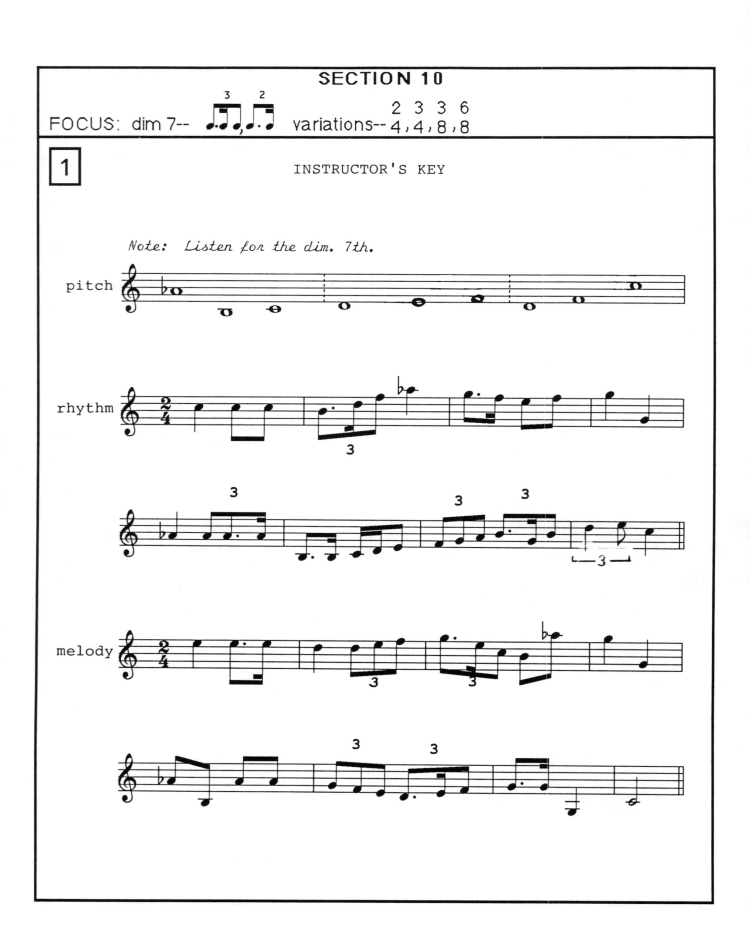 variations-- $\frac{2}{4}, \frac{3}{4}, \frac{3}{8}, \frac{6}{8}$

1  INSTRUCTOR'S KEY

Note: Listen for the dim. 7th.

312

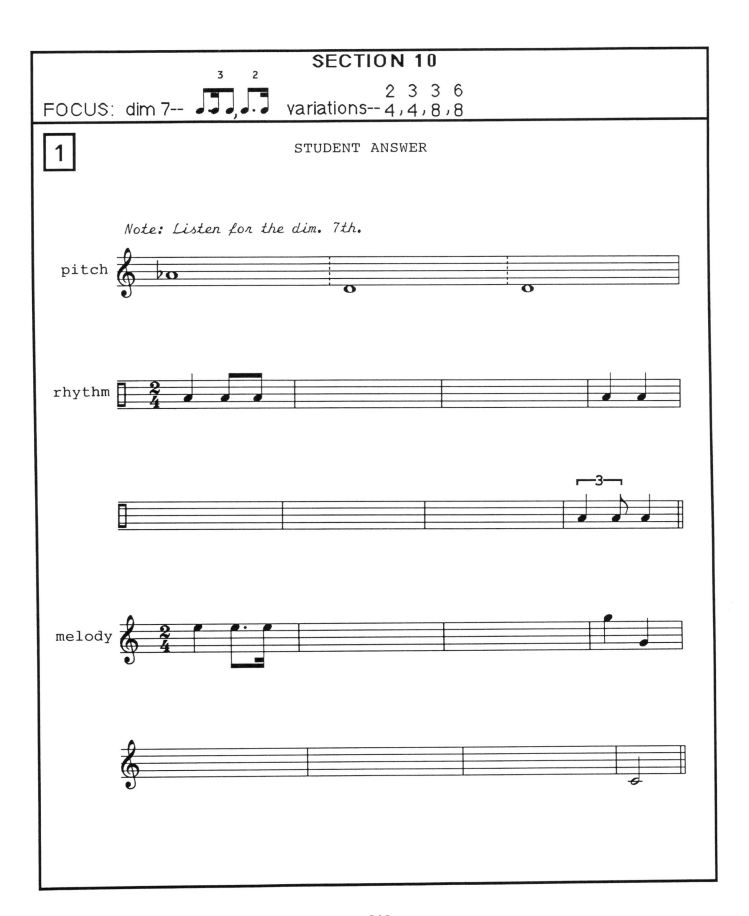

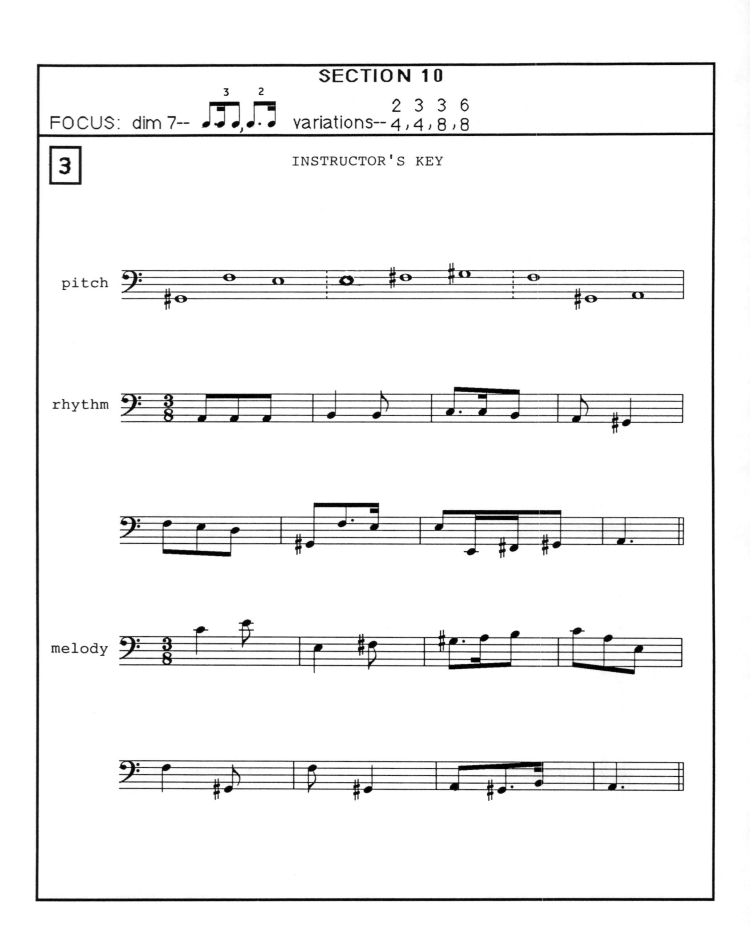

316

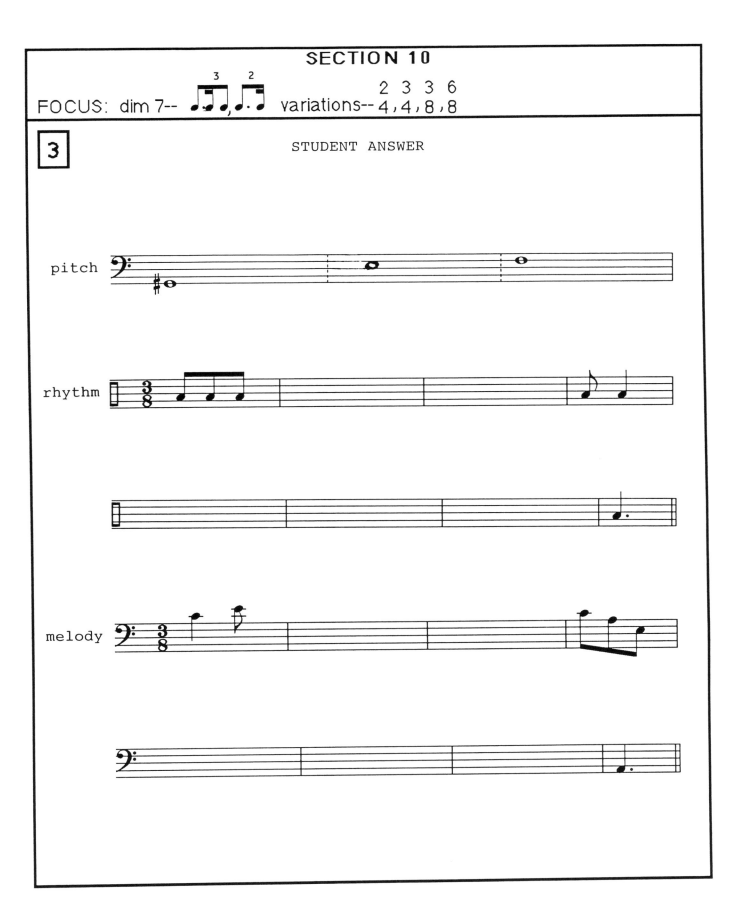

# SECTION 10

318

# SECTION 10A

**FOCUS:** Inversions of Half-Diminished
and Fully-Diminished Sevenths

| INSTRUCTOR'S KEY: | STUDENT ANSWER: |
|---|---|

1  C: I    vii$\emptyset{}^6_5$    I$^6$

1  C: ___  ___  ___

2  C: I$^6$    vii$\emptyset{}^4_3$    I$^6$

2  C: ___  ___  ___

3  C: V$^6$    vii$\emptyset{}^2$    I$^6_4$    V

3  C: ___  ___  ___  ___

4  C: I    vii$°{}^6_5$    I$^6$    IV

4  C: ___  ___  ___  ___

5  C: vii$°{}^4_3$ I$^6$    vi    IV

5  C: ___  ___  ___  ___

6  C: vii$°{}^4_3$  vii$°{}^6_5$  vii$°{}^4_2$  I$^6_4$

6  C: ___  ___  ___  ___

# SECTION 10A

FOCUS: Inversions of Half-Diminished
and Fully-Diminished Sevenths

| INSTRUCTOR'S KEY | STUDENT ANSWER |
|---|---|

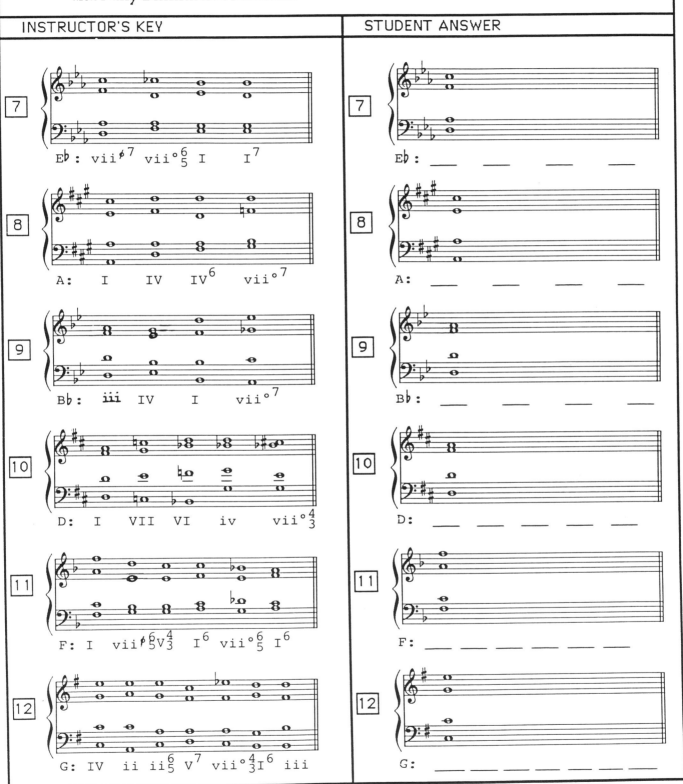

7  Eb: vii⌀7  vii°6/5  I  I7

Eb: ___ ___ ___ ___

8  A:  I  IV  IV6  vii°7

A: ___ ___ ___ ___

9  Bb: iii  IV  I  vii°7

Bb: ___ ___ ___ ___

10  D:  I  VII  VI  iv  vii°4/3

D: ___ ___ ___ ___ ___

11  F:  I  vii⌀6/5 V4/3  I6  vii°6/5  I6

F: ___ ___ ___ ___ ___ ___

12  G:  IV  ii  ii6/5  V7  vii°4/3 I6  iii

G: ___ ___ ___ ___ ___ ___ ___

321

# SECTION 10B

FOCUS: Inversions of Fully-
Diminished Sevenths

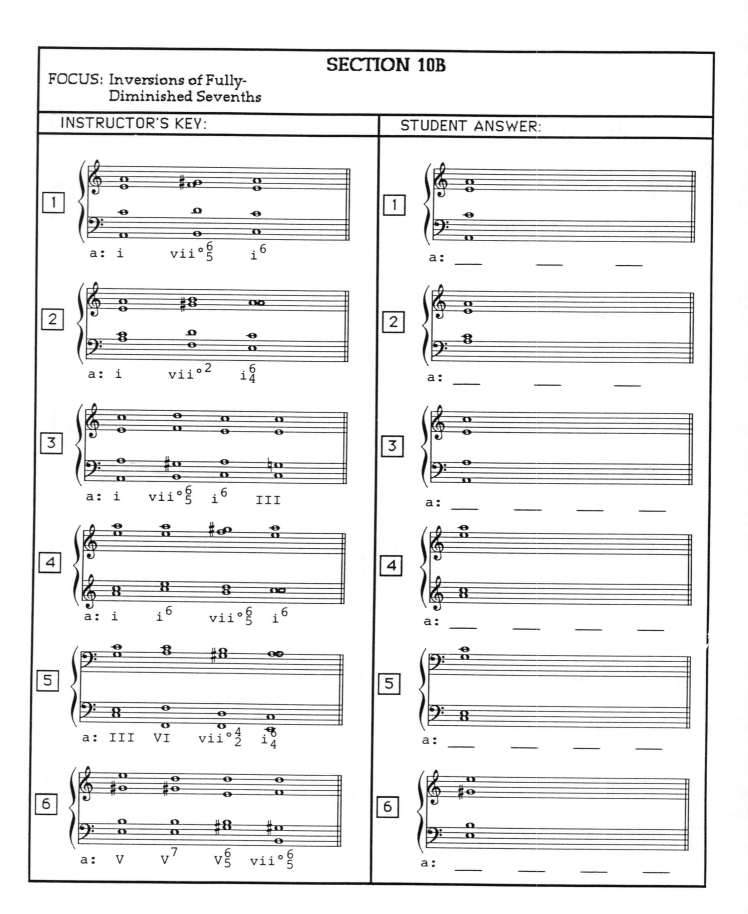

INSTRUCTOR'S KEY:

1. a: i    vii°$^6_5$    i$^6$

2. a: i    vii°$^2$    i$^6_4$

3. a: i    vii°$^6_5$    i$^6$    III

4. a: i    i$^6$    vii°$^6_5$    i$^6$

5. a: III   VI   vii°$^4_2$   i$^6_4$

6. a: V   V$^7$   V$^6_5$   vii°$^6_5$

STUDENT ANSWER:

1. a: ___    ___    ___

2. a: ___    ___    ___

3. a: ___    ___    ___    ___

4. a: ___    ___    ___    ___

5. a: ___    ___    ___    ___

6. a: ___    ___    ___    ___

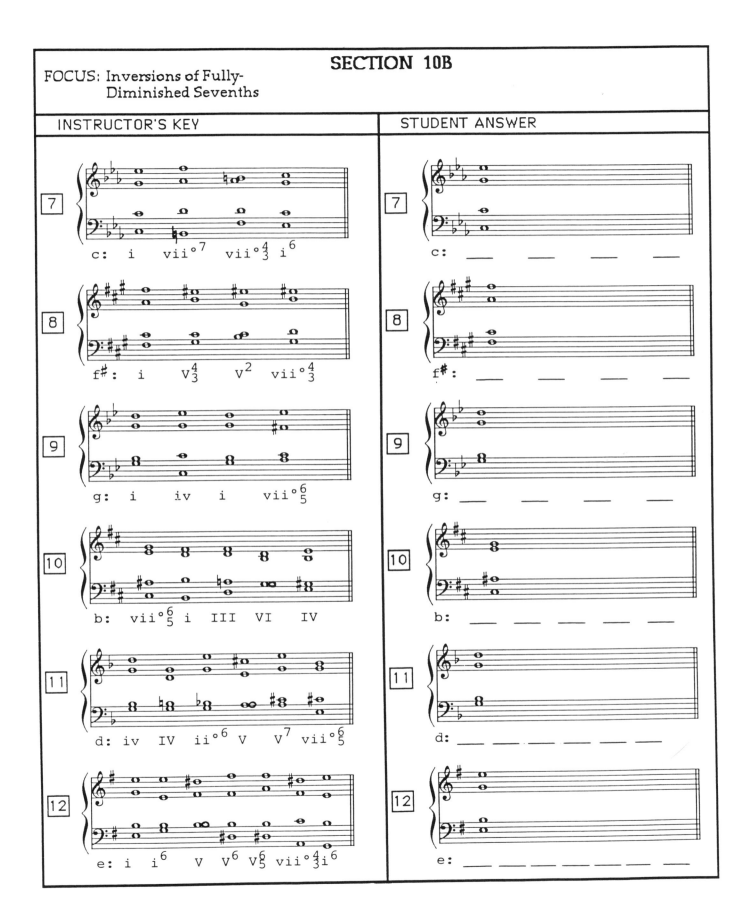